PENGUIN  CLASSICS

THE HISTORIES

ADVISORY EDITOR: BETTY RADICE

CORNELIUS TACITUS was born about A.D. 55 and probably survived the emperor Trajan who died in 117. In a Rome keenly appreciative of elegance in the spoken and written word he gained distinction as an impressive orator, and one of his three surviving monographs, the *Dialogue*, is an historical survey of changes in oratorical style. His political career as a senator began under Vespasian (69–79), and developed under Titus (79–81) and Domitian (81–96). Despite the alleged reign of terror at the end of this period, he survived to enjoy the consulship in 97, and, fifteen years later, the highest civilian provincial governorship, that of Western Anatolia ('Asia'). His other monographs, the biographical *Agricola* and the ethnographical *Germany*, appeared within a short time of each other in 98. Of his later and major works, the *Histories* were intended to cover the years from Nero's death in 68 to that of Domitian in 96, and the *Annals* those from A.D. 14 to 68. Both books have survived, though mutilated. Tacitus was a friend of Pliny the Younger, who greatly admired him. He was married to the daughter of a native of Fréjus, Julius Agricola, governor of Britain in the seventies and eighties. But the historian is generally reticent about himself, and we do not even know his place of origin, though Italy and southern France are possible candidates for this honour.

•

KENNETH WELLESLEY was, until 1981, Reader in Humanity (Latin) at the University of Edinburgh. As a scholar of Peterhouse he read classics at Cambridge, then enjoyed some years' schoolmastering before and after the Second World War. He has contributed a number of papers to learned journals on various aspects of Roman history and literature, and has recently been engaged in a textual, literary and historical study of the *Histories* of Tacitus. In 1972 he pubished a new text of the Third Book with commentary, and in 1975 an up-to-date narrative, *The Long Year: A.D. 69*. Most of the sites mentioned in the *Histories* are familiar to the translator from personal knowledge. He is co-editor of the forthcoming new edition of the standard Teubner text of Tacitus (Leipzig).

# TACITUS

---

# THE HISTORIES

A NEW TRANSLATION
BY
*Kenneth Wellesley*

PENGUIN BOOKS

PENGUIN BOOKS

Published by the Penguin Group
27 Wrights Lane, London w8 5tz, England
Viking Penguin Inc., 40 West 23rd Street, New York, New York 10010, USA
Penguin Books Australia Ltd, Ringwood, Victoria, Australia
Penguin Books Canada Ltd, 2801 John Street, Markham, Ontario, Canada l3r 1b4
Penguin Books (NZ) Ltd, 182–190 Wairau Road, Auckland 10, New Zealand

Penguin Books Ltd, Registered Offices: Harmondsworth, Middlesex, England

This translation first published 1964
Reprinted 1968
Reprinted (with Bibliography) 1972
Reprinted (with revisions) 1975
Reprinted 1976, 1978, 1980, 1982, 1984
Reprinted (with revisions) 1986
Reprinted 1988

Printed and bound in Great Britain by
Cox & Wyman Ltd, Reading
Set in Monotype Bembo

# CONTENTS

Introduction                                    9

## BOOK ONE

1–11   The Setting of the Story               21
12–50  The Murder of Galba                    29
51–90  The Vitellian Advance                  52

## BOOK TWO

1–10   Flavian Caution                        81
11–45  The First Battle of Cremona            88
46–56  Otho's Suicide                         109
57–73  Vitellius in Northern Italy            115
74–86  Vespasian Emperor                      125
87–101 Rome under Vitellius                   134

## BOOK THREE

1–35   The Second Battle of Cremona           145
36–48  A World Convulsed                      167
49–86  The March on Rome                      175

## BOOK FOUR

1–11   A Divided Senate                       203
12–37  Civilis Revolts                        211
38–53  The New Year, A.D. 70                  230
54–80  The Rhineland Recovered                242
81–86  Signs and Wonders                      263

## BOOK FIVE

| | | |
|---|---|---|
| 1–13 | The Jews | 271 |
| 14–26 | The Collapse of Civilis | 280 |
| | Bibliography | 289 |
| | Key to Technical Terms | 309 |
| | Key to Place-Names | 313 |
| | Index of Personal Names | 319 |
| | Maps | 326 |

# MAPS

1 Northern Italy                                    326–7
2 The Postumian Way, Cremona-Bedriacum   228–9
3 The Vitellian Camp at Cremona              328
4 The Second Battle of Cremona               329
5 Central Italy                                        330
6 Gaul and Upper Germany                      331
7 Lower Germany                                    332
8 The Battle of Rigodulum                        333
9 The Battle of Trier                                333
10 Rome: the Centre                                334–5
11 Rome: the Environs                            336

# Introduction

IN the troubled history of Europe the Roman Empire seems an era of comparative order, peace and legality. It can hardly fail to exert a certain fascination amid the turmoil of the present century. If the average man is content to view the Romans through the eyes of the novelist and film-director, the curious observer will have questions to ask. He will wish to get a little nearer to the sources of our knowledge. He will turn in the first instance to the *Annals* of the senator Cornelius Tacitus. Now mutilated, the *Annals* originally comprised sixteen or eighteen short 'books', spanning the fifty-four years from the accession of the second emperor, Tiberius, to the death of the fifth, Nero (A.D. 14–68). Not less instructive, however, is an earlier work of Tacitus, the *Histories*. These deal with the three short-lived emperors of A.D. 69, Galba, Otho and Vitellius, and with the three emperors of the succeeding Flavian dynasty (Vespasian, 69–79; Titus, 79–81; and Domitian, 81–96). Originally twelve or fourteen books in length, the *Histories* survive to the extent of the first four and a portion of the fifth, covering the 'Year of the Four Emperors' A.D. 69, and some nine months of A.D. 70. Tacitus seems to have been planning the work as early as A.D. 98, and it may have been published, perhaps in instalments, between A.D. 105 and 108.

It follows that the scale of treatment was more generous in the *Histories* than in the *Annals*, and is most generous of all in the surviving portion of the former translated in the present volume. The reason for this abundance is not hard to guess. The year 69, 'that long but single year' as Tacitus had earlier called it, offers a wealth of dramatic incident. After the solid and prosperous security of the first or Julio–Claudian dynasty, the ground opens. The vast edifice of the world empire is shaken. Pretender rises against pretender. The frontier armies move on Rome from Spain, Germany, the Balkans and the East. The frontiers themselves are breached by the barbarian. There

9

are palace conspiracies, sudden assassinations, desperate battles, deeds of heroism and perfidy. The scene shifts continually from one end of the empire to the other, from Britain to Palestine, from Morocco to the Caucasus. Three emperors – Galba, Otho and Vitellius – meet their end. The fourth, Vespasian, survives by fate or chance or merit, and founds his dynasty for good or ill. Here, in the clash of Roman with Roman, the civilized world seemed for the moment about to perish. Ancient or modern, the reader who delights in history as story could scarcely find the narrative dull, however inexpert the narrator. And the narrator is Tacitus. He rises to his theme, and as stylist, statesman and critic of human nature has the skill and knowledge to make words live.

In all the records of Rome there can scarcely be another year that is so full of calamity, or that displays so clearly the strength and weakness of the Romans. In the *Histories* we can follow events from month to month, from day to day, sometimes even from hour to hour. We stand close to the picture. The canvas is restricted but the details fascinate. Nor are broader masses and more distant perspectives lacking.

At first names crowd upon us. Tacitus must set the scene. The actors are numerous, the plot already thick. He starts at 1 January 69, the year of destiny, with backward glances at the six months or so that have elapsed since Nero's death. We too must look back, and a little further.

Since the Battle of Actium in 31 B.C., the Roman world has been ruled by Augustus and his family, the Julio-Claudians. The ruler is called *imperator* ('commander') or *princeps* ('leader'). The principate is an autocracy with some republican trappings. As in the days of the republic a hierarchy of elected officials ('magistrates') continues to hold office in Rome and act as army commanders or provincial governors for longer or shorter periods thereafter. The senate, a chamber composed of these officials and numbering some 500 members, continues to handle a considerable mass of public business. Many rich and important provinces, with Italy itself, still lie under its superintendence. But the armed forces are now controlled by the emperor, and with them the provinces in which these forces are stationed, mostly on the periphery of the empire. Such are Britain, the Rhineland, the Danubian countries, Egypt and the East. In a state where an official career alternates between civil and military appointments, the emperor's patronage is essential to advancement. In the association of *princeps* and senate, the former is inevitably the dominant partner. As brake or spur, the effectiveness of the senate depends upon its own cohesion and public spirit. As for the 'people of Rome', the full citizens living in Italy or scattered throughout the empire, their political power has shrunk almost to nothing, and that of non-Romans has never existed except at the level of local politics. The positions of eminence are occupied by senators, who in private life are rich landed gentry, and by knights (the 'equestrian order'), who possess a less exalted birth and are delimited by a lower property qualification. Both these orders have open to them official careers in which merit may rise in regular but flexible patterns of promotion. We must add to them a class hardly less important, that of the imperial freedmen, ex-slaves often of Eastern origin, men of talent acting as imperial civil-servants under the immediate control of the emperor.

Augustus and Tiberius were cautious and intelligent rulers, under whom Rome and her dominions prospered. The calm of a benevolent autocracy had succeeded the fever and anguish of the last century of the free republic. But Gaius, Claudius and Nero were less successful. Eccentric or megalomaniac in their various ways, these men, and particularly Nero, brought the Julio-Claudian dynasty – and to a certain degree the principate itself – into disrepute. The execution in A.D. 67 of a distinguished commander in the East, Domitius Corbulo, was an indication of the sort of gratitude that prominent Romans could expect of a suspicious and unbalanced tyrant. There were conspiracies. In March 68 came the rebellion of the governor of Central Gaul, Julius Vindex, himself of Gallic origin. But there was a more important malcontent. In early April, the governor of Nearer Spain, Sulpicius Galba, member of an ancient aristocratic family, was hailed as emperor by his troops. Vindex, who had only a local militia at his disposal, was soon crushed by the governor of Upper Germany, Verginius Rufus. But on 9 June, Nero, feeling his position desperate, committed suicide. Thereupon, Galba was recognized as *princeps* by the senate.

The credentials of a historian who is our main source for this period must be scrutinized. In writing the *Histories*, Tacitus enjoyed many advantages. He was himself a senator whose official career had begun and developed under the Flavians. He must necessarily have known much of the political history of the time at first hand. In the Year of the Four Emperors, he was only a boy of fourteen. But of course sources were plentiful. The events of A.D. 69 evoked a rich literature in both Greek and Latin, much of it tendentious and propagandist. There is no reason to doubt that Tacitus faithfully consulted these written sources, noting agreements and discrepancies. Two writers only are mentioned by name; others can be guessed. But in A.D. 98–105, when Tacitus was planning and writing his work, oral testimony was available from many survivors. Such was Vestricius Spurinna, a soldier with a long and distinguished career whose beginning Tacitus gracefully notices. Like many other possible informants, Spurinna was on friendly terms with the younger Pliny, and hence probably with his friend Tacitus. Pliny speaks warmly of the old man's character and love of reminiscence. Much of the detailed information in Books Two and Three concerning events in Liguria Tacitus may have retained from recollections of talk with his father-in-law Agricola, who was there at the time. Some state papers were certainly available to one who was a senator, particularly the Roman Hansard, the Transactions of the Senate – obviously put to good use in Book Four. These he seems to have supplemented by the evidence of surviving participants.

How conscientious and unbiased is he? Can we rely upon the facts, if not the interpretations that he provides? Any answer to this question must face the basic difficulty that the historian's sources, both primary and secondary, are lost to us. We have neither the Transactions of the Senate nor the historical works of the elder Pliny or Messalla. Independent evidence – a coin, an inscription, an archaeological find – is too slight to provide an effective criterion. Comparisons with parallel authorities are favourable to Tacitus. By and large, we must judge by internal evidence.

No reader of the *Histories* can be in doubt that the writer's emotions are involved in his account of the recent and controversial past, written, it may be, with an eye to the present and to the inscrutable and perhaps ominous future. There are King Charles's heads, themes that recur with suspicious and predictable frequency: the irresponsibility and corruption of the metropolis, the excessive influence of imperial freedmen, the selfish ambitions of competing courtiers, a senate riven and helpless, an emperor suspicious and uncertain. Some small slips in matters of fact may be detected, but they are few. The love of speed and brevity, or an assumption of knowledge in the reader, leads to omissions. There are sentences of Delphic ambiguity and antitheses more striking than clear. Epigram is not likely to be the best vehicle of truth. We may lament, while we enjoy, a sly innuendo. But these defects, if defects they are, lie on the surface. The more we study Tacitus, the more he rises in our esteem.

It would, however, be optimistic to suppose that his historical research was more than superficial. It is true that he consulted his friend the younger Pliny concerning the circumstances of the death of the latter's uncle in the eruption of Vesuvius in A.D. 79: the source was excellent and close at hand. In areas of dispute, however, he more than once tells us that inquiries would be difficult or impracticable. His task, it seemed to him, was to denounce implicitly or explicitly the grosser lies of partisan historians. When conflicting versions baffled solution, it was fairest and certainly easiest to state the alternatives, perhaps with a hint of what the writer himself considered most credible in the light of general probability. This preference is often, though not always, given to the less flattering version.

Since Tacitus cannot fall back upon his own research, many small and some vital issues remain in doubt. Was the acclamation of Vespasian engineered or spontaneous? Who was responsible for the sack of Cremona? Who for the firing of the amphitheatre at Placentia or of the Capitol at Rome? Did Vespasian connive at the incitement of Civilis to rebel? Was Antonius Primus the victim of Mucianus' jealousy, or was his fall from favour richly deserved? This and much else remain obscure. But the reason is not only the difficulty of establishing the truth. It is also a conviction that truth is not simple. Motives are complex, chance unpredictable, fate or the gods supreme. Will it not be better, where so much is dark, to leave the reader to ponder?

Sometimes Tacitus' accuracy can be submitted to objective tests. How far is the narrative consistent with itself? Prolonged and peevish criticism has revealed very little amiss. Even when Tacitus does not state a thing, it may sometimes be deduced that he knows it, and that his knowledge is sound. The chronology of Book Three, whose events form a closely interwoven and integrated whole, can be worked out in detail, though few dates are given by the historian. The sequence of events is found to be feasible in itself, and consistent with the data of topography, astronomy, speed of march and so on. Or we may appeal to witnesses who are still with us: rivers, mountains, tracks, gradients, towns. The story of the minor engagement described in Book Four, 71, is a case in point. By good fortune, Tacitus happens to specify the locality: Rigodulum (Riol) near Trier. This gives us our opportunity. The battle reads at first like a hundred other skirmishes in Roman historians, and is dismissed accordingly. But it has detailed features and clear phases. We need the River Mosel, a mountain, a road to Trier, a road-block, a quarry for stones, sloping ground, a steep point of vantage for the enemy, and contours which permit the Roman cavalry to approach Riol from the east without being seen. It gives the student of Tacitus peculiar satisfaction to follow the Mosel to the Kammerwald east of Riol, trace the course of the Roman road, identify the obvious site of the road-block, climb the sloping ground and then the steeper mountain-side, pass the stone-quarry, and follow the cavalry's route to the road-junction where one party rode right and uphill to bundle the Gauls from their perch, while the other followed the lower contours and approached by a track, still used, to within 1,000 yards of Riol unobserved. Thus what seemed merely an imaginative reconstruction by a rhetorical historian fits exactly and convincingly into the modern landscape. It may be doubted whether Tacitus himself had ever seen Riol; but he has faithfully preserved the information of a good source (probably the elder Pliny), abbreviating it almost to the point of obscurity. The same concision and the same reliability can be demonstrated in his accounts of the two battles of Cremona (or Bedriacum), and the Battle of Trier. The presumption must be that Tacitus is careful, though brief, in his reproduction of his source material. Where this is good, he will give it shapeliness and polish. Where it is not, his narrative is unlikely to find support in personal research. The account of the Jews is a fascinating farrago of truth and lies.

Indeed, the academic pursuit of knowledge for its own sake appeared to Tacitus, as to many of his countrymen, a dangerous form of dilettantism. Philosophy is particularly suspect if it fails to result in good works. Men often devote their gifts to it, he says, in describing the character of Helvidius Priscus, in order to disguise ease and idleness under a pretentious name. Those who claim to teach the art of living may be wolves in sheep's clothing, like Publius Celer, or out of touch with the hard realities of life, like Musonius Rufus, who preached peace to men who carried arms. So with learning in general. When the world needs leaders, study cannot be disinterested. Historians must not be antiquaries. They must teach by examples, denouncing evil and honouring virtue. One or other of the seven deadly sins – pride, covetousness, lust, envy, gluttony, anger and sloth, to which we may add an eighth, cowardice – confronts us on almost every page of the *Histories*. But the vices of the early empire are known to us chiefly through the Roman delight in self-criticism. In a moment of gloom Tacitus suggests that the moral climate of A.D. 69 was such as to render any possibility of a peaceful settlement between the Othonian and Vitellian forces quite chimerical. This is special pleading, belied by the context. In any case such generalizations are practically meaningless. They belong to the tradition of Roman puritanism and the doctrine of progressive and galloping decline from an idealized past. It is in accordance with this moralizing attitude that the civil war is represented less as a political hazard than as evidence of the corruption of the age.

The desire to preach sometimes comes close to malice. Tacitus finds some good things to say even of Vitellius: he was generous, and a good family man, however poor an emperor. But the historian presses home the charge of gluttony in season and out. Along the roads of Italy clatter the wheels of his commissariat. This keynote is struck early, at the very beginning of the reign. News of the revolt of the legions of Upper Germany from Galba reaches Vitellius in the governor's palace at Cologne after dark on 1 January 69: the messenger has ridden hard all day to cover the 105 miles from Mainz. But Tacitus cannot resist the temptation to add that Vitellius is at the dinner table. The information is gratuitous, the insult studied. Before entering Rome the Vitellian troops receive an issue of rations. Nothing, one would think, could be more normal, nor better designed to forestall hunger or looting. But this will not do for our moralist. Vitellius, he writes, 'was engaged in issuing haversack rations as if he were fattening up a lot of gladiators'. Some of these absurdities may be plausibly attributed to Flavian pamphleteers anxious to stress the enormities of an emperor against whom Vespasian rebelled. Tacitus realizes that much contemporary history is propagandist, but does not always succeed in freeing himself of its influence. Some of the mud sticks.

Nor, as Tacitus himself admits, is the picture one of unrelieved gloom. The world is naughty, but good deeds shine out. The reader is duly reminded of examples of patriotism, loyalty, friendship, independence of spirit, modesty, courage. The names of those faithful unto death are carefully recorded, or regret expressed if the names have perished. The lower the station of the hero, the greater the gratification of his historian. Senators are expected to set an example; they often fail to do so. How much the more must we admire the sacrificial devotion of a governor's slave or the courage of a defence-less woman of Liguria!

The story of A.D. 69–70 is a complex web of contemporary events widely separated in space, yet possessing a causal or chronological relationship to one another. Their interaction must be made clear. Selection, grouping, arrangement and emphasis present the historian with manifold difficulties and opportunities. Tacitus dominates the chaos with an unfaltering hand. The annalistic tradition of Roman historiography made it natural that each year should be introduced by the mention of its consuls, that is, its date. Within the year, it was necessary to find some compromise between two conflicting ideals – strict chronological sequence and the grouping of events into episodes. Tacitus' method is to present us with a succession of longer or shorter 'chapters': the murder of Galba, the march on Rome, the Jews, and so on. Matter which coheres he is reluctant to break up without strong reasons. Neighbouring chapters precede, succeed or overlap each other in time. Transitions are often ably managed; the reader moves in imagination from place to place in the company of imperial couriers. There are surprisingly few explicit dates, and we are not even told, though we can deduce, when the battles of Cremona were fought, and this too, despite the stern reproof administered to Vitellius for forgetting a fatal anniversary – that of the Battles of the Allia and Cremera. Yet the historian is always conscious of his time-scale, and examination shows that he is faithful to it and that it is substantially correct. Literary critics are sometimes puzzled by the sudden and brief intrusion of Titus at the beginning of Book Two. Should this not have been relegated to a later point – the description of the rise of Vespasian? The truth is that the journey of Titus took place in the early months of A.D. 69: it cannot be postponed to mid-summer.

Once the arrangement of his material had been planned, it remained to render it in words harmoniously, pointedly and with variety. The leading characters – the emperors and their chief supporters – are kept well to the foreground. Their salient attitudes are repeatedly stressed.

Behind them stand a host of lesser figures, sketched in rapidly but incisively. Particular attention is paid to the psychology of hope and fear. The atmosphere is highly charged with emotion. At times, the imaginative reconstruction borders upon the technique of the historical novelist. No conceivable source except his own imagination can have told Tacitus the thoughts that passed through the mind of Vespasian as he hesitated before the fateful decision to rebel. But this is what brings history to life, and no Roman critic could have taken exception to it. In the same way, and in accordance with a convention of high ancestry, eloquent and impressive speeches are invented with the greatest freedom. They serve to clarify issues, relieve the monotony of factual narration, and allow the orator Tacitus to speak at once in the person of his hero and of himself. There are other devices to secure variety. Certain scenes of terror and pathos lend themselves to highlighting. Striking or casual phrases disclose the visual imagination of the artist and the poet. Nor does Tacitus deny himself the wilful digression: Paphos, Veleda, Serapis, the Jews. Indeed the Year of the Four Emperors offered infinite possibilities. Later, when Tacitus came to write the history of the Julio-Claudians, the long catalogue of the Tiberian treason-trials seemed tedious even to their narrator. He looked back regretfully to the colourful scenes of the *Histories*: 'Descriptions of foreign parts, the fluctuating tide of battle, great men dying in glory – these are the themes that hold and refresh the reader's interest.'

A well-constructed book conceals the art of its construction. The reader of Tacitus' Latin is much more immediately aware of his verbal dexterity and of a style almost without parallel in the literature of his nation. The formal patterns and figures which the concise and unambiguous inflexions of the Latin language permit and encourage are employed by Tacitus with consummate skill. In a modern English setting these adornments – parallelism, variation, alliteration, chiasmus and a dozen more – are inevitably sacrificed or retain only a ghostly existence. How far they are to be allowed to survive is a question of taste or prejudice where scarcely two critics will agree. I have tried to keep as close as possible to the brevity, point and speed of the original.

My occasional departures from the standard texts of Fisher (1910), Giarratano (1939) and Koestermann (1961) have not been noted: they are obvious to those familiar with the Latin, and of little interest to others. A few footnotes (the translator's) provide a bare minimum of comment or explanation. I am most grateful to my Edinburgh colleagues Mr W. K. Smith, Mr D. A. West, Dr T. J. Cadoux and Dr P. G. Walsh, and also to my daughter Inga, for the acute and helpful scrutiny with which they have read various portions of the translation. Thanks to them many blemishes have been removed, and they are in no way responsible for such infelicities and inaccuracies as remain. For the typing of my manuscript I am indebted to Mrs A. M. Cochrane and Miss E. L. A. Inglis.

No translator of Tacitus can view his labours without some feeling of guilt and remorse. He may prove to have butchered his victim. He has inevitably robbed the original of its peculiar virtue, the living word. 'A language is expressive and beautiful in the country that produced it,' wrote George Moore in his *Epistle to the Cymry*. 'As soon as a language passes beyond its natural frontier it weakens, disintegrates, decays; Asiatics cannot express themselves in English, and what we say in French is not worth saying. The thought that sustains a book is but a small part of the book; a thought is common property, but the words belong to the writer. ... An idea is mine today, it is yours tomorrow, the day after tomorrow it belongs to the whole world, but a beautiful sentence is always the property of him who made it.'

1963                                                                        K. W.

### Note on the 1972 reissue

This reissue incorporates a bibliography on all aspects of the *Histories* except the purely textual and linguistic. I have also made half-a-dozen minor changes reflecting a different interpretation or punctuation of individual sentences.

                                                                            K. W.
March 1972

### Note on the 1975 reissue

In this reissue the bibliography has been brought up to date as far as possible, and some minor changes have been made in the text and notes.

                                                                            K. W.
May 1975

### Note on the 1986 reissue

The bibliography has again been updated and a few notes added. I have also made some alterations in the body of the translation to accommodate the findings of recent research.

October 1986                                                                K. W.

*Book One*

# The Setting of the Story

1. I shall begin my work with the year[1] in which Servius Galba and
Titus Vinius were consuls, the former for the second time. My choice
of starting-point is determined by the fact that the preceding period
of 820 years dating from the foundation of Rome has found many
historians. So long as republican history was their theme, they wrote
with equal eloquence of style and independence of outlook. But when
the Battle of Actium had been fought and the interests of peace
demanded the concentration of power in the hands of one man, this
great line of classical historians came to an end. Truth, too, suffered in
more ways than one. To an understandable ignorance of policy,
which now lay outside public control, was in due course added a
passion for flattery, or else a hatred of autocrats. Thus neither school
bothered about posterity, for the one was bitterly alienated and the
other deeply committed. But whereas the reader can easily discount
the bias of the time-serving historian, detraction and spite find a ready
audience. Adulation bears the ugly taint of subservience, but malice
gives the false impression of being independent. As for myself, Galba,
Otho and Vitellius were known to me neither as benefactors nor as
enemies. My official career owed its beginning to Vespasian, its
progress to Titus and its further advancement to Domitian. I have no
wish to deny this. But partiality and hatred towards any man are equally
inappropriate in a writer who claims to be honest and reliable. If I live,
I propose to deal with the reign of the deified Nerva and the imperial
career of Trajan. This is a more fruitful and less thorny field, and I
have reserved it for my declining years. Modern times are indeed
happy as few others have been, for we can think as we please, and
speak as we think.

2. The story upon which I embark is one full of incident, marked by
bitter fighting, rent by treason, and even in peace sinister. Four

1. A.D. 69.

emperors perished violently.[1] There were three civil wars,[2] still more campaigns fought against the foreigner, and often conflicts which combined elements of both. Success in the East was balanced by failure in the West. The Balkans were in turmoil, the Gallic provinces wavered in their allegiance, and Britain was left to fend for itself no sooner than its conquest had been completed.[3] The Sarmatian and Suebian peoples rose upon us, the Dacian distinguished himself in desperate battles won and lost, and thanks to the activities of a charlatan masquerading as Nero, even Parthia was on the brink of declaring war.[4] Finally, Italy itself fell victim to disasters which were quite unprecedented or had not occurred for many centuries. Whole towns were burnt down or buried throughout the richest part of the coast of Campania, and Rome suffered severely from fires that destroyed its most venerable temples, the very Capitol being set alight by Roman hands. Things holy were desecrated, there was adultery in high places. The Mediterranean swarmed with exiles and its rocky islets ran with blood. The reign of terror[5] was particularly ruthless at Rome. Rank, wealth and office, whether surrendered or retained, provided grounds for accusation, and the reward for virtue was inevitable death. The profits made by the prosecutors were no less odious than their crimes. Some helped themselves to priesthoods and consulships as the prize of victory. Others acquired official posts and backstairs influence, creating a universal pandemonium of hatred and terror. Slaves were suborned to speak against their masters, freedmen against their patrons, while those who had not an enemy in the world were ruined by their friends.

3. However, the period was not so barren of merit that it failed to teach some good lessons as well. Mothers accompanied their children in flight, wives followed their husbands into exile. There were resolute kinsmen, sons-in-law who showed steadfast fidelity, and slaves whose loyalty scorned the rack. Distinguished men driven to suicide

1. Galba on 15 January 69; Otho on 16 April 69; Vitellius on 20 December 69; and Domitian on 18 September 96.

2. Otho *v.* Vitellius, Vitellius *v.* Vespasian and Domitian *v.* Antonius Saturninus (January 89).

3. This reference to the striking advance into Scotland under Tacitus' father-in-law Agricola, followed by a degree of disengagement, is exuberant rather than exact.

4. About A.D. 88; cf. p. 85.

5. Especially in Domitian's last years, A.D. 93–6.

faced the last agony with unflinching courage, and there were death-scenes not inferior to those held up to our admiration in the history of early Rome. In addition to manifold tragedy on the human plane, signs and wonders occurred in heaven and earth, premonitory lightnings and tokens of things to come, auspicious or ominous, doubtful or manifest. In short, Rome's unparalleled sufferings supplied ample proof that the gods are indifferent to our tranquillity, but eager for our punishment.

4. However, before embarking on my theme, it seems desirable to go back a little and survey the state of public opinion at Rome, the mind of the army, the attitude of the provinces, and the elements of strength and weakness throughout the Roman world. In this way it may be possible to appreciate not only the actual course of events, whose outcome, whether good or ill, is often dictated by chance, but also their underlying logic and causes.

The death of Nero[1] had been welcomed initially by a surge of relief. But it had also evoked a variety of emotions in the senate, the populace, and the garrison of the capital, as well as in all the many legions and legionary commanders. A well-hidden secret of the principate had been revealed: it was possible, it seemed, for an emperor to be chosen outside Rome. But the senators were delighted, and promptly permitted themselves considerable freedom of speech in their negotiations with an emperor who was new to his task and absent from the capital. The leading members of the equestrian order were hardly less gratified than the senators. Hopes were raised among respectable middle-class Romans who had ties of duty towards the great families, as among the dependants and freedmen of condemned persons and exiles. The riff-raff haunting the circus and theatres, and the scum of the slave population, or those spendthrifts and bankrupts who had been the recipients of Nero's degrading charity were filled with gloom and hungry for the latest rumours. 5. The city garrison, for its part, had a long tradition of sworn allegiance to the Caesars, and had been induced to desert Nero more by cunning and suggestion than from any inclination of its own. It now discovered that payment of the bounty promised in the name of Galba was not forthcoming, and that there would not be the same scope for great services and rewards in peace as in war. These troops also realized that it was too late for them to ingratiate themselves with an emperor who owed his elevation to

1. See Introduction, p. 11.

the legions. Already disaffected, they were made still more restless by the unscrupulous intrigues of their prefect, Nymphidius Sabinus, who was plotting to make himself emperor. It is true that Nymphidius was caught in the act and disposed of. But though the arch-rebel had been removed, many of the troops retained a guilty conscience.

There were rumours, too, about Galba's brutality and miserliness. His strictness had once been well spoken of and held up to admiration in military circles, but it now irritated men who would have nothing to do with the discipline of the past and who, in the course of fourteen years under Nero, had come to like the vices of emperors no less than they had once feared their virtues. To crown all, there was the famous remark by Galba – 'I select my troops, I don't buy them.' Impeccable as a statement of public policy, the epigram proved a two-edged weapon so far as Galba himself was concerned, for the rest of his behaviour failed to measure up to this standard. 6. Old and feeble, Galba was dominated by Titus Vinius and Cornelius Laco. The former of these was the most vicious of men, the latter the most idle. Between them, they saddled the emperor's reputation with crimes that caused public revulsion, and then ruined it altogether by an indolence that earned contempt.

Galba's march[1] had been slow and bloodstained. In the course of it, he had executed Cingonius Varro, a consul-designate, and the consular Petronius Turpilianus. The grounds were that the former was a confederate of Nymphidius and the latter a commander appointed by Nero. Allowed no proper trial or defence, these two had perished by what seemed a miscarriage of justice. An ominous gloom was cast over the emperor's entry into Rome by the massacre of thousands of unarmed troops, appalling even to the perpetrators. Owing to the arrival of the Spanish legion[2] and the retention in Rome of the formation raised by Nero from the fleet, the capital was crowded with a quite unusual garrison. In addition, there were numerous drafts from Germany, Britain and the Balkans. It was Nero who had selected these and sent them on ahead to the Caspian Gates for the campaign which he was mounting against the Albani, but had later recalled them to deal with the revolt of Vindex.[3] Here was fuel in plenty for a new outbreak,

1. From Spain to Rome, late summer and autumn, A.D. 68.
2. The Seventh (Galbian) Legion recruited by Galba in Spain in June 68. Shortly after its arrival in Rome, it was posted to Carnuntum in Pannonia under the command of Antonius Primus.
3. See Introduction, p. 11.

lacking indeed a clear-cut preference for any one leader, but nevertheless readily available to any unscrupulous incendiary.

7. As it turned out, the news of the executions of Clodius Macer and Fonteius Capito arrived simultaneously. Macer, obviously bent on causing trouble in Africa, had been put to death by the imperial agent Trebonius Garutianus on the orders of Galba.[1] Capito, who harboured similar designs in Germany,[2] had been assassinated by the legionary commanders Cornelius Aquinus and Fabius Valens, who did not wait for instructions. Some people believed a different story. According to this, despite his unsavoury reputation for money-grubbing and immorality, Capito had nevertheless had no idea of rebelling. But when his legionary commanders found him unresponsive to their suggestions for an armed revolt, it was alleged that they had put their heads together, accused Capito himself of sedition, and then treacherously murdered him, whereupon Galba's lack of firmness, or perhaps his anxiety not to probe too deep, had approved what could not be altered, however suspicious the circumstances.

Whatever the truth of the matter, both executions were ill received, and once the emperor had made himself unpopular, good deeds and bad brought him equal discredit. Everything had its price. The imperial freedmen wielded excessive influence and Galba's own servants had itching palms eager to catch at an unexpected windfall, for they knew their time was short in view of the emperor's age. The new court exhibited the same evils as the old – equally serious, but not equally tolerable. The very fact that Galba was getting on in years provoked sneers and discontent among a populace which was used to the young Nero, and compared the two emperors, as the crowd will, for their looks and personal attractions.

8. So much for public opinion at Rome, naturally complex in view of the large numbers of people involved. Of the provinces, Spain was governed by Cluvius Rufus, a fine orator, who was tried in the arts of peace, but untried in wars.[3] The Gallic provinces were linked to the régime by their memory of Vindex, and, in addition, by the recent grant of Roman citizenship and the corresponding prospect

1. Macer as commander of the legion stationed in Africa (see Key to Place-Names) staged a revolt in A.D. 68 and attempted to put pressure on the capital by holding up supplies of corn.

2. Capito was governor of Lower Germany in the same year.

3. Consul before A.D. 41, and Galba's successor as governor of Nearer Spain. He wrote a history of Nero's reign, now lost.

of tax relief. But the Gallic communities closest to the military districts of Germany had not been so well treated. Some had actually suffered loss of territory and derived as little comfort from viewing the concessions accorded to others as from an estimate of their own sufferings.

The mood of the armies of Germany presented a particular danger in view of their strength. Anxious and resentful, they plumed themselves on their recent success, yet feared the consequences of having backed the wrong side. They had been slow to abandon Nero, nor had Verginius declared for Galba immediately.[1] Whether his ambitions extended to becoming emperor himself is doubtful, but it was common knowledge that the troops had offered him the position. Fonteius Capito's assassination still rankled, even with those who were in no position to complain. What was lacking was a leader, for Verginius had been removed, amid protestations of imperial favour. The troops, observing that he had not been sent back to Germany and indeed faced prosecution, felt that they were incriminated themselves. 9. The upper army despised its commander-in-chief, Hordeonius Flaccus. Elderly and lame, Flaccus lacked personality and prestige. Even when the troops were quiet, he was unable to maintain discipline; and by the same token, if the men were in an ugly mood, his feeble attempts to control them merely added fuel to the flames. The legions of Lower Germany were left without a governor for some time. Finally Galba's nominee appeared – Aulus Vitellius, son of the Vitellius who had held the censorship and three consulships. These, it seemed, were qualifications enough.

In the army of Britain there were no hard feelings. Indeed, throughout the period of civil war, no other legions acted with greater propriety. The reason may lie in the fact that they were far away, beyond the barrier of the North Sea; or perhaps they had learnt from continual campaigning to reserve their hatred for the enemy. There was peace, too, along the Danube, though the legions mobilized by Nero had sent deputations to sound Verginius during their period of waiting in Italy. But the formations were widely dispersed (always a very sound method of ensuring the loyalty of troops) and there was no concentration of forces or failings.

10. The East remained as yet quiescent. Syria, with four legions, was

---

1. i.e. immediately after Nero's death and the recognition of Galba by the senate.

governed by Licinius Mucianus. He was a man much talked of, in fair days and foul alike. In his youth, he had courted the great with an eye to his own advancement. Then he ran through a fortune and his standing became precarious, for even Claudius was thought to disapprove of him. Removed to an isolated corner of Asia, he came as near to being an exile as later to being emperor. Mucianus' character was a compound of self-indulgence and energy, courtesy and arrogance, good and evil. A libertine in idle moments, he yet showed remarkable qualities once he had set his hand to a thing. To the world, his activities might seem laudable; but there were ugly rumours about his private life. Yet by a supple gift for intrigue he exercised great influence on his subordinates, associates and colleagues, and found it more congenial to make an emperor than be one.

The conduct of the Jewish War,[1] with the command of three legions, lay in the hands of Nero's nominee, Flavius Vespasian. That he had neither the wish nor the intent to oppose Galba is shown by his having sent his son Titus to do homage and pay his respects to the emperor, as I shall record in the appropriate context.[2] It may be that mysterious prophecies were already circulating, and that portents and oracles promised Vespasian and his sons the purple; but it was only after the rise of the Flavians that we Romans believed in such stories.

11. Egypt, together with the forces designed to keep it in order, has been governed ever since Augustus' day by Romans of equestrian rank acting as successors to the Ptolemies. It seemed policy that a province of this sort – difficult of access, exporting a valuable corn-crop, yet divided and unsettled by strange cults and irresponsible excesses, indifferent to law and ignorant of civil government – should be kept under the immediate control of the imperial house. It was ruled at the moment by Tiberius Alexander, himself an Egyptian.

As for Africa and the legions in it, they had lived to see the execution of Clodius Macer and were content with any kind of emperor after experiencing a lesser master. The two Mauretanias, together with Raetia, Noricum, Thrace and the other minor commands, took their cue from the various armies near them, and were driven willy-nilly into support or hostility by the contact of more powerful influences. The ungarrisoned provinces – and above all Italy itself, the

1. A.D. 66–73.
2. See p. 81.

helpless victim of every overlord – were doomed to be the spoils of war.

This, then, was the state of the Roman Empire when Servius Galba entered upon his second consulship as the colleague of Titus Vinius, at the start of a year which brought about their death and the near-destruction of Rome.

# The Murder of Galba

12. A few days after 1 January, word came from Pompeius Propinquus, the imperial agent in Belgica, that the legions of Upper Germany had broken their oath of loyalty and were calling for a change of emperor, though they resigned the choice of the new ruler to the Senate and People of Rome in order to mitigate the offence. This event accelerated a measure which Galba had for some time been debating in his own mind and with his friends – the adoption of an heir. In recent months, the matter had undoubtedly been the main topic of discussion throughout the country, for in the first place, there was opportunity, as well as an unhealthy craving, for such talk, and in the second, Galba was old and failing. Few Romans had any capacity to judge or real desire for the public good. But many day-dreamers talked glibly of the chances of this candidate or that in order to curry favour with a friend or a patron, or else to vent their spite on Titus Vinius, whose daily-growing influence only rendered him daily more detested.

The fact was that Galba's courtiers had tasted success, and the emperor's indulgence merely whetted their appetite for more. So weak and credulous a ruler made wrongdoing both safer and more lucrative. 13. The power that properly belonged to the emperor was in fact shared between the consul Titus Vinius and the pretorian prefect Cornelius Laco. No less influential was Galba's freedman Icelus, who had been given the status of knight and as such was commonly called 'Marcianus'. These three were at loggerheads, and each pursued an individual policy in minor matters. But on the question of electing a successor to Galba they were divided into two factions. Vinius supported Marcus Otho, while Laco and Icelus agreed in rejecting him, though they had no one alternative candidate in mind. Galba himself was not blind to the friendship existing between Otho and Titus Vinius, while wagging tongues could not resist prophesying that, as Vinius had an unwedded daughter and Otho was single, a marriage would conveniently seal the alliance.

I believe that Galba had begun to be anxious, too, about the welfare of his country, for it was little use having seized power from Nero if this were to pass to Otho. After all, the latter had spent a thoughtless childhood and riotous youth, winning Nero's favour because he mimicked his vices. This was why the emperor, until such times as he could get rid of his wife Octavia, had planted his mistress Poppaea Sabina on Otho, who knew all about the affair. Later he suspected him of falling in love with this same Poppaea, and packed him off to the province of Lusitania in the guise of its governor. Otho administered his province with courtesy, and was the first to side with the revolt.[1] So long as the campaign lasted he showed energy, and held the leading position among those in personal attendance upon Galba. He had hoped to be adopted from the start, and now each passing day saw his ambition intensified. He had the support of a majority among the troops, and Nero's courtiers naturally fell for one who resembled him.

14. But once informed of the army revolt in Germany, Galba was anxious about the extent of the outbreak, although so far there was no certain information about Vitellius. The emperor had no confidence in the city garrison either. He therefore resorted to what he believed to be the one and only cure for the disease – an imperial election. He summoned Marius Celsus (one of the consuls-designate) and Ducenius Geminus (the city prefect) as well as Vinius and Laco, and after a few prefatory remarks about his advancing years, sent for Piso Licinianus. It is not clear whether this was his own choice, or whether, as some have believed, it was the result of pressure from Laco, who had made friends with Piso at the house of Rubellius Plautus. However, in supporting him Laco astutely pretended that he was a stranger, and Piso's reputation made the policy plausible enough. As the son of Marcus Crassus and Scribonia, Piso came of distinguished parentage on both sides. His severe expression and general appearance belonged to an earlier age and on a just estimate suggested strictness of principle, though carping critics found him too straitlaced. If this aspect of his character awoke some misgivings in the pessimists, it won the approval of his adoptive father.

15. So it seems that Galba took Piso's hand and spoke to him in terms

1. Of Galba in Spain, April 68.

which may be paraphrased as follows: 'If I were a private citizen adopting you in the traditional way before the pontiffs with due legislative forms, it would have been gratifying to me to have a descendant of Gnaeus Pompey and Marcus Crassus entering my family, and you in your turn would have found it an honour to enhance your own distinctions with those of the Sulpicii and Lutatii. But as things are, the unanimous will of heaven and earth has called me to supreme power, and it is rather your character and patriotism which have impelled me to offer you the principate. For this power, our forefathers fought on the battle-field, and I myself won it by the sword. But I now give it to you in time of peace, following the precedent set by Emperor Augustus. He it was who promoted to a position immediately below his own his sister's son Marcellus, then his son-on-law Agrippa, later his own grandsons, and finally Tiberius Nero, his step-son. But Augustus looked for a successor within his family: I have done so in the country at large. This is not because I have no relatives or army colleagues. But it was not from selfish motives that I accepted office myself, and the nature of my present choice should be plain from the fact that, for your sake. I have passed over the claims not only of my relatives but of yours. Your brother is as nobly born as you, and older. He, too, could worthily fill the part, were you not the better man.

'You are old enough now to have escaped the waywardness of youth, and you have nothing to apologize for in your past. Until today, misfortune was all you had to bear. But success probes a man's character more keenly. Men put up with bad times, but prosperity spoils us. Loyalty, independence and friendship are the finest flowers of human character. These qualities you will of course continue to display as sturdily as ever. But others will seek to weaken them by a cringing attitude. You will have to face up to flattery, honied words and the poison most fatal to sincerity – individual self-interest. Even if you and I are today conversing with perfect frankness, the world will prefer to address us as emperors, not as ourselves. Persuading a ruler to adopt the right course is a fatiguing business, but to flatter him regardless of his character is a mechanical exercise which presupposes no real affection.

16. 'If it were possible for our gigantic empire to stand erect and keep its balance in the absence of a ruler, I should be the right sort of person to hand over power to a republican form of government. But

in fact we have long ago reached a point where drastic measures are necessary. Hence my declining years can make Rome no greater gift than a good successor, nor your youth any greater gift than a good emperor. Under Tiberius, Gaius and Claudius, the principate was the heirloom of a single family, so that the introduction of the principle of choice will mean liberty. The dynasty of the Julii and Claudii has come to an end, and the best man will be discovered by the process of adoption. To be born and bred of emperors is a matter of chance and is valued accordingly. But adoption implies the unfettered exercise of judgement. Moreover, if one wants guidance in this choice, public opinion points the way. Remember Nero, who prided himself on being the heir of a long line of Caesars. It was not Vindex with his undefended province, nor I with my one legion,[1] who dislodged this incubus from the shoulders of Rome. His own monstrous excesses and life of pleasure did so, though there was no precedent at that time for the condemnation of an emperor. We ourselves, who owe our promotion to armed force and critical scrutiny, are bound to be the target of envious glances, whatever our merits. However, you must not lose confidence if two legions[2] have not yet recovered their steadiness after the shock which the Roman world has suffered. My accession too was far from tranquil. Besides, once men hear of your adoption they will cease to view me as an old man – the only criticism they can level at me now. Nero will always be missed by the riff-raff. It is your task and mine to see to it that he is not missed by good men as well.

'This is not the moment for further words of advice, and indeed every precaution has been taken if I did right in choosing you. The most practical and also most rapid criterion of good and bad policy is to reflect what actions you would yourself approve or disapprove of if another were emperor. Rome is not like primitive countries with their kings. Here we have no ruling caste dominating a nation of slaves. You are called to be the leader of men who can tolerate neither total slavery nor total liberty.'

Such was the tenor of Galba's remarks. They sounded as if he were still in the process of creating an emperor. But the tone the

---

1. Galba was saluted as emperor by the Sixth Legion; but while still in Spain he raised the Seventh, which bore his name, as well as other troops.
2. The Fourth and Twenty-Second in Upper Germany: see p. 56.

rest took towards Piso showed that they regarded the process as complete.

17. We are told that the new Caesar betrayed no indication of emotion or exultation to his immediate audience or afterwards to the general public who riveted their gaze upon him. He addressed his father and sovereign in suitably respectful language, and referred to himself modestly. His unaltered looks and manner seemed to imply that he had the ability rather than the desire to be emperor.

It was then debated whether the right place for an official proclamation of the adoption would be the rostra, the senate or the pretorian barracks. It seemed best to proceed to the barracks. This, it was felt, would be a tribute to the army, whose favour ought not to be sought by bounties and cajolery, but was not to be despised if won by honourable means. Meanwhile, the palace had been surrounded by an expectant public impatient to hear the great secret, and attempts to suppress rumours which had leaked out merely intensified them.

18. The tenth of January was an unpleasantly rainy day, abnormally disturbed by thunder, lightning and a threatening sky. From time immemorial this had been interpreted as an omen calling for the cancellation of political assemblies, but it did not frighten Galba from making his way to the barracks. He despised such things as being the blind forces of nature; or perhaps the future is predestined and inevitable whatever the premonitory signs. His proclamation, addressed to a massive parade of the troops, was marked by the brevity befitting a supreme commander. He said that in adopting Piso he was acting in accordance with the precedent of Emperor Augustus and the military practice whereby one man used to pick another.[1] Furthermore, in order to stop exaggerated versions of the revolt by speaking frankly, he went out of his way to insist that the aberrations of the Fourth and Twenty-Second Legions had not exceeded mere words and slogans, and they would soon return to their duty. Nor did he round off the speech by pandering to the troops or bribing them. Despite this, the tribunes, centurions and front-ranks raised a gratifying cheer by way of response. But throughout the rest reigned gloom and silence, as if they felt that active service had lost them the bounty customarily exacted even in peace-time. There is general agreement that it would have been quite possible to win them over by a mere token act of generosity on the part of the niggardly old emperor. His

1. An ancient Italian method of levying troops was by personal co-optation.

old-fashioned rigidity and excessive strictness spelt ruin, for we cannot rise to these standards nowadays.

19. Then came a meeting of the senate. Its members heard from Galba some remarks as simple and brief as those he had addressed to the troops. Piso made a courteous and formal speech, which went down well. Many senators felt genuine good will, those who had opposed him spoke even more effusively, and the uncommitted majority were quick to grovel. They were too busy calculating their private prospects to worry about the public interest. In the following four days, the time which intervened between his adoption and murder, Piso made no public utterance or move.

As reports of the German revolt increased day by day in a country prepared to hear and believe all the latest news if it is bad, the senate had determined to send a mission to the army of Germany. The question of Piso's joining the embassy was ventilated in secret. This would look more impressive: the others would carry the authority of the senate, Piso the prestige of a Caesar. They decided to include Laco, the pretorian prefect; but he promptly vetoed this plan. Besides, the selection of the other commissioners, which had been entrusted by the senate to Galba, was marked by scandalous indecision. Men were nominated, and then allowed to withdraw or suggest substitutes, according as each man's fears or hopes induced him to pull strings in an endeavour to secure exemption from the mission or inclusion in it.

20. The next matter to be dealt with was finance. A comprehensive survey showed that the fairest thing would be to demand repayment from those who were responsible for the crisis. Nero had squandered 2,200 million sesterces in largesse. Galba ordered the recipients to be sent individual demand-notices, on the understanding that each was to retain one tenth of what he had received. But the people concerned had barely this amount left, for they had spent other men's money as lavishly as their own. The really greedy and unprincipled beneficiaries no longer disposed of any landed property or capital investments: only the minor trappings of depravity remained. The collection of the money was to be supervised by an equestrian committee of thirty. Their functions were without precedent, and rendered onerous by interest and numbers. The auctioneer and the dealer in confiscated property were everywhere, and Rome was distracted by lawsuits. Yet there was also intense jubilation at the

thought that the recipients of Nero's bounty would henceforth be as poor as those he had robbed.

In the course of these days some tribunes were cashiered: Antonius Taurus and Antonius Naso of the Pretorian Guard, Aemilius Pacensis of the Urban Cohorts, and Julius Fronto of the Watch. No steps were taken against the rest. This only gave rise to the feeling that, if individual offenders were being timidly and cunningly removed, all were suspect.

21. Otho had nothing to hope for from settled conditions, and his whole policy was based on exploiting chaos. By this time he was responding to a number of irritants: dissipation such as would have imposed a strain even upon an emperor's pocket, poverty which even a private individual could scarcely stand, malice towards Galba and jealousy of Piso. To stimulate his ambition, he conjured up imaginary dangers, too. He told himself that Nero had found him too much of a burden, and he could not expect a second Lusitania and appointment to another exile. Suspicion and hatred must always be the reaction of rulers towards the man talked of as the next in the succession. It was this, he reflected, that had prejudiced his chances with an elderly emperor, and it would do so even more with an ill-natured youth soured by prolonged exile. His assassination, Otho reflected, was always a possibility. So he must be up and doing, while Galba's popularity was fading and Piso's had not yet established itself. There was scope for great enterprises when power changed hands, and hesitation was misplaced where inaction could do more harm than recklessness. Death came equally to all men as a condition of their existence: it was differentiated only by oblivion or fame in after times. If guilty and innocent must await the same end, it showed more spirit in a man to die for a purpose.

22. Otho's character was not as flabby as his physical condition, and it was exploited by his confidential freedmen and slaves, who were given a freer hand than one expects in a private household. These creatures dangled alluring prospects before his greedy gaze: a court and life of pleasure like Nero's, liaisons, marriages and all the gratifications of tyranny. These could be his if he had the courage. If he did nothing, the taunters added, these prizes would go to someone else. Further pressure came from the astrologers, who asserted that their observation of the stars heralded change and a year of glory for Otho. Such men mislead the powerful and deceive the ambitious, practising

a profession which our country will always be outlawed and always maintained. The backstairs intrigues of Poppaea had employed a number of astrologers whose nefarious activities secured her marriage to the emperor. One of these, Ptolemaeus, had gone with Otho to Spain. He had promised that his patron would survive Nero, and the fulfilment of the prophecy established his reputation. Now, proceeding by guesswork and the calculations of gossips who worked out Galba's age and compared it with Otho's, he had managed to persuade the latter that he would be called to be emperor. But in accepting these predictions, Otho imagined they were based on knowledge and the voice of destiny, man's character being such that he will always prefer to believe in mysteries. Ptolemaeus pressed his advantage and proceeded to urge Otho to take the fatally easy step from evil ambition to evil deeds.

23. But whether the plot was the result of a sudden impulse may be questioned. Otho had been angling for the support of the troops for some time, in the hope of succeeding to the principate or in preparation for a coup. On the move from Spain, whether during the march or at halting places, he made it a practice to address the oldest[1] soldiers by name, and talked of 'their service together' – an allusion to attendance upon Nero. He greeted some as old friends. He asked after the occasional absentee. He gave assistance in the form of money or favours, often dropping complaints and double-edged remarks about Galba and employing all the other incitements of the mob agitator. The tiring marches, short rations[2] and strict discipline were not well received by men who were used to travelling to the lake district of Campania and the cities of Greece on board ship, but who now found themselves plodding wearily over the Pyrenees and Alps and along interminable roads under the weight of their arms and equipment.

24. The smouldering discontent of the troops was fanned to a blaze by one of Tigellinus' cronies, Mevius Pudens. Getting hold of the men who were most easily led, or who were short of money and therefore ready for any desperate plunge, he worked upon them little by little and finally went so far as to hand out a tip of 100 sesterces to each and every member of the cohort on duty whenever Galba dined with Otho, ostensibly for their meal. This semi-official bounty

1. As governor of Lusitania from A.D. 58 to 68, Otho had long been out of touch with the pretorians.
2. Or 'lack of leave'.

was backed by more confidential rewards to individuals. His methods of corruption were enterprising. A member of the emperor's personal bodyguard called Cocceius Proculus happened to be in dispute with a neighbour over part of the latter's land. Otho bought up the whole of this neighbour's farm out of his own pocket, and presented it to Proculus as a free gift. Such things were only rendered possible by the inefficiency of the pretorian prefect, who was blind to everything, whether it was common knowledge or a secret.

25. Anyway, Otho now put his freedman Onomastus in charge of the plot. The latter introduced two members of the bodyguard, a corporal called Barbius Proculus and a warrant-officer, one Veturius. In the course of a discursive interview Otho found out that they were competent and unscrupulous, and doled out bribes and promises on a lavish scale. Money was given them to enable them to bid for wider support. Thus two non-commissioned officers undertook to dispose of the empire which belonged to Rome. In this they were completely successful. Only a few confederates were let into the secret. As for the rest, Proculus and Veturius employed a variety of ingenious methods to prod the hesitant, dropping hints to senior N.C.O.s that they were under a cloud because Nymphidius had promoted them, and inducing in the remainder, that is the majority, a mood of anger and despair at the repeated postponement of the bounty. If a few regretted Nero and missed the slack discipline of the past, all without exception were panic-stricken at the prospect of being posted to less favoured units.

26. The rot spread to the legionaries and auxiliaries, already demoralized by the spread of news about the crumbling loyalty of the army of Germany. The mischief-makers were ready for mutiny, and even the better sort were prepared to connive at it. Indeed, on the following day[1] they were on the point of carrying Otho off to their barracks as he was returning home from a dinner, but were scared off by the uncertainties of night-time, the scattered location of the troops throughout Rome, and the difficulty of achieving co-ordination between men who were the worse for drink. It was not their country they were worried about, for they were preparing in sober earnest to desecrate it with the blood of their emperor. But there was a real fear that in the darkness any chance person who met the Pannonian or German units might be mistaken for Otho, who was not personally known to most people. There was plenty of evidence of this incipient outbreak, but those in the

1. 11 January.

know hushed it up. A few hints which reached Galba's ears were side-stepped by the prefect Laco, who was quite out of touch with what his men thought, regularly opposed any plan, whatever its excellence, which he had not himself proposed, and showed a stubborn disregard for expert opinion.

27. On 15 January, Galba was offering sacrifice in front of the Temple of Apollo.[1] The soothsayer Umbricius pronounced the entrails of the victim to be ill-omened, and predicted the imminence of a plot and the presence of a traitor within the palace. As Otho was standing next to Galba, he overheard this and gleefully interpreted it in the contrary sense as favourable to his own designs. A few minutes later, his freedman Onomastus brought him a message: the architect and builders were waiting for him. This was the prearranged code indicating that the troops were already assembling and the plot ripe. Some asked Otho why he was leaving. In reply, he pretended that he was buying some dilapidated property which had to be surveyed before the deal was complete. Arm-in-arm with his freedman, he made his way through the Palace of Tiberius into the Velabrum, and from there to the Golden Milestone near the Temple of Saturn. Here twenty-three members of the bodyguard gave him the imperial salutation. Otho was appalled that they were so few in number, but they quickly placed him in a chair, drew their swords and hurried him off. Roughly the same number of soldiers joined the party on the way – some privy to the plot, many bewildered, a proportion shouting and flourishing their swords, others again maintaining silence, with the intention of suiting their reaction to the event.

28. The duty-officer at the barracks was the tribune Julius Martialis. It is hard to say whether he was overwhelmed by the mere idea of such an immense and wicked enterprise, or whether he feared that the rot went deeper among the men and that resistance on his part might spell death. In any case, he gave many people the impression that he was in the plot. The other tribunes, and the centurions, also preferred the advantage of the moment to the incalculable risks of honour. Their mood may be summed up thus: a shocking crime was committed on the unscrupulous initiative of few individuals, with the blessing of more, and amid the passive acquiescence of all.

29. Meanwhile, Galba was unaware of what was afoot. Preoccupied with the sacrifice, he continued to offer his importunities to the gods of

1. On the Palatine Hill near the palace; its site is disputed.

an empire no longer his. Suddenly word came that some senator – it was not known who – was being hastily carried to the pretorian barracks. After a while, the man was identified as Otho. News came from every part of Rome at once, brought by whoever had met the procession. Some of these informants were panicky, and gave an exaggerated account. A few used understatement, unable even at the eleventh hour to forget the habit of flattery. A consultation was held. It was decided to test the attitude of the cohort that was on duty in the palace area, while not exposing Galba in person. The prestige of the emperor was to be reserved intact to deal with some more drastic situation. So it was Piso who addressed the parade from the steps of the palace in a speech whose substance I reproduce:

'This is the fifth day, men, since I was created a Caesar by adoption. I was ignorant of what was to come. Perhaps this name was one to covet; perhaps it was to be dreaded. What in fact this implies for my family and for the state is a matter which rests with you. Not that I have any fears of a grimmer upshot on my own account. I have experienced adversity already, and this very moment teaches me that success itself is no less dangerous. But I am indeed sorry for my father, the senate and the empire itself, if we must either suffer death today or, by a dispensation equally grievous to good men, inflict it. In the last crisis, we found comfort in the circumstance that there was no bloodshed in the capital and that the transference of power was undisputed. In this case, the fact of adoption appeared sufficient guarantee against fighting, even after Galba's reign comes to an end.

30. 'I shall make no claims for myself in point of ancestry or good character. After all, there is no need for a catalogue of virtues when the comparison is with Otho. His sole boast is a vicious life, which involved the downfall of an emperor even when Otho passed himself off as the emperor's friend. Are we to believe that he earned the principate by his mincing airs? Or by his characteristically effeminate love of finery? The public are mistaken: they are imposed upon by a prodigal wearing the mask of generosity. Otho will be skilled in squandering, but not in giving. At this moment seduction, revelry and sex are the things that engage his imagination. These he takes to be the spoils of the imperial office, whose lusts and pleasures are to be his, their shame and degradation everyone's. No one has ever made good use of power evilly gained.

'Galba was called to be a Caesar by the unanimous voice of the whole world, and I by Galba with your approval. If "constitution", "senate" and "people" are merely empty phrases, it is up to you, men, to see that the emperor is not created by the dregs of the army. We have sometimes heard stories of legionaries rising in mutiny against their commanders, but your reliability and reputation have never been in question until today. Even Nero himself deserted you; you did not desert him. We are faced with less than thirty renegades and deserters – men in whom no one would tolerate the claim to appoint a centurion or a tribune. Are they to have an empire in their gift? Are you going to concede this precedent, and make yourselves accessories to the act by doing nothing about it? These liberties will spread to the provinces, and the upshot will be death for us and warfare for you. Murdering your emperor brings no greater reward than keeping your hands clean, and from us you will get as generous a bonus for loyalty as you would from others for treason.'

31. The men of the bodyguard had slipped away,[1] but the rest of the cohort took no exception to Piso's speech. They prepared for action with heightened excitement, increased confusion and yet still with a degree of loyalty; some were in genuine ignorance of what was afoot, others (as was afterwards believed) were traitors putting on an act. Marius Celsus, too, was sent off to negotiate with the Balkan contingents quartered in the Porticus Vipsania,[2] and instructions were given to two senior warrant-officers, Amullius Serenus and Domitius Sabinus, to bring up the troops of the army of Germany from Freedom Hall.[3] Little confidence was placed in the naval legion, for the men still resented the butchery of their comrades by Galba on the very first occasion of his entering Rome.[4] In addition to these measures, the tribunes Cetrius Severus, Subrius Dexter and Pomponius Longinus went off to the pretorian barracks to see if the still incipient outbreak could be made to yield to saner counsels before it was too late. Of the tribunes, Subrius and Cetrius were given a threatening reception by the troops, while Longinus was actually manhandled, arrested and disarmed. This was because his loyalty to his emperor depended less on rank than friendship with Galba, and so rendered him particularly suspect in the eyes of the rebels. The naval legion promptly went over to the pretorians, and

1. See p. 38.

2. A portico in the northern part of the city near the point where the modern Via del Tritone meets the Via del Corso.

3. Perhaps behind the Senate House near the Forum.    4. See pp. 24 and 43.

the drafts from the army of the Balkans drove Celsus away at the
point of their pikes. The detachments from Germany wavered for
some time, being still physically unfit, as well as amiably disposed.
They had formed the advance-party sent on to Alexandria by Nero,
and as their health had been impaired by the long return voyage,
Galba had made a point of nursing them back into condition.

32. By this time, the palace area was jammed by the mob, consisting
of the lower classes in full strength, with some slaves. Discordant
shouts were raised demanding Otho's head and the execution of the
conspirators, as if the crowd were clamouring for some sort of entertainment in the circus or theatre. There was no question of their
expressing a considered or sincere opinion, for on the very same day
they were to make diametrically opposed demands with equal alacrity. This was merely the accepted tradition whereby any emperor,
no matter who he was, was acclaimed with extravagant applause and
empty demonstration.

Meanwhile Galba was hesitating between two proposals. Titus
Vinius urged staying in the palace, using the household slaves as a
screen, barricading the doors, and avoiding contact while tempers
ran high. Galba, he said, should give the offenders an opportunity to
repent, and loyal subjects a breathing space to adopt concerted action.
What made crime effective was the element of surprise. Honest
counsels profited from delay. Finally, the emperor would still be in a
position to venture out at will later, if this seemed policy, but if he
were to do so and regret it, any return to the palace would lie at the
mercy of others.

33. The remainder of the council were for speedy action to anticipate
the growth of the conspiracy, which was so far a feeble business confined to a few plotters. Otho, too, was likely to be in a panic, they
pointed out. He had left furtively and been carried off to men who
were strangers to him. But the idle advocates of procrastination and
time-wasting were at this very moment giving him a chance to learn
the part of emperor. They must not wait for him to establish his hold
on the barracks, invade the Forum and enter the Capitol under
Galba's nose, while the doughty emperor and his heroic courtiers –
doughty and heroic as far as the door, at any rate – bolted and barred
the palace with the evident intention of submitting to a siege. Much
help would they get from the slaves, once the united will of the great
crowd and its all-important initial outburst of indignation were

allowed to flag! Such a policy was as dangerous as it was degrading. Even if they were fated to die, it was best to meet danger half-way. This would win Otho the greater infamy, and themselves honour.

Vinius' opposition to this plan provoked a furious onslaught from the blustering Laco. The latter was backed by Icelus, who obstinately persisted in a private vendetta to the ruin of his country.  34. Galba for his part hesitated no longer, and gave his casting vote in favour of their plan: it looked better. However, Piso was told to go on ahead to the barracks as being a young man of great name recently promoted, and an opponent of Titus Vinius. (Whether he was such in fact, or whether malignant critics merely wanted him to be, is not clear; but a quarrel seems the more likely supposition.)

Piso had scarcely left the palace when word came that Otho had been killed in the barracks. At first the rumour was vague and uncertain. Then, as so often is the case with brazen falsehoods, certain individuals asserted that they had been present when the deed was done and had witnessed it. The story was lapped up by a jubilant and uncritical public. Many people held that the rumour had been invented and swollen by means of Othonian agents who had already insinuated themselves among the crowd and spread the bogus good news in order to lure Galba out of his palace.

35. This was the signal for a burst of applause and exaggerated enthusiasm, which was not confined to the populace and the ignorant lower classes. Many of the knights and senators threw fear and caution to the winds. Forcing the doors of the palace, they poured into the apartments, and presented themselves before Galba with the complaint that they had been forestalled in their revenge. The greatest cowards among them – those who, as events proved, were to lose their nerve in the moment of danger – expressed themselves in violent language, and played the hero with their tongue. Ignorance and assertion went hand in hand everywhere. Finally, the absence of reliable information and the united chorus of delusion proved Galba's undoing. He buckled on his breastplate, and being too old and too infirm to resist the pressure of the crowd as it surged in, was placed in a chair and raised shoulder-high. While still in the palace area, he was confronted by one of his bodyguard called Julius Atticus, who flourished a blood-stained sword and cried out that he had killed Otho. Galba's immediate retort was: 'Who gave you the order, my man?' This remark shows his striking determination to check

indiscipline. Indeed, threats left him unafraid, and in the face of flatterers he retained his integrity.

36. By this time all hesitation had vanished in the pretorian barracks. So great was the enthusiasm that the men were not content with escorting Otho and crowding round him. They put him, amid massed flags and standards, on a dais which had recently supported a gold statue of Galba. The tribunes and centurions were allowed no access to Otho, and in any case the other ranks warned him to be on his guard against the officers. The whole place re-echoed with shouting, tumult and mutual encouragement. It is not unusual for the civilian populace and the lower classes to voice their idle flattery by means of confused cries. But this was quite different. Whenever the troops noticed a fresh adherent coming over to them, they shook him by the hand, put their arms around his neck, placed him near Otho and administered the oath of allegiance, praising the emperor to his troops in one breath and the troops to their emperor in the next. Otho, too, played his part well. He would hold out his hands, bow to the mob and throw them kisses, in everything aping the slave in order to become the master. When the naval legion had taken the oath down to the last man, he began to feel sure of himself. Believing that individual inducement should be backed up by a general appeal, he took up a position on the wall surrounding the barracks, and addressed the pretorians as follows:

37. 'I find it hard to say in what capacity I stand before you, men. I can scarcely call myself a subject after you have nominated me as emperor. Nor can I describe myself as emperor while another rules. Your own designation will be just as ambiguous so long as it is not clear whether the man you are harbouring in your barracks is the ruler of Rome or a traitor. Do you hear them? They are calling in the same breath for my punishment and your execution. This makes it quite obvious that we stand or fall together.

'Knowing Galba's clemency, one can guess that he has already undertaken to carry out the sentence. After all, he slaughtered thousands of completely inoffensive troops when no one asked him to. I shudder when I think of his grisly occupation of Rome – the only victory Galba ever won – in which he gave orders that men who had surrendered, thrown themselves on his mercy and been accepted as his loyal followers, should suffer decimation before the gaze of the capital. After this auspicious entry, what prestige did he confer upon the office of emperor other than that of having executed Obultronius

Sabinus and Cornelius Marcellus in Spain, Betuus Cilo in Gaul, Fonteius Capito in Germany, Clodius Macer in Africa, Cingonius on the march, Turpilianus at Rome, Nymphidius in the barracks? What province is there throughout the world, what army barracks, which is not stained and polluted with blood, or, to use Galba's phrase, "reformed and straightened up"? Treatment which others call criminal he calls remedial. By a misuse of language, he describes cruelty as severity, greed as economy and the execution and insults you have suffered as a lesson in discipline.

'Barely seven months have passed since the death of Nero, and in this time Icelus has stolen more money than was ever squandered by creatures like Polyclitus, Vatinius and Egnatius.[1] The exactions of Titus Vinius would have displayed less greed and lawlessness if he had been emperor himself. As it is, he has both kept us in subjection as if we were his chattels, and held us cheap as though we belonged to another. His mansion alone is enough to provide that bounty which is still denied, yet forms the text of daily sermons.

38. 'What is more, to make sure that we should not pin our hopes upon his successor, Galba has restored from exile the one man who in his opinion most closely resembled himself for surliness and avarice. You have observed, men, the remarkable storm by which even the gods signified their disgust at this ill-omened adoption. The same mood animates the senate. The same mood animates the Roman people. All they are waiting for is your courageous intervention, for you alone can make good policies effective, and without you the best endeavours are paralysed.

'I am not calling upon you to fight a war or risk your lives. The armed forces without exception are on our side. As for the one solitary cohort in civilian dress manning the palace, its function is not so much to protect Galba as to keep him in custody. When this unit catches sight of you, when it receives my signal, the only struggle that will take place will be a competition to see who can earn my deepest gratitude. In an enterprise that can only win praise if it is carried to a successful conclusion, there is no room for hesitation.'

Otho then ordered the arsenal to be opened. Weapons were hastily grabbed. Tradition and discipline went by the board. The troops disregarded the distinctions of equipment between pretorians and legionaries, and seized helmets and shields meant for auxiliaries. All

1. Influential freedmen of Nero.

was confusion. No encouragement came from tribunes or centurions. Each man followed his own lead and prompting, and the worst elements found their chief stimulus in the sorrow of the good.

39. By this time Piso was seriously alarmed by the mounting tumult and cries of mutiny, audible even in Rome itself. He joined Galba, who had in the interval left the palace and was approaching the Forum. Celsus, too, returned with bad news. Some of Galba's suite suggested returning to the Palatine. Others wanted to make for the Capitol. A number of them were for securing the rostra. The majority, however, confined themselves to denouncing the views of their companions, and as so often happens when things go wrong, regretted they had not done what it was now too late to do. It is said that Laco, without telling Galba, toyed with the idea of killing Titus Vinius. If so, it is hard to say whether he thought his execution would mollify the troops, or believed him Otho's confederate, or in the last resort merely hated him. The time and the place gave him pause. Once killing starts, it is difficult to draw the line. Anyway, Laco's plan was upset by the alarming news and the flight of his associates. Indeed, all those keen supporters who had ostentatiously paraded their loyalty and courage at the start now lost heart.

40. By this time, Galba was being carried hither and thither by the irregular impact of the surging multitude. Everywhere the public buildings and temples were crowded with a sea of faces. The crowd was thrilled to be witnesses of a solemn moment. Not a cry came from the mass of the people or the lower classes. Their faces betrayed astonishment, their ears were strained to catch every sound. There was neither disorder nor quiet, but only the hush typical of great fear or great anger.

Otho, however, was informed that the mob were being armed. He ordered his men to move in at full speed and seize the danger-points. Thus it was that Roman troops made ready to murder an old, defenceless man who was their emperor, just as if they were set on deposing a Vologaeses or Pacorus from the ancestral throne of the Arsacids.[1] Forcing their way through the crowd, trampling the senate under foot, with weapons at the ready and horses spurred to a gallop, they burst upon the Forum. Such men were not deterred by the sight of the Capitol, the sanctity of the temples that looked down upon

1. The dynasty that ruled Parthia from the third century B.C. to the third century A.D.

them, nor the thought of emperors past and emperors to come. They were bent upon the commission of a crime that is inevitably avenged by the victim's successor.

41. On catching sight of the approaching party of armed men, an ensign belonging to the cohort which formed Galba's escort – Atilius Vergilio, according to the tradition – ripped from his standard the effigy of Galba and dashed it to the ground, a clear indication that all the troops supported Otho. It was also a signal for a mass exodus of the civilian populace from the Forum. Swords were drawn to deal with recalcitrants. Near the Basin of Curtius, the panic of his bearers caused Galba to be flung sprawling from his chair. His last words are variously recorded by the conflicting voices of hatred and admiration. Some say that he grovelled, and asked what he had done to deserve his fate, begging a few days' grace to pay the bounty. The majority of the historians believe that he voluntarily bared his throat to the assassins, telling them to strike and be done with it, if this was what seemed best for the country. Little did the murderers care what he said.

The identity of the killer is in doubt. Some authorities speak of a veteran called Terentius. Others mention one Laecanius. The more usual version holds that a soldier of the Fifteenth Legion named Camurius thrust his sword deep into Galba's throat. The rest of them, with revolting butchery, hacked at his legs and arms, as these (unlike his body) were not protected by armour. These sadistic monsters even inflicted a number of wounds on the already truncated torso.

42. Then they turned upon Titus Vinius. Here, too, accounts differ. Was he rendered speechless by a paroxysm of fear? Or did he call out that Otho had given no instructions that he was to be murdered? Whether this remark was in fact an invention due to fear or a confession that he was in the plot, his life and reputation incline me to think that he had prior knowledge of a crime he certainly caused. In front of the Temple of Julius Caesar he was struck down by a blow on the back of the knee, followed by a thrust from a legionary, Julius Carus, which pierced him from side to side.

43. This day's work has provided modern times with the spectacle of a real act of heroism. The hero was Sempronius Densus, a centurion who belonged to one of the pretorian cohorts and had been appointed by Galba to watch over Piso's safety. With dagger drawn, he advanced to meet his fully armed enemies and denounced their mutiny. His words and actions diverted the attention of the assassins upon

himself. This gave Piso a chance to escape, wounded though he was. He got away to the Temple of Vesta, where the state slave who was its guardian, taking pity on him, gave him shelter and concealment in his humble room. Thus, for a while, Piso managed to postpone the fatal moment, not thanks to the sanctity of the building or its daily ritual, but by lying low. But then came two of Otho's emissaries bent hot-foot upon their murderous errand. One of these was Sulpicius Florus of the auxiliary cohorts serving in Britain. (Only recently, he had been given Roman citizenship by Galba.) The other was the imperial bodyguard Statius Murcus. These two dragged out Piso and murdered him at the door of the temple.

44. It is said that Otho was especially gratified to hear of Piso's death, and studied the victim's severed head with peculiar malevolence, as if his eyes could never drink their fill. Perhaps this was because the last weight had now been lifted from his mind and he felt free to exult. Or perhaps the reason lay in the contrast with the fate of Galba and Titus Vinius. There the thought of his treason towards the former and his friendship for the latter had cast a shadow over Otho's spirit, for all its ruthlessness. But the doom of an enemy and rival like Piso may have seemed a right and proper reason for satisfaction.

The heads of the victims were impaled and carried in procession, backed by the cohort standards and a legionary eagle. The mutineers vied with each other in displaying the blood dripping from their hands, whether they had actually done the killing or had merely witnessed it, and whether their boastful claim to what they called a fine and memorable deed was true or false. More than 120 individuals presented petitions demanding a reward for some noteworthy service on this day. These documents later fell into the hands of Vitellius, who gave instructions that all the petitioners were to be rounded up and put to death. This was not meant as a tribute on his part to Galba: it was the traditional method by which rulers secure self-defence for the present and warn of retribution in the future.

45. A complete transformation seemed to have taken place in both senators and people. They were now a mob stampeding in the direction of the barracks, each man trying to outstrip his neighbour in the race and catch up with those who led the field. They cursed Galba, complimented the soldiers on their choice, and covered Otho's hand with kisses. These demonstrations were multiplied in proportion to their insincerity. Otho for his part welcomed even single individuals who came up to him, and restrained the greed and menaces of his men

47

by word and look. The consul-designate Marius Celsus had shown Galba affection and loyalty to the bitter end. For this the soldiers now demanded his head, for they resented his energy and high principle as if they were faults of character. It was only too obvious that they were looking for an excuse to set about bloodshed and plunder and the annihilation of every decent Roman. But Otho was not yet in a position to prevent outrage – though he could already command it. So he pretended to be angry, and by ordering Celsus to be put in irons and undertaking that he would receive a heavier punishment later on, rescued him from immediate death.

46. After that, the troops got their way in everything. They chose their own pretorian prefects. One was Plotius Firmus. After serving in the ranks at one time, this man had been given command of the Watch and had joined the faction of Otho while Galba's position was still sound. His colleague was Licinius Proculus, whose close association with Otho suggested that he had encouraged his designs. As city prefect, the troops chose Flavius Sabinus. In this they followed Nero's lead, for Sabinus had held the same post under that emperor. In making this choice many of them had their eye on his brother, Vespasian.

There was a demand for the remission of the payments traditionally made to centurions to secure exemption from duty. This was a kind of annual tax payable by the other ranks. As much as a quarter of a company's strength would be scattered high and low on leave or loitering in the actual barracks, so long as they squared the company commander. The extent of these exactions and the methods employed to meet them were nobody's business. Highway robbery, theft or taking on jobs as servants were the means by which they paid for their time off. Besides this, the richer a soldier was, the more he was subjected to fatigues and ill-treatment until he agreed to purchase exemption. Finally, when his money had given out and he had got into an idle and unhealthy state, he would return to his unit, reduced from affluence to poverty and from vigour to sloth. This process was repeated interminably; and the same destitution and indiscipline ruined man after man, driving them herd-like down the slope that leads to mutiny, dissension and, in the last resort, civil war. However, Otho had no wish to alienate his centurions by bribing their men. So he promised that the annual leave should be paid for by the imperial exchequer.[1]

1. The payment was to be made directly to the centurions by their commanding officers as a charge on the legionary chest.

There is no doubt that this was a beneficial reform, and in the course of time the practice hardened into a recognized part of the military system under the good emperors who succeeded.

The prefect Laco was given the impression that he was being exiled to an island. In fact, he was struck down by a veteran whom Otho had already sent ahead to murder him. Marcianus Icelus was a freedman, and, as such, he was publicly executed.

47. The long day of villainy drew to its end. There remained the last horror – a mood of jubilation. The senate was summoned by the urban praetor, the other magistrates surpassed each other in feats of flattery, and the senators hurried hot-foot to the meeting. A decree was passed giving Otho the tribunician power, the title 'Augustus' and all the imperial prerogatives. Everybody made a desperate effort to obliterate the taunts and insults which had been freely bandied about; no one was actually made to feel that they rankled in Otho's mind, and whether in fact he had renounced revenge or merely postponed it was a question which remained unanswered owing to the shortness of his reign.

The forum was still bloodstained and littered with bodies when Otho was carried through it to the Capitol, and from there to the palace. He allowed the remains to be handed over for burial and to be cremated. Piso was laid to rest by his wife Verania and his brother Scribonianus, Titus Vinius by his daughter Crispina. They had to search for the heads and pay a ransom for them, as the assassins had kept them in order to do a deal.

48. At the time of his death, Piso was nearing his thirty-first birthday. He was a man whose reputation was better than his luck. Two of his brothers had been executed: Magnus by Claudius and Crassus by Nero. He himself was for long an exile, and for five days a Caesar. His hurried adoption gave him one advantage, and one only, over the elder brother to whom he was preferred: he was the first to be murdered.

As for Titus Vinius, during a lifetime lasting forty-seven years he played many parts, both good and evil. His father came of a family which had produced praetors, and his grandfather on his mother's side was a victim of the proscriptions.[1] His first tour of military service won him notoriety. The wife of his commanding officer Calvisius Sabinus had an unfortunate passion for inspecting the camp-

1. Of the Triumvirs, 43 B.C.

site. One night, she entered it disguised as a soldier, and with no less effrontery forced herself upon the pickets and other military activities. Finally, she had the shamelessness to commit adultery, in the head-quarters building of all places. The man involved was proved to be Titus Vinius. So he was put under close arrest by order of Gaius Caesar,[1] but when times changed soon afterwards, he was given his freedom, rising smoothly in the public service as praetor, and then as a legionary commander who proved his worth. His reputation was later sullied by a scandal unworthy of a gentleman. He was alleged to have stolen a gold cup at a banquet given by Claudius. Indeed, on the day after, the emperor gave orders that Vinius alone of all his guests was to be served on earthenware. Still, he proved a strict and honest proconsul of Narbonese Gaul, and after that his friendship with Galba carried him irresistibly into the abyss. Unscrupulous, cunning and quick-witted, when and as he made up his mind he could be either vicious or hard-working, with equal effectiveness.

While Titus Vinius' enormous wealth caused his will to be set aside, Piso's last wishes were respected because he was poor.

49. The body of Galba lay disregarded for many hours, and under cover of night marauders offered it repeated outrage. Finally his steward Argius, an old retainer of his, buried it in a humble grave in the grounds of Galba's private villa. The head fell into the hands of army sutlers and servants, who were responsible for impaling and mutilating it. It was only on the following day that it was found in front of the tomb of Patrobius, a freedman of Nero who had been sentenced by Galba. It was then laid with the ashes of the body, which had already been cremated.

Such was the fate of Servius Galba. In the course of seventy-three years he had lived a successful life spanning the reigns of five emperors – reigns which proved luckier for him than his own. He came of a family that could boast ancient nobility and great wealth. His own personality was something of a compromise: while free from serious faults, it scarcely achieved real virtues. Having won a reputation, he neither despised nor exploited it. He harboured no designs upon other people's property, was thrifty with his own, and where the state was involved showed himself a positive miser. A tolerant attitude towards courtiers and officials attracted no censure when they happened to be honest; but his lack of perception if they were not was quite inexcusable. How-

1. Caligula, emperor A.D. 37–41.

ever, distinguished birth and the alarms of the time disguised his lack of enterprise and caused it to be described as wisdom. In the prime of life he attained military distinction in the Rhineland; as proconsul, he administered Africa with moderation, and his control of Nearer Spain in his latter years showed a similar sense of fair-play. Indeed, so long as he was a subject, he seemed too great a man to be one, and by common consent possessed the makings of a ruler – had he never ruled.

50. In Rome, public opinion was nervous. Men were not merely aghast at the grisly crimes which had just been committed; they also feared Otho's character, which they knew from the past. An additional source of anxiety was the fresh news about Vitellius. This had been hushed up before Galba's assassination, so that the mutiny was thought to be confined to the army of Upper Germany. Here then were the two most despicable men in the whole world by reason of their unclean, idle and pleasure-loving lives, apparently appointed by fate for the task of destroying the empire. It was the realization of this that now evoked unconcealed regret not only from the senate and knights, who had some stake and interest in the country, but from the man in the street as well. Conversation no longer centred on recent episodes which illustrated the brutality of peace. Minds went back to the civil wars, and they spoke of the many times Rome had been captured by its own armies, of the devastation of Italy, of the sack of provinces, of Pharsalia, Philippi and famous names associated with national disasters. The whole world, they reflected, had been practically turned upside down when the duel for power involved honourable rivals. But the empire had survived the victory of Julius Caesar and that of Augustus. The republic would have done the same under Pompey and Brutus. But were they now to visit the temples and pray for Otho? Or rather for Vitellius? Intercession for either would be equally impious, and vows equally blasphemous. In any struggle between the pair, the only certainty was that the winner would turn out the worse. Some observers pointed to the possibility of intervention by Vespasian and the forces of the east, and though Vespasian was better than either Otho or Vitellius, yet they were terrified of fresh hostilities and fresh disasters. There were in fact conflicting stories about Vespasian, and he alone – unlike all the emperors before him – changed for the better.

# The Vitellian Advance

51. I shall now explain the origin and causes of the movement in favour of Vitellius. The destruction of Julius Vindex and his entire force had given the Roman army a taste for loot and glory. This was only natural, for without exertion or danger it had gained the victory in a war that proved exceedingly profitable. The men now wanted campaigns and set battles, as the prizes here were more attractive than their normal pay. For long they had put up with hard and unrewarding service in an uncongenial area and climate, under strict discipline. But discipline, however inflexible in peace-time, is relaxed in civil conflicts, where agents are ready to encourage disloyalty on either side, and treachery goes unpunished.

Recruits, equipment and mounts were in ample supply, whether for use or show. Besides, before the war with Vindex, the men had only been familiar with their own company or troop, as the two armies were kept apart by the provincial boundaries.[1] But now the concentration of the legions to deal with Vindex had enabled them to take stock of themselves and of the Gallic provinces. Hence they began to look around for fresh trouble and new quarrels. No longer, as in the past, did they refer to the provincials as 'allies', but as 'the enemy' or 'the defeated side'. In this they were supported by the Gallic communities bordering the Rhine. These threw in their lot with the Roman garrisons, and now venomously incited them to attack those of their fellow countrymen whom in their contempt for Vindex they labelled 'Galba's lot'. Thus the troops came to look upon the Sequani, Aedui and a series of wealthy communities as their enemies. Their imaginations greedily lapped up the idea of a succession of sacked cities, plundered countryside and rifled homes. Greed

1. The boundary between Upper and Lower Germany was formed by the Vinxtbach near Niederbreisig, between Remagen and Andernach.

and arrogance are always characteristic of the stronger side, and it was only logical that the Roman troops should be annoyed by the insolence of Gauls who insulted the army by boasting that Galba had excused them a quarter of the tribute and made grants of territory to their states.

These motives were reinforced by a rumour cunningly circulated and rashly credited. The legions, it was alleged, were being decimated and the most enterprising centurions cashiered. On every hand there were ill tidings. Reports from Rome boded no good. The city of Lyons was disaffected, and its persistent loyalty to Nero made it a hotbed of rumours. But it was the camps themselves that contained the richest material for imagination and credulity. Here were hatred, fear and the conviction, as they realized their power, that the risk was slight.

52. Shortly before 1 December in the previous year,[1] Aulus Vitellius had entered Lower Germany as its governor and made a thorough visit of inspection to the legionary headquarters. A number of centurions were given back their rank, discharged men were reinstated and sentences reduced. In general these changes reflected a desire to curry favour. But some showed judgement and constituted an honest reform of the money-grubbing methods with which Fonteius Capito had soiled his hands when promoting officers or reducing them. Whatever he did was interpreted not in the light of what is appropriate in a governor-general but as a hint of something greater. This ingratiating attitude lowered Vitellius in the eyes of strict disciplinarians. Well-wishers, however, described as 'affability' and 'good nature' the excessive and imprudent generosity with which he squandered both what was his to give and what was not. Besides, his men were eager enough for favours, and this eagerness caused them to take his very faults for virtues. Both armies contained many orderly, quiet soldiers. But there were also many disgruntled and active ones. But for boundless ambition and a notable lack of scruple two men stood out above the rest – the legionary commanders Alienus Caecina and Fabius Valens.

Valens for his part was the bitter enemy of Galba. He felt that the emperor had been ungrateful for his services in uncovering Verginius' reluctance and crushing Capito's plots. So he proceeded to work upon Vitellius, pointing out how keen the troops were. Vitellius, he said, was well spoken of everywhere, and Hordeonius Flaccus could

I. A.D. 68.

do little to hold things up. Britain would rally to them, and the German auxiliaries would follow their lead. There was disaffection in the provinces. The old emperor held power on sufferance, and this power would in any case soon pass to another. The wind of change was favourable. Vitellius should crowd on all canvas, and sail forward to meet success halfway. It was understandable, he added, that Verginius should have had his hesitations. He came of an equestrian family, and his father was a nobody. Such a man might well think it presumptuous to accept the principate, whereas there was safety in refusal. But in Vitellius' case his father's record as consul on three separate occasions, as censor and as the colleague of a Caesar[1] had long since imposed upon the son the qualifications proper to an emperor and robbed him of the comfortable feeling that he was safe as a subject.

Vitellius was a man of lazy temperament, but he wavered under the strong impact of these arguments. The result was an idle longing rather than real hope.

53. In Upper Germany, however, it was Caecina who had coaxed support from the troops. He was young, good-looking, tall and upstanding, as well as possessing inordinate ambition and some skill in words. As quaestor in South Spain he had eagerly joined Galba's party, and for this was rewarded at an early age with the command of a legion. But Galba later learnt that he had misappropriated public funds, and ordered him to be prosecuted for malversation. This was not to Caecina's liking. He made up his mind to cause general chaos and use his country's sufferings to disguise his own predicament. In the army, too, there was no dearth of the raw materials of disturbance. The whole force had been involved in the campaign against Vindex; it had not gone over to Galba until after Nero's death; and finally, when it did take the oath, its accession had been anticipated by the units in Lower Germany. Apart from this, the Gallic communities such as the Treveri and Lingones, at whom Galba had struck hard by means of severe edicts or loss of territory, lie in specially close contact with the legionary camps. All this gave rise to seditious talk between the two parties, a further sapping of the troops' loyalty by contact with civilians, and the likelihood that the support offered to

1. Vitellius' father had been consul in A.D. 34, 43, and 47. This was a signal distinction, and in A.D. 47–51 he was censor as colleague of the emperor Claudius.

Verginius would be a valuable tool at the disposal of any other pretender.

54. The civic authorities of the Lingones had sent the legions the traditional token of mutual hospitality – symbolic 'hands'.[1] The representatives who brought them carefully assumed the guise of mourning and woe, and paraded through the headquarters building and the barrack blocks dwelling alternately upon their own sufferings and the privileges granted to their neighbours. When the story found a ready hearing among the troops, the Lingones went on to lament the dangers and humiliation to which the army itself was exposed. This agitation promised to be successful, and the troops were on the point of mutiny when Hordeonius Flaccus ordered the envoys to go, telling them to leave the camp at night in order that their departure should attract less attention. But this only led to a shocking rumour. It was widely held that the men had been murdered, and that, unless the troops took steps to defend themselves, their most vocal representatives, who had denounced the present state of affairs, would be put to death when it was dark and the rest know nothing. The legions bound themselves by a secret understanding to act together. This was extended to cover the auxiliary units. The latter were at first looked upon with suspicion as their cohorts and cavalry regiments had been moved up and it was believed that an attack on the legions was being planned. But in due course the auxiliaries showed themselves keener plotters than their companions. Scoundrels find it easier to agree on warlike measures than on means to achieve harmony in peacetime.

55. However in Lower Germany the legions were made to take the usual New Year oath of loyalty to Galba on 1 January, though they showed considerable reluctance. Here and there individuals in the front ranks spoke up audibly, but the rest of the troops did not open their mouths. Everybody was waiting for a bold move from his neighbour, for it is only human nature to be quick to follow a lead, however much we dislike taking it. But the various legions did not see eye to eye themselves. The men of the First and Fifth were quite out of hand – indeed some of them stoned the portraits of Galba. The Fifteenth and Sixteenth Legions, on the other hand, confined themselves to muttering threats and looked around for others to start the outbreak.

1. Clasped hands of bronze or silver.

But in the upper army the Fourth and Twenty-Second Legions, who were billeted in the same cantonments, tore the portraits of Galba to pieces. This actually happened on 1 January. At first the Fourth took the initiative, while the Twenty-Second was relatively backward. Later they acted in concert. Not wanting to abandon all fealty to the empire, they introduced the now outworn formula of 'the Senate and People of Rome' into their oath of allegiance. None of the senior officers made any effort on Galba's behalf, and some of them, true to form, attracted attention by the prominent part they played in a scene of general chaos. However, no one got up and addressed the troops collectively – after all, there was as yet no emperor with whom they could ingratiate themselves.   56. Looking on at this disgraceful scene stood the governor, Hordeonius Flaccus. He made no attempt to coerce the rioters, rally waverers or encourage those who were loyal. Too frightened to lift a finger, he avoided offence by doing nothing. Four centurions of the Twenty-Second Legion – Nonius Receptus, Donatius Valens, Romilius Marcellus and Calpurnius Repentinus – tried to protect the portraits of Galba, but the troops made a rush at them and hustled them off to a place of confinement. After that, there was no question of any man's showing loyalty or remembering his previous oath, and the mutiny followed the classical pattern of all mutinies: the view of the majority was suddenly found to be the view of everybody.

After dark on 1 January, the city of Cologne was entered by a standard-bearer from the Fourth Legion. He brought word to Vitellius, who was dining at the time, that the Fourth and Twenty-Second Legions had thrown down the portraits of Galba and sworn allegiance to the senate and people of Rome. It was felt that this oath meant nothing; they should strike while the iron was hot and offer the troops an emperor. Vitellius sent information to his legions and their commanders that the upper army had risen against Galba, and put it to them that they must either fight the rebels or else, if they preferred agreement and peace, they must nominate an emperor. He added that the prompt choice of a ruler would be safer than a prolonged search for one.

57. The nearest camp was that of the First Legion, and the quickest legionary commander off the mark was Fabius Valens. On the following day, entering the city of Cologne at the head of the cavalry component of his legion and of its auxiliaries, he greeted Vitellius as

emperor. His example was followed with remarkable eagerness by the legions of the lower province, while the upper army dropped its lip-service to 'the Senate and People of Rome' and on 3 January went over to Vitellius. Whatever authority they had recognized during the preceding two days, it had obviously not been that of a republican government. No less enthusiastic than the armies were the people of Cologne, as well as the Treviri and Lingones. They offered to contribute reinforcements, horses, equipment and money in accordance with their various physical, material and moral resources. This spirit of sacrifice was not confined to the leaders in the cities and army camps, who had the means to give ready money and could look forward to handsome dividends when victory was theirs. Even ordinary privates in the companies handed over their savings or, in lieu of cash, their sword-belts, medals and silver parade equipment, under the stimulus of others' encouragement or their own initiative and greed.

58. So Vitellius, gratefully acknowledging the prompt response of his men, saw to it that court functions normally carried out by freedmen were distributed among knights, paid the centurions for their men's leave out of the imperial exchequer, confirmed on more than one occasion a number of vindictive sentences demanded by his troops, and only now and again foiled them by the pretence of awarding a term of imprisonment. Pompeius Propinquus, the imperial agent in Belgica, was immediately executed, but Vitellius managed to get away by a ruse the commander of the German Fleet, Julius Burdo. The army was violently incensed with Burdo because they thought he had engineered a false accusation against Capito and backed it up by conspiracy. Of Capito they had kindly recollections, and in their present savage mood executions could be carried out in public, but acts of mercy only by stealth. So the accused was kept in confinement, and only let out when the hour of victory had struck and the resentment of the troops had subsided. In the meantime, to propitiate them, the centurion Crispinus was handed over to the men. In a murderer whose hands had actually dripped with the blood of Capito the public clamour saw a more obvious target and the agent of retribution[1] a victim less worth saving.

59. The next to be pardoned was Julius Civilis. He carried great weight among the Batavians, and it seemed desirable to avoid

1. i.e. Vitellius.

alienating a high-spirited nation by executing him. Besides, there were eight cohorts of Batavians stationed in the territory of the Lingones. These formed an auxiliary force normally attached to the Fourteenth Legion, but in this troubled period they had separated from their parent formation, and their friendship or hostility was likely to have a serious effect on the balance of power. I have already referred to the centurions Nonius, Donatius, Romilius and Calpurnius. Vitellius now ordered their execution as being guilty of loyalty – a most serious charge in the eyes of rebels. The faction of Vitellius found two new adherents in Valerius Asiaticus, governor of the province of Belgica and soon to be selected by Vitellius as son-in-law, and in Junius Blaesus, who was in charge of Central Gaul. The latter brought over the Italian Legion and the Taurian Cavalry Regiment, both stationed at Lyons. The garrison of Raetia was also prompt in its adhesion.

60. Even in Britain there was no sign of hesitation. Its governor was Trebellius Maximus, whose greed and miserliness had earned him the contempt and dislike of his army. His unpopularity was enhanced by the attitude of the commander of the Twentieth Legion, Roscius Coelius. The two men had long been on bad terms, but the convenient accident of civil war had intensified the quarrel. Trebellius accused Coelius of disloyalty and disrespect towards his superior. Coelius replied by pointing to the despoiled and impoverished state of the legions. Meanwhile, this scandalous feud between two senior officers prejudiced the discipline of the army. The situation became so bad that the auxiliaries in their turn denounced Trebellius and refused to have anything to do with him. The cohorts and cavalry regiments went over to Coelius' side, and the discomfited governor had to take refuge with Vitellius. Despite his removal, the province carried on quietly. It was administered by the legionary commanders, theoretically on an equal footing, though Coelius' lack of scruple gave him greater pull.

61. The adhesion of the army of Britain raised Vitellius' resources of manpower and material to an imposing level. He now decided on two commanders and a two-fold advance. After winning over the Gallic provinces by diplomacy, or, if they refused, by devastation, Fabius Valens was to invade Italy by way of the Cottian Alps. Caecina was told to take a shorter route which would bring him down into the flat country via the Pennine Range. Valens received some contingents drawn from the lower army, together with the H.Q. and main

party of the Fifth Legion and a force of auxiliary cohorts and cavalry. This amounted to about 40,000 armed men in all. As for Caecina, he was given 30,000 troops from Upper Germany, the Twenty-First Legion forming the main element. Each commander was also allotted German auxiliary units, and Vitellius used the same source to provide a stiffening for his own force. He was to follow with the total war potential.

62. The army and its emperor presented a remarkable contrast. The impatient troops demanded action while the Gallic provinces were still unnerved and the Spanish ones undecided. They were not going to be held up by winter or the slow pace of unheroic peace. It was vital, they held, to invade Italy and get hold of the capital. In civil war, speed was the only safe policy, and deeds were wanted, not deliberation. Vitellius dozed away his time. Quick to take advantage of the privileges of an emperor, he gave himself up to idle pleasures and sumptuous banquets. Even at midday he was the worse for drink and over-eating. Yet, despite this, their keenness and vigour made his men carry out the duties of their commander as well as their own, just as though he were there to give them their orders and afford the active or lazy the stimulus of hope or fear. Ready and at the alert, they clamoured for the signal to start, and gave Vitellius the title 'Germanicus' on the spot, though he refused to allow them to address him as 'Caesar' even after his final victory.[1]

A happy augury was vouchsafed to Fabius Valens and the army he led off to war. On the very day they started, an eagle floated effortlessly forward in front of the advancing column, as if guiding it on its way. For many miles the neighbourhood resounded with the shouts of the exultant soldiers, and for as many the bird maintained its flight, calm and undisturbed. This was interpreted as an omen clearly presaging a great and successful enterprise.

63. Indeed, as far as the Treveri were concerned, the army felt it had nothing to worry about upon entering what it took to be allied territory. At Divodurum, the capital of the Mediomatrici, it was received with every civility. But in spite of this, a sudden panic gripped the troops, and they hastily seized their arms with the intention of spilling the blood of an inoffensive community. In this they were prompted not by rapine or a taste for plunder, but by hallucination, frenzy and motives which defy analysis. The illogicality of their attitude made it all the harder to cope with, though in

1. This reference to titles is out of context and belongs to the second sentence of Ch. 57, p. 57, top.

the end they were mollified by their commander's appeals and refrained from utterly wiping out the population. Still, almost 4,000 people lost their lives, and after this the Gallic provincials were so alarmed that on the approach of the marching column whole cities would go out to meet it with their magistrates, armed with pleas for mercy. Women and children prostrated themselves along the highways, and every conceivable concession was made which could placate an angry foe, in order to secure peace in the absence of war.

64. News of Galba's murder and Otho's accession reached Fabius Valens when he was at the capital of the Leuci. His troops were neither pleased nor frightened. What they were interested in was war. But the Gauls bestirred themselves briskly. For Otho and Vitellius they felt equal hatred – but the latter inspired fear as well. The next community, that of the Lingones, was faithful to the Vitellian cause. The army received a cordial welcome, and tried to repay its hosts by behaving well. But the general rejoicing was cut short by the insubordination of those cohorts which, as I have already described, had cut adrift from the Fourteenth Legion, and which Fabius Valens had incorporated in his force. Initial exchanges of abuse developed into a free fight between the Batavians and the legionaries which practically assumed the proportions of a battle as the two sides were joined by their respective partisans among the troops at large. But Valens dealt with the trouble by punishing a few of the offenders in order to remind the Batavians of what they had forgotten – that they were under his command.

An attempt to pick upon the Aedui failed. Over and above the money and equipment requisitioned from them, they offered food supplies without payment. What the Aedui had done from fear, the people of Lyons did with pleasure. But the Italian Legion and the Taurian Cavalry Regiment were withdrawn from the city, though it was decided to leave the Eighteenth Cohort[1] at Lyons, where it was normally stationed in winter. The commanding officer of the Italian Legion, Manlius Valens, got no credit from Vitellius despite his services to the cause. This was because Fabius had made allegations against him behind his back. Manlius knew nothing of this, and was lulled into a false sense of security by the praises showered upon him in public.

65. For many years the cities of Lyons and Vienne had been on bad

1. Probably one of the Urban Cohorts on detachment.

terms. Their differences were inflamed by the recent fighting. Both had given as many knocks as they had received, and incidents had occurred with a frequency and venom out of all proportion to a mere battle on behalf of Nero and Galba. Moreover, in a fit of pique, Galba had sequestrated the revenues of Lyons to the imperial treasury, while according great attention to Vienne. Hence sprang rivalry, envy and a hatred that locked together cities parted by a single river.[1] So the inhabitants of Lyons began to work upon individual soldiers and urge them to sack the rival city. They reminded them that Vienne had subjected Lyons to a siege, assisted the rebel Vindex, and in the recent past recruited legionaries to protect Galba. After these plausible excuses for hatred, they passed on to unfold the immense possibilities of loot. By this time, private approaches had been reinforced by an official appeal, which called upon the troops to rise up and destroy the stronghold of Gallic rebellion. At Vienne, it was claimed, the whole atmosphere suggested foreigners and enemies, but Lyons was a Roman city closely connected with the army.[2] It would hold fast through thick and thin, and the Vitellians must not leave it at the mercy of a resentful foe in case luck decided against them.

66. These arguments, and more of the same kind, had been effective. Indeed, even the senior officers and leading supporters of Vitellius thought that it would be impossible to cool down the heated feelings of the troops. Meanwhile, the people of Vienne were well aware of the peril in which they stood. Headed by white flags and tokens of surrender, they went out to meet the troops, who were already on the march towards them, and managed to soften their hearts by laying their hands in a gesture of entreaty upon the soldiers' weapons and by grovelling at their feet. Valens helped on the good work by giving each man a bounty of three hundred sesterces. Then – and only then – were they influenced by the fact that Vienne was a historic and imposing city, and Fabius' appeal that there should be no loss of life or damage to property was given an unprejudiced hearing. However, as a community Vienne was disarmed, and the inhabitants gave the troops all sorts of unofficial gifts. But the rumour persisted that

1. Roman Lyons (Lugdunum) lay on the hill of Fourvière west of the Rhône, Vienne twenty miles downstream on its east bank; the antithesis is forced.

2. Because it was a garrison town through which supplies and reinforcements passed, and where time-expired veterans tended to settle. But Vienne had also the honourable status of a 'Roman city', *colonia*.

Valens had himself been heavily bribed. Long miserably poor, he found it hard to conceal his sudden translation from shabbiness to affluence. Greedy desires had been inflamed by protracted need. These were now given full scope, and the man who had been a penniless youth became a spendthrift in middle age.

Valens then marched his force slowly forward through the lands of the Allobroges and Vocontii, actually auctioneering the length of the day's march and the moves from one camp to another, and striking discreditable deals with farmers and local officials. Menaces were employed, too. For instance, at Lucus, a town in the territory of the Vocontii, he threatened to set fire to the place until he got a sweetener. When money was not available, he could be bribed with women. In such fashion they made their way as far as the Alps.

67. Caecina proved more predatory and bloodthirsty. Always on the look-out for trouble, he had fallen foul of the Helvetii. This is a Gallic tribe once famous for its fighting qualities; in more recent times it has lived on its reputation. These people knew nothing of Galba's murder and refused to recognize Vitellius as emperor. Hostilities were provoked by the greedy and precipitate action of the Twenty-First Legion in stealing a sum of money sent to provide pay for the garrison of a fort[1] which the Helvetii themselves maintained with their own levies and at their own expense. The Helvetii were not prepared to put up with this. They detained some dispatches which were being delivered in the name of the army of Germany to the legions in Pannonia, and put the centurion and his small escort under arrest. Caecina was spoiling for a fight and eager to punish the first offender he could find before a change of heart took place. Suddenly moving camp, he devastated the countryside and plundered a spa which, over the long years of peace, had developed into a fair-sized town attracting a number of visitors who came to take the waters in agreeable surroundings.[2] Instructions were sent to the auxiliaries in Raetia to attack the Helvetii in the rear as they turned to face the legion.

68. The natives were bold carpet-knights, but they proved cowards in the hour of danger. When the alarm was first sounded, they had put themselves under the command of one Claudius Severus. But they showed a total lack of military skill, discipline and coordination.

1. Perhaps the Eppenberg, 3 km south of Aarau.
2. Baden a.d. Limmat.

An encounter with veteran troops was inevitably fatal, and as their forts were now crumbling and decayed, it was impossible to risk a siege. They were caught in a trap. On one side was Caecina at the head of his powerful army, on the other the cavalry and infantry auxiliaries from Raetia, supported by the local Raetian levies who were used to fighting and had been well trained. Everywhere the scene was one of devastation and slaughter. Drifting helplessly between the two enemy forces, the Helvetii threw away their arms and made for the depths of the Mons Vocetius, many of them wounded or stragglers. Thereupon a cohort of Thracians was promptly directed to the area, and the fugitives were dislodged. Then the troops from Germany and Raetia tracked them down from one end of the forest to the other, and indeed killed them in the very hiding-places in which they lurked. Many thousands fell, and as many were sold into slavery.

After the mopping-up operations were complete, a reinforced body of Roman regulars marched towards the capital, Aventicum. Thereupon a deputation was sent out to offer the surrender of the town, and this was accepted. Caecina made an example of their chief Julius Alpinus, whom he regarded as responsible for the rebellion. The rest he left to Vitellius' mercy or vindictiveness, so that the Helvetian envoys had to confront the emperor and his troops. 69. It is hard to say which they found the more implacable. The troops demanded the destruction of the town, and thrust their weapons and fists under the delegates' noses. Even Vitellius permitted himself to bluster and threaten. But one of the representatives called Claudius Cossus was a well-known speaker. An apt display of nervousness helped to conceal the artifices of oratory, and rendered them correspondingly effective. His intervention was successful in mollifying the troops. The mob was typically temperamental. Once exaggeratedly vindictive, the men were now equally ready to sympathize. Tears coursed down their cheeks, and their greater insistence on better treatment secured Aventicum pardon and survival.

70. Caecina spent a few days in Helvetian territory waiting for word of Vitellius' decision on this matter, and using the time in preparing for the passage of the Alps. It was now that he received from Italy the cheering news that a unit stationed in the Po valley had declared for Vitellius. This was the Silian cavalry regiment, which had served in the province of Africa during Vitellius' period as governor. Later

mobilized by Nero as part of the advance force sent to Egypt, it had
been recalled owing to the rebellion of Vindex, and at the moment
was marking time in Italy. Its officers knew nothing about Otho, but
felt a moral obligation to support Vitellius. They laid repeated
emphasis on the strength of the legions advancing on them, and the
reputation which the army of Germany enjoyed. At their instigation,
the regiment went over to Vitellius and by way of making a presen-
tation to their new emperor handed over to him the most considerable
towns in the Transpadane Region – Mediolanum, Novaria, Eporedia
and Vercellae. Caecina was informed of this by the unit itself, and
since a single cavalry regiment could not possibly defend such an
extensive portion of Italy, he sent ahead cohorts of Gauls, Lusitanians
and Britons as well as some German horse and the Petrian cavalry
regiment. As regards his own plans, he hesitated for a time. Ought he
not to make a détour over the mountains of Raetia into Noricum in
order to deal with its governor, Petronius Urbicus, who had mustered his auxiliary forces, cut the bridges over the rivers and thus
looked as if he proposed to be loyal to Otho? On reflection this seemed
a dangerous move. He might lose the infantry and cavalry already
sent on ahead. He also reflected that there was more glory to be won
by consolidating his Italian gains. In any case, wherever the issue was
fought out, Noricum would rank among the other prizes of victory.
So he decided on the Great St Bernard route, and led his main body
and the heavy legionary force across the Alps while they were still in
the grip of winter.

71. Meanwhile, to everybody's surprise, Otho did not sink into a
lethargic mood of hedonism and idleness. Amusements were postponed, indulgence disguised, and his whole behaviour was adjusted
to the high standards expected of a ruler. But this merely increased
misgiving about virtues that were fictitious and vices that promised
to return.

Marius Celsus the consul designate had been saved from the venom
of the troops by a pretence of imprisonment.[1] He was now summoned
to the Capitol on Otho's orders. The emperor's intention was to
acquire a reputation for clemency in his treatment of a famous man
who was a political opponent. Celsus sturdily admitted the charge of

1. Cf. p. 48. In the following sentence, the Capitol should be understood as
the scene of a sacrifice of thanksgiving offered by Otho at daybreak on 16
January.

keeping faith with Galba, and indeed claimed credit for setting a good example. Nor did Otho merely behave like the average man who forgives. He called heaven to witness their mutual reconciliation, and immediately treated Celsus as an intimate friend, and later as one of his war leaders. In his turn Celsus re-enacted for Otho what seemed his predestined role in life – the part of loyalty, sincere but unlucky. Greeted with jubilation by leading Romans and much discussed by the general public, Celsus' pardon was not unpopular even with the troops, who admired the very quality that irritated them.

72. Then came a similar gratification, though for different reasons. Otho was persuaded to put Ofonius Tigellinus to death. A man of humble birth, vicious childhood and dissolute maturity, he had achieved among other things the command of the Watch and of the Pretorian Guard. These are normally the rewards of virtue, but Tigellinus found it quicker to win them by vice. In due course he took to less effeminate forms of immorality, such as cruelty and greed. While tempting Nero to every form of wickedness, he ventured on some crimes without his knowledge, and finally deserted and betrayed him. Hence the exceptional insistence with which his punishment was called for, for the demand sprang from two opposite moods – hatred of Nero and regret that he was no more. During Galba's reign, he was sheltered by the influential Titus Vinius, whose excuse was that Tigellinus had saved his daughter's life. No doubt he had done so, though the act cannot have been prompted by mercy in view of Tigellinus' record of murder: the intention was to provide an escape-route for the future, for a criminal distrusts the present and is led by his fear of changed circumstances in the future to lay in a stock of private gratitude as a protection against the detestation of the public. This is why there can be no question of Tigellinus' having wished to keep his hands clean: he merely hoped for a similar immunity in exchange. This only made the public more bitter. To their old hatred for Tigellinus was added the recent unpopularity of Titus Vinius. All Rome gathered to the Palace and the squares, and overflowing into the circus and theatres, where the mob can demonstrate with the greater impunity, raised a seditious clamour. In the end, Tigellinus received the order to commit suicide while he was taking the waters at Sinuessa Spa. In an atmosphere of lechery, kissing and nauseous hesitations, he finally slit his throat with a razor and

crowned a disreputable life with new infamy by quitting it too late
and with dishonour.

73. An emphatic public demand was voiced at this time for the
execution of Calvia Crispinilla. But she was saved from this fate by
various manoeuvres on the part of Otho, whose lack of sincerity
evoked hostile comment. This woman had been Nero's tutor in vice
before going over to the province of Africa to instigate Clodius
Macer to revolt. Her plan was quite obvious – a blockade of Rome.
Later she became a popular figure throughout the country as a whole,
securing her position by marriage to a senior statesman, and the
successive régimes of Galba, Otho and Vitellius brought her no harm.
In after days she enjoyed great influence as a wealthy woman who
had no heirs – for, whether times are good or bad, such qualities
retain their power.

74. Meanwhile Otho kept up a lively correspondence with Vitellius.
His letters were disfigured by alluring and unmanly bribes – money,
influence and a quiet spot to be selected at will for a life of indulgence.
Similar baits were held out by Vitellius, with some degree of restraint at first, so long as the rivals still maintained a foolish and
degrading hypocrisy. Then, like men quarrelling, they accused each
other of debauchery and wickedness. Here at least both were in the
right.

Otho recalled the mission sent by Galba and dispatched a fresh
deputation, chosen ostensibly from the senate, to approach both
armies in Germany, the Italian Legion and the forces at Lyons. With
an alacrity which belied any notion of compulsion, these envoys
threw in their lot with Vitellius. But the pretorian escort provided
by Otho as a guard of honour was hurriedly returned to Rome[1] before
it could come into contact with the legionaries. Fabius backed this
move up by giving them a letter addressed in the name of the army
of Germany to the pretorian and urban cohorts. In this he boasted
of the strength of the Vitellian side and offered an understanding. But
he also quite unnecessarily criticized them for conveying the office of
emperor to Otho long after it had been entrusted to Vitellius.  75. In
this way both promises and threats were brought to bear on the city
garrison: outclassed in a military sense, it was not likely to lose anything by making peace. Despite this, the pretorians remained
inflexibly loyal.

1. Presumably at the instigation of its own officers.

But that was not all. Assassins were sent by Otho to Germany, and by Vitellius to the capital. Both parties failed to achieve anything, Vitellius' agents going undetected and unpunished because they were lost amid the vast population of Rome, all strangers to one another. But the Othonians were fresh faces in a community where each man knew his comrades personally, and their identity was thus betrayed. Vitellius framed a letter to Otho's brother Titianus in which he threatened to put the latter and his son to death in the event of any harm befalling his own mother and children. In fact, both families survived, thanks perhaps to menaces so long as Otho was emperor: when Vitellius won, he was credited with clemency.

76. The first event to give Otho confidence was the news from the Balkans that the legions of Dalmatia, Pannonia and Moesia had acknowledged him as emperor. Identical reports came from Spain, and a proclamation was issued praising Cluvius Rufus. Yet in no time at all it was discovered that Spain had gone over to Vitellius. Even Aquitania soon shifted its ground, despite the oath of loyalty to Otho imposed by Julius Cordus. Nowhere could one rely on loyalty or affection: fear and compulsion were the pressures that swayed them this way and that. The same sort of panic impelled the Narbonese province to rally to Vitellius: it took the easy step of joining neighbours stronger than itself. The distant provinces and such forces as lay overseas remained true to Otho, less from enthusiasm for his cause than because of the considerable prestige exercised by the mere name of Rome and the imposing façade of senatorial support. In any case, Otho had already established his position psychologically, for he had been heard of before Vitellius was. The army of Judaea had the oath of allegiance to Otho administered to it by Vespasian, the legions of Syria by Mucianus. At the same time, the authorities in Egypt and all the eastern provinces expressed nominal support. Africa was no less complaisant. Here the initiative came from Carthage, which did not wait for a lead from the governor, Vipstanus Apronianus. One of Nero's freedmen, Crescens – for even these creatures claim to be part of the body politic when times are bad – had offered the public a feast in celebration of the recent accession, and the reckless populace committed itself in a number of ways with immoderate haste. The example of Carthage was followed by the remaining cities in the province.

77. This split in the armies and provinces meant that Vitellius was

compelled to fight for the position of emperor. Otho, however, went on with his imperial duties as if there were not a cloud in the sky. He sometimes displayed a proper sense of statesmanship, more often an unseemly haste based on a policy of quick returns. With his brother Titianus he took over the consulship until 1 March, making some attempt to mollify the army of Germany by allotting the succeeding months to Verginius, whose colleague was to be Pompeius Vopiscus, allegedly because he was an old friend, though many took this as a compliment to Vienne. So far as the remaining consulships were concerned, no alteration was made in the scheme as drawn up by Nero or Galba. Thus Caelius Sabinus and Flavius Sabinus were to hold office until 1 July, and Arrius Antoninus and Marius Celsus until 1 September. Even Vitellius refrained from vetoing these arrangements after his victory. Otho also made appointments to the colleges of pontiffs and augurs as a crowning distinction for men with a long career of public service behind them, or afforded young men of rank recently back from exile the solace and satisfaction of occupying priesthoods held by their fathers and grandfathers. Membership of the senate was restored to Cadius Rufus, Pedius Blaesus and Scaevinus Propinquus,[1] who had been condemned for extortion under Claudius and Nero. In pardoning them, the senators decided to find a new name for 'rapacity' (for that is what their conduct had been in plain language) and to regard it as 'treason', a charge then so hated for its misuse that even salutary laws[2] became a dead letter.

78. The same lavishness marked Otho's approaches to civic communities and provinces. At Hispalis and Emerita additional families of settlers were incorporated, the Lingones received a block grant of Roman citizenship, and the province of Baetica was assigned some Moorish communities. New constitutions devised for both Cappadocia and Africa looked well but were fated to be short-lived. Amid all these proposals, for which the nature of his immediate predicament and imminent worries offered some extenuation, Otho still remembered his amours. He secured by senatorial decree the restoration of the statues of Poppaea. It was believed that he even contemplated some ceremony in memory of Nero, in order to entice the mob. Indeed, some Romans did exhibit portraits of Nero, and on certain occasions the populace and the troops actually saluted the emperor as

1. The name is quite uncertain.
2. e.g. those punishing extortion.

'Nero Otho' as if this represented an additional ennoblement. Otho left the matter in the air, for he was afraid of saying 'no' or else ashamed to acknowledge the title.

79. Preoccupation with civil war led to some slackness in the face of danger from abroad. The Rhoxolani, a Sarmatian tribe, had cut to pieces two auxiliary cohorts in the previous winter, and they were now encouraged to stage an ambitious invasion of Moesia. Their forces mumbered some 9,000 wild and exulting horsemen, keener on booty than battle. These unwary rovers were suddenly set upon by the Third Legion, with its auxiliaries. On the Roman side all was set for the encounter. Not so the Sarmatians. Dispersed for plunder, laden with heavy spoils, and unable to profit by their horses' pace because the tracks were slippery, they were delivered as sheep to the slaughter. It is indeed curious to observe how completely the formidable Sarmatians depend on extraneous aids. An engagement on foot finds them utterly ineffective, but when they appear on horseback, there is scarcely a line of battle that can stand up to them. But this particular day was wet, and a thaw had set in. Neither their lances nor their enormous two-handed swords were of any use, because the horses lost their footing and the dismounted warriors were weighed down by their body-armour. This protective clothing is worn by the chiefs and notables and consists of iron-plating or toughened leather. Proof against blows, it is cumbersome when a man tries to get up after being unhorsed by an enemy charge. Moreover, the Sarmatians were time and time again swallowed up in the deep, soft snow. The Roman troops on the other hand wore breastplates allowing easy movement. They moved up, throwing their javelins or using their lances and, as occasion required, their light-weight swords to close in and wound the unprotected Sarmatians, who do not normally carry shields. Finally, the few survivors took refuge in swampy country, where they succumbed to the severity of the weather or their wounds.

When news of this reached Rome, Marcus Aponius, the governor of Moesia, was granted a triumphal statue,[1] and the legionary commanders Aurelius Fulvus, Tettius Julianus and Numisius Lupus received consular decorations.[2] Otho was delighted, and plumed

---

1. A statue of the officer in triumphal dress, erected in the Forum of Augustus at Rome.

2. The right (enjoyed by a consul) to the use of a ceremonial chair, *sella curulis*, inlaid with ivory, and of a bordered toga, *toga praetexta*.

himself on the victory as if he had won it himself and exalted his
country by means of commanders and armies that were his.

80. Meanwhile a mutiny occurred which had almost fatal consequences for the capital, though it arose out of a trifling incident where
no danger was anticipated. Otho had ordered the Seventeenth Cohort[1]
to move to Rome from the city of Ostia, and a pretorian tribune
named Varius Crispinus was charged with the task of issuing arms to
it. Anxious to carry out his orders with greater freedom from distraction
while the pretorian barracks were quiet, he had the armoury opened
and the cohort's transport loaded up at nightfall.[2] The hour aroused
suspicion, the motive was misconstrued, and the bid for peace and
quiet led to uproar. Seeing the arms, some drunken pretorians felt an
urge to get hold of them. The troops raised a clamour and accused the
tribunes and centurions of a treasonable plot to arm the household servants of the senators and murder Otho. Some of the pretorians were
ignorant of the real circumstances and befuddled with drink, the riff-
raff seized the chance of loot, and the mass of the men were, as usual,
ready for any kind of excitement. Besides, the willingness of the better
men to obey orders had been neutralized by the darkness. The tribune
and the strictest disciplinarians among the centurions offered resistance,
but were struck down. The men helped themselves to the arms, drew
their swords and rode off to Rome and the palace.

81. Otho was entertaining a large dinner party of society men and
women. The guests were at their wits' end. Was this a meaningless
outbreak on the part of the troops or trickery on the part of Otho?
Would it be more dangerous to stay and be caught, or escape and
scatter? At one moment, they assumed a nonchalance they were far
from feeling. At the next, their fears betrayed them. They eyed
Otho's expression. As is the way with suspicious minds, although
Otho felt alarm, he also inspired it. However, in his concern – as
much for the senators as for himself – he had promptly sent off the
pretorian prefects to calm down their angry men. He also told all his
guests to hurry away from the banqueting room. This was the signal
for a general stampede. Magistrates threw away their badges of
office, and eluded the masses of retainers and servants who were

1. See p. 60, n. 1.
2. The cohort's arms, or some of them, were evidently stored in the armoury
of the pretorian barracks in Rome. It looks as if the unit were under orders to
move northwards to the front.

waiting upon them. With the womenfolk and old gentlemen they vanished down the darkened streets of the capital in every direction. One or two made for their mansions, the vast majority for the homes of their friends and humblest dependants, where they could lie low without anyone being the wiser.

82. Even the doors of the palace could not stop the troops surging irresistibly into the banqueting-hall with a demand that Otho should show himself to them. A tribune, Julius Martialis, and a legionary prefect, Vitellius Saturninus, were wounded in their attempt to stem the rush. The whole building was a hubbub of weapons and threats. In one breath the men denounced the centurions and tribunes, in the next the senate at large. Their blind and panic-stricken frenzy, finding no single target for its anger, clamoured for a clean sweep of everybody. Finally Otho threw imperial dignity to the winds, clambered up on a couch, and with some difficulty restrained the mutineers by means of tears and entreaties. So they returned to barracks, but grudgingly and with bad consciences. Rome resembled a captured city on the next day. The great houses were shuttered, the streets almost empty, the populace in mourning. The downcast glances of the troops displayed sullenness rather than regret. Company by company, they were addressed by their prefects, Licinius Proculus and Plotius Firmus, with the differing degrees of severity that reflected the characters of the two men. The upshot of their remarks was that each soldier was to be paid 5,000 sesterces. Only then did Otho venture into the barracks. He was immediately surrounded by the tribunes and centurions, who stripped off their uniform, and asked to be retired from the forces and granted their lives. The troops were sensitive to this reflexion upon themselves. They returned to their duty in an orderly way and, without prompting, demanded the execution of the ringleaders in the mutiny.

83. Otho felt that he must do something about this breach of the peace. Opinion among the troops was divided. The best of them wanted the present wave of indiscipline effectively dealt with. The average man, that is, the majority of them, delighted in mutiny and in a leadership that worked by bribery. A career of riot and looting was just the thing to acclimatize them to the idea of civil war. But Otho also reflected that a usurper whose hands are none too clean cannot maintain control by sudden doses of discipline and old-fashioned strictness. On the other hand, he was worried at the

insecurity to which Rome was exposed and the threat to the senate's existence. In the end he made a speech to the troops on these lines:

'I have not come, men, to fire your hearts with affection for me or spur your spirit to heroism. You have both these qualities already to a marked degree. On the contrary, I have come to ask you to keep your valour under control and to restrain your friendly feelings for me. Yesterday's riot was not prompted by the cupidity or bad blood that have encouraged disorder in many armies. Nor was it prompted by a cowardly refusal to face danger. Your excessive devotion provided a stimulus that was keen but misguided. If honest intentions are not backed up by sound judgement, the consequences are often fatal.

'You and I are setting out on a campaign. Do you imagine that every intelligence report can be read in public and every plan studied in a council-of-war embracing the whole army? The need for carefully weighing up the situation and arriving at a quick decision when the hour strikes makes such a thing impossible. In some respects, ignorance is no less desirable in the ordinary soldier than knowledge. The nature of a general's authority and of the strict observance of discipline requires that even centurions and tribunes should frequently obey without question. If every single individual is to have the right to ask the why and the wherefore of his orders, then the habit of obedience is sapped, and with it the whole principle of command. Are we still going to have men rushing to arms in the middle of the night when we are in the field? Suppose there are a couple of drunken louts – for I feel sure that those who went mad in last night's affair were no more in number: are a few such men to stain their hands with the blood of a centurion and a tribune? Are they to force their way into their general's tent?

84. 'Of course you aimed at my protection by your action. But commotion, darkness and general confusion may also provide an opening for my assassination. If Vitellius and his gang could put upon us any sort of spell they chose, surely the very attitude of mind they would pray for would be mutiny and dissension, that the private should disobey his centurion and the centurion his tribune, that in an inextricable chaos of infantry and cavalry we should rush blindly to our destruction. Successful fighting, men, depends on obedience, not on questioning orders, and the bravest army in the hour of danger is the one that is best behaved before that hour strikes. Arms and courage

should be your business: the job of planning policy and guiding your gallantry must be left to me.

'A few individuals only were to blame: two only shall suffer. It is up to the rest of you to wipe out the memory of an awful night.

'I only hope that no army in the world hears the dreadful words you uttered against the senate! To call for violent measures against the supreme council of state, which is recruited from men of distinction in every province of the empire, is a type of behaviour which even the Germans whom Vitellius is mustering against us at this very moment would surely not permit themselves. Can any son of Italy, any true Roman warrior, cry out for the butchery of an order whose radiance and glory enable us to blind the obscure and shabby following of Vitellius? True, he has got hold of a few native tribes. He has some poor apology for an army. But on our side is the senate. So the state takes its stand here: there, over against us, are the enemies of that state. Do you really imagine that the splendour of the capital stands or falls with mansions, buildings and piles of masonry? These are dumb, lifeless things – their collapse or restoration means nothing. But the survival of our empire, peace between the nations, and your life as well as mine find a firm support in the continued preservation of the senate. The senatorial order was solemnly instituted by the patriarch and founder of our city.[1] From the regal period up to the principate it has survived in unbroken continuity. We received it from our fathers. Let us as surely transmit it to our sons. You are the source of new blood for the senate, and the senate in its turn supplies our emperors.'

85. This speech, nicely calculated to reprimand the troops and calm their feelings, and also Otho's moderate display of severity – no more than two men were to be punished – were well received. For the moment some degree of order had been achieved among troops who could not be dealt with firmly. However, peace and quiet had not returned to the capital, which clattered with arms and bore the look of war. The soldiers caused no concerted disorder. But they had insinuated themselves into all the great houses disguised as civilians, and kept a jealous eye upon all whose station, wealth or some other uncommon distinction exposed them to gossip. It was commonly believed too, that Vitellian soldiers had entered Rome to explore the degree of support for their cause. The whole atmosphere was heavy

1. Romulus.

with suspicion. Even the privacy of the home was hardly secure. But in public, anxiety reached a climax. Men had constantly to attune their attitudes and expressions to the latest rumour: it would not do to appear too upset by bad tidings and insufficiently gratified by good. But it was above all when the senate was assembled in the chamber that the task of steering a course between Scylla and Charybdis presented a continual hazard. Here silence might seem rebellious and free speech suspect. Otho had recently been an ordinary senator and had used the same language as his peers. So he knew all about flattery. In making their speeches, therefore, the senators tacked and veered and trimmed their sails to suit the moment. They denounced Vitellius as a traitor to the country that had bred him. But wary politicians with an eye to the future confined themselves to perfunctory abuse. Certain others did not mince matters, yet took care to time their denunciations for moments of uproar when everyone was on his feet, or else blurted them out in an incoherent torrent of words which nobody could quite catch.

86. There were alarming prodigies, too. News of these flowed from a number of independent sources. At the entrance to the Capitol, it was said, the reins of the chariot in which Victory rides had slipped from her grasp; an apparition of superhuman size had suddenly emerged from the Chapel of Juno; on a sunny, windless day the statue of Julius Caesar on the Tiber Island had turned round so as to face east instead of west; an ox had spoken in Etruria; there had been monstrous animal births and numerous other signs and wonders of the kind that in primitive centuries were noted even in peacetime, but are now only heard of when men are afraid. But the most serious panic was caused by a disaster which combined immediate destruction with the threat of trouble in the future. This was the flooding of the Tiber. A tremendous rise in its level caused the collapse of the Pile Bridge. Its ruins obstructed the flow of the river, which inundated not only the flat and low-lying parts of the capital, but also areas held to be immune from disasters of this kind. A number of Romans were swept away in the streets, and even more were cut off without warning in their shops and beds. Unemployment and food shortages caused famine in the poorer classes, and the standing flood water sapped the foundations of large tenement blocks, which collapsed as the river retreated. No sooner had the public recovered from this shock than it was faced by another. As Otho got together his expe-

ditionary force, it was found that the Campus Martius and the Flaminian Way were blocked. This was the route to the front, and though the obstruction sprang from chance or natural causes, the mere fact of its occurrence was interpreted as a sign from heaven and an omen of imminent disaster.

87. Otho held a service of purification throughout the city, and sized up his plans of campaign. As the Pennine and Cottian Alps and all the other landward approaches to the Gallic provinces were closed[1] to Vitellius' armies, he decided to invade Narbonese Gaul with the help of his powerful navy. This was loyal, because the survivors of the Milvian Bridge massacre,[2] imprisoned by the spiteful Galba, had been placed by Otho on the nominal roll of a legion, while the rest of the navy men received a promise of promotion to the senior service in due course. Otho reinforced his fleet with urban cohorts and a sizable contingent of pretorians. These were to form the spearhead, and give the generals the benefit of their advice and protection. The expedition was commanded by Antonius Novellus and Suedius Clemens, who were senior centurions, and by Aemilius Pacensis, to whom Otho had restored the tribune's rank of which Galba had deprived him. The naval side continued to be the responsibility of the freedman Moschus, who was appointed as a sort of commissar to spy upon the loyalty of his superiors.

Suetonius Paulinus, Marius Celsus and Annius Gallus were earmarked to lead the main force of infantry and cavalry. But the real position of trust was occupied by Licinius Proculus, the pretorian prefect. The latter had been active during his period of service in the capital, but possessed no experience in the field. However, by criticizing Paulinus, Celsus and Gallus despite their respective qualifications – reputation, energy and seasoned judgement – this evil and designing man had little difficulty in getting the upper hand of his restrained and honest colleagues.

88. These events coincided with the banishment of Cornelius Dolabella to the city of Aquinum. He was not subjected to close or humiliating custody, and no charge was brought against him. But critics had pointed to his ancient lineage and close connexions with Galba.

Otho now gave instructions that many of the magistrates and a large proportion of the senior statesmen were to prepare themselves to accompany him, ostensibly as his suite, not as active participants

1. By the winter snow.     2. See p. 40.

or aides in the campaign. Even Lucius Vitellius was included in their number, for he was treated no differently from the rest and not as the brother of an emperor – or of a traitor.

All this caused a wave of anxiety in the capital, where none of the upper classes of society was exempt from fear or danger. The leading senators were incapacitated by age or enervated by a long peace, the nobility lazy and unwarlike, the knights without experience of active service. The more these people strove to hide and conceal their fear, the more obvious it became. On the other hand there were fools who tried to cut a dash by purchasing showy arms and equipment, fine horses and even, in some cases, canteens of lavish tableware and the means to titillate the appetites, as if these were weapons of war. Sensible men were worried about peace and the state of the country, the irresponsible and the improvident were puffed up with idle hopes, and many bankrupts, at their wits' end in peace, drew new vigour from confusion, and found their greatest safeguard in insecurity.

89. Political issues are usually above the heads of the lower classes and the man in the street owing to their complexity. But now the masses gradually began to be sensible of the hardships of war. Owing to the channelling of all available money into the war effort, there was a rise in the cost of food. This was a burden whose effects on ordinary people had been much less crushing during the revolt of Vindex, for at that time there had been no direct threat to Rome. The fighting had been restricted to the provinces, and was tantamount to a foreign war, as it only involved the legions and Gaul. Indeed, ever since the Augustan settlement, the Caesars alone had reaped the worry and glory of Rome's distant wars. Under Tiberius and Gaius the only disasters that affected the public were those of peace. The plot of Scribonianus[1] against Claudius was no sooner reported than crushed, and Nero was driven to abdication by messages and rumours rather than by force of arms. But now legions and fleets were taken into the front-line. So indeed were the pretorian and urban troops, whose employment on active service is almost unparalleled. Behind them were arrayed the East and the West with all their respective forces. If further commanders were to enter the lists, there was the making of a long war.

Some advisers pressed upon Otho the need for postponing his

1. A governor of Dalmatia who staged a short-lived revolt in A.D. 42, but was abandoned by his own troops (see pp. 125ff.) and soon met his death.

departure on religious grounds, for the ceremony of Laying up the Shields[1] had not yet been completed. But Otho was impatient to be off at all costs, for he felt that it was delay of this kind that had been Nero's undoing. The fact that Caecina had by now crossed the Alps was another strong argument for speed. 90. On 14 March, Otho formally handed over the civil administration to the senate, and as a gratuity to those recalled from exile gave them the residue of the proceeds from the sale of Nero's donations, in so far as they had not been paid into the treasury. This concession was perfectly fair, and it looked generous, though in fact it yielded little as the confiscations had been pushed on for some time at top speed.

Otho then summoned a meeting of the whole populace, in which he stressed the prestige of the capital and the united support of senate and people as factors which told in his favour. His references to the Vitellian faction were restrained. He blamed the legions for ignorance rather than presumption. No allusion was made to Vitellius himself. This may have been self-control on Otho's part, or possibly the man who wrote his speech for him was led to refrain from abuse of Vitellius by fear for his own skin. The latter explanation may well be true, for just as Otho relied upon Suetonius Paulinus and Marius Celsus in military matters, so he was thought to employ Galerius Trachalus to advise him on affairs at Rome. Indeed, some hearers professed to detect the authorship of the speech on the mere strength of its style, for it was familiar from Trachalus' frequent appearance in the courts, and his ample and sonorous Latin was admirably designed to satisfy popular taste.

The cheers and cries of the crowd followed the usual pattern of flattery in being overdone and insincere. Everyone tried to outbid his neighbour in enthusiasm and good wishes, as if they were seeing off Julius Caesar or Emperor Augustus. Neither fear nor affection was involved. The passion for self-abasement operated as it does among domestic slaves, for each individual was prompted by selfishness, and the decencies of public life now meant nothing. On leaving Rome, Otho resigned the policing of the capital and the day-to-day responsibilities of an emperor to his brother Salvius Titianus.

1. During the month of March, a mysterious ceremony took place. Priests paraded through the city from point to point, carrying ancient magical shields, singing hymns and dancing in honour of a god 'Mamurius' (= Mars).

*Book Two*

# Flavian Caution

1. In a very different part of the world fortune was already planning the initial moves and motives for the creation of a new dynasty, whose varied complexion was to signify both happiness and misery for the state, and personal success or disaster for its rulers.[1] Titus Vespasianus had been sent off from Judaea by his father while Galba was still alive. The young man alleged that his journey was prompted by a desire to pay homage to the emperor and to stand for the public offices for which he was now of age to be a candidate.[2] But an imaginative public had spread the story that he had been summoned to Rome to be adopted as the emperor's heir. Such gossip found fuel in the fact of Galba's advanced age and childlessness, as well as in Rome's weakness for speculating on the chances of many possible candidates until such time as the successful one is chosen. Titus' reputation was rated all the higher because of his personal qualities. His intelligence fitted him for the most exalted station, while he had good looks, too, and a certain dignity of manner. Moreover Vespasian had been successful, prophecies were favourable, and a credulous society was disposed to regard even chance events as omens. At the city of Corinth in Achaia he was reliably informed of Galba's death, and met those who assured him that Vitellius was arming for war. In perplexity, he gathered round him a few friends and examined all the possibilities on either side. If he went on to the capital, he could expect no thanks for a gesture designed to honour another, and would merely be a hostage in the hands of either Vitellius or Otho. If, on the other hand, he returned to Judaea, the new emperor would undoubtedly take umbrage when he was victorious, though so long

1. The first two Flavian emperors, Vespasian and Titus, were popular; the third, Domitian, was severely autocratic (see p. 239 and n. 1) and was finally assassinated (see p. 22, n. 1).
2. Titus was just twenty-nine years old; a candidate for the praetorship must be in his thirtieth year or older.

as victory was still undecided and provided his father joined the winner, he, the son, would be forgiven. If, however, Vespasian claimed the principate, such slights would inevitably be forgotten in the bustle of war.

2. These and similar arguments kept him hovering uneasily between hope and fear. Finally, hope triumphed. Some have held that his passion for Queen Berenice[1] made him turn back. It is quite true that she attracted the young man, but practical efficiency never suffered from this. (Titus led a life of pleasure in his youth, and proved more self-disciplined during his own reign than during his father's.) So he sailed along the coasts of Achaia and Asia, skirting the gulfs to the left[2] and making for the islands of Rhodes and Cyprus, and then, by the open sea, for Syria. He could not resist the temptation to go and visit the Temple of Venus at Paphos, which is famous among natives and visitors alike. It may perhaps be of some interest to say a few words about the origin of this cult, the temple ritual, and – since this is quite unique – the form in which the goddess is represented.

3. An ancient tradition declares that the temple was founded by King Aerias,[3] while some authorities say that this is the name of the goddess herself. A more recent version tells us that the temple was consecrated by Cinyras and that it was here that the goddess landed after her birth from the sea. But the knowledge and skill of divination, it seems, was introduced from abroad by Tamiras of Cilicia, and it was agreed that control over ceremonial should be exercised alike by the descendants of both families. Later, to avoid a situation in which the royal line enjoyed no advantage over foreigners, the immigrants renounced the control of the very lore they had introduced, and now the only priest consulted is a descendant of Cinyras. The worshipper selects whatever sort of victim he has vowed to give, but the choice is restricted to male animals. The livers of kids are held to offer the surest prediction. Spilling blood upon the altar is forbidden. All that is offered upon it is prayer and pure fire, and despite its situation in the open, it is never wetted by rain. The goddess is not portrayed in

1. Berenice, now forty, daughter of Agrippa I of Judaea, had been married to Herod King of Chalcis and then to Polemo of Cilicia. Her brother was Agrippa II, who accompanied Titus on this journey and went on to Rome when his companion turned back; see p. 130.

2. The gulfs of Güllük (Mandalya), Gökova (Kerme) and Hisarön, for which see H. M. Denham, *The Aegean*[4] 1979, 176 ff.     3. The names are mythical.

the likeness of a human. Her image resembles a truncated cone, tapering from a broad circular base to a top of slender circumference. The reason for this is obscure.

4. Titus examined the rich treasures, which included gifts from kings and other objects for which the antiquarianism of the Greeks claims an origin lost in the mists of the past. Then he put his first question, which dealt with his voyage. On being assured of a clear passage and calm sea, he inquired in veiled language of his own future, offering a number of victims. Sostratus – for so the priest was named – observed that in every case the entrails showed favourable indications. The goddess was clearly intent on giving her blessing to a great enterprise. So for the time being he made a short and conventional reply, but asked for an interview in secret, and in this disclosed the future. Heartened by these assurances, Titus sailed on to rejoin his father. Amid the mood of uncertainty prevailing throughout the provinces and armies, his arrival inspired a surge of confidence.

The back of the Jewish War[1] had already been broken by Vespasian. There remained the siege of Jerusalem, which promised to be a hard and uphill task, more because of the peculiar character of its mountain site and the bigotry of its inhabitants than because it had the means to endure a desperate struggle. I have already mentioned that Vespasian himself had three seasoned legions. Four others were commanded by Mucianus. These had seen no active service, but rivalry and the distinction of the neighbouring army of Judaea had put them on their mettle. If Vespasian's troops owed their toughness to danger and exertion, their rivals had acquired an equal degree of vigour from uninterrupted peace and the attractiveness of war to those who have no experience of it. Each of these two armies had its auxiliary cohorts and cavalry regiments, its fleets and client-kings and a great name based upon differing reputations.

5. Vespasian was a born soldier, accustomed to march at the head of his troops, to choose the place where they should camp, and to harry the enemy day and night by his generalship and, if occasion required, by personal combat, content with whatever rations were available and dressed much the same as a private soldier. In short, if one excepts his meanness in money matters, he was a worthy successor to the commanders of old. Mucianus was quite different, owing his eminence to lavish generosity, great wealth, and the lordly scale upon

1. See pp. 27 and 277.

which he did everything. Happier in his choice of words as an orator than was Vespasian, he was an expert at manipulating a given political situation, and at foreseeing a future one. Freed of their several weaknesses, the combined virtues of these two would have comprised to a remarkable degree the qualities demanded of an emperor. However, as governors of Syria and Judaea respectively, Mucianus and Vespasian had been divided by the jealousy which is typical of the administration of neighbouring provinces. It was Nero's death that finally healed the breach and led to close collaboration, initially at staff level. Then Titus did much to inspire confidence. He managed to remove petty friction by an appeal to their common interests, and in him a nice admixture of frankness and diplomacy was able to fascinate even the sophisticated Mucianus. The support of tribunes, centurions and other ranks was secured by playing upon their industry and licence, their virtues and vices. Motives were as mixed as characters.

6. Before Titus' return, both armies had taken the oath to Otho. His accession had of course been speedily reported, and the massive machinery of civil war was slow to gather momentum. In any case this was the first occasion upon which the long peaceful and dormant East had embarked upon such a war. In the past, the great conflicts of Roman with Roman had started in Italy or Gaul, relying upon the resources of the West. Pompey, Crassus, Brutus and Antony, who drew civil war in their wake across the sea, had come to an unlucky end, and in Syria and Judaea the Caesars had been spoken of more often than seen. The legions had avoided mutiny and reserved their hostility for the Parthians, with varying success. In the most recent civil war,[1] turmoil elsewhere contrasted with unbroken peace here, followed by allegiance to Galba. Later, when it became generally known that Otho and Vitellius proposed to tear the Roman state to pieces in a sacrilegious war, the troops began to fear that others would earn the prizes of empire and themselves nothing but the compulsion of slavery. So they proceeded to agitate and to count their own strength. For a start, there were seven legions as well as Syria and Judaea with their considerable auxiliary forces. On one side and in immediate proximity stood Egypt and its garrison of two legions, while on the other lay Cappadocia and Pontus and the fringe of camps facing Armenia, together with Asia and the other rich and populous provinces, all the islands in the Eastern Mediterranean, and finally that sea itself,

1. The revolt of Vindex and Galba against Nero.

which offered support and protection during the interim period of mobilization.

7. The commanders were perfectly aware that the troops wanted action, but so long as the others were fighting they decided to play a waiting game in the conviction that the winning and losing sides in a civil war never form a sincere and durable union. It made no difference whether it was Vitellius or Otho who happened to survive. Success rendered even good generals conceited, and their troops riotous. Thus idleness, high living and their innate viciousness would destroy one of the rivals in the fighting and the other in the day of victory. For these reasons, then, they proposed to hold their hand until the moment was propitious. The decision to fight was a recent one so far as Vespasian and Mucianus were concerned. The rest had long since decided, though their motives were mixed. Men of the highest character acted from love of their country. Many were stimulated by the attractive prospect of making a fortune, others again by financial embarrassment. Thus there were good men and bad, but for a variety of reasons and with equal enthusiasm all of them wanted a war.

8. About this time Achaia and Asia were upset by a false alarm. It was rumoured that Nero was on his way to them. There had been conflicting stories about his death, and so numbers of people imagined – and believed – that he was alive. I shall describe the adventures of the other claimants in their chronological context as my story develops. On this occasion the man concerned was a slave from Pontus, or, according to other accounts, a freedman from Italy. The circumstance that he was a harpist and singer by profession, when added to a facial resemblance, made the imposture all the more plausible. He was joined by some army deserters who had been roaming about in destitution until he bribed them to follow him by lavish promises.

With these men he embarked on board ship. A storm forced him to land on the island of Cythnus, where he recruited some troops returning from the east on leave, or had them murdered when they refused. He also robbed businessmen and armed the sturdiest of their slaves. A centurion named Sisenna, representing the army of Syria, happened to be bringing some symbolic 'hands'[1] to the pretorians as a token of friendship. He was subjected to a variety of artful approaches, but finally slipped away from the island and fled in fear of

1. See p. 55 and n. 1.

his life. This caused a wave of panic, and many restless or discontented creatures rallied with eagerness to a famous name. The bubble reputation, daily increasing, was abruptly pricked by one of the chances of history.

9. Galba had appointed Calpurnius Asprenas governor of the province of Galatia and Pamphylia. He had been given two triremes from the Ravenna fleet as escort, and with these he travelled east, putting in at the island of Cythnus. Here agents of the self-styled Nero invited the captains of the triremes to join him. Assuming a pathetic air, the fellow appealed to 'the allegiance of his former soldiers' and asked them to land him in Syria or Egypt. Half-convinced, or to trick him, the captains declared that they would have to talk to their crews, and would return when they had got them all into the right frame of mind. But in fact, as in duty bound, they made a full report to Asprenas, at whose instance the ship was overwhelmed, and the man of mystery put to death. His body, which arrested attention by the eyes, hair and savage expression, was taken to Asia and thence to Rome.

10. In a capital riven by dissension and hovering between liberty and licence as one emperor followed on the heels of another, even trivial matters were dealt with in a highly emotional atmosphere. Vibius Crispus, whose wealth, influence and intelligence classed him among Romans of distinction rather than merit, attacked Annius Faustus, a knight who had repeatedly acted as prosecutor in Nero's day. He impeached him before the senate, since, in the early days of Galba's reign, the fathers had resolved that the professional prosecutors should be put on trial. This senatorial decree had led to controversy. Ineffectual when a powerful man was accused, operative when the defendant was helpless, it still retained some power of intimidation. Besides, Crispus was a man to be reckoned with on his own account. He used all his powers to bring about the downfall of his brother's accuser, and had managed to bully a considerable proportion of the senate into demanding a sentence of execution without defence or hearing. Other members however, viewed the matter differently. For them a strong argument in favour of the accused was the undue influence wielded by the prosecutor. They voiced the opinion that notice should be given, the heads of indictment published, and a proper hearing granted in accordance with tradition, however unpopular and vicious the accused might be. Indeed, this view prevailed at first, and the case was post-

poned for a few days. But then came Faustus' condemnation, though this was far from commanding the kind of backing from the public which he had richly deserved in view of his evil character. The trouble was that they remembered that Crispus himself had made a fortune by acting as prosecutor in the very same way, and their disapproval applied less to the fact than to the instrument of retribution.

# The First Battle of Cremona

11. Meanwhile, the opening of the campaign augured success for Otho. At his command, armies had moved up from Dalmatia and Pannonia. They comprised four legions, from each of which 2,000 men were sent ahead. The main parties followed at no great distance. The formations concerned were the Seventh, raised by Galba, and three veteran legions – the Eleventh, the Thirteenth, and above all the Fourteenth, whose men had covered themselves in glory by quelling the rebellion in Britain.[1] Nero had enhanced their reputation by singling them out as his best troops – hence their protracted devotion to him and their lively enthusiasm for Otho. But excellent fighting qualities were offset by a corresponding fault bred of over-confidence: they were slow to move. As they marched, the legions were preceded by auxiliary cavalry and infantry, and from the capital itself came a sizable contingent consisting of five pretorian cohorts and some squadrons of cavalry, together with the First Legion.[2] In addition, there were 2,000 gladiators – an ill-favoured force to call upon, though employed in the civil wars even by strict commanders. These troops were placed under the command of Annius Gallus, who was sent ahead with Vestricius Spurinna to secure both banks of the Po in view of the fact that the original plan had fallen through owing to the passage of the Alps by Caecina, whom the emperor had at first hoped to contain within the Gallic provinces. Otho himself was attended by a personal bodyguard of picked physique and the remaining pretorian cohorts, by veterans of the Pretorian Guard, and by a large naval brigade. Nor did he travel slowly in luxurious comfort. He wore a steel cuirass, and marched on foot before the standards, ill-shaven, unkempt and belying his reputation.

12. At first fortune smiled on Otho's strategy. His ships and his command of the sea enabled him to dominate the greater part of Italy

1. The rebellion of Boudicca; see *Annals* xiv, 34ff.
2. The First (Support) Legion: cf. pp. 96 and 106.

right up to the frontier with the Maritime Alps. He had selected Suedius Clemens, Antonius Novellus and Aemilius Pacensis for the task of raiding this province and threatening Narbonese Gaul. But Pacensis was put under arrest by his unruly men, and Antonius Novellus was a mere cipher. Control lay with the ambitious Suedius Clemens. Though susceptible to pressure in a way prejudicial to good discipline, he was spoiling for a fight. One would never have guessed that it was against Italy or the towns and homes of the mother country that the invasion was directed: it looked as if these were foreign shores and cities of the enemy. For they proceeded to burn, devastate and plunder them with a savagery rendered more frightful by the total lack of precautions everywhere against such an emergency. The men were in the fields, the farmhouses open and defenceless. As owners ran out with wives and children, they met their end, victims of war in what they thought was peace.[1]

The then governor of the Maritime Alps was Marius Maturus. He raised the alarm among the natives (there was, of course, a militia force), and prepared to man the frontiers of his province against the Othonians. But at the first charge the hill-folk were cut down and scattered. This was only to be expected of hastily gathered levies with no idea of what is meant by entrenching a camp or obeying orders, men who took no pride in victory and saw no dishonour in defeat.

13. This encounter provoked Otho's men into venting their spite on the town of Albintimilium. They had taken no booty in the fighting, as the countryfolk were poor and their accoutrements valueless. Nor indeed was it possible to capture tribesmen who were fleet of foot and knew the area intimately. But greed was satisfied at the cost of the inoffensive civilians. What intensified bitterness was the exemplary courage of a Ligurian woman. She hid her son, and when the soldiers, thinking that money was secreted with him, asked her under torture where she was concealing him, she pointed to her womb, and said 'Here'. No subsequent frightfulness, not even death, could make her modify this heroic reply.

14. The news that the Narbonese province, which had been made to swear allegiance to Vitellius, was threatened by Otho's fleet reached Fabius Valens on the lips of quaking messengers. Representatives of the more important towns presented themselves with requests for

1. Among the victims at Albintimilium was Agricola's mother: Tacitus, *Agricola* 7.

help. Fabius sent off two Tungrian cohorts, four squadrons of cavalry and a whole regiment of Treviran horse, with its commander Julius Classicus. A portion was kept in the rear at Forum Julii, because if the whole force had been thrown into the advance by land, the Othonian fleet might have sailed rapidly on through undefended waters. Twelve squadrons of cavalry and details from the cohorts made for the enemy, supported by a cohort of Ligurians which had long formed the local garrison, and 500 Pannonians not yet regularly embodied. Battle was not long delayed. The Othonian front was drawn up as follows: some of the naval personnel, together with an admixture of civilians, occupied rising ground on the hills near the sea; the flat land between the hills and the coast was held in strength by the pretorians, and on the sea, maintaining contact and ready for action, the fleet provided a menacing screen of prows turned towards the enemy. The Vitellians, inferior in infantry but well provided with horse, placed their Alpine troops on the neighbouring hills, and their cohorts in close order behind the cavalry.

The Treviran squadrons charged the enemy recklessly, and met stiff resistance from the veterans, while on the flank they suffered severely under a hail of stones hurled by the civilians. Even they were quite adept at this sort of thing, and being interspersed among troops, showed the same daring in the moment of victory, whatever their prowess or lack of it. The shattered troops were further demoralized when the fleet delivered an attack on their rear while they were still fighting. Thus encircled on every hand, the whole force would have been annihilated had not the winning side been hampered by dusk, which covered the escape of the fugitives.

15. The Vitellians were not idle either, despite their beating. They brought up reinforcements and fell upon an enemy whom success had rendered complacent and too slack. The sentries were cut down, the camp was penetrated, and panic reigned by the ships. Gradually the alarm ebbed, and after rallying on a near-by hill the Othonians went over to the offensive. In this they inflicted severe losses, and the commanders of the Tungrian cohorts, who made a prolonged effort to hold out, were finally overwhelmed by a rain of missiles. Even the Othonians did not score a bloodless victory. Some of them launched a blind pursuit, and the cavalry faced about and surrounded them. A tacit truce was then concluded, and to obviate any surprise move by the fleet on the one side or the cavalry on the other, the Vitellians

returned to Antipolis in Narbonese Gaul and the Othonians to Albingaunum further back in Liguria.

16. Corsica, Sardinia and the other Mediterranean islands in adjacent waters were kept on Otho's side by the prestige of the victorious fleet. But Corsica nearly came to grief through the recklessness of its governor Picarius Decumus. In fact, though his intervention in such a massive conflict was bound to be ineffectual, it proved fatal to himself. Hating Otho, he determined to help Vitellius by mobilizing the resources of Corsica – trumpery aid even if the enterprise had succeeded. He summoned the leading personalities of the island and explained his plan. Those who ventured to demur – Claudius Pyrrhicus, captain of the galleys stationed off Corsica, and Quintius Certus, a Roman knight – he caused to be executed. This unnerved those who were there, and their fears communicated themselves to a spineless throng of people who did not know what was afoot. All of them promptly swore allegiance to Vitellius. But when Picarius began to enlist troops and burden primitive people with military duty, these unaccustomed exertions proved unpopular. They reflected on their powerlessness, telling themselves that they were islanders, while Germany and the might of the legions were far away. Even those who had cohorts and cavalry to protect them had been plundered and devastated by the fleet. There was a sudden change of mood, though without any public outbreak: they chose rather to strike in secret. When Picarius' following had left him and he was naked and helpless in the baths, he fell to an assassin's blow, and his staff shared his fate. Their heads, like those of outlaws, were taken to Otho by the murderers in person. But they got neither reward from Otho nor punishment from Vitellius, for in the world-wide upheaval of the time they were inextricably lost amid greater enormities.

17. As I have mentioned above,[1] the Silian cavalry regiment was the unit responsible for opening the door to Italy and bringing the war south of the Alps. Otho was not popular with anyone. Yet the reason was not to be found in any preference for Vitellius. A long period of peace had made the Italians ready to submit tamely to any master. They were fair game for the first-comer, and had no interest in the relative merits of the rivals. As some cohorts sent ahead by Caecina had also arrived, the forces of Vitellius now controlled the most prosperous area of Italy, including all the flat country and the cities

1. See pp. 63ff.

between the Po and the Alps.[1] A cohort of Pannonians was captured at Cremona. A hundred cavalrymen and 1,000 sailors were rounded up between Placentia and Ticinum. These successes meant that the Vitellian army found its way no longer barred by enemy forces upon the Po or along its banks. Indeed, the mere presence of the river was a challenge to the Batavians and the Germans from beyond the Rhine. They crossed it without warning, opposite Placentia, and by surprising a few reconnaissance troops so demoralized the rest that they brought back a false and panic-stricken report that Caecina's whole army was at hand.

18. Spurinna, who held Placentia, was quite certain that Caecina was not yet in the offing, and if the enemy did approach, he had made up his mind to keep his men behind the fortifications and avoid exposing to a seasoned army his own force – three pretorian cohorts, 1,000 infantry drafted from the legions, and a small cavalry contingent. But the men were out of hand, and had seen no active service. Seizing the standards and flags, they ran amuck and offered violence to their general as he tried to restrain them, without bothering about the centurions and tribunes. Indeed they kept howling that treachery was afoot against Otho, and that Caecina had been invited into Italy. Then they marched off recklessly, and Spurinna went with them. He did so at first under compulsion, but later feigned acquiescence so that his views should carry more weight if the mutiny petered out.

19. When the Po was sighted[2] and night drew on, it was decided to entrench camp. The physical labour (a novelty for troops normally stationed in the capital) effectually broke their spirit. Then the older men began to denounce their own credulity, and point out the critical danger of their position if Caecina and his army surrounded their slender force of cohorts in the open plain. By this time sober language was heard throughout the camp, and when the centurions and tribunes went among the ranks, there was praise for the foresight of a commander who had chosen a populous and wealthy city as his strongpoint and headquarters. Finally Spurinna addressed them in a tone of explanation rather than criticism, and leaving a reconnaissance

1. An exaggeration: the area controlled by the Vitellian forces was little more than the Transpadane Region, for which see p. 64 and map 1.

2. The pretorians marched westward and then branched off to the right, following the road to Ticinum which crossed the Po about twenty miles from Placentia.

party behind, marched the rest back to Placentia in a less disorderly mood, ready to listen to orders. The city-walls were reinforced, parapets added, towers increased in height, and provision and preparation made in respect both of arms and of military obedience and discipline – the only thing the Othonian side lacked, since they could have no regrets on the score of courage.

20. As for Caecina, he seemed to have left violence and licence behind north of the Alps, and marched through the Italian countryside in an orderly fashion. His manner of dress was interpreted by the townsfolk as arrogance, for he made speeches to toga-clad audiences while himself wearing exotic garb – a parti-coloured cloak and trousers.[1] His wife Salonina attracted attention, too, by riding on horseback in a purple dress. No offence was meant, but the Italians took it as an insult. It is only human nature to submit fortune's latest favourite to a penetrating scrutiny, and a modest use of success is above all expected of those whom their critics have seen on a level with themselves.

Having crossed the Po, Caecina tried to lure the Othonians from their allegiance by negotiation and promises, and was himself subjected to the same process. At first some pretentious language about 'peace' and 'concord' was bandied about to little purpose. Then he tried intimidation, and directed all his plans and endeavours to the siege of Placentia. He was perfectly aware that the degree of success achieved in the opening phase of the campaign would determine his prestige later.

21. The first day's action, however, was marked by a vigorous offensive rather than by the skilled techniques of a seasoned army. The enemy approached the walls carelessly without cover, after heavy eating and drinking. It was in the course of this fighting that the fine amphitheatre outside the walls went up in flames, though it is an open question whether it was set on fire by the besiegers as they hurled torches, slingshots and incendiary missiles at the besieged, or by the latter as they responded. The ordinary townsfolk, always ready to suspect the worst, believed that inflammable material had been furtively brought into the building by certain people from neighbouring cities who were jealous and envied them the possession of an edifice unrivalled for size throughout Italy. Whatever the cause of the

---

1. Trousers were worn by Germans or Orientals; the toga was the formal and ceremonial dress of Rome.

disaster, it was made light of so long as worse was to be feared, but once their worries were over they felt they could have suffered no heavier blow, and deeply regretted it. However that may be, Caecina was repulsed with serious casualties, and the night was spent in preparing siege-equipment. The Vitellians got ready screens, hurdles and mantlets in order to undermine the walls and protect the assault parties, while the Othonians provided themselves with stakes and immense masses of stone, lead and bronze designed to crush and annihilate the enemy. Both armies felt the call of honour and glory, but derived encouragement from different sources. One side stressed the military prowess of the legions and the army of Germany, the other the prestige attaching to the garrison of the capital and the pretorian cohorts. The Vitellians dismissed their opponents as a flabby and idle crew of circus-fans and theatregoers, and the Othonians spoke scornfully of the enemy as a lot of foreigners and aliens. The cult or criticism of Otho and Vitellius provided an added stimulus, less fruitful of praise than of mutual abuse.

22. Soon after first light, the walls were crammed with shock-troops, and the plains glittered with arms and men. The legionaries in close formation and the auxiliary forces in extended order assailed the top of the walls with arrows or stones and closed in upon stretches which had been neglected or were crumbling with age. The javelins hurled down by the Othonians gathered more momentum and found their target more surely amid the rashly advancing cohorts of Germans who, with wild battle-songs and bodies bared in traditional fashion, clashed their shields together with upraised arms. The legionary troops, protected by screens and hurdles, undermined the walls, built an earthen siege-mound, and attacked the gates with crow-bars. The pretorians facing them rolled down millstones disposed at various points along the wall for this purpose. Their weight and the consequent crashes were terrific. Some of the men at the foot of the walls were crushed to pieces, others hit, struck senseless or maimed. Panic made the slaughter worse and only served to intensify the effect of the murderous fire from the walls. The consequent retreat was a severe blow to the reputation of the Vitellians, and Caecina, who was ashamed of his reckless and ill-considered attack, and anxious not to encamp in the same spot to no purpose amid the jeers of his beholders, recrossed the Po and made for Cremona. As he departed, he received the surrender of Turullius Cerialis with a number of naval personnel and

of Julius Briganticus with a few cavalrymen. The latter officer was a cavalry prefect of Batavian birth, the former a senior centurion known to Caecina because he had commanded a company in Germany.

23. On learning of the enemy's approach, Spurinna informed Annius Gallus[1] in writing of his measures to defend Placentia, the events of the past days, and Caecina's intentions. Gallus was at that moment leading the First Legion to the relief of Placentia, having no confidence in the ability of such a small number of cohorts to face a prolonged siege and the powerful army of Germany. When he heard that the discomfited Caecina was making for Cremona, he held back his legion. This was a difficult achievement, and the troops were on the brink of mutiny in their burning eagerness to fight. The place at which he halted them was Bedriacum, a village between Verona and Cremona, which thanks to two Roman catastrophes is now famous

In the course of these same days, Martius Macer scored a success near Cremona. This enterprising general ferried his gladiators across the Po and staged a lightning raid on the opposite bank. Some Vitellian auxiliaries there were thrown into disorder, and when the rest of them fled to Cremona, those who had stood firm were cut to pieces. But the offensive was kept within bounds in case the enemy brought up reinforcements and turned the tables upon the victors. This created suspicion among the Othonian troops, who put an unfavourable construction on everything their generals did. Cowardly and loud-mouthed elements among them vied with each other in assailing Annius Gallus, Suetonius Paulinus and Marius Celsus, who had also been given command by Otho. The accusations were varied, but the most violent incitement to mutiny and sedition was offered by the murderers of Galba, who were crazed by guilt and fear. These men caused chaos, both by provocative remarks openly made and by communicating secretly with Otho. The emperor was always ready to listen to the lowest of the low, and it was good advice he feared. He now fell into a panic, being a man who was thrown off his balance by success and did better in the thick of disaster. So he summoned his brother Titianus and made him commander-in-chief. In the meantime, a brilliant action was fought under the command of Paulinus and Celsus.

1. Gallus appears to have been in the Mantua–Verona area; Tacitus has forgotten to keep us informed of his whereabouts. Chronological considerations compel us to suppose two different messages from Spurinna to Gallus, though Tacitus is far from clear on this.

24. Caecina had been tortured by the failure of all his moves and the fast-fading laurels of his army. Driven from Placentia, his auxiliaries lately cut to pieces, he had not even held his own in a series of brushes fought between patrols and scarcely worth mentioning. Fabius Valens was near, and to prevent the whole credit for the campaign going to him, Caecina hastened to retrieve his reputation with more greed than judgement. At a point called the 'Castores',[1] twelve miles from Cremona, he posted his most spirited auxiliaries in a hiding place afforded by some woods close to the road. The cavalry were told to go further forward, provoke a battle, and by voluntarily beating a retreat induce the enemy to gallop after them far enough for the auxiliaries to take them by surprise. This plan was betrayed to the Othonian leaders. Paulinus and Celsus assumed responsibility for the infantry and cavalry respectively. The advance-party of the Thirteenth Legion, with four cohorts of auxiliaries and 500 horse, was posted on the left. Three pretorian cohorts held the high road on a narrow front. On the right, the First Legion moved forward with two auxiliary cohorts and 500 horse. In addition, 1,000 cavalrymen drawn from the Pretorian Guard and the auxiliaries were set in motion as a reserve to put the finishing touches to a victory or help any troops in trouble.  25. Before the two sides made contact, the Vitellians turned about. Celsus knew this was a trick, and held back his men. But the Vitellians rashly issued from their ambush, and as Celsus slowly retreated, they followed him too far, and of their own accord fell headlong into the trap themselves. They had the cohorts on their flanks, the legions opposite them; and by a sudden dividing movement the cavalry had surrounded them in the rear. Suetonius Paulinus did not immediately give the infantry the signal to engage. He was by nature dilatory – the sort of man that prefers a cautious, well-considered plan to the luck of the gambler. So he had the ditches filled, the flat ground opened up, and the line extended, thinking that it would be soon enough to start winning when precautions had been taken against defeat. This delay gave the Vitellians a chance to retreat to a vineyard where a complex network of trellised vines impeded movement. There was a small wood close by, too. From this they ventured to stage a counter-attack, and in so doing managed to kill the most eager of the pretorian troopers. Among the wounded was Prince

1. Here there was a small wayside chapel dedicated to the gods of travel, the Dioscuri, Castor and Pollux; see Key to Place-Names.

Epiphanes,[1] who was eagerly leading his men into battle on Otho's side. 26. Then the Othonian infantry charged. The enemy line was trodden under foot, and the rout communicated itself to their reinforcements as they arrived. Caecina had not summoned his cohorts simultaneously, but one by one. This increased the panic and confusion on the field of battle, for the scattered groups, nowhere in strength, were borne away one after another by the stampede. Besides this, there was mutiny in the camp,[2] caused by the discontent of the army at not being led out to battle *en masse*. They confined the camp-commandant, Julius Gratus, on the grounds that he was concerting treachery with his brother, who was serving with Otho. As it happened, the brother, a tribune named Julius Fronto, had been put in irons by the Othonians on the very same charge. However, there was such consternation everywhere among the fugitives and those who sought to make headway against them, in the front line no less than outside the camp, that it was rumoured on both sides that Caecina might have been destroyed with all his forces had not Suetonius Paulinus sounded the retreat. Paulinus for his part asserted that he had shrunk from making further demands on his men in the way of heavy fighting and a long pursuit, as the Vitellian troops might have fallen upon the wearied Othonians while themselves fresh from camp, and there would have been no reserve to back them up in the event of disaster. A few critics approved of the general's reasoning, but it was not well received by the rank-and-file.

27. This defeat caused some dismay among the Vitellians, but it was still more effective in restoring discipline. This is true not only of the army of Caecina, who threw the blame upon his men, as being readier to mutiny than fight: Fabius Valens, too, who had by this time reached Ticinum, found that his forces no longer underestimated the enemy and in their eagerness to retrieve their reputation obeyed his orders with greater respect and consistency.

Anyhow, there had previously been a serious outbreak of indiscipline. To explain its origin, it will be necessary for me to revert to an earlier stage in the narrative, as it would have been wrong to interrupt the sequence of Caecina's operations. I have already described how, during the fighting in Nero's reign, the Batavian cohorts separated

1. Son of King Antiochus (see p. 129 and n. 2). He was at Rome at the moment of Otho's accession.
2. At Cremona; see map 3, and cf. pp. 161 ff.

themselves from the Fourteenth Legion and were on their way to Britain when they heard of Vitellius' moves and joined Fabius Valens in the territory of the Lingones. These Batavians now started to behave arrogantly. They would go up to the lines of each of the legions in turn and boast that they had put the Fourteenth in its place, robbed Nero of Italy and now held the whole issue of the war in the hollow of their hand. This attitude was an affront to the legions bitterly resented by their commander. Discipline was prejudiced by disputes and brawls. In the end, their insubordination led Valens to suspect treachery.    28. So when news came that the Treviran cavalry regiment and the Tungrians had been routed by Otho's fleet and that Narbonese Gaul was being isolated, Valens, anxious both to protect allied communities and by a clever stratagem to split up unruly cohorts that could be dangerous if united, ordered some of the Batavians to go to the rescue. When this leaked out and became common knowledge, it evoked regrets from the auxiliaries and protests from the legions. They complained that they were being deprived of the help of the best troops. Now that the enemy were within sight, the seasoned heroes who had won so many battles were to be practically withdrawn from the front-line! If a mere province were more important than the capital and the safety of the empire, then they should all follow the Batavians to Gaul. But if victory hinged on the preservation of Italy, the body of the army must not be mutilated by the amputation of its strongest limbs.

29. They aired these grievances in violent language, and when Valens started to check the mutiny by sending his lictors to make arrests, they attacked him personally, bombarded him with stones, and chased him as he ran for it, yelling out that he was hiding the Gallic loot and the gold of Vienne, which they had earned by their own exertions. They ransacked the general's kit, rummaged his tent and poked about in the very ground with spears and lances. Valens meanwhile was hiding in a cavalry officer's quarters, disguised as his servant. Then, as the mutineers gradually cooled down, the camp-commandant, Alfenus Varus, helped on the good work by a sensible decision. He told the centurions not to make their usual inspection of the pickets, and omitted the trumpet-calls which summon the troops to their duties. They all seemed paralysed into inaction as a result, looking round at each other in bewilderment, and unnerved by the mere fact that there was no one to give orders. Their silence,

their submissiveness, and in the last resort their appeals and tears pleaded for pardon. But the climax came when Valens came out of hiding in his mean garb, weeping and surprised to find himself alive: their reaction was one of relief, sympathy and good will. The ordinary man always goes from one emotional extreme to the other, and there was now a revulsion of feeling. They exultantly gathered the eagles and standards about him and bore him to the dais in the square amid praise and congratulation. Valens was wise enough to avoid severity. He refrained from demanding that anyone should be executed, but in order not to increase suspicion by obvious insincerity, he denounced a few men as trouble-makers. He knew perfectly well that in a civil war the troops can take more liberties than their commanders.

30. His men were entrenching camp at Ticinum when word came of Caecina's defeat. The mutiny almost repeated itself, for there was an impression that they had been kept away from the scene of the fighting by Valens' underhand methods and repeated time-wasting. There was no question of the troops' wanting a rest or waiting for the general to act – they were off in advance of the standards, telling the bearers to get a move on. A rapid march brought them up with Caecina.

Valens was not highly thought of by Caecina's troops. They complained of having been left to face an enemy in the full vigour of his first engagement though themselves far inferior in numbers. In the same breath, they made a flattering estimate of the strength of the newcomers too. This was done in self-defence – they did not want to be looked down upon as men who were beaten and cowardly. Besides, although Valens disposed of a more powerful force and almost twice the number of legions and auxiliary units, yet the troops liked Caecina better. He was thought to be readier to show kindliness, and he was also a tall and well-built man in the prime of life, and possessed a sort of superficial charm. This was why the generals were jealous of each other. Caecina dismissed his rival as a disreputable money-grubber, and Valens responded by deriding the other as a pompous ass. But they concealed their enmity for the time being and pursued their common advantage, writing a stream of insulting letters to Otho. In so doing, they burnt their boats behind them, whereas the leaders of the Othonian faction abstained from abusing Vitellius, though the field for invective was an exceedingly rich one. 31. Admittedly, until the hour of death, in which Otho won glory and

Vitellius infamy, the idle pleasures of Vitellius seemed less dangerous than Otho's complete lack of self-control. The latter had also earned himself men's dread and hatred by murdering Galba, whereas no one held Vitellius responsible for beginning the fighting. As the slave of his belly and his palate, he was felt to have brought discredit chiefly upon himself, while the pleasure-seeking, cruel and unscrupulous Otho seemed a deadlier threat to the community.

After the rendezvous of the armies of Caecina and Valens, the Vitellians had no further inducement to delay committing their combined forces. But Otho held a council of war to decide whether to wage a long campaign or try his luck immediately.  32. At this meeting Suetonius Paulinus thought he owed it to his military reputation – second-to-none at that time – to review the whole strategic position. He made a speech explaining that haste would serve the enemy's purpose and a waiting game their own. Vitellius' army had now arrived in full, but was weakly supported in the rear since the Gallic provinces were restive and it would be inadvisable to abandon the Rhine frontier when one must reckon with raids by bitterly hostile tribes. The garrison of Britain could not intervene because of its enemies and the sea. The Spanish provinces had practically no troops to spare. Narbonese Gaul, invaded by the fleet and defeated in battle, had received a severe shock. The Transpadane Region of Italy was enclosed by the Alps and could not be reinforced by sea, while the mere passage of an army through its countryside had wrought havoc. There was no corn available to the enemy army anywhere, and without supplies an army could not be kept together. Even the Germans, the most dreaded troops on the other side, would not stand up to the change of latitude and climate. If the war were prolonged to the summer, their health was bound to be impaired. A powerful initiative had often come to nothing in a context of boredom and delay. On their own side, all was different. The picture everywhere was one of abundant resources and confident devotion. They disposed of Pannonia, Moesia, Dalmatia and the East, with armies fresh and unimpaired; of Italy and the city which was the capital of the world; of the Roman senate and people – great names whose halo, if sometimes overshadowed, was never eclipsed. They could call upon official and private resources, and those boundless riches which are more effective in civil dissension than the sword; upon soldiers whose constitutions were inured to Italy or else to tropical heat. They had the River Po to protect them, and cities

securely defended by men and walls. That none of these would go over
to the enemy was abundantly clear from the defence of Placentia.¹
Otho should therefore avoid an immediate decision. In a few days,
the Fourteenth Legion would appear on the scene – itself famous and
now supplemented by forces from Moesia. Then the emperor would
consider the situation afresh, and if he decided on battle, they would
fight with augmented strength.

33. The views of Paulinus were echoed by Marius Celsus and Annius
Gallus (the latter had been injured a few days before by a fall from
his horse, but messengers were sent to inquire what he thought and
had already returned with his approval). Otho for his part was set
upon forcing a decision. His brother Titianus and the pretorian prefect
Proculus, with the eagerness of ignorance, claimed that fortune,
heaven and Otho's guardian angel smiled upon their plans and would
smile upon their performance: they had fallen back on flattery to prevent any attempt at opposition.

Once the decision to fight had been taken, the council of war
considered whether it would be better for the emperor to be present
at the battle or not. Reluctant to appear to expose him to danger,
Paulinus and Celsus raised no further objections, and the same group
of mistaken advisers induced Otho to retire to Brixellum and hold
himself in readiness to take the supreme decisions, undisturbed by the
alarms of battle. This day's work marked the beginning of the end
for the Othonian cause. Not only did a strong force of pretorians,
bodyguards and cavalry go with the emperor as he departed, but
those who remained behind lost heart. This was because the generals
were regarded with suspicion, and Otho had left the chain of command in uncertainty as he trusted no one but the troops and alone
enjoyed their confidence.

34. All this was well known to the Vitellians, thanks to the continual
desertions to be expected in civil war. Besides, the Othonian reconnaissance was so eager to discover the enemy's intentions that it failed
to conceal its own. Coolly and calmly, Caecina and Valens kept their
eyes open for the moment when the enemy would rush blindly to
destruction. They had at least sense enough to wait for others to play
the fool. They began bridge-building and made a feint of crossing the
Po, ostensibly in order to deal with the company of gladiators² on

1. But Cremona had fallen to the Vitellians: see pp. 94 and 97.
2. See p. 95.

the other bank and save their own troops from suffering the effects of idleness. A line of pontoons was arranged facing against the current, equally spaced and secured by heavy timbers fore and aft. The structure was held rigid by anchors planted upstream with sufficient slack on the anchor-cables to allow the boats to ride the mounting waters without losing formation.[1] A tower was put on board to enclose the further end of the bridge, and with the addition of each successive pontoon it was transferred to it. This was designed as a platform from which artillery of various kinds could keep the enemy at bay.

The Othonians, meanwhile, had erected a tower on the bank and were discharging stones and firebrands. 35. There was also an island in midstream to which both sides found their way, the gladiators by hard rowing, the Germans[2] swimming down with the current. It happened on one occasion that the latter had got across in some strength. Macer then manned some galleys and attacked them, using the keenest of his gladiators. But the latter did not exhibit the same steady courage as the regulars, and found it harder to shoot effectively from the heaving decks than did their enemies, who had a firm footing on the bank. As the frightened men shifted their position, so the boats swayed with their movements, and the rowers and fighters fell over each other in confusion. The Germans seized their chance. They plunged into the shallow water, held the ships back by the sterns, climbed on board the gangways or drowned their opponents in hand-to-hand tussles. The whole scene was played out under the eyes of the two armies. The Vitellians were delighted, and with corresponding bitterness the Othonians cursed the cause and architect of their defeat. 36. So far as the fighting was concerned, the surviving ships managed to get away and the retreat marked its end. But the gladiators clamoured for Macer's head. After wounding him with a lance thrown from some distance, they made to close in with drawn swords, but the tribunes and centurions intervened and rescued him. It was not long before Vestricius Spurinna arrived with his cohorts in accordance with Otho's orders, having left a small garrison to hold Placentia. Then Otho sent the consul-designate Flavius Sabinus to take over the force previously commanded by Macer. The troops were delighted at the change of general, and owing to the continual

1. The melting of the Alpine snows may cause a rise of 6–9 m. in the level of the Po in April.
2. i.e. Batavians; cf. pp. 92 and 107.

mutinies the generals were not keen on service under such vexatious conditions.

37. I find it stated by certain writers that in their dread of war or contempt for both emperors – whose wickedness and degradation became in fact daily more notorious – the two armies wondered whether they should not conclude an armistice under which they could either negotiate on their own or leave the choice of an emperor to the senate. According to these authorities, this was why the Othonian leaders suggested waiting for a while: Paulinus, it is alleged, was particularly keen on this because he was the senior officer of consular rank and had made a name for himself by service in the British campaigns. For myself, I am quite prepared to grant that in their heart of hearts a few men may have prayed for peace in preference to strife and for a good and honest ruler instead of two worthless and infamous scoundrels. Yet in an age and society so degenerate, I do not believe that the prudent Paulinus expected the ordinary soldier to exercise such self-control as to lay his arms down from an attachment to peace after disturbing the peace from love of war. Nor do I think that armies so different in tongue and habit[1] were capable of a union of this kind, or that officers and generals whose consciences were in most cases burdened with the recollection of a life of pleasure, bankruptcy and crime would have tolerated as emperor any other than a disreputable character from whom they could demand payment for the services they had rendered.

38. From time immemorial, man has had an instinctive love of power. With the growth of our empire, this instinct has become a dominant and uncontrollable force. It was easy to maintain equality when Rome was weak. World-wide conquest and the destruction of all rival communities or potentates opened the way to the secure enjoyment of wealth and an overriding appetite for it. This was how the smouldering rivalry between senate and people was first fanned into a blaze. Unruly tribunes alternated with powerful consuls. Rome and the Roman forum had a foretaste of what civil war means. Then Gaius Marius, whose origin was of the humblest, and Lucius Sulla, who outdid his fellow nobles in ruthlessness, destroyed the republican constitution by force of arms.[2] In its place they put despotism. After

---

1. Tacitus is thinking of native (auxiliary) soldiers, not all of whom had a perfect knowledge of Latin, and who sometimes retained their peculiar local dress.

2. Gaius Marius (157–86 B.C.) was seven times consul; his rival, Cornelius Sulla (138–78 B.C.) was master of Rome in the years 82–79 B.C.

them came Gnaeus Pompey, who, though more secretive, was no better, and from then on the one and only aim was autocracy. Roman legions did not shrink from civil war at Pharsalia or Philippi,[1] and there is even less likelihood that the armies of Otho and Vitellius would have made peace voluntarily. Now, as in the past, it was the same divine wrath, the same human infatuation and the same background of evil deeds that drove them to conflict. That each round of the contest was decided by a knock-out blow was merely the consequence of the feebleness of these rulers. But my reflections on the characteristics of ancient and modern times have made me digress too far. I shall now return to the chronological sequence of events.

39. After Otho's departure for Brixellum, the outward trappings of command were assumed by his brother Titianus, effective power and control by the prefect Proculus. Celsus and Paulinus, whose prudent advice fell on deaf ears, were generals in name only, serving as a screen to hide the criminal folly of others. The attitude of the tribunes and centurions was ambiguous, since the best of them were passed over and power lay with the worst. The ordinary soldiers showed enthusiasm, but of a kind that preferred to criticize the orders of generals rather than obey them.

It was decided to advance to a point four miles from Bedriacum (incidentally, the movement was carried out so unskilfully that they suffered from lack of water despite the fact that it was spring and there were plenty of rivers in the area), and once there they wondered whether to fight. Otho's dispatches pressed for speed, while the troops wanted the emperor's presence on the field and many demanded that the forces south of the Po should be brought up. It is hard to decide what would have been the best policy in the circumstances, but it is easy to conclude that the one adopted was the worst possible. 40. As the cumbrous army set itself in motion, an observer might have been pardoned for thinking that it was setting out for a campaign, not a battle. Its objective was the confluence of two rivers[2] sixteen miles

1. The Battle of Pharsalia was fought in 48 B.C. between Pompey and Caesar, while at Philippi in 42 B.C. Antony and Octavian defeated the republican army under Brutus and Cassius.

2. The River Po and the now canalized tributary that flows into it a mile or so south-east of Cremona (already described as 'Naviglio' in a map of 1440).

away. Celsus and Paulinus were against exposing a footsore and heavily laden army to a foe who would not fail to seize his chance. In light battle-order, he would have barely four miles to advance[1] in order to fall upon the Othonians while they were still marching undeployed or else scattered and bent upon entrenching camp. Titianus and Proculus were outvoted in the council-of-war, but overruled opposition. It is true that a Numidian horseman had galloped up hotfooted with strongly worded instructions from Otho in which he denounced the generals for their slowness and commanded them to risk an action. Delay was torture to him, and he found the tension too much to bear.

41. On the same day, the commanders of two pretorian cohorts approached Caecina while he was busy with the construction of the bridge,[2] and asked for an interview. He was on the point of listening to their proposals and making counter-suggestions, when his scouts hurried to him with the news that the enemy were at hand. The tribunes' remarks were cut short, which is why it was difficult to say with certainty whether they had in mind a trick or the surrender of their troops or else some scheme which was aboveboard.[3] Dismissing the officers, Caecina rode back to camp and found that Fabius Valens had issued the signal for battle and that the troops were under arms. While the legions were drawing lots to determine the sequence of march, the cavalry galloped out of the camp. Surprisingly enough, they were repulsed by an inferior number of Othonians and would have been forced back against the rampart but for the courage of the Italian Legion,[4] whose men drew their swords and compelled the retreating troops to retrace their steps and resume the engagement. The Vitellian legions deployed without fuss, for though the enemy was near, it was impossible to see any sign of an armed force owing to the densely planted trees that served as vine-props. The Othonians afforded a different spectacle – frightened generals who were unpopular with their men, a confusion of vehicles and camp-followers, and a

1. i.e. along the Postumian Way from the camp outside Cremona to the point at which the Othonians were likely to turn off from the highroad towards the bridge under construction by Caecina. Otho obviously thought it necessary at all costs to stop a crossing of the Po by the enemy.

2. Near the confluence: see pp. 101 and 107. The date is 14 April.

3. The probability is that the tribunes wished to conclude an agreement of the kind declared to be impracticable at p. 103.

4. See p. 60.

road which, thanks to the sheer ditches which accompanied it on either side, would have been somewhat narrow even for a column advancing calmly. Some of the Othonian troops were massed round their respective standards, others were looking for them. Everywhere there was a confused hubbub of rushing and shouting men. Under the impulse of recklessness or fright, they would surge forward or drift back, making for front or rear.

42. The sudden threat had clearly caught them on the wrong foot. In this state of mind, a false piece of good news served merely to sap initiative. Certain individuals circulated a lying report that the Vitellian army had repudiated its emperor. It has not been fully established whether this rumour was spread by the Vitellian scouts or actually arose on Otho's side, either by design or chance. Whatever the facts, the Othonians lost all heart for fighting and took it into their heads to cheer their opponents. They were booed in reply, and as a number of troops on their own side did not know the reason for the cheers, all they succeeded in doing was to make men fear treachery. At this moment, the enemy advanced with unbroken ranks. In fighting qualities and numbers he had the advantage. As for the Othonians, scattered, outnumbered and weary as they were, they went into action gallantly enough. Indeed, as the battle was fought over a wide area thickly planted with a maze of vines and vine-props, it presented a variety of aspects. The two sides made contact at long and short range, in loose or compact formations. On the high road, Vitellians and Othonians fought hand-to-hand, throwing the weight of their bodies and shield-bosses against each other. The usual discharge of javelins was scrapped, and swords and axes used to pierce helmets and armour. Knowing each other,[1] watched by their comrades, they fought the fight that was to settle the whole campaign.

43. As it turned out, two legions made contact in open country between the Po and the road.[2] They were the Vitellian Twenty-First (Hurricane), long known and famous, and on the Othonian side the First (Support) Legion, which had never fought before,[3] but was in high spirits and avid of distinction in its first action. The First overran the front ranks of the Twenty-First, and carried off their eagle. Smarting under this humiliation, the latter got their own back by charging the First, who lost their commanding officer, Orfidius Benignus, and a great number of standards and flags. In another part of the field, the

1. The First (Italian) Legion (see pp. 60 and 105) and the pretorians had both served in Italy.    2. The Postumian Way.    3. Untrue: cf. pp. 96 f.

Fifth pushed back the Thirteenth Legion, while the contingent from the Fourteenth was outnumbered and rolled up. Long after the Oththonian commanders had fled, Caecina and Valens were still bringing up reinforcements to strengthen their men. Then, at the eleventh hour, came the Batavians, after routing the force of gladiators. These had crossed the Po in their ships only to be done to death in the very water by the cohorts confronting them. As the sequel to this success, the Batavians now delivered their onslaught on the Othonian flank.

44. The penetration of the centre led to a general retreat in the direction of Bedriacum. The distance was enormous,[1] the roads choked with heaps of dead. This only increased the casualties. After all, in civil war you cannot make money out of prisoners.[2] Suetonius Paulinus and Licinius Proculus escaped by different routes, and kept away from the camp. Vedius Aquila, the commander of the Thirteenth, was so scared that he lost his head and exposed himself to the resentment of his troops. Entering the camp-defences late in the evening, he was immediately surrounded by a noisy mob of troublemakers and runaways, who raised a deafening clamour. He was insulted, roughly handled and labelled deserter and traitor. He was not himself at fault, but the men accused others of their own infamous conduct. This, of course, is typical of the mob. Titianus and Celsus were lucky enough to arrive in the dark. By this time, sentries had been posted and the troops got under control by Annius Gallus, who by words of advice and appeal, and thanks to the respect he commanded, managed to persuade them not to aggravate the losses of defeat by butchering each other. Whatever happened, he remarked – whether this was the end of the war or whether they made up their mind to fight again another day – the losers could find relief only by acting together.

In general, the men were thoroughly dispirited. But the pretorians angrily protested that they had been beaten by treachery, not courage. Even the Vitellians, they added, had bought their victory dearly, as their cavalry had been routed and a legionary eagle captured. But the Oth'onians still had Otho himself and the troops that formed his escort south of the Po. The legions from Moesia were on their way and a large part of the army had stayed behind at Bedriacum. These at any rate had not been beaten and would find a more honourable

1. About eighteen miles.
2. See p. 166.

grave, if need be, on the field of battle. Such then were the thoughts that embittered or dismayed them. But their utter desperation bred dogged resentment more often than fear.

45. However, five miles from Bedriacum, the Vitellian army bivouacked. Their commanders were chary of attacking the camp the same day, and they also hoped that the enemy would surrender of their own accord. The Vitellians had no entrenching-tools, having marched out with the sole intention of fighting an engagement; but arms and victory were their safeguard.[1] On the next day, the attitude of the Othonian army was not in doubt, and the wilder elements had come to their senses. So a deputation was sent to the Vitellian leaders. They for their part had no hesitation in granting peace. The envoys were held up for a time, and this caused some suspense as the Othonians did not know whether their request had been granted or not. Later, the mission was sent back and the camp opened up. Then victors and vanquished alike burst into tears, cursing with melancholy delight the civil war to which fate had doomed them. They shared tents and nursed their wounded brothers or relatives. Hopes and rewards seemed problematic, but death and bereavement were sure. Everybody was involved in the tragedy and had someone's death to mourn. A search was made for the body of the legionary commander Orfidius, and it was cremated with the customary honours. A few were buried by their own kith and kin, but the vast majority of the dead remained lying where they had fallen.

1. In the field, a Roman army normally entrenched camp at night. Failure to do so was regarded as highly dangerous: cf. pp. 92, 161, and 258.

## Otho's Suicide

46. Otho's mood as he waited for news of the battle was one of
calm resolve. He had made up his mind what to do. First came an ugly
rumour, then fugitives from the battle-field revealed the full extent
of the disaster. So eager were Otho's men that they did not wait for
the emperor to make any announcement. They told him to be of
good cheer, pointing out that his new armies were still intact and
that they themselves were prepared to do or die. Nor was this flattery.
Some strange, consuming madness and infatuation prompted them to
join the fight and restore the fallen fortunes of their side. Distant observers hailed Otho with outstretched hands. The nearest bystanders
threw themselves at his feet. First and foremost among them was
Plotius Firmus. As pretorian prefect, he appealed to the emperor
again and again not to abandon a devoted army and soldiers who had
done yeoman service. It was nobler, he said, to endure adversity than
evade it. Brave and active men were true to their hopes even in the teeth
of misfortune, and only weaklings and cowards hurried headlong to
despair through fear. During this speech, whenever Otho's looks
relaxed or hardened, they cheered and groaned. Nor did encouragement come merely from Otho's personal troops, the pretorians. Forward elements from Moesia informed him that the advancing armies
were just as determined, and that some legions had entered Aquileia.
No one therefore doubts that there might well have been a resumption
of desperate and costly fighting, hazardous to victors and vanquished
alike.

47. Otho's reply showed that he had turned his back on all such
thoughts. 'This spirit,' he said, 'this courage of yours, must not be
exposed to further danger. That, I consider, would be too high a price
to pay for my life. You hold out great hopes, in the event of my
deciding to live on: they merely serve to make death finer. We have
sized each other up, fortune and I. Nor must you calculate my reign

in terms of time. It is harder for a man to observe moderation in success when he thinks he will not enjoy it for long. Civil war began with Vitellius, and with him lies the responsibility for our embarking on an armed struggle for supremacy. I too can set an example by preventing its repetition. Let this be the act by which posterity judges Otho. Vitellius shall live to have the society of his brother, wife and children: I require neither vengeance nor consolation. It may well be that others have held the principate longer, but I shall make sure that no one quits it more courageously. It is not for me to allow all these young Romans, all these fine armies, to be trampled underfoot a second time, to their country's loss. Let your devotion accompany me, just as if you had in fact died for my sake – but live on after me. I must not impede your chances of survival, nor you my resolution. To waste further words on death smacks of cowardice. Here is your best proof that my decision is irrevocable: I complain of no one. Denouncing gods or men is a task for one who is in love with life.'

48. After this speech, he summoned his staff in order of age and rank, and addressed some kind words to them. They were to be off with all speed and avoid irritating the victor by hanging back. The young ones felt bound to obey because they looked up to him, the old because he appealed to them to act as he wished. His look was calm, his words intrepid, and when his courtiers wept, he restrained their untimely emotion. He allocated ships and vehicles for their departure. Any petitions or letters that showed outspoken support of himself or criticism of Vitellius he destroyed. He distributed money sparingly, quite unlike a man facing death. Then he dealt with a young lad called Salvius Cocceianus, his brother's son. The boy was afraid, and broken-hearted. Otho went out of his way to comfort him, praising his family affection but reproving his fear. Did he really imagine that Vitellius was such an ogre that he would refuse to make this slight return for the immunity granted to his whole family? He, Otho, was doing his best to earn the victor's mercy by committing suicide quickly. For it was not in a moment of final desperation, but amid the clamour of his troops for battle that he had chosen to absolve his country from the ultimate catastrophe. He had won enough of a name for himself, enough distinction for his descendants. After all the Julians, Claudians and Servians[1] he had been the first to win the imperial dignity for a new family. So the young lad must face life with

1. A rhetorical plural: Servius Sulpicius Galba is meant.

head erect. That Otho had been his uncle was a fact that he must never forget – nor remember too well.

49. After this, he dismissed everyone from his presence and rested for a while. He was already turning over in his mind the terms of his last will and testament when he was distracted by a sudden disturbance. He was told that the troops were desperate and beyond control. They kept threatening to murder the departing courtiers, reserving the most scandalous display of violence for Verginius, who was held prisoner within the walls of his house. Otho reprimanded the ringleaders, and returning to his quarters insisted upon having a word with each of his officials as they left, until such time as they had all got away unmolested. Towards evening, he quenched his thirst with a draught of cold water. Then two daggers were brought to him. He tried both, and placed one beneath his pillow. Then, having made quite sure that his suite had gone, he went to bed, passing a quiet night and by all accounts enjoying some sleep. At dawn[1] he fell upon his dagger. Hearing the dying man's groan, his freedmen and slaves entered his room with the pretorian prefect Plotius Firmus. They found a single wound, in the chest.

The funeral was performed without delay. This had been his urgent request, for he feared that his head might be cut off and exposed to insult. As the body was borne by the pretorian cohorts amid tributes and tears, they kissed his wound and hands. Some of the troops committed suicide beside the funeral pyre, not because they were beholden to him or feared his successor but because they loved their emperor and wished to share his glory. Afterwards, at Bedriacum, Placentia and other camps, high and low made away with themselves in the same way. Otho received a tomb of modest structure, destined to endure. Such then was his end, in his thirty-seventh year.

50. He came from the town of Ferentis. His father had attained the rank of consul, his grandfather that of praetor. On his mother's side his birth was less distinguished, but not lowly. His childhood and youth were such as I have described.[2] Two actions of his, one appalling, one heroic, have earned him in history an equal meed of fame and infamy.

Though I feel that a wilful search for old wives' tales and the use of fiction to divert the reader is quite inappropriate in a serious work of this type, I hesitate all the same to be sceptical about events widely

1. 16 April.     2. See p. 30.

believed and handed down. According to local accounts, on the day that the Battle of Bedriacum was fought a bird of a species never before seen perched in a busy spot at Regium Lepidum. Thereafter, neither the staring crowds nor the flocks of birds that circled around succeeded in scaring it or driving it away, until the moment of Otho's suicide. Then, so the story runs, it vanished from sight, and a calculation of dates and times showed that the appearance and disappearance of the portent coincided with Otho's last days.

51. At his funeral the grief and misery of the troops led to renewed trouble, and this time there was no one to check it. They betook themselves to Verginius and demanded with menaces that he should assume the principate or else go and act as their spokesman in negotiations with Caecina and Valens. Verginius slipped away by the back of the house and so foiled the men just as they broke in at the front.

The cohorts stationed at Brixellum got Rubrius Gallus to convey their appeal for grace to the victor. It was immediately granted. Flavius Sabinus arranged the hand-over of the forces under his command.   52. Hostilities had now ceased everywhere, but a large number of senators found themselves in an exceedingly dangerous position. Quitting Rome in Otho's company, they had been left behind at Mutina. It was here that news of the defeat reached them. But the troops thought that the rumour was false and refused to credit it. Believing that the senators were opposed to Otho, they spied on their conversation and put a forced and distorted construction on their looks and demeanour. Finally, by means of insults and abuse, they tried to pick a quarrel which would have a fatal ending. Apart from this, another peril loomed over the senators. Now that the Vitellian side was all-powerful, they might be thought to have been dilatory in welcoming the victory. They had thus a double reason for fear and anxiety when they met to consider their course of action. No one was ready to take the initiative on his own, and all felt they would be safer if the blame were shared among many. The worries of the unhappy senators were aggravated by an offer of arms and money from the town-council of Mutina, which addressed them by the formal title of 'Conscript Fathers'. The compliment was ill-timed.

53. There was one notorious dispute. Licinius Caecina denounced Eprius Marcellus for making an evasive speech. Not that the rest revealed their real sentiments; but as men remembered Marcellus'

activity as prosecutor all too well, his very name aroused violent feelings and offered a handle for attack. This was inducement enough for Caecina, who, as a newly-fledged senator of unknown family, wanted to make his mark by engaging in controversy with a prominent personality. The two antagonists were parted by the good sense of the moderate senators.

Indeed, the whole group now moved back to Bononia, intending to hold a second meeting there. It was also hoped that more information would become available in the interval. At Bononia, pickets were posted on the various approaches to question each traveller as he arrived. One of Otho's freedmen was asked the reason for his departure from Brixellum and replied that he was the bearer of his master's last wishes. When he left Otho, it seemed, the emperor was still alive, but concerned only with making provision for his heirs, since life had no more attractions for him. This account evoked admiration and an understandable reluctance to probe further. Mentally, all the senators now made their peace with Vitellius. 54. His brother Lucius was present when they met to deliberate and was already courting their flattery when Nero's freedman Coenus suddenly appeared and caused general consternation by telling an appalling lie. He asserted that the Fourteenth Legion had turned up and after making junction with the forces from Brixellum had defeated the victorious Vitellians and reversed the balance of advantage between the two sides. This fabrication was designed to enable the travel-warrants[1] franked by Otho, which were now being disregarded, to regain their validity upon the receipt of better news. True enough, Coenus succeeded in getting to Rome at full speed – only to be punished a few days later on Vitellius' instructions. But the senators found themselves in a still more ugly situation because the Othonian troops thought the news was true . What intensified the senators' alarm was the thought that the departure from Mutina and abandonment of Otho's cause looked like official acts. Henceforward, they held no more meetings, and each senator did what he thought best on his own account. Finally, a dispatch from Fabius Valens set their fears at rest. Indeed, the nobility of Otho's death helped to spread the news of it like wildfire.

1. Permits to use the imperial posting system were issued by the emperor or a governor acting in his name. The news of Otho's death invalidated these permits and prevented Coenus getting remounts at the staging-points.

55. At Rome, however, all was quiet. The festival of Ceres was being celebrated with the usual shows.[1] When reliable informants brought word to the theatre that Otho was dead and that the city prefect Flavius Sabinus had made the garrison of Rome take the oath to Vitellius, the audience applauded the mention of the new emperor. Adorned with laurel and flowers, the people made the round of the temples carrying busts of Galba, and piled up their garlands in a great funeral mound near the Basin of Curtius at the spot stained with the blood of the dying Galba. In the senate all the prerogatives accumulated during the long reigns of previous emperors were decreed forthwith. They were supplemented by congratulations and thanks to the armies of Germany, and a deputation was sent off to convey a dutiful expression of delight. A letter which Fabius Valens had written to the consuls was read in the senate. This was framed in moderate language, but the members preferred the restraint shown by Caecina in not writing at all.[2]

56. Italy, on the other hand, suffered more severely and dreadfully than it had during the fighting. Scattered throughout the various towns, the Vitellian troops embarked on a career of spoliation, violence and licentiousness. Greedy or venal to the point of utter lack of scruple, they spared nothing, whether sacred or profane. There were also civilians who disguised themselves as soldiers to make away with their enemies. The soldiers did their bit, too. Those who were familiar with the local geography selected prosperous farms and rich landowners as targets for plunder, or, in case of resistance, death. Their generals lay under an obligation to them, and were in no position to stop these proceedings. Caecina was the less avaricious of the two, but more given to popularity hunting. Valens had a bad name for love of money and rapacity, and for this reason was prepared to connive at the offences of others as well as his own. Long since impoverished, Italy found it hard to put up with such hordes of infantry and cavalry, and with violence, financial loss and acts of lawlessness.

1. Theatrical performances on 12–18 April, and circus games on 19 April.
2. Military commanders were merely deputies of the emperor, and as such reported to him, and not directly to the senate via the consuls.

## Vitellius in Northern Italy

57. Meanwhile Vitellius, unaware that he had won, was concentrating what remained of the pick of the German garrison under the impression that all the fighting lay ahead. A small number of men who had seen many years' service was left in the permanent forts, and recruiting was stepped up in the Gallic provinces in order to bring up to strength the legions that were staying behind, now reduced to skeleton formations. Responsibility for the Rhine frontier was entrusted to Hordeonius Flaccus. Vitellius supplemented his own army with 8,000 men drawn from the garrison of Britain. He had only completed a few days' march when he was informed of the victorious Battle of Bedriacum and that resistance had collapsed on the death of Otho. His reaction was to hold a parade and praise the valour of the troops fulsomely. The army asked him to give his freedman Asiaticus the rank of knight, but he checked this degrading flattery. Then he changed his mind with characteristic inconsistency. Taking advantage of the privacy of a dinner-party to grant the very concession he had publicly refused, he loaded the fellow with the knight's rings. This Asiaticus was a repulsive and designing creature who was eager to rise in the world by underhand means.

58. These events coincided with the news that both provinces of Mauretania had gone over to Vitellius as a sequel to the murder of their governor Albinus. Lucceius Albinus had been given Mauretania Caesariensis by Nero, Galba adding the control of Tingitana. The forces at the governor's disposal were considerable – nineteen cohorts, five cavalry regiments and a large force of Moorish irregulars who had acquired some military aptitude from their addiction to brigandage and robbery. On Galba's death, Albinus was inclined to back Otho, and, not content with Africa, threatened to invade Spain from which he was divided by a narrow strait. This alarmed Cluvius Rufus, who moved the Tenth Legion down to the coast as if in preparation

for a crossing. Centurions were sent ahead to win over the Moors to Vitellius. This was indeed no very arduous matter in view of the fact that the army of Germany enjoyed a great reputation in every province. A rumour was also spread to the effect that Albinus, despising the title 'governor', had assumed the royal crown and the name 'Juba'.[1] 59. There was a revulsion of feeling, and the cavalry commander Asinius Pollio, one of Albinus' sturdiest supporters, and Festus and Scipio, two cohort commanders, were assassinated. Albinus himself, who was on his way from Tingitana to Mauretania Caesariensis, was murdered when he put in to land. His wife threw herself upon the assassins and met the same fate, though Vitellius made no investigation into the details of what had occurred. However important the news, he dismissed it with a brief hearing, being unequal to the more serious responsibilities of his position.

He ordered his army to proceed by road, while himself travelling by boat down the River Saône. His progress was remarkable for the straitened circumstances which he inherited from his past rather than for the pomp associated with an emperor. But in due course, the governor of Central Gaul, Junius Blaesus, who was a man of high birth, open-handed generosity and corresponding wealth, supplied the emperor with a suite of servants and accompanied him with a retinue worthy of a gentleman. This, however, earned him little gratitude, though Vitellius concealed his resentment beneath cringing compliments. At Lyons, the leaders of the victorious and vanquished sides waited upon him. Valens and Caecina received a glowing tribute from Vitellius at a military parade, and were stationed close to his official chair. Then he ordered the whole army to march out to meet his infant son, who was solemnly conducted to the spot and enveloped in a general's cloak. Holding the child in his arms, Vitellius gave him the name 'Germanicus' and surrounded him with all the emblems of imperial rank. This lavish honour in the hour of victory proved fatal to the child when trouble came.[2]

60. Then the leading Othonian centurions were executed. This act, above all else, made enemies for Vitellius throughout the Balkan armies, while contact with troops from Germany, and bitter feelings towards them, helped to encourage a war mood in the other legions too. As for Suetonius Paulinus and Licinius Proculus, Vitellius kept the accused waiting in wretched suspense for quite a time before

1. The name borne by the last king of independent Mauretania.
2. Cf. p. 261.

finally granting an audience. Here the pleas to which they were reduced did them little credit. They actually claimed credit for betraying their own side. The long march which preceded the battle, the exhaustion of the Othonians, the chaotic confusion of marching men and vehicles and a number of circumstances which were purely accidental were attributed by the defendants to their own duplicity. Vitellius promptly took them at their word in the matter of treachery, and acquitted them of good faith. Salvius Titianus was not in danger, for his indolence and the obligations he owed his brother Otho secured him a pardon. Marius Celsus retained his consulship. But it was commonly believed, and afterwards alleged in the senate to the prejudice of Caecilius Simplex, that the latter had been willing to purchase the office by a bribe and also at the cost of Celsus' life. Vitellius resisted this, and later awarded Simplex a consulship which cost him neither murder nor money. Trachalus was protected from his accusers by Vitellius' wife Galeria.

61. While great men went in peril of their lives, it cannot be recorded without a blush that a humble member of the Boian tribe,[1] a certain Mariccus, had the impudence to try to sneak into prominence and challenge the armed might of Rome by pretending to be divine. This self-styled 'champion of Gaul' and 'god' had raised a force of 8,000 men and was already making some impression on the neighbouring Aeduan cantons when the central authorities among the Aedui, showing a great sense of responsibility, called up their best militiamen and with the assistance of some cohorts assigned them by Vitellius scattered the mob of zealots to the four winds. In the fighting, Mariccus was captured. Later, he was thrown to the beasts, but they refused to tear him to pieces. This made the ignorant lower classes think that he bore a charmed life – until he was executed before the eyes of Vitellius.

62. No further measures of a severe kind were taken against the rebels or any man's property. Due effect was given to the wills of those Othonians who had fallen in battle, or else the law of intestacy was applied. Indeed, there was no reason to fear Vitellius' cupidity, if only he had been less addicted to high living. For rich fare he displayed a revolting and insatiable appetite. Delicacies were carted all the way from Rome and Italy to tickle his palate, and the routes which lead from the Tuscan and Adriatic Seas were loud with the

1. A tribe long settled in the territory of the Aedui.

sound of traffic. Leading members of the various cities found the provision of sumptuous banquets a heavy drain on their pockets, and the very cities were reduced to beggary. The Vitellian troops became flabby and work-shy as they acquired a taste for indulgence and a contempt for their leader.

Vitellius forwarded to Rome a decree postponing his acceptance of the title 'Augustus'[1] and refusing that of 'Caesar', though he made no abatement of the powers implied thereby. Astrologers were expelled from Italy, and strict orders issued that Romans of equestrian rank were not to disgrace themselves by performing in the games and the arena. Previous emperors had driven them to this kind of thing by offering payment or, more often, by the use of force, and a number of Italian towns vied with one another in holding out financial inducements to undesirables among the younger generation.

63. With the arrival of his brother and the intrusion of crawlers who gave him lessons in tyranny, Vitellius became more overbearing and brutal. He gave orders for the execution of Dolabella, whose banishment to the city of Aquinum I have already recorded.[2] Dolabella had found his way into the capital on learning of Otho's death, and this action had been the object of a charge which Plancius Varus, an ex-praetor and close intimate of Dolabella, laid before the city prefect Flavius Sabinus. The allegation was that he had broken out of custody in order to make a bid for the leadership of the beaten side. The accuser added that an attempt had been made to seduce the cohort stationed at Ostia. These serious charges were entirely unsupported, and Varus in due course repented of his action and begged for forgiveness. But it was too late, and the evil had been done. As Flavius Sabinus hesitated as to the course he should pursue in such grave circumstances, Lucius Vitellius' wife Triaria displayed a venom scarcely credible in a woman and worked upon his fears by hinting that he had no business to win a reputation for clemency by endangering the emperor's life. Sabinus was naturally a mild man, but his resolution was easily broken by threats. Fearing for his own skin in a situation which carried deadly menace for another, he contributed the final push which sent the unfortunate man headlong to his doom. 64. So it came about that Vitellius, who feared and hated Dolabella because he had married his divorced wife Petronia, summoned him by letter, and gave orders that

1. Until June; as for 'Caesar', see p. 181.
2. See p. 75.

the traveller should turn off from the busy Flaminian Way to Interamna, where he was to be put to death. This seemed too long-winded a business to the executioner. On the journey, he threw his victim to the ground in a wayside inn and cut his throat. The murder brought great discredit upon the new régime, for this was the first incident that afforded an insight into its character. Moreover the uncontrollable passions of Triaria were set in an unfavourable light by the proximity of one who was a pattern of moderation. This was the emperor's wife Galeria, who was not mixed up in these grim events. No less virtuous was Sextilia, the mother of the two Vitellii, who belonged to the old school. On first hearing from her son of his accession, she was said to have remarked that she had borne a 'Vitellius', not a 'Germanicus'. No subsequent allurements of rank, no flattering attentions from the public overcame this prejudice of hers or made her happy. It was merely the calamities of her house that touched her.

65. After Vitellius had departed from Lyons, he was overtaken by Cluvius Rufus, who had left Spain to look after itself. Rufus' face wore an expression of delight and congratulation, but at heart he was worried and aware that charges had been levelled at him. An imperial freedman named Hilarus had alleged that on hearing of the elevation of Vitellius and Otho, Rufus had planned to make a bid for power himself with the Spanish provinces as his base. This, it was explained, was why the governor had not endorsed his travel-warrants with the name of any emperor. The accuser also quoted some passages from his speeches which he interpreted as insults towards Vitellius and claptrap in favour of himself. But Cluvius was too respected a figure, and Vitellius actually had his own freedman punished, while Cluvius was given a place in the emperor's suite without losing Spain, which he governed by proxy. A precedent for this was supplied by Lucius Arruntius, but this governor was kept at court by Tiberius because he feared him, whereas Vitellius was not frightened of Cluvius. The same concession was not made to Trebellius Maximus, who fled from Britain in the face of his troops' resentment. He was replaced by Vettius Bolanus, one of the courtiers in attendance.

66. Vitellius was worried by the attitude of the beaten legions, which was far from submissive. They were scattered throughout Italy in close association with the victors, and their language was the language of enemies. Particular defiance was shown by the Fourteenth Legion, whose men would not agree that they had been beaten. At the Battle

of Bedriacum, they asserted, their advance-party alone had been
routed, and the main body of the legion had not been present. It was
decided that they should be returned to Britain, from which Nero
had summoned them. In the meantime, they were to share camp with
the Batavian cohorts, because the latter had long been on bad terms
with them. Soon the bitter hostility between the groups of armed
soldiers led to a breach of the peace. One day, a workman at Turin
was being abused by a Batavian for cheating him, and defended by
a legionary billeted on him. The two opponents were joined by
their respective comrades, and from abuse the men passed to bloodshed. Indeed, desperate fighting would have broken out, had not two
pretorian cohorts joined in on the side of the Fourteenth and thus
encouraged them and intimidated the Batavians. Vitellius attached
the latter to his column of march as a sign that he valued their loyalty,
and ordered the legion to cross the Alps by the Little St Bernard and
take a roundabout route avoiding Vienne, which was also regarded
as a danger-point. On the night of their departure the legionaries
left fires alight everywhere, and a part of the city of Turin was burnt
down. The memory of this havoc, like that of many calamities in
war, has been effaced by the more dreadful fate of other cities. When
the Fourteenth had descended from the Alps into lower country, the
most unruly elements in the legion tried to lead the way to Vienne,
but the more level-headed men got together and stopped this. So the
legion crossed over into Britain without incident.

67. The next source of anxiety for Vitellius was provided by the
pretorian cohorts. The men were first split up, and then offered the
consolation of an honourable discharge from the forces. So they
proceeded to hand in their equipment to their commanding officers,
and this continued until Vespasian's bid for power gathered momentum. Then they rejoined the service, and formed a major factor in
the Flavian strength.

The First (Naval) Legion was sent to Spain to cool down in an
atmosphere of peace and quiet. The Eleventh and Seventh were
returned to their respective permanent stations, while the Thirteenth
was instructed to build amphitheatres, as Caecina and Valens were
preparing to exhibit gladiatorial shows (at Cremona and Bononia
respectively) and Vitellius was never so preoccupied by the cares of
office as to forget his pleasures.

68. So far as the vanquished were concerned, Vitellius had managed

to split them up without resorting to extreme measures. But there was trouble among the victors. Its origin was trifling, had not the number of dead lent one more sinister note to a sinister campaign. Vitellius was holding a dinner-party at Ticinum, Verginius being among the guests. Army officers take their cue from the behaviour of the supreme commander, copying his strictness or indulging in lengthy mess-dinners. By the same token the ordinary soldier either does his duty conscientiously or gets out of hand. In Vitellius' circle, all was chaos and drunkenness, an atmosphere approximating more closely to late hours and wild orgies than to discipline and normal camp life. Thus it happened that two soldiers – one belonging to the Fifth Legion, the other a Gallic auxiliary – were induced by high spirits to engage in a bout of wrestling. The legionary took a fall, and the Gaul jeered at his discomfited opponent. Thereupon the spectators who had gathered round took sides, the legionaries set about the auxiliaries, and two cohorts were annihilated. This alarming outbreak was cured by a second alarm. In the distance could be seen a cloud of dust and the glint of arms. The sudden cry went up that the Fourteenth Legion had turned on its tracks and was coming to the attack. But the troops were in fact the rearguard of Vitellius' army, and their recognition as such set minds at rest.

Meanwhile a slave of Verginius happened to appear on the scene. He was accused of planning to murder Vitellius, and the troops proceeded to invade the officers' mess, clamouring for Verginius' head. Even Vitellius, who was terrified by the slightest hint of a conspiracy, had no doubt that he was innocent. But it was difficult to restrain these men, who pressed for the execution of a senior statesman who had once been their own commander. Indeed, Verginius more than anybody else was the target of every act of insubordination. The great man still retained his magic, but the troops hated him because they felt he had slighted them.

69. On the next day Vitellius heard an address from a deputation of the senate which had been told by the emperor to await him at Ticinum. He then went over to the camp and made a point of praising the troops for their devotion, though the auxiliaries noisily protested at the free hand now accorded to the arrogant legionaries. To prevent the Batavian cohorts venturing upon some even more truculent act, they were sent back to Germany. By this move destiny paved the way for what was to be at once a civil war and a war fought against a

foreign foe.[1] The Gallic auxiliaries were returned to their various communities. They formed a numerous contingent whose help had been accepted at the very beginning of the Vitellian uprising as a form of military window-dressing. However, to enable the now depleted resources of the empire to meet the drain of lavish bounties, Vitellius ordered the strength of legionary and auxiliary units to be reduced by a veto on recruiting, and men were offered their discharge right and left. This policy was fatal to the country and unpopular with the troops, who found that the same number of fatigues and duties had to be performed by a small number of men, so that danger and toil came round with greater frequency. Moreover their vigour was sapped by pleasures, in a way totally at variance with old-fashioned ideas of discipline and tradition, which found a better basis for Roman steadiness in character than in money.

70. From Ticinum Vitellius took the branch road to Cremona, and after viewing Caecina's gladiatorial show, insisted on walking over the battlefield of Bedriacum and inspecting the traces of the recent victory. It was a dreadful and revolting sight. Less than forty days had elapsed since the engagement, and mutilated corpses, severed limbs and the decaying carcasses of men and horses lay everywhere. The ground was bloodstained and the flattened trees and crops bore witness to the frightful devastation. Not less callous was the spectacle presented by the high road, which the Cremonese had strewn with laurel and roses, building altars and sacrificing victims after the fashion of an Oriental monarchy. These trappings afforded pleasure for the moment, but were soon to prove their undoing. Valens and Caecina were in attendance, pointing out the various localities connected with the battle: this was the starting point for the legions' forward thrust; from that point the cavalry had fallen upon the foe; and in a third place the auxiliary forces had surrounded their victims. Even the regimental officers contributed their quota, each magnifying his own performance in a hotchpotch of lies, truth and exaggeration. The ordinary soldiers, too, turned off the high road with shouts of glee, retracing the extent of the fighting and gazing admiringly at the heaps of equipment and corpses littering the plain. There were indeed some few observers who were deeply affected by the diverse influences exerted by an inscrutable destiny. They were moved to tears

1. The revolt of the Batavian Civilis and of the Gauls, to be described in Book Four.

and pity. But not Vitellius. His gaze was unaverted, and he felt no horror at the multitude of fellow Romans lying there unburied. Blatantly exulting, and little knowing how near the day of judgement was, he proceeded to offer a sacrifice to the gods of the place.

71. After this, a gladiatorial show was put on by Fabius Valens at Bononia, the decorations being brought from the capital. Indeed, with every mile travelled towards Rome, the emperor's progress became more riotous. It was joined by actors and gangs of eunuchs and all the other idiosyncrasies of Nero's court. For Vitellius was a personal devotee of Nero. He had been in the habit of attending the emperor's song recitals, not – like the better sort – under compulsion, but as the slave and hireling of pleasure and gluttony.

Desiring to find some spare months to accommodate Valens and Caecina in the consular list, Vitellius cut short the tenure of office of others, passing over that of Martius Macer on the ground that he had been a leading supporter of Otho, and postponing the consulship to which Valerius Marinus had been nominated by Galba. Valerius had done nothing to annoy Vitellius, but he was a mild man prepared to swallow any affront. The name of Pedanius Costa was omitted from the list because he had earned the emperor's ill will by his activities against Nero and support of Verginius, though the reasons adduced by Vitellius in public were different. That the emperor was thanked as well was a sign of the habitual servility of the time.

72. A case of impersonation now occurred. This proved merely a nine-days' wonder, though it evoked intense excitement at first. A man had turned up who alleged that he was Scribonianus Camerinus.[1] During Nero's reign of terror, Scribonianus had taken hiding in Histria, because in this area there were still some retainers and estates belonging to the ancient clan of the Crassi, whose name was one to conjure with. So the fellow got together some riff-raff to give colour to his story, and the gullible lower classes, together with some of the troops, started to flock around him eagerly, whether genuinely deluded or bent on mischief. But the man was brought before Vitellius and asked his identity. As his statement rang false and he was recognized by his master as a runaway slave called Geta, he was executed in the manner appropriate to persons of servile condition.[2]

1. A son of Licinius Crassus Frugi, who was consul in A.D. 64 and one of Nero's victims.
2. Crucifixion.

73. It is hard to credit the degree of self-satisfaction and indolence assumed by Vitellius when officials from Syria and Judaea brought word that the East had recognized him as emperor. For there was gossip and rumour concerning Vespasian, however vague and ill-authenticated, and Vitellius usually showed alarm at the mention of his name. But now he and the army felt the way was clear, and in tyranny, debauch and rapine gave full rein to excesses that were quite un-Roman.

## Vespasian Emperor

74. As for Vespasian, he was engaged in taking careful stock of the military situation and the forces available to him far and near. The personal devotion of the troops to him is shown by the fact that when he dictated the formula of the oath of allegiance and prayed for Vitellius' success, they listened to him in silence. Mucianus, while not unfriendly to Vespasian, was still more attached to Titus. The prefect of Egypt, Tiberius Alexander, had already come to an understanding. Then there was the Third Legion. This Vespasian reckoned his own because before its transfer to Moesia it had been stationed in Syria. There were prospects that the remaining legions in the Balkans would follow any lead it gave, as the whole garrison had been furious at the arrogant behaviour of the bullying and blustering troops who came from Vitellius and derided everyone else as their inferiors. But men usually hesitate before assuming such crushing military responsibilities, and whatever his moods of optimism, Vespasian would sometimes reflect on the possibility of disaster. What would the day of decision mean to them – the day on which he committed his sixty years and two young sons to the hazards of war? One could press on or draw back in a private enterprise, and commit oneself more deeply or less at will, in accordance with the prospects of the moment. But in the pursuit of an empire there was no mean between the summit and the abyss. 75. Vespasian could clearly picture to himself the fighting qualities of the German garrison. Such things were naturally familiar to a military man. His own legions had no experiecne of civil war, while those of Vitellius had been victorious in it; and the beaten side was querulous rather than strong. When a country was divided, military loyalty was a precarious thing, and solitary assassins presented a danger. What was the use of cohorts and cavalry regiments if one or two men decided to earn easy money from the other side by murdering him at the first convenient occasion? That was

how Scribonianus had met his end under Claudius, and how his
assassin Volaginius had risen from the ranks to the highest posts in
the army. It was easier to set whole armies in motion than avoid the
lone killer.

76. Such were the fears that swayed Vespasian. Among the officers
and friends who tried to reassure him was Mucianus. After many
confidential discussions, he finally made a direct appeal to Vespasian. Its tenor was as follows:

'All who plan great enterprises must calculate the degree to which
their initiative is helpful to their country, creditable to themselves,
and easily attainable or at least not unduly difficult. At the same time
one must carefully scrutinize the advocate of any particular policy to
see whether he is willing to back it by action involving danger to
himself, and one must consider who is likely to gain the highest
distinction in the event of success.

'I call upon you, Vespasian, to assume the position of emperor and
so perform an act which is beneficial to our country and does honour
to yourself. Under heaven, it lies within your grasp. There is no need
for you to fear what might seem mere flattery: it is perhaps as much
an insult as a compliment to be chosen to succeed Vitellius. We are
not rising in revolt against the subtle statesmanship of Augustus, nor
against the elaborate precautions of the elderly Tiberius, nor even
against Gaius or Claudius or Nero, whose power was firmly based on
a long dynasty. You yielded even to Galba's aristocratic pretensions,
but further passivity in the face of a process in which our country
suffers defilement and decay would smack of sloth and feebleness,
even if such discreditable servility afforded you corresponding protection. But the time has gone and is now long past when it was
possible for you to pretend to be indifferent to power. At the moment
it is your only refuge. Have you forgotten the murder of Corbulo?
It is true that he came of a more distinguished family than either of us,
but Nero, too, was more highly born than Vitellius. In the eyes of a
suspicious monarch no suspect can be too humble.

'Besides, the lesson that an army can create an emperor is one that
Vitellius can learn from his own accession. He could boast no active
service nor military distinction, and owed his promotion entirely to
the unpopularity of Galba. Nor indeed was Otho beaten by generalship or overwhelming odds, but by his own premature despair, and
Vitellius has now made his predecessor seem a great emperor whose

loss is regretted. Meantime he is scattering his legions, disarming his cohorts and sowing every day fresh seeds of conflict. Whatever keenness and dash his troops had in the past is being steadily dissipated in cafés and in drinking and imitation of their emperor. You, Vespasian, can draw on Judaea, Syria and Egypt for nine legions. These are formations which are unimpaired, without battle casualties, united. Your troops are in good training and have successfully fought a foreign foe; and to these must be added other powerful resources in the shape of fleets, cavalry regiments and cohorts, devoted native kings, and your own unrivalled experience.

77. 'For myself I shall make no greater claim than that of precedence over Valens and Caecina. But still you must not despise Mucianus as an ally because you have not to face him as a rival. I rank myself before Vitellius and after you. Your family can boast the distinctions of a triumph and the presence of two young men, one of whom is already competent to hold the position of supreme commander, and in the first years of his military career won distinction in the eyes of the very armies of Germany. It would be illogical not to concede the imperial supremacy to one whose son I should set about adopting if I were emperor myself. However, our relative positions will not be the same in success as in failure. If we win, I shall enjoy such status as you choose to give: the risk and dangers we shall share alike. Better still, you should concern yourself with the supreme command of your armies, and entrust to me the fighting and uncertainties of battle.

'At this moment the vanquished are better disciplined than the victors, for resentment, hatred and the thirst for vengeance kindle their courage, while boredom and insubordination continue to blunt the efficiency of the Vitellians. The hidden and festering scars of the victorious side will be revealed and reopened by the mere fact that they have to fight. Your faculties of watchfulness, restraint and wisdom give me great confidence; even greater is that which I derive from Vitellius' sloth, ignorance and malice. But our prospects are better if we declare war than they would be if we kept the peace, for those who plan rebellion are already rebels.'

78. After Mucianus' speech, the rest clustered round Vespasian with greater unreserve, encouraging him with reports of the prophecies of soothsayers and the conjunctions of the stars. That such superstitious beliefs had some hold on Vespasian is evident from the fact that a little

later, when he had gained supreme power, he openly kept at court one Seleucus, an astrologer, to guide him and give him knowledge of the future. His thoughts now went back to omens from the past, for instance the sudden fall of a remarkably tall cypress tree on his estate. On the following day it had sprung up again at the same spot, and in due course grew as lofty as ever, spreading its boughs even more widely and luxuriantly. The seers were unanimous that this was a notable sign of future prosperity, and it seemed that the highest honours were promised to Vespasian while he was still a very young man. But at first the omen appeared to find its fulfilment in his triumphal awards, the consulship and the renown of his Jewish victory. Once these were achieved, he thought he was fated to be emperor.

Between Judaea and Syria lies a mountain called Carmel, which is the name of the local god. Yet traditionally this god boasts neither image nor temple, only an altar and the reverence of his worshippers. Here Vespasian had offered sacrifice when he was turning over in his mind his secret ambitions. The priest Basilides time and again examined the entrails of the victims. Finally he declared: 'Whatever you are planning, Vespasian – be it the building of a house, an addition to your estate, or engaging more servants – this is granted you. You shall have a great mansion, far-flung boundaries and a host of people.' This ambiguous statement had been immediately pounced upon by gossip, and was now given great publicity. Indeed ordinary people talked of little else. Still more lively was the discussion in Vespasian's immediate circle, for hope is eloquent. With minds made up, they parted company, Mucianus going to Antioch and Vespasian to Caesarea. These are the capitals of Syria and Judaea respectively.

79. The first move to convey imperial status to Vespasian took place at Alexandria. This was due to the eagerness of Tiberius Alexander, who caused his legions to swear allegiance to the new emperor on 1 July. The date was afterwards honoured as that of his accession, though on 3 July the army of Judaea had taken the oath before Vespasian in person. Such was the enthusiasm that they acted without even waiting for the arrival of his son Titus, who was on his way back from Syria, where he had acted as the link between Mucianus and his father in their negotiations. The whole affair was carried through by a spontaneous move on the part of the troops, and there was no time to weigh up the situation or concentrate the scattered legions.

80. It all happened while a search was still being made for a suitable time and place, and above all, for the mechanism of the initial acclamation – no easy matter this in such a delicate situation. Their imagination was dominated by hopes and fears, by calculation and the unpredictable. One day, as Vespasian came out of his bedroom, a small guard of honour who had been paraded to greet him in the usual way as provincial governor, substituted for this title that of 'emperor'. Then the rest hurried to the spot and heaped upon him all the imperial titles, including those of 'Caesar' and 'Augustus'. In a flash his supporters had moved from trepidation to confidence.

Vespasian for his part gave himself no airs. Though the situation was changed, there was no change in his modest bearing. For a moment a mist swam before his eyes at the thought of the giddy heights of power. But as soon as this cleared, he addressed his men in soldierly accents, and was greeted with universal congratulation and offers of support. Shortly afterwards, Mucianus, who had been waiting for just this, made his troops swear loyalty to Vespasian. They were nothing loath. Then he entered the theatre at Antioch, which is regularly used for their political meetings, and made a speech to the concourse which had flocked to the spot with flattering effusiveness. Mucianus was quite a graceful speaker, even in Greek, and had the art of displaying to advantage whatever he said and did. One thing in particular kindled intense indignation in province and garrison alike. Mucianus asserted that Vitellius had made up his mind to transfer the legions of Germany to a lucrative and quiet station in Syria, while those in Syria were to be moved to the bases in Germany, where the climate was severe and conditions hard. The fact is that even the provincials liked to deal with troops they were used to, and there was a good deal of intermarriage between the two. The troops, again, felt at home in the camp where they had served so long and for which they had acquired a real affection.

81. By 15 July the whole of Syria had taken the oath of allegiance to Vespasian. He had also gained the adhesion of Sohaemus and his kingdom,[1] whose resources were not to be despised, and that of Antiochus,[2] who had great inherited wealth and was the richest

1. Emesa (Homs).
2. King of Commagene, on the west bank of the Upper Euphrates.

client-king of all. Then Agrippa[1] arrived after a fast voyage from
Rome, where secret emissaries from his people had brought him news
which recalled him home while Vitellius was still in the dark. Equal
enthusiasm marked the support given to the cause by Queen Berenice.
She was in her best years and at the height of her beauty, while even
the elderly Vespasian appreciated her generosity. All the coastal
provinces up to and including Asia and Achaia, and the whole
Roman territory[2] extending inland towards Pontus and Armenia
acknowledged Vespasian as emperor. But these lands were controlled
by governors who had no troops at their disposal, since at this date
Cappadocia had not been given a legionary garrison. A council was
held at Berytus to decide the main lines of policy. To this city came
Mucianus with his legionary commanders and regimental officers, as
well as the leading centurions and other ranks. The army of Judaea
sent a distinguished representation. The accumulated array of infantry, cavalry, and client-kings, outbidding each other in splendour,
provided a truly imperial setting.

82. First and foremost, the war effort demanded the levying of troops
and the recall of reservists. A number of wealthy cities were selected
for the manufacture of armaments. At Antioch gold and silver curren-
cies were struck. All these endeavours were rapidly put in hand
in the various localities under the supervision of appropriate officials.
Vespasian personally assumed the task of inspection and encouragement, praising the efficient and spurring rather than correcting the
idle. He preferred to hide the weaknesses of his friends rather than
their merits. In a bid for popularity he made many of them prefects
and procurators, and a number were granted senatorial rank. These
were men of exceptional calibre, who were soon to rise to high place.
With a few it was a question of money rather than solid merit. As for
a bounty to the troops, Mucianus had only held out the prospect of a
modest sum at the initial parade, and even Vespasian offered no more
under conditions of civil war than others had in peacetime. Here he
set an excellent example by his strong opposition to any bribery of
the troops, and this was in itself enough to secure a better army. A

---

1. Agrippa II, brother of Berenice and ruler of territory east of Galilee; see
p. 82, n. 1.
2. Tacitus seems to allude to the provinces of Galatia and Cappadocia. Of
these, Galatia already had a garrison of auxiliary units, and Cappadocia received a legionary garrison in A.D. 70.

mission was sent to Parthia and Armenia, and steps taken to safeguard the rear of the legions while they were preoccupied with the civil war. It was decided that Titus should keep up the pressure on Judaea while Vespasian secured Egypt, which held a key position. It seemed that a fraction of the forces available would be adequate to deal with Vitellius, given the abilities of Mucianus as a general, the magic of Vespasian's name and the irresistible trend of destiny. Letters were sent off to all the various armies and commanders with instructions to stimulate recruitment among the pretorians who hated Vitellius. They were to be offered an attractive bait – readmission to the Guard.

83. Mucianus set off with a force in battle-order, behaving as the emperor's colleague rather than as his subordinate. He avoided marching slowly, for he had no wish to give the impression of dawdling. Nor on the other hand did he show great haste, allowing mere distance to amplify the stories of his strength. He realized only too well that his force was a slender one, but that the public forms inflated ideas of what it cannot see for itself. But behind him marched an impressive array – the Sixth Legion and a composite force of 13,000 men drafted from its fellow formations. He had ordered the fleet to sail from the Black Sea and concentrate on Byzantium. He was still undecided whether to carry on with his original plan, which was to by-pass Moesia and strike rapidly at Dyrrachium with his cavalry and infantry, at the same time employing warships to blockade the Adriatic. In this case, he need have no fears for Achaia and Asia in his rear. Otherwise these provinces, having no garrison, were likely to be at Vitellius' mercy unless specially reinforced. Another argument in favour of the plan was that Vitellius would not know which part of Italy to protect if Brundisium, Tarentum and the coasts of Calabria and Lucania were all to be exposed to invasion by sea.

84. So the eastern provinces now hummed with the preparation of ships, armies and equipment. The most exhausting imposition, however, was the financial levy. According to Mucianus, money was the sinews of civil war, and in his assessments he had eyes only for the depths of a man's purse, not for equity or truth. On every side accusers came forward, and the richer classes were plundered unmercifully. These grievous and intolerable burdens might be defended on the ground of military exigency, but they continued to be imposed even when peace came. At the beginning of his reign, Vespasian was not personally so set on retaining abuses, but in time the smiles of

fortune and the instruction of evil tutors found in him an apt and willing pupil. Mucianus also helped the war effort with his own fortune. A lavish expenditure of private means gave him an excuse for helping himself to public money even more liberally. Of the rest who followed his lead in contributing their wealth, very few had the same opportunities to recoup themselves.

85. Meanwhile Vespasian's initial plans were accelerated by the eagerness with which the Balkan garrison came over to his side. The Third Legion set an example to its fellows in Moesia. These were the Eighth and Seventh (Claudian). They had taken no part in the First Battle of Bedriacum, though dyed-in-the-wool Othonians. On that occasion they had advanced as far as Aquileia. Messengers bringing news of Otho's defeat were roughly handled, and their flags, which displayed the name of Vitellius, torn to pieces. Finally the Moesian troops stole their money and divided it among themselves. In all these ways they had shown by their actions that they were Vitellius' enemies. This bred fear of the consequences, and in its turn fear generated policy. Actions for which it would be necessary to apologize to Vitellius could win gratitude from Vespasian. So the three legions in Moesia communicated with the garrison of Pannonia, suggesting that the latter should join in. They also prepared themselves to employ force to guard against a refusal. In this fluid situation, Aponius Saturninus, the governor of Moesia, ventured to commit an appalling act. He sent a centurion to assassinate the commander of the Seventh Legion, Tettius Julianus. The motive was a private dispute, camouflaged as a bid to help the Flavian cause. Julianus discovered he was in danger, and seeking the aid of natives who knew the geography of the area intimately, made his escape through the trackless wilds of Moesia to the region south of the Balkan range. Thereafter he took no part in the civil war, finding a number of excuses for spinning out his journey to Vespasian and in response to the latest news alternately loitering or hurrying forward.

86. In Pannonia, however, the Thirteenth and Seventh (Galbian) Legions declared for Vespasian promptly. They still felt badly about the Battle of Bedriacum, and their attitude was strongly influenced by the impetuous Antonius Primus.[1] This man had a criminal record,

1. The hero of Book Three. Antonius Primus, nicknamed 'Beaky', was born about A.D. 20 at Tolosa (Toulouse), and to this city he returned after his fall from favour.

and in Nero's reign had been sentenced for forgery. It was one of the unfortunate results of civil war that he had managed to get back his rank as senator. By Galba he was given command of the Seventh Legion. It was believed that he had written more than once to Otho volunteering his assistance as a party leader, but the offer was disregarded, and he rendered no service in the Othonian campaign. Switching his allegiance to Vespasian as Vitellius' star waned, he gave a powerful impetus to the Flavian movement. A man of drive and eloquence, a skilful propagandist who came into his own in a period of dissension and revolt, light-fingered and open-handed, he was at once a vicious influence in peacetime and a general to be reckoned with in war.

In due course the joint action of the garrisons of Moesia and Pannonia induced the troops in Dalmatia to fall into line, although the governors of these provinces took no part in the movement. Pannonia and Dalmatia were governed respectively by Tampius Flavianus and Pompeius Silvanus, who were rich and elderly. But at their elbow stood the imperial agent Cornelius Fuscus. He was now in the prime of life, and came of a good family. In early youth Fuscus had resigned from the senatorial order because he had no ambition for an official career. Yet he induced his home town[1] to go over to Galba, and for these services won the office of procurator. Once he had rallied to the Flavian side, his fanaticism did much to touch off the campaign. Exulting less in the prizes that danger wins than in danger for its own sake, he sacrificed the assured gains of the past to a novel and hazardous gamble. So these two – Primus and Fuscus – set to work everywhere to fish in troubled waters. Letters were despatched to the Fourteenth Legion in Britain and the First in Spain, because both these formations had supported Otho and opposed Vitellius. Messages were sent off to every quarter of the Gallic provinces, and in no time a great holocaust of war had been ignited. The Balkan armies were now in open rebellion, and the rest were likely to follow their lead if they proved successful.

1. Perhaps Pompeii or Forum Iulii.

# Rome under Vitellius

87. While Vespasian and his leaders were thus employed in the various provinces, Vitellius was moving ponderously towards Rome. Day by day more despicable and lazy, he made a point of stopping at every pleasant town and country seat. In his train followed 60,000 armed men, dissolute and undisciplined. Even larger was the number of soldiers' servants, and the camp-followers were remarkable even among slaves for their overbearing manners. So numerous was the escort of officers and courtiers that it alone would have presented problems of discipline, even of this had been strictly enforced. The unwieldy mob was further encumbered by a number of senators and knights who came out from the capital to meet it. Some had been induced to come by fear, many were prompted by the wish to flatter, while the rest, and in due course all of them, joined in because they did not want to be left behind. There was also an influx of members of the lower classes who had made Vitellius' acquaintance by rendering him disreputable services. Such were the buffoons, actors and charioteers, whose degrading friendship gave him extraordinary pleasure. It was not only the towns that were exhausted by the necessity of supplying the multitude with food: the very land-workers and the fields now ready for harvest were stripped bare, as if this were enemy soil.[1]

88. There were many dreadful instances of bloody quarrels among the troops, for the legionaries and auxiliaries still did not see eye to eye after the original outburst at Ticinum. When it came to attacking civilians, however, they agreed well enough. But the loss of life was severest at a point seven miles from Rome. Here Vitellius was one day engaged in issuing haversack rations as if he were fattening up a lot of gladiators, and the lower classes had poured out from the capital and were milling about everywhere in the camp. Taking advantage of the fact that the vigilance of the troops was relaxed, some crude

1. This whole account reflects Flavian propaganda. Vitellius reached Rome about 21 June.

practical jokers managed to cut off their belts without the victims' knowledge, and then kept asking them where their equipment was. The soldiers were not used to be jeered at and took the joke badly, attacking the unarmed populace with their swords. Among other casualties, the father of one of the soldiers was killed in the company of his son. Then his identity was realized, and the news of his death halted the onslaught on the hapless civilians.

However, there were anxious moments inside Rome, as the troops rapidly pressed forward at every point. They made chiefly for the forum, being eager to see the spot where Galba had fallen. No less grim was the spectacle they themselves presented, thanks to the shaggy hides of wild beasts and the long deadly weapons which they wore. Not being used to crowds, they did not bother about avoiding collisions, and sometimes fell over because the road was slippery or someone had jostled them. When this happened, the answer was abuse, developing in its turn into fisticuffs and sword-play. The officers, too, added to the general confusion by dashing about here, there and everywhere with armed escorts.

89. Vitellius himself, once the Milvian Bridge[1] was reached, mounted a fine charger, armed and wearing the full panoply of a general. In this guise he drove the senate and people before him like a herd of cattle. However, his entourage deterred him from entering Rome as if it were a conquered city; so he exchanged his uniform for a bordered toga, and marched at the head of his troops in good order. The front of the column displayed four legionary eagles surrounded by four flags representing the other legions. After that came twelve cavalry standards and the serried ranks of the infantry, followed by the cavalry. Then followed thirty-four auxiliary cohorts grouped according to nationality and type of equipment. In front of the eagles went the camp commandants, regimental staff officers and senior centurions in white raiment, the rest marching with their respective companies in full dress uniform with medals worn. The troops, too, were resplendent in their various decorations. It was a noble sight, and an army worthy of an emperor – though not when that emperor was Vitellius. In this fashion, then, he entered the Capitol and there embraced his mother and honoured her with the title 'Augusta'.

1. The bridge (still 'Ponte Milvio' and still in use) by which the Flaminian Way crosses the Tiber two miles north of Rome; see map 11.

90. On the following day he delivered a boastful speech about himself as if he were addressing the senate and people of a foreign state. In this he dwelt upon his own energy and restraint, despite the fact that his scandalous behaviour was only too obvious to the audience and indeed to the whole of Italy through which he had made his lamentable way in sleep and revelry. The lower classes, however, are irresponsible and unable to discriminate between counterfeit and true. Adept in offering the usual flattery, they shouted and yelled their approval, and though Vitellius rejected the title 'Augustus', they compelled him to assume it. The acceptance was as pointless as the refusal.

91. One action of Vitellius' was regarded as ill-omened by a capital which reacted to every event. After assuming the office of Pontifex Maximus, he issued a decree concerning public worship. But he did this on 18 July, a date which from time immemorial has been regarded as unlucky because it is the anniversary of the defeats on the Cremera and the Allia.[1] This was typical of his ignorance of all law, human and divine. Equal indifference was displayed by his officials and courtiers, and the administration seemed to function in an atmosphere of carouse. But he carried out the consular elections in the presence of the candidates with constitutional formality, and lost no chance of wringing every plaudit from the lowest classes by appearing at the theatre as a member of the audience and at the race-course as a punter. If prompted by respectability, this would certainly have been a welcome and democratic gesture, but the memory of his past deprived it of credit and value. He made a habit of attending the senate even when the agenda was trivial. On one occasion, as it happened, the praetor-designate Helvidius Priscus[2] had proposed a course of action which conflicted with Vitellius' own wishes. He was put out at first, though merely appealing to the tribunes of the plebs to take up this insult offered to the tribunician power of the emperor. But in due course his courtiers, who feared his deeper resentment, succeeded in mollifying him, and Vitellius remarked that there was nothing new in a difference of opinion between two senators on a matter of politics.

1. In 477 B.C. the Romans were defeated by the Veientines on the River Cremera, and in 390 or 387 B.C. by the Gauls on the River Allia. Both these streams are in the neighbourhood of Rome.

2. Cf. p. 206.

He added that he had himself been in the habit of voicing his opposition to Thrasea.[1] A number of his hearers sneered at this impudent claim to be such a man's rival, while others approved of his choosing Thrasea rather than any of the favourites of the moment as the pattern of true glory.

92. To command the pretorian guard he had selected Publilius Sabinus, who had been prefect of an auxiliary cohort, and Julius Priscus, at the moment a centurion. Priscus could rely on the support of Valens, and Sabinus upon that of Caecina. In this conflict of rivals Vitellius was a mere pawn. The imperial functions were in fact discharged by Caecina and Valens. They had long warily watched each other with a hostility scarcely veiled by the exigencies of war and military requirements. Their enmity had grown even more deadly in the environment of a vicious entourage and of a capital prolific in intrigue. The struggle between these two found its measure in the flattery of their attendants and the endless queues of the levee. Vitellius supported now one, now the other, for rank autocracy is never confident of itself. An emperor who thus hovered between sudden offence and ill-timed complaisance was regarded with alternate fear and contempt. This, however, had not stopped Valens and Caecina laying hands on mansions, parks and the riches of the empire, though the tearful and destitute throng of nobles who had been allowed by Galba to return home from exile with their children got no pity or assistance from the emperor. One decision was welcome to the leaders of society, and approved by the populace too. Vitellius had allowed returned exiles to resume the rights they had enjoyed over their freedmen, though these wily creatures tried to stultify the concession in every conceivable way by hiding fortunes under fake bank accounts or by buying favour. Some of them transferred to the imperial household and became more powerful than their erstwhile masters.

93. But the troops were everywhere. The barracks could not accommodate all of them, so they roamed about the porticoes or temple precincts, and throughout the capital. There was no question of parades, proper sentry duty or a training programme. Amid the lures of the capital and pursuits too shocking to be described, they ruined their physique by idleness and their morals by indulgence. Finally, careless of life itself, many of them encamped in the unhealthy

1. A member of the Stoic opposition and victim of Nero: Tacitus, *Annals* xvi, 21–35.

Vatican district. This caused an epidemic. The Tiber flowed near at hand, and the Germans and Gauls, who are in any case susceptible to illness, found their resistance further impaired by a passion for swimming, and by their inability to stand heat. What is more, the whole military organization was thrown into confusion by misguided policy or selfish ambition. Sixteen pretorian and four urban cohorts were formed, each a thousand strong.[1] Valens showed the less scruple in levying these troops because he felt that it was he who had saved Caecina from disaster.[2] It cannot be denied that Valens' arrival upon the scene had put fresh heart into the Vitellians, and the bad name he had won by marching so slowly had been effaced by victory. In any case all the troops from Lower Germany swore by Valens. It was this circumstance, as it was believed, that first caused Caecina's loyalty to flag.

94. However, Vitellius' indulgence towards his generals was as nothing compared with the licence accorded to the troops. Every man was allowed to pick his own arm of the service. The most worthless characters were taken on the strength of the garrison of Rome if that was their preference. On the other hand really deserving soldiers were permitted to stay with the legions or cavalry if they so desired. There was no dearth of such volunteers among those who were sick and blamed the extremes of the Italian climate. Nevertheless the legions and cavalry lost the pick of their men, and the prestige of service at Rome suffered a severe shock, for a procedure whereby 20,000 men were taken from the army as a whole was not selection, but chaos.

One day, during a speech made by Vitellius, a demand was raised for the execution of the Gallic leaders Asiaticus, Flavus and Rufinus. The ground was that they had fought for Vindex. Vitellius made no attempt to curb outcries of this sort. Quite apart from his constitutional indolence, the realization that a bounty was expected for which he had not the money made him lavish every other sort of concession on the troops. The freedmen of leading Romans were told to pay an extraordinary tax scaled in proportion to the number of their slaves. Vitellius himself was bent solely upon spending. He constructed larger stables for his charioteers, filled the circus with gladiatorial and wild-beast shows, and embarked on a spending spree as if his purse were bottomless.

1. The number of pretorian cohorts was normally nine.        2. See p. 99.

95. Indeed, Caecina and Valens celebrated Vitellius' birthday[1] by giving gladiatorial shows throughout Rome and in every quarter of the city. Such lavish displays had rarely been seen before. To the delight of the rabble and with the disapproval of honest citizens, the emperor had organized a memorial service for Nero. Altars were set up in the Campus Martius, and sacrificial victims slaughtered and burnt at the public expense. The torch was applied to the pyre by the Augustales, a college of priests which Emperor Tiberius had instituted for the worship of the Julian clan, in imitation of Romulus' foundation in honour of King Tatius.

Four months had not yet elapsed since the advent of the new régime, yet Vitellius' freedman Asiaticus had already rivalled the efforts of Polyclitus, Patrobius[2] and the hated names of the past. At such a court no one sought distinction by honesty or hard work. The one and only avenue to influence was to glut the insatiable appetites of Vitellius with lavish junketing, expenditure and debauch. The emperor himself, content to enjoy the present and thoughtless of the morrow, is held to have squandered 900 million sesterces in a very few months. Huge and helpless, the Roman state had suffered an Otho and a Vitellius within a single year; it had had to endure a varied and ignominious fate as the helpless victim of men like Vinius, Fabius, Icelus and Asiaticus. In the end these yielded to Mucianus and Marcellus and a change of individuals rather than of outlook.

96. The legion whose defection was first to be announced to Vitellius was the Third, for Aponius Saturninus sent a letter with the news before he, too, joined Vespasian's side. But Aponius had not given a full account of what had happened. He was unnerved by the abruptness of the blow, and the courtiers of Vitellius played down the news with honied tongues. Only one legion was disaffected, they assured him, and the rest of the troops were unshakably loyal. This was also the line which Vitellius adopted in a speech to the troops. In this he denounced the recently dismissed pretorians as rumour-mongers, and asserted that there was no danger of civil war. Any reference to Vespasian was censored, and troops patrolled the capital to stop the public gossiping. It was this that chiefly served to encourage rumours.

97. However, Vitellius called up reinforcements from Germany, Britain and the Spanish provinces, though in a dilatory fashion and

1. 7 or 24 September.　　　2. See pp. 44 and 50.

without admitting the urgency of the situation. The governors and provinces were equally slow to act. Hordeonius Flaccus was by now suspicious of the Batavians and worried at the prospect of having a war on his own doorstep, while Vettius Bolanus felt that Britain was never a really peaceful country. Both alike were in two minds about supporting Vitellius. Nor did the Spanish provinces show any alacrity, as there was no governor there at the time. The three legionary commanders were on an equal footing, and while they would have competed in subservience if Vitellius had looked like winning, they were unanimous in their reluctance to back a loser. In Africa, the legion normally stationed there, together with the cohorts recruited by Clodius Macer and later disbanded by Galba, once more assumed action stations at Vitellius' command, and at the same time the residue of the men of military age signed on promptly. The reason for this was that while Vitellius had won golden opinions as an honest governor of Africa, Vespasian's tenure of office there had earned him discredit and unpopularity. So the provincials argued that they would display the same qualities as emperors. But experience showed otherwise. 98. Indeed, at first the legion's commander, Valerius Festus, faithfully supported the enthusiasm of the provincials. As time went on, however, he wavered. In official correspondence and proclamations he sided with Vitellius, but maintained secret contact with Vespasian, intending to champion the winning side. In various parts of Raetia and the Gallic provinces, a certain number of soldiers and centurions were arrested in possession of letters and proclamations of Vespasian. They were sent to Vitellius, and put to death. Even more avoided detection thanks to loyal friends or their own cleverness. In this way, Vitellius' measures became known, but on the whole Vespasian's intentions remained wrapped in mystery. This was partly due to Vitellius' slackness, but also to the fact that the blockade of the Pannonian Alps[1] held up news. Conditions in the Mediterranean helped, too: the Etesian winds provided an easy passage to the East and hampered the voyage in the opposite direction.

99. It was only when the invasion began[2] that the alarming news from every quarter finally shocked Vitellius into ordering Caecina and Valens to mobilize. Caecina was sent on ahead. At the time, Valens was just getting on his feet after a severe illness, and convalescence

1. The Julian Alps barring the way to Pannonia from Northern Italy.
2. Early September, A.D. 69.

held him up. There was a vast alteration for the worse in the appearance of the army of Germany as it left the capital. Enfeebled and dispirited, the depleted ranks struggled slowly along. Their arms and equipment were sloppy, their horses lazy. The men were unable to stand up to sun, dust and bad weather. With this blunting of the will to face hardship went a corresponding readiness to make trouble. Then there was Caecina. He had always had an eye to his own advantage, but was now seized with something new – apathy. Indulgence in the spoils of power had turned him into a flabby pleasure-seeker, or perhaps he was toying with treachery and thought that sapping the army's morale was just another clever thing to do. Many have held the view that Caecina's loyalty was undermined by the policy of Flavius Sabinus, Rubrius Gallus acting as the go-between in their negotiations. In the course of these, Caecina was assured that any deal involving a change of side would be upheld by Vespasian. He was also reminded of the dislike and jealousy he felt for Fabius Valens. If his rival stood higher with Vitellius, it was up to Caecina to establish his position by courting a new emperor.

100. Caecina was given an effusive and gratifying send-off by Vitellius. On leaving the emperor, he sent part of his cavalry on in advance to make sure of Cremona. This force was followed by drafts from the First, Fourth, Fifteenth and Sixteenth Legions, and later by the Fifth and Twenty-Second. The rearguard was formed of the Twenty-First (Hurricane) and First (Italian), accompanied by elements of the three legions forming the British garrison and by selected auxiliaries. Once Caecina had gone, Fabius Valens sent orders to the army which had been under his command to wait for him on the road. This, he said, was what he had agreed on with Caecina. But the latter was on the spot, and could exercise more control. So he pretended that this plan had been altered so as to permit of their deploying their full forces against the enemy penetration. Thus some of the legions were ordered to hurry on to Cremona, others to make for Hostilia. Caecina himself branched off to Ravenna, ostensibly to address the fleet. Later, it leaked out that he had aimed at a secret interview in order to concoct treachery. His partner was Lucilius Bassus. This officer, after commanding a cavalry regiment, had been appointed by Vitellius admiral of both the Ravenna and the Misenum fleets. He quite unjustifiably took umbrage because he had not been made pretorian prefect immediately, and was now planning this

dastardly treachery as his revenge. Nor indeed can we be sure whether it was he who induced Caecina to desert, or whether – since evil minds think alike – the same wicked impulse affected both.   101. Historians of this war who wrote during the Flavian dynasty have flatteringly described the motives of these men as 'concern for peace' and 'patriotism'. My own view is that in addition to a natural instability of character and the cheapening of loyalty which was a consequence of their betrayal of Galba, a jealous fear that rivals would outpace them in Vitellius' affections induced them to ruin Vitellius himself. Caecina overtook the legions, and employed various devices to undermine the obstinate devotion of the centurions and troops to Vitellius. Bassus had less difficulty in engineering a similar plot – the loyalty of the fleet had no very firm footing as it had not forgotten its recent campaign on behalf of Otho.

*Book Three*

## The Second Battle of Cremona

1. Better luck and loyalty attended the leaders of the Flavian interest as they proceeded to form their plan of campaign. They had met at Poetovio, the winter-quarters of the Thirteenth Legion. There they debated whether to decide on closing the Pannonian Alps[1] until such time as their forces were massed behind them in full strength, or whether it would show more spirit to grapple with the enemy in a struggle for Italy. Those who preferred to await reinforcements and fight a long war stressed the power and reputation of the legions of Germany and the subsequent arrival of Vitellius with a picked force from the army of Britain. The Flavian legions, on the other hand, were fewer in number and had been recently driven from the field. For all their bluster, beaten troops were inevitably inferior in morale. But once the Alps were held, they could expect Mucianus to arrive with the forces of the East. Moreover Vespasian controlled the Mediterranean with its various fleets and enjoyed the support of the provinces. Thanks to these he could open a second front on a massive scale. Thus delay would be their salvation: it would mean the arrival of new forces, and no loss of the old.

2. In reply to these arguments, the keenest advocate of war, Antonius Primus,[2] urged that speed would be helpful to themselves and fatal to Vitellius. The winning side had grown slacker, not more confident, for they were not held at short call and accommodated in barracks. Billeted in idleness in all the towns of Italy, formidable only to their hosts, they had grasped at unfamiliar pleasures with a greed that matched their previous violence. The circus, too, and the theatres and amenities of the capital had made them soft or ailing. Given a breathing-space, however, they too would recover their toughness under training. Germany, the source of their strength, was not far off. Britain lay across the narrow waters of the Channel. The Gallic

1. See p. 140 and n. 1.    2. See p. 132 and n. 1.

and Spanish provinces were close at hand, and from both came men, horses and money. Then there was Italy itself and the wealth of Rome. Finally, if the Vitellians wanted to take the offensive, they could rely on two fleets[1] and a defenceless Adriatic. What good would the control of the Alps be then, or the prolongation of fighting to the next summer? Where meanwhile were the Flavians to get money and supplies? Surely it would be better to profit from the very fact that the Pannonian legions[2] had been cheated of victory rather than beaten in fair fight and were eager to have their own back, while the powerful armies of Moesia would come fresh to the attack? If one counted men rather than legions, their own side was the stronger, as well as being undemoralized by pleasure. Besides, their very humiliation had helped discipline. The cavalry, furthermore, had not been beaten even at Cremona. Despite a difficult situation it had pierced Vitellius' front line. 'In that encounter,' Antonius exclaimed, 'two Pannonian and Moesian cavalry regiments cut their way through the enemy: now sixteen will mass their colours and by their impact and din, by the very clouds of dust they raise, will bury and overwhelm riders and horses that have forgotten battle. Give me a free hand and I will be responsible for both planning and performance. You, gentlemen, who have a reputation to maintain, may hold the legions in reserve: all I want are cohorts in battle order. Soon you shall hear that the gates of Italy have been unlocked and Vitellius' fortunes shattered. You will be glad enough to follow, and tread in the footsteps of the victor.'

3. These and similar remarks Antonius poured out with flashing eyes and strident voice. He wanted to be audible in the farthest corner of the council-of-war, supplemented as it was on this occasion by the centurions and some of the rank-and-file. The effect was electric. He swept even cautious and wary officers off their feet, while the ordinary soldiers and the rest of the staff were deaf to less vigorous advice, and hailed Antonius as the one real man and leader. This indeed was the reputation he had already won at the initial parade when Vespasian's letter was read out. Instead of confining his remarks, like the majority of the speakers, to ambiguities which he could later interpret to suit

1. At Misenum and Ravenna.
2. The Seventh (Galbian) and Thirteenth (Twin); the latter had been present at the First Battle of Cremona, but the former had probably arrived too late to participate in it. Both might claim that they had been cheated of victory.

events, he was felt to have shown his hand openly, and to that extent he carried greater weight with the troops as their partner in crime – or glory.

4. After Antonius, the most influential officer was the imperial agent Cornelius Fuscus, whose habitual and bitter criticism of Vitellius had sealed his fate if things went wrong. Then there was Tampius Flavianus. By nature dilatory, and not less so with increasing years, he was distrusted by the troops, who suspected that he could not forget that he was a relative of Vitellius. Moreover by disappearing when the legions first grew restive and then returning of his own free will, he was believed to have tried to secure an opportunity of betraying them. After resigning command of Pannonia, Flavianus had sought refuge in Italy. But then his restless ambition had induced him to resume the title of governor and join in the civil war. He had done so at the prompting of Cornelius Fuscus – not that the latter stood in need of such vigour as Flavianus could offer: his intention was that the name of a senior officer should lend the incipient Flavian movement an air of respectability.

5. However, in order to reduce the risk and exploit the advantage of transferring operations to Italy, written instructions were sent to Aponius Saturninus to move up quickly with the army of Moesia, and in case the now defenceless provinces should be exposed to the attentions of barbarian tribes beyond the frontier, the rulers of the Sarmatian Iazyges, who hold absolute power in their community, were enrolled in the Flavian army. They also volunteered to raise a mass levy as well as a force of cavalry, their one effective arm; but the offer was rejected for fear that they might take advantage of our dissensions to organize an attack on the empire, or play false if offered better terms by the other side. The Flavians secured the support of the Suebian kings, Sido and Italicus,[1] who had shown long-standing compliance to Rome and whose people were more disposed to keep faith than break it. Auxiliary forces were posted on the flank in view of the hostility of Raetia under its governor Porcius Septiminus, a staunch adherent of Vitellius. This was why Sextilius Felix, with the Aurian cavalry regiment, and some Norican levies, was sent to hold the bank of the River Inn,[2] which forms the boundary between

---

1. Rulers of a small kingdom in Moravia.

2. e.g. at Innsbruck–Wilten (Veldidena) or Langenpfunzen near Rosenheim (Pons Aeni).

Raetia and Noricum. Neither side showed fight in this theatre, and the success of the Flavians was decided elsewhere.

6. Antonius began his lightning invasion of Italy with the help of detachments from the cohorts and a part of the cavalry.[1] He was accompanied by Arrius Varus, an officer who had gained a reputation for vigour, thanks to service under Corbulo and the successes in Armenia.[2] But there was a rumour that he had criticized Corbulo's ability in the course of private conversations with Nero, and though he ingratiated himself with the emperor by this discreditable behaviour and so obtained promotion to senior centurion, the immediate advantage was later to prove his undoing.

However, Primus and Varus occupied Aquileia, and in the neighbouring towns, and at Opitergium and Altinum, they were warmly welcomed. Altinum was garrisoned against a possible threat from the Ravenna fleet, whose defection had not yet been heard of. They then received the adhesion of Patavium and Ateste. At the latter place it was learnt that three Vitellian cohorts and a regiment of cavalry (the Sebosian) were encamped by a bridge which they had built at Forum Alieni. This seemed a good chance to strike at an unwary foe, for such they were said to be. At first light the Flavians fell upon the enemy while they were still mostly unarmed. Instructions had been given that only a few should be killed and the rest frightened into changing sides; and in fact some surrendered immediately, though more succeeded in halting their opponents' advance by cutting the bridge.

7. When this success became public knowledge and the first engagement in the war was seen to have been decided in favour of the Flavians, the Seventh (Galbian) and Thirteenth (Twin) Legions, with the latter's commander Vedius Aquila, moved briskly to Patavium. There a few days were passed resting, and Minicius Justus, the camp commandant of the Seventh, a disciplinarian who kept the troops on too tight a rein for civil war, was relieved of his appointment to save him from the fury of the men, and sent to Vespasian. A step was then taken which was considered long overdue, and indeed the comment it aroused lent it a prestige which was out of all proportion to the occasion. In every town, the portraits of Galba, which had been taken down owing to the troubles, were restored to honour on the instructions of Antonius, who believed that it would be creditable to the

1. The date is mid-September 69.        2. See Introduction, p. 11.

cause if the public thought that Galba's reign was approved and that his followers were regaining influence.

8. The next problem was the selection of a base. Verona seemed preferable because the extensive plains in the vicinity lent themselves to cavalry operations, in which the Flavians excelled. Moreover, to deprive Vitellius of a rich city seemed to be good policy and good propaganda. Vicetia was occupied by the advancing troops without a blow being struck. This was a small incident in view of the modest resources of the town, but significant in the eyes of observers who reflected that Caecina was born there and that the enemy commander had thus lost control of his native place. Verona was a real prize. Its populace helped the Flavian cause by their example and material support: and the army had at one swoop seized a central strategic position that closed the door upon Raetia and the Julian Alps, and denied the armies of Germany transit through them.

These steps were taken without the knowledge of Vespasian or else against his instructions, for his orders at this time were that the advance was to be halted at Aquileia to allow Mucianus to catch up. They were reinforced by an explanation of his strategy. Now that he commanded both Egypt, with its control of the corn supply, and the revenues of the richest provinces of the empire,[1] the army of Vitellius could be forced to its knees merely by lack of pay and supplies. The same advice was conveyed in repeated dispatches from Mucianus, who, while ostensibly advocating a bloodless victory, the need for keeping casualties down and so on, was in fact greedy of glory and anxious to monopolize any distinction the campaign afforded. However, the great distances involved meant that official instructions arrived when events had already taken place.

9. . . . so[2] Antonius overran the enemy outposts by a sudden assault, and the fighting spirit of the combatants was tested in a brush from which neither side emerged victorious. After this, Caecina planted a strongly entrenched camp between Hostilia (a village in the territory of Verona) and the marshes of the River Tartaro, choosing a site protected in the rear by a river[3] and on the flanks by a barrier of marshland. Had he possessed loyalty as well, there were two possibilities: either the concentrated Vitellian forces would have been in

---

1. Egypt supplied one-third of the corn imported into Italy, and among the richest provinces were Asia and Syria.

2. There appears to be a short lacuna here.      3. The Po.

a position to inflict a crushing blow on two solitary legions[1] not yet
reinforced by the army of Moesia; or else the Flavians would have
been driven back and ignominiously compelled to evacuate Italy.
But Caecina allowed the enemy to gain the initiative in the opening
phases of the campaign by procrastinating in various ways and denouncing in official messages an army which he could readily have
routed by force of arms. His aim was to conclude a traitorous deal with
the enemy by means of his emissaries. During this lull, Aponius
Saturninus arrived on the scene. With him came the Seventh (Claudian) Legion commanded by Vipstanus Messalla, a distinguished member of a famous family, and the only man to contribute an element of
integrity to this campaign. This then was the force – far inferior to the
Vitellian and still only numbering three legions – to which Caecina
sent his letters. In these he criticized the folly of fighting for lost causes
and in the same breath lavishly praised the high morale of the army of
Germany, with only a slight and perfunctory reference to Vitellius
and an absence of all abuse of Vespasian. In this there was absolutely
nothing which was calculated either to entice or to frighten the
enemy. In their reply, the Flavian commanders made no attempt to
apologize for failure in the past. They spoke up for Vespasian with
pride and for their cause with assurance, confident in their army and
displaying undisguised hostility towards Vitellius, though they offered
tribunes and centurions the hope of retaining any concessions made
by him. As for Caecina, he was openly urged to desert. The public
reading of this correspondence in the parade-ground raised Flavian
morale, since it was clear that Caecina's tone was cringing, as if he
were afraid to offend Vespasian, whereas their own officers had not
minced their words, and gave the impression of offering Vitellius a
direct insult.

10. When in due course two more Flavian legions appeared – the
Third, led by Dillius Aponianus, and the Eighth, led by Numisius
Lupus – the decision was taken to make a show of strength and provide
Verona with an outer rampart.[2] It so happened that the task of build-
ing this rampart on the side facing the enemy was allotted to the
Seventh (Galbian) Legion, and when some allied cavalry were sighted

1. The Pannonian legions, Seventh (Galbian) and Thirteenth (Twin).
2. Verona had expanded beyond its city-walls and the rampart was designed
to protect the exposed southern suburbs. It followed the line Castel Vecchio-
Via Pallone.

in the distance and taken for the enemy, a false alarm was raised.
Fearful of treachery, the legionaries seized their arms and turned the
full weight of their anger on Tampius Flavianus. There were no solid
grounds for such an accusation, but he had long been unpopular, and
they now raised a frenzied clamour for his head. Shouts were heard
denouncing him as a relative of Vitellius, a traitor to Otho, and a
man who had pocketed the bounty meant for themselves. He was
given no opportunity to defend himself, though he appealed for
mercy with outstretched hands, almost prostrate on the ground, his
clothes torn, his chest heaving and his lips quivering with inarticulate
sobs. This in itself incited the men to even greater hostility, for in their
eyes his complete loss of nerve was the sign of a guilty conscience.
Aponius tried to speak to them, but was unable to make himself
heard amid the yelling men. Other officers were rebuffed with jeers
and shouts; and Antonius alone managed to get a hearing, for he not
only had eloquence and the trick of quietening a mob, but inspired
respect as a leader. When the mutiny began to get out of hand and
the troops passed from abuse and insult to arms and action, he ordered
Flavianus to be put in irons. The soldiers saw through the farce, and
thrusting aside the guards around the officers' platform prepared to
resort to lynch-law. Antonius pushed forward to meet them with
drawn sword, assuring them that he would die by the hand of the
troops or by his own. Whenever his eye fell upon a soldier known to
him personally and wearing some decoration for valour, he appealed
to him by name for help. Then, turning to the standards and the gods
of war,[1] he prayed that they might deflect such discord and infatuation
upon the armies of the enemy. Gradually the mutiny began to peter
out, and with the gathering dusk the men separated to their several
tents. Flavianus left the same night and was rescued from danger
by a dispatch from Vespasian, whose bearer he encountered on the
way.[2]

11. The rot was infectious, for the legionaries now advanced upon
Aponius Saturninus, commanding the forces from Moesia. Their
violence was accentuated by the fact that tempers had flared up at
midday – not, as previously, in the evening, when they were exhausted by the physical labour of digging. The cause was the

1. The legionary eagles as cult-objects.
2. Vespasian must have summoned or complimented Flavianus, who was
allowed to go on his way unmolested.

publication of some correspondence which Saturninus was supposed to have had with Vitellius. Once Roman soldiers had competed in courage and discipline. Now their rivalry was one of insolence and insubordination – they must be sure to clamour for Aponius' death as violently as they had done for Flavianus'. The Moesian legionaries remembered that they had assisted the men of Pannonia to settle scores, and the Pannonians felt that the mutiny of others excused their own. Hence it was only natural that they were both ready to commit a second offence. They made for the mansion in which Saturninus was staying. Primus, Aponianus and Messalla did their best, but it was not so much their efforts that saved Saturninus as the dark hiding-place in which he was skulking – he had concealed himself in the furnace-house in a villa that happened to be untenanted. Afterwards, he got rid of his lictors and made his escape to Patavium. Thanks to the departure of the two senior governors, Antonius now had effective control of both armies, for his brother-officers took second place and the troops backed him with enthusiasm. But there were some critics who held that Antonius had incited both these mutinies in order to have a free hand in the campaign.

12. On the Vitellian side, too, there were restless spirits. Here the turmoil and dissension were even more fatal, since they sprang less from the suspicions of the men than from the treachery of their leaders. The Ravenna fleet was commanded by Lucilius Bassus. His men were luke-warm in their allegiance, for many came from Dalmatia and Pannonia and these provinces were now held in Vespasian's name. So the admiral had brought them over to the Flavian cause. The act of treachery was to be performed after dark, so that the conspirators could hold a meeting in the headquarters building without the presence or knowledge of others. Bassus himself was ashamed of what was afoot or afraid of how it would turn out. So he awaited the upshot in his house. The captains staged a wild onslaught upon the portraits of Vitellius, and when the few who offered resistance had been cut down, the men at large, who wanted a change, came over to Vespasian. At this point Lucilius appeared and publicly put himself at the head of the movement. But the sailors offered the command of the fleet to Cornelius Fuscus, who speedily hurried to the base.[1] As for

1. He must have been waiting near Ravenna in accordance with arrangements negotiated between Antonius and Caecina, or between Antonius and Bassus.

Bassus, he was taken in a fast flotilla under open arrest as far as Atria. Here he was closely confined by Memmius Rufinus, who commanded a regiment of horse in the town. But his fetters were promptly struck off by the intervention of the imperial freedman Hormus: he, too, passed for one of the leaders.

13. To return to Caecina: when the defection of the fleet became common knowledge, he called a meeting of the senior centurions and a few of the rank-and-file at his headquarters, choosing a time when the camp was quiet and the rest of the troops were scattered on their various duties.[1] He there spoke highly of Vespasian's qualities and the strength of his following. The fleet, he pointed out, had changed sides, supplies were short, the Gallic and Spanish provinces hostile, and the capital thoroughly disaffected. All his allusions to Vitellius, too, were uncomplimentary. Then those of his hearers who were in the plot took the lead in swearing allegiance to Vespasian, and before the rest had recovered from their surprise, Caecina made them do so too. In the same instant, Vitellius' portraits were torn down and the news sent to Antonius. However, the treasonable act became the talk of the entire camp, and as the men rushed back to the headquarters building, they saw that Vespasian's name had been written up and Vitellius' portraits thrown down. At first, there was a great and dreadful hush, then one great explosion of protest. Had the credit of the army of Germany sunk so low, they cried, that they were tamely to put their hands into fetters and surrender their weapons to the captors without striking a blow? After all, what sort of legions could the other side boast of? Were they not beaten ones? Besides, the only good formations in Otho's army, the First and Fourteenth, were not there, though even these they had routed and cut to pieces on those very plains. Were many thousands of armed men to be handed over as a gift to the outlaw Antonius, like a gang of slaves bought and sold in the market? It seemed that eight legions were to be bargained away as a make-weight to one miserable fleet! This, then, was the deliberate policy both of Bassus and of Caecina – after stealing palaces, villas and fortunes from Vitellius, they were now bent on robbing the troops of their emperor, and the emperor of his troops! Unscathed and unscarred, cheap even in the eyes of the Flavians, what would they say to those who legitimately demanded to see the balance sheet of victory or defeat?

1. The date is 18 October 69.

14. Such were the cries of indignation that sprang from one and all. Following the lead given by the Fifth Legion, they restored the portraits of Vitellius to their place, put Caecina under arrest, elected as their leaders Fabius Fabullus, commanding officer of the Fifth, and the camp-commandant, Cassius Longus, and massacred the crews of three galleys who chanced to cross their path, ignorant and innocent of what had happened. Then, striking camp and cutting the bridge,[1] they marched back to Hostilia and thence to Cremona to join the First (Italian) and Twenty-First (Hurricane) Legions, which Caecina had sent ahead with part of the cavalry to hold Cremona.

15. When news of this reached Antonius, he decided to close with the enemy while their two forces were separated and their purpose disunited. He could not wait until their leaders recovered their hold and the troops their discipline, or until a rendezvous restored confidence. He guessed that Fabius Valens had left Rome, and would increase his pace on learning of Caecina's betrayal. The fidelity of Fabius to Vitellius, his skill as a general, and the possible advance of large masses of Germans through Raetia were frightening thoughts. As a matter of fact, Vitellius had indeed called for reinforcements from Britain, Gaul and Spain. A war of boundless havoc seemed imminent. But Antonius, anticipating this, snatched a timely victory by forcing an engagement. A two days' march from Verona[2] brought him to Bedriacum with the whole of his army. On the following morning,[3] keeping his legions back to entrench camp, he sent his auxiliary cohorts into the territory of Cremona, ostensibly to forage, actually to acquire a taste for plundering Roman civilians. He himself, with 4,000 cavalry, moved forward to a point[4] eight miles from Bedriacum to give the spoilers greater scope. Reconnaissance parties made the usual sorties farther afield.

16. It was approximately 11 a.m. when a rider galloped up with the news: the enemy were approaching, headed by a small advance party, and movement and tumult could be heard over a wide area. While Antonius was still debating a plan of action with his staff, Arrius Varus, who was impatient for results, dashed out with a spearhead of cavalry and threw the Vitellians back. But he inflicted only slight losses. For as greater numbers hastened to the scene, the tables were

1. On the Po at Hostilia, after crossing to the south bank so as to avoid contact with Antonius.
2. The distance is forty (Roman) miles.   3. 24 October 69.   4. See map 2.

turned, and the most eager of the pursuers now found themselves at
the rear of the retreat. Such haste had not been Antonius' wish, and
he had all along been expecting what had in fact happened. Telling
his men to engage the enemy with stout hearts, he moved his troops
of horse to the flanks and left a free passage in the middle for Varus
and his unit. The legions were told to arm.[1] A trumpet call was sounded throughout the area to indicate that the various parties of foragers
should drop their hunt for spoil and make for the fighting at the
nearest point. Meanwhile, in some disorder, the frightened Varus
linked up with the main body of cavalry, infecting it with his own
panic. Wounded and whole, they all fled, jostling each other because
of their loss of nerve and the narrowness of the roads.   17. In this
chaos Antonius did whatever a steadfast officer or brave soldier could
do, confronting the panic-stricken and restraining the fugitive. Where
most effort was required, or there was any opening, however slight,
his words, deeds and presence of mind made him a marked man in the
eyes of friend and foe alike. Finally he was so carried away that he
thrust a spear through a retreating ensign, then caught up the flag
and turned it to face the enemy. Some troopers numbering no more
than a hundred were shamed by this incident into standing their
ground. The place helped them, owing to the narrowing of the road
at that point and the demolition of a bridge over a stream[2] which
flowed between the two armies and by its slippery bed and steep
banks rendered escape difficult. This circumstance – whether we call
it necessity or luck – gave fresh heart to a side which seemed already
beaten. They formed up, closed ranks, and presented a solid front to
the rash and scattered charges of the Vitellians. It was now the
enemy's turn to suffer disaster. Antonius was quick to press his advantage home and ride down resistance, while his troops, following their
bent, plundered the fallen, took prisoner the survivors, and deprived
the enemy of arms and mounts. Indeed, their exulting cries alerted
those who, only minutes before, had been scattering over the countryside for their lives, and they too now joined in the victorious action.
18. Four miles from Cremona, the glint of standards marked the
approach of the Hurricane and Italian Legions, which had marched
out as far as this during the initial success of their cavalry. But when

   1. Even in the field, Roman troops were not fully armed unless fighting was
imminent; cf. p. 105.
   2. The stream is the Delmona, not then canalized.

luck turned against them, they did nothing. They did not form open order. They failed to give shelter to their disorganized comrades. They did not advance to take the initiative against an enemy exhausted by marching and fighting over a distance of so many miles.[1] Had they done so, they would have had a fair chance of victory. When things went well, they had not seriously felt their lack of a commander: now, in the hour of defeat, they realized it to the full. The front ranks wavered, and the victorious cavalry charged into them, closely followed by the tribune Vipstanus Messalla leading the auxiliaries from Moesia, whose rapid pace was matched by many of the legionaries. Thus a mixed force of infantry and cavalry broke through the Vitellian legions. The nearby walls of Cremona, too, gave them greater hope of escape and correspondingly lessened their will to resist. Nor did Antonius press home his advantage, thinking of the exhaustion and wounds inflicted on riders and mounts by a fight in which, despite final success, the chances had been so evenly balanced.

19. As the light faded, the Flavian army arrived in full strength. Once they began to march over the heaps of dead and the fresh traces of bloodshed, they thought that the fighting was over and clamoured to press on towards Cremona to receive, or enforce, the surrender of the beaten enemy. This at any rate was what they said openly, and it sounded well. But what each man thought in his heart was something different. A city on flat ground could be rushed, and an army which forced an entry during the hours of darkness would have just as much dash, and enjoy greater licence to plunder. But if they waited for the dawn, it would be too late: there would be peace-terms and appeals for mercy. In that case, the only recompense for their wounds and exertions would be the empty credit of clemency, while the riches of Cremona would be pocketed by the auxiliary and legionary commanders. When a city was stormed, its booty fell to the troops; when surrendered, to the commanders. With these reflections, they brushed aside centurions and tribunes, and drowned any protests by clashing their arms as a sign of their intention to mutiny if they were not ordered to march on.

20. Then Antonius pushed his way into the thick of the companies. When his appearance and prestige had secured silence, he assured his hearers that he had no intention of robbing such deserving troops of

1. Ten.

credit or reward. But commanders and men had different functions to perform. A fighting spirit was excellent in soldiers, but commanders more often rendered service by deliberation and caution than by recklessness. In the past he had made his contribution to victory, and had done so sword in hand. In the future he would serve them by calculation and planning, which were the proper attributes of a leader. There were no two questions about the dangers confronting them – darkness, an unfamiliar city, and, within it, an enemy enjoying every facility for surprise. Even if the gates were wide open, it would be wrong to enter except after a reconnaissance, and by day. Or did they propose to begin the attack blindfold, without knowing the favourable approaches or the height of the walls, or whether the assault upon the city called for guns and missiles or siege-works and mantlets? Antonius then tried an individual approach. He asked one man after another whether he had brought with him axes and picks and all the other equipment necessary for storming cities. When they shook their heads, he retorted: 'Can brute strength breach and undermine walls with swords and javelins? Suppose it proves necessary to build a mound, suppose we must shelter behind screens and hurdles: are we going to stand about helplessly like an improvident mob, admiring the height of the towers and our opponents' defences? Why not wait just for one night, bring up the guns and engines, and then sweep forward carrying terror and triumph with us?' And so, without more ado, Antonius sent the sutlers and batmen with the freshest part of the cavalry back to Bedriacum to bring up supplies and anything else likely to be of use.

21. This indeed was almost too much for the men. They were on the verge of mutiny when the cavalry, riding right up to the walls of Cremona, captured some stray townsfolk from whom they got word that six Vitellian legions, comprising the whole army previously stationed at Hostilia, had covered thirty miles[1] that very day, and on hearing of the defeat of their comrades were now arming for battle and would turn up at any moment. It was this threat that opened the deaf ears of the troops and made them ready to listen to their commander's advice. He ordered the Thirteenth Legion to take up a position[2] astride the actual embankment of the Postumian Way. In

1. The average distance covered by heavily-laden legionaries in a day on good roads was 18–20 (Roman) miles.
2. One mile north of Longardore (Comune di Sospiro): see map 4.

contact on its left stood the Seventh (Galbian) on open ground, then the Seventh (Claudian), its front protected by one of the drainage ditches characteristic of the area.[1] On the right were the Eighth, deployed along a side-road without cover, and after that the Third, interspersed among a dense plantation of trees used as vine-props. (This at least was the order in which the eagles and standards were placed; the troops themselves were mixed up haphazardly in the darkness.) The contingent of pretorians lay next to the Third, the auxiliary cohorts held the extremities of the line, and the cavalry protected the flanks and rear. The Suebians, Sido and Italicus, patrolled the front line with a picked force of their countrymen.

22. As for the Vitellian army, reason dictated that it should rest at Cremona. After some food and sleep to recover its strength, it could have attacked the shivering and hungry enemy on the next morning with dire and devastating effect. But it had no leader and no plan of action. At about 8.30 p.m., by which time the Flavians were ready and in position, the Vitellians hurled themselves violently on their foe. I should hesitate to be dogmatic about the Vitellian order of battle because fury and darkness confused it, although others[2] have recorded that their right front was held by the Fourth (Macedonian), their centre by the Fifth and Fifteenth supported by detachments of the Ninth, Second and Twentieth Legions from Britain, and their left front by the men of the Sixteenth, Twenty-Second and First Legions. Elements of the Hurricane and Italian Legions had attached themselves to all the companies, while the cavalry and auxiliaries chose their own posts.

Throughout the night, the fighting was varied, indecisive and bitter, inflicting destruction on either side in turn. Clear heads and strong arms availed nothing, and even eyes were helpless in the dark. On both sides weapons and uniform were identical, frequent challenges and replies disclosed the watchword, and flags were inextricably confused as they were captured by this group or that and carried hither and thither. The formation under heaviest pressure was the Seventh Legion recently raised by Galba. Six centurions of the leading companies were killed, and a few standards lost. Even the eagle was only saved by Atilius Varus' desperate

1. The Dugale Gambalone.
2. Authors other than Tacitus or other than his source, Vipstanus Messalla? In any case the information appears to be sound.

execution upon the enemy and at the cost, finally, of his own life.
23. Antonius stiffened the wavering line by bringing up the pretorians. After relieving the Seventh, they drove the enemy back,
only to be driven back themselves. The reason for this was that the
Vitellians had concentrated their artillery[1] upon the highway so as to
command an unobstructed field of fire over the open ground. Their
shooting had at first been sporadic, and the shots had struck the vine-
props without hurting the enemy. The Sixteenth Legion had an
enormous field-piece which hurled massive stones. These were now
mowing down the opposing front-line, and would have inflicted
extensive havoc but for an act of heroism on the part of two soldiers.
They concealed their identity by catching up shields from the fallen,
and severed the tackle by which the engine was operated. They were
killed immediately and so their names have perished, but that the
deed was done is beyond question.

Neither side had had the advantage until, in the middle of the
night,[2] the moon rose, displaying – and deceiving – the combatants.
But the light favoured the Flavians, being behind them; on their side
the shadows of horses and men were exaggerated, and the enemy fire
fell short though the gunlayers imagined that they were on target.
But the Vitellians were brilliantly illuminated by the light shining full
in their faces, and so without realizing it provided an easy mark for an
enemy aiming from what were virtually concealed positions.
24. Antonius and his men could now recognize each other. So he
seized the chance of spurring them on, some by taunts and appeals to
their pride, many by praise and encouragement. all by hope and
promises. Why, he asked the Pannonian legions, had they taken up
arms in their resentment?[3] These were the very battlefields which
offered them a chance to wash away the stain of past humiliation and
regain their credit in men's eyes. Then, turning to the troops from
Moesia, he called on them as the leaders and authors of the campaign:[4]
they had challenged the Vitellians by threats and words, but this
meant nothing if they were not going to endure their deeds and looks.
Such were his arguments to the successive contingents as he reached
them; but he spoke at greater length to the soldiers of the Third,

---

1. See map 4. Each legion now normally had an artillery component of fifty-
five catapults, mounted on carts and possessing an effective range of not more
than 400 yards.

2. At 9.40 p.m. 24 October.    3. See p. 108.    4. See p. 132.

reminding them of their early and recent history, how under Mark Antony they had routed the Parthians, under Corbulo the Armenians, and in the immediate past the Sarmatians.[1] Then he spoke with greater sharpness to the pretorian guards. 'As for you,' he said, 'you are finished as soldiers unless you beat the enemy. What other emperor and what other camp is there to which you can transfer? There, among the foe, are the standards and equipment which are really yours, and for the beaten the sentence is death. Dishonour you have drunk to the dregs.'[2]

Everywhere there were cries of enthusiasm, and as the sun rose, the Third greeted it with cheers in accordance with Syrian custom.[3]

25. This led to a vague rumour (perhaps intentionally spread by the Flavian commander) that Mucianus had arrived and that the cries were greetings exchanged by the two armies. The men moved forward under the impression that they had been reinforced by fresh troops, the Vitellian line being now thinner than before, as one might expect of a force which in the absence of all leadership bunched and spread according to individual impulse or panic. When Antonius sensed that the enemy were reeling, he proceeded to throw them into confusion by the use of massed columns of troops. The loosely-knit ranks broke, and could not be closed again owing to the obstacles presented by vehicles and guns. Down the long straight road, drawing away from each other in the fervour of pursuit, charged the victors.

An event which made the slaughter more dreadful was the death of a father at the hands of his son. I record the incident and the names on the authority of Vipstanus Messalla. A recruit to the Hurricane Legion, one Julius Mansuetus from Spain, had left a young lad at home. Soon after, the boy came of age, and having been called up by Galba for service in the Seventh,[4] chanced to encounter his father in this battle and wounded him seriously. As he was searching the prostrate and semi-conscious figure, father and son recognized each other. Embracing the dying man, the son prayed in words choked by sobs that his father's spirit would be appeased and not bear him ill-will as a parricide: the act was not a personal one, and one single soldier

1. In February–March 69; see p. 69.

2. By betraying Galba for Otho, and failing Otho in the war against Vitellius, whom they were now attacking in support of Vespasian.

3. During its long stay in Syria from the time of Mark Antony the legion had learnt to worship some solar deity.

4. See p. 24.

was merely an infinitesimal fraction of the forces engaged in the civil war. With these words, he took up the body, dug a grave, and discharged the last duty to his father. Some nearby troops noticed this, then more and more; and so throughout the lines ran a current of wonder and complaint, and men cursed this cruellest of all wars. However, this did not stop them killing and robbing relatives, kinsmen and brothers: they said to each other that a crime had been done – and in the same breath did it themselves.

26. A new and formidable task confronted the Flavians when they reached Cremona. During the campaign with Otho, the troops from Germany had built a camp near the walls of Cremona and a rampart round the camp;[1] and since then, they had strengthened these defences still further. This sight gave the victors pause. Their officers were uncertain what orders to issue. To begin the assault with an army exhausted by a long day and night seemed difficult, and, if no reserves were standing by, dangerous. If, on the other hand, they were to go all the way back to Bedriacum, the march would be intolerably fatiguing and involved throwing away their victory. Even entrenching camp was a perilous business in such close proximity to the enemy, for there was the threat that scattered parties of men engaged in digging would be thrown into disorder by a sudden sortie. But above and beyond all these factors, the generals were frightened of their own troops, who preferred risk to waiting. Playing safe was dull, taking a chance offered possibilities. Whatever the cost in death and wounds and bloodshed, it counted for nothing when weighed against their appetite for spoil.

27. Antonius was inclined to agree, and ordered a ring of troops to be thrown around the fortified camp. The first phase of the battle was a distant exchange of arrows and stones, resulting in greater damage to the Flavians, who were exposed to the full force of the plunging fire. But then Antonius assigned the various sectors of the rampart and gates to different legions so that a division of labour might distinguish the brave from the cowardly, and the men find stimulus in the mere competition for honour. The area nearest to the road to Bedriacum was allotted to the men of the Third and Seventh Legions, and the wall further to the right to the Eighth and Seventh (Claudian); the companies of the Thirteenth advanced impetuously as far as the

---

1. See map 3.

Brixia gate.[1] A slight pause followed, while some of the legionaries collected axes in the adjacent countryside, and others scythes and ladders. Then, lifting their shields above their heads, they moved up in a tight 'tortoise'.[2] Both sides displayed the fighting skill of Rome. The Vitellians rolled down heavy stones on their opponents, and then, when the 'tortoise' was split and wavering, probed it with lances and poles until the compact structure of shields fell to pieces and they could flatten their bleeding or maimed opponents with deadly effect. The Flavian attack began to slacken. Their commanders, finding the men worn out and deaf to exhortations they believed useless, pointed to Cremona as the prize of victory. (28. Whether this ingenious suggestion came from Hormus, as Messalla tells us, or whether we should attach greater weight to the authority of Gaius Plinius, who accuses Antonius,[3] I find difficult to decide. One can only say that, whichever of the two it was, he did not bely his reputation and way of life by this appalling crime.) Henceforward bloodshed and wounds could not check the troops' determination to undermine the rampart and shatter the gates. Climbing on one another's shoulders and mounting on top of the re-formed 'tortoise', they clutched at the enemy's weapons and shoulders. Locked together in a fatal embrace, the whole with the wounded, the maimed with the stricken, they rolled down in a shifting kaleidoscope of death and destruction.

29. The hardest fighting fell to the Third and Seventh Legions, and the commander Antonius at the head of a picked auxiliary force pressed the attack in this sector. Their grim rivalry in the offensive was too much for the Vitellians, while the missiles hurled down on the 'tortoise' glanced harmlessly off. So in the end the defenders tipped over the great gun itself upon the enemy beneath. For the moment this made a gap, as it crushed the men on whom it fell. But it also took with it in its fall the merlons and the upper part of the wall, and in the same instant an adjacent tower succumbed to a hail of stones. Here, while the men of the Seventh pressed the attack in

1. The northern gate of the camp, nearest to the Brixia road.

2. A closely-bunched party of men interlocking their semi-cylindrical shields above their heads to form a screen against missiles.

3. Vipstanus Messalla appears to have written a memoir of this campaign. The Elder Pliny composed a history in thirty-one books, now lost, dealing with part or all of Nero's reign, the year 69 and part of the reign of Vespasian. It was published posthumously in A.D. 79, and is probably Tacitus' main source. It was no doubt pro-Flavian.

close formation, those of the Third managed to beeak a way through the gate with their axes and swords. According to the unanimous testimony of our authorities, the first to penetrate the camp was Gaius Volusius, a private of the Third Legion. He climbed up to the wall, threw down any men still attempting resistance, and waving and yelling to attract attention, cried out 'The camp is ours'. His comrades, now that the Vitellians were on the run and were jumping down from the wall, surged through to join him. Heavy losses were inflicted on the enemy throughout the open space between the camp and the fortifications of Cremona.[1]

30. And now for the second time their eyes fell upon a battle setting entirely new to them: lofty town-walls, towers of masonry, gates with iron portcullises, a garrison flourishing its weapons and Cremona's teeming populace, which was deeply attached to the Vitellian cause – to say nothing of the large number of visitors from the rest of Italy who had flocked to the fair regularly held at that time of year, their numbers a help to the defence and their wealth an allurement to the assailants. Antonius ordered torches to be produced and applied to the most attractive suburban houses. The idea was that the loss of their property might induce the Cremonese to change sides. Such buildings as stood close to the walls and overtopped them he manned with his best troops, who dislodged the first line of the defence with joists, tiles and firebrands.

31. Some of the legionaries were already forming up for the 'tortoise' and others discharging missiles and stones, when the morale of the Vitellians gradually began to crack. The higher the rank, the less the will to resist the inevitable. They feared that if Cremona too were taken by storm, there would be no further question of quarter and the conqueror's anger would fall entirely upon the tribunes and centurions who were worth killing rather than upon the multitude who had nothing to lose. But the ordinary soldier stood firm, for he cared nothing for the future and thought himself relatively safe, because unknown. Roaming through the streets or hidden in houses, these men refused to ask for peace even when they had ceased to wage war. The camp commandants took down the portraits of Vitellius and the indications of his name. Caecina, who was still in confinement, was released from his shackles and requested to plead for the

---

1. The remains of two Vitellian *ballistae* (one from IV Macedonia) were found in 1887 in this area: see map 3.

Vitellians. He stood on his dignity and refused, but they wore down his resistance with tearful entreaties, presenting the degrading phenomenon of many fine soldiers invoking the aid of a single traitor. Soon after, the white flag was displayed prominently from the walls. Antonius signalled the cease-fire, and the Vitellians brought out the standards and eagles. These were followed by a dejected column of disarmed men with downcast eyes. The victors had formed up to receive them, and at first jeered and thrust at them with their weapons. But after a while, when the beaten men faced their insults without flinching and impassively endured everything, their tormentors remembered that this was the army which, not long previously, had refrained from pressing home its victory at Bedriacum.[1] But when Caecina, distinguished by bordered toga and lictors, thrust aside the throng and made his way forward in his capacity as consul, the victors were in an uproar. They taunted him with conceit and malevolence, never attractive vices, and treachery as well. Antonius intervened, and giving him an escort sent him off to Vespasian.[2]

32. Meanwhile scuffles were developing between the Cremonese populace and the armed troops, and it was only when a massacre was imminent that the appeals of their leaders succeeded in pacifying their men. Moreover Antonius held a parade, addressing the victors proudly, and the vanquished with clemency, without referring to Cremona either way. Quite apart from its natural taste for plunder, the army had old scores to settle, and was bent on wiping out the Cremonese. It was held that they had once before supported the Vitellian side, in the war against Otho;[3] and later the men of the Thirteenth, left there to build an amphitheatre,[4] had been the target of their mockery and insults, this behaviour being typical of the impudent attitude of city mobs. The feeling against them was aggravated by a gladiatorial show Caecina had given at Cremona, its renewed employment as a base, and the way in which they offered the Vitellians food in the fighting line.[5] This had involved the death of certain women whose enthusiasm for the cause was such that they made their way out to the scene of battle. Moreover it was the season of the fair, and this filled a city which was in any case opulent with

---

1. See p. 108.
2. By whom he was well received.    3. See p. 94.    4. See p. 120.
5. The legions coming from Hostilia had given themselves no time to eat before marching out to battle; see pp. 157ff.

an even greater display of wealth. The other generals were shadowy figures, but Antonius' success and status had placed him full in the public gaze. He hurried off to the baths to wash away the stains of battle, and there, as he criticized the temperature, he was over-heard to say: 'Luke-warm! We'll be in hot water soon, though.' This cheap witticism fastened in him the whole odium of the affair, for people thought that he had given the word to fire Cremona, which was in fact already burning.

33. Forty thousand armed men forced their way into the city, with batmen and sutlers in greater numbers and even more viciously addicted to lust and violence. Neither rank nor years saved the victims from an indiscriminate orgy in which rape alternated with murder and murder with rape. Greybeards and frail old women, who had no value as loot, were dragged off to raise a laugh. But any full-grown girl or good-looking lad who crossed their path was pulled this way and that in a violent tug-of-war between the would-be captors, and finally drove them to destroy each other. A single looter trailing a hoard of money or temple-offerings of massive gold was often cut to pieces by others who were stronger. Some few turned up their noses at the obvious finds, and inflicted flogging and torture on the owners in order to rummage after hidden valuables and dig for buried treasure. In their hands they held firebrands, which, once they had got their spoil away, they wantonly flung into the empty houses and rifled temples. It is not surprising that, in an army of varied tongues and conventions, including Romans, allies and foreigners,[1] there was a diversity of wild desires, differing conceptions of what was lawful, and nothing barred. Cremona lasted them four days. While all its buildings, sacred and secular, collapsed in flames, only the temple of Mefitis[2] outside the walls remained standing, defended by its position or the power of the divinity.

34. This, then, was the fate of Cremona, 286 years after its foundation. It had been planted in the consulship of Tiberius Sempronius and Publius Cornelius at the time when Hannibal was menacing Italy,[3] to serve as a bulwark against the Gauls living north of the Po or any other violent irruption by way of the Alps. As it turned out, the

1. See p. 103 and n. 1.
2. A goddess of pestilential vapours placated in many parts of Italy. The site of this temple is unknown.
3. 218 B.C.

abundance of settlers, the convenient presence of rivers,[1] and the fertility of its territory, as well as kinship and intermarriage with the local tribes, conspired to favour the growth and prosperity of a city immune from foreign invasion and unlucky only in civil wars.

Antonius, thoroughly ashamed of the dreadful deed and worried by the mounting scandal which it caused, issued a proclamation that no one should keep prisoner a citizen of Cremona. Indeed, the troops had already found their booty useless to them owing to a concerted refusal throughout Italy to buy slaves of this sort, and they began to murder them. When this leaked out, the unfortunate men were stealthily ransomed by those who were their relatives by blood or marriage. In due course, the surviving inhabitants returned to Cremona. The squares and temples were restored thanks to the generosity of other Italian towns; and Vespasian gave the work his blessing.[2]

35. However, it was impossible to encamp for long by the ruins of the dead city owing to the infected ground. They moved out three miles, and formed up the frightened and straggling Vitellians in their respective units. To prevent any suspicious behaviour on the part of the defeated legions while the civil war was still raging, they were dispersed throughout the Balkans. Next, messengers were sent with the news to Britain and the Spanish provinces. Julius Calenus, a tribune, was dispatched to Gaul, and Alpinius Montanus, a cohort commander, to Germany. The intention was to impress public opinion, for the latter came from Trier, Calenus was an Aeduan, and both had been supporters of Vitellius. At the same time, the Alpine passes were manned in view of the threat that Germany would prepare to come to the rescue of the defeated emperor.

1. See p. 104 and n. 3.
2. He was accused of meanness: see p. 131.

# A World Convulsed

36. A few days after Caecina's departure,[1] Vitellius induced Fabius Valens to leave for the front. This done, he concealed his anxieties behind a smoke-screen of dissipation, neither making preparations for war, nor stiffening morale among the troops by appeals and training, nor keeping himself in the public eye. Hidden in the shady arbours of his villa he had consigned past, present and future to universal oblivion – like those miserable animals that are content to lie and doze so long as food is put in front of them. And there, among the groves of Aricia, in the midst of sloth and languor, the treachery of Lucilius Bassus and the defection of the Ravenna fleet came on him as a sudden shock. Soon after, reports arrived of Caecina, good news and bad together, telling both of his desertion and of his arrest by the army. In a character so feeble, satisfaction outweighed concern. Exultantly he rode back to the capital, and before a crowded audience made a speech fulsomely praising the devotion of his troops. Publilius Sabinus, the pretorian prefect, was put under arrest by the emperor in view of his friendship with Caecina, Alfenus Varus taking his place.

37. Vitellius then addressed the senate in a speech carefully designed to impress, and was extolled by its members with studied flattery. A move for a severe resolution on Caecina came from Lucius Vitellius. It was taken up by the rest, who affected to be scandalized by the thought that the state had been betrayed by its consul, the emperor by his general, and a friend by one upon whom he had lavished wealth and honour. They were pretending to protest on behalf of Vitellius, but really voiced their own annoyance. Not a single speaker reproached the Flavian leaders. Criticizing the armies for their error and lack of vision, they used elaborate circumlocution in their anxiety to avoid mentioning Vespasian. One senator actually wheedled himself into the one-day consulship left vacant by Caecina's disgrace.

1. From Rome: p. 141.

This earned both donor and recipient profound contempt. On 31 October, Rosius Regulus entered – and resigned – office. Constitutional experts noted that never before had a suffect magistrate[1] been appointed without the passing of a formal act of abrogation. The shortness of the term was not in itself a novelty, as Caninius Rebilus had been consul for one day[2] in the dictatorship of Julius Caesar when rewards for services in the civil war were being hurriedly distributed.

38. It was at this period that Junius Blaesus died. The news caused a great stir. The account which has come down to us is the following. Vitellius was lying seriously ill in the Servilian Park[3] when he noticed that a tall mansion in the neighbourhood was ablaze throughout the night with many lights. On inquiring the reason, he was told that Caecina Tuscus was holding a large dinner-party, and that the guest of honour was Junius Blaesus. The picture was filled in with an exaggerated account of lavish display and an atmosphere of licence. Critics readily came forward to denounce Tuscus himself and others for spending their days in merriment during their emperor's illness. These charges were levelled with particular venom at Blaesus. There are always courtiers who keep an eye open for an emperor's displeasure. When these were satisfied that Vitellius was offended and that Blaesus could be disgraced, the role of informer was given to Lucius Vitellius. He was Blaesus' enemy, bitterly jealous of him because his own scandalous life contrasted infavourably with the other's excellent reputation. Lucius suddenly flung open the door of the emperor's room and knelt down before him, clasping Vitellius' young son in his arms. He was asked what the trouble was. He had come with appeals and tears, he replied, not because of his own personal fears and private anxieties, but from concern for the good of his brother and his brother's children. There was no point in being afraid of Vespasian: from him they were shielded by the many legions of the garrison of Germany, by many loyal and stout-hearted provinces, and by vast areas of land and sea. It was in the capital and his own intimate circle that the emperor must guard against a traitor who boasted that he was descended from the Junii and Antonii, and who by affability and free spending sought to gain publicity among the troops as member

1. A 'magistrate' elected in place of another who retires before the expiry of the full (annual) term of office.

2. His consulship was a by-word, for he held office from 12.45 p.m. until midnight on 31 December 45 B.C.          3. In southern Rome.

of a ruling family. He was the centre of public attention, while Vitellius, heedless of friends and enemies alike, nursed a rival who contemplated the emperor's sufferings from the convenient distance of a banqueting table. Such untimely festivity should be repaid by a night of misery and death, in which he would learn to his cost that Vitellius was still alive and still emperor, and in the event of death had a son to succeed him.

39. His hearer hesitated between murder and fear. If he postponed Blaesus' execution, he might incur speedy ruin himself; while to order it openly would cause a terrible scandal. Finally he decided to use poison. What made people believe him guilty was the noticeable pleasure he took in visiting Blaesus. Indeed, Vitellius was heard to make a most inhuman remark: he boasted in so many words that 'he had feasted his eyes on the spectacle of his enemy's death.'

Blaesus possessed not only distinction of birth and the manners of a gentleman, but also unshakable loyalty. Even before the Vitellian position became precarious, he was approached by Caecina and other prominent members of the party who were already turning against the emperor; but he persisted in refusing to join any plot. Despite a good life, a dislike for trouble-making and a lack of all ambition for sudden preferment to any post, let alone the principate, he had failed to avoid the danger of being thought worthy of it.

40. Meanwhile Fabius Valens, with a long and luxurious train of harlots and eunuchs, was advancing at a pace too sluggish for a campaign when he was informed that the Ravenna fleet had been betrayed to the enemy by Lucilius Bassus. The news had travelled posthaste, and if Valens, who had just started on his journey, had hurried forward, he could have caught Caecina in time while the latter was still wavering, or else have overtaken the legions before the decisive battle. Some of his advisers did in fact suggest that he should take his trustiest men by secret tracks across the mountains,[1] avoid Ravenna, and make straight for Hostilia or Cremona. Others again thought it best to summon the pretorians from Rome and force a way through in strength. Valens himself merely waited, which was useless, and frittered away in deliberation days that called for action. Then, rejecting both proposals, he hit upon the worst possible solution in a crisis, that of compromise, and so failed to achieve the necessary degree either of boldness or of caution. 41. He wrote to Vitellius

1. The Apennines in the Florence–Bologna area.

to ask for help, and received three cohorts[1] together with a cavalry regiment from Britain. This was a contingent too large to escape detection and too small to cut its way through.

Even at such a critical moment, ugly stories still circulated about Valens. Men were convinced that he was grasping at forbidden pleasures while there was still time, and dishonouring the homes of his hosts by intrigues with their wives and daughters. He certainly had the power of compulsion, money and the urge of a doomed man to have a final fling.

It was only when the infantry and cavalry arrived that the wrongness of his strategy became obvious. He could not move straight through enemy territory with such a small force, however trusty. In fact, it turned out that the newcomers were of questionable loyalty. However, a sense of shame and the respect inspired by the presence of their commander restrained them for the time being – though these were no very lasting ties for men who were afraid of danger and cared nothing for dishonour. This was what Valens feared, and why he chose to be accompanied by only a few companions who were steadfast amid disaster. The cohorts he sent on to Ariminum, and told the cavalry regiment to watch the rear, while he himself with his small party left the main road and made for Umbria and then Etruria. In Etruria he heard the result of the battle of Cremona, and decided on a plan of action which showed some spirit and would have had dreadful consequences if it had been successful. This was to get hold of some shipping, land somewhere or other in the province of Narbonese Gaul, and incite the Gallic provinces, the armies and the German tribes to renew hostilities.

42. When Valens had left them, his demoralized forces garrisoned Ariminum, but Cornelius Fuscus moved up troops, dispatched a fast naval force along the adjacent coast, and cut the Vitellians off by land and sea. The victors now proceeded to occupy the Umbrian plain and the Adriatic seaboard of Picenum, so that Italy as a whole was divided between Vespasian and Vitellius by the Apennines. Fabius Valens set sail from Portus Pisanus, but was compelled by sluggish seas or contrary wind to put in at Portus Herculis Monoeci. Nearby were the headquarters of a staunch Vitellian, the governor of the Maritime Alps, Marius Maturus. Despite the hostility of the whole

1. Auxiliary cohorts, not pretorian, despite the reference to the latter in ch. 40.

area around him, this man had not yet forgotten his oath of allegiance. He gave Valens a courteous welcome, but his advice deterred his guest from the rash step of entering Narbonese Gaul. What is more, the loyalty of Valens' followers was now sapped by fear. The prospect was indeed black.    43. So far as the neighbouring communities were concerned, the imperial agent[1] Valerius Paulinus, an energetic soldier, had made them swear obedience to Vespasian, whose friend he had been even before the latter's rise to power, and after recruiting all those who had been discharged from the Pretorian Guard by Vitellius and were only too ready to flock to the colours, he now held in force the town and naval base of Forum Julii. Paulinus' lead was readily followed because this was his native town, and he was looked up to by the pretorians whom he had once commanded as tribune. The civilians, too, were well-disposed towards a fellow-townsman, and hoped that he would be in a position to pull strings for them in the future. They thus supported the cause with enthusiasm. All this was a formidable show of strength, and rumour magnified it. As its impact upon the wavering minds of the Vitellians increased, Fabius Valens, accompanied by four bodyguards, three friends and the same number of centurions, returned to the ships. Maturus and the rest were content to stay behind and take the oath to Vespasian. As for Valens, the sea seemed less dangerous than the coast and its towns, but his future plans were undecided, and it was easier for him to know what to avoid than whom to trust. In the event, bad weather forced him to land in the Stoechades Islands which belonged to Marseilles, and there a flotilla of fast galleys sent by Paulinus effected his arrest.

44. With the capture of Valens the whole Roman world rallied to the winning side. The movement began in Spain with the First (Support) Legion, which remembered Otho and disliked Vitellius: its lead was followed by the Tenth and Sixth. Nor were the Gallic provinces reluctant. Britain joined in as well. Here the balance of opinion was already in favour of Vespasian, who had been posted to the country by Claudius to command the Second Legion and had fought there with distinction.[2] But there was some restlessness among the other legions in Britain, for they contained a number of centurions and N.C.O.s who owed their promotion to Vitellius and were doubtful about accepting a new emperor in exchange for one they knew.

45. These differences, and the spate of rumours about civil war,

1. In Narbonese Gaul.    2. In south and south-west England.

emboldened the Britons to pluck up their courage and follow a man called Venutius, who, quite apart from a violent character and a hatred of all things Roman, was goaded to fury by a personal feud with Queen Cartimandua. She had been for some time ruler of the Brigantes, and was a princess of high birth and hence influence. This she had increased thanks to her treacherous capture of King Caratacus, an action by which she was generally thought to have set the seal upon Claudius' triumph.[1] Hence came wealth and the self-indulgence of prosperity. She tired of Venutius, who was her consort, and gave her hand and kingdom to his armour-bearer, one Vellocatus. This scandal immediately shook the royal house to its foundations. The discarded husband could rely on the support of the Brigantian people, the lover upon the infatuation of the queen and her ruthless cruelty. So Venutius summoned help from outside, and a simultaneous revolt on the part of the Brigantes themselves reduced Cartimandua to a position of acute danger, in which she appealed for Roman assistance. In the event, our cohorts and cavalry regiments did succeed, at the cost of desperate fighting, in rescuing the queen from a tight corner. Venutius inherited the throne, and we the fighting.

46. It was at this same time that there was trouble in Germany, and the slackness of our commanders, the mutiny of our legions, foreign invasion and allied treachery nearly caused the downfall of Rome. This war, with its various causes and incidents – for it was a long business – I shall deal with in due course.[2] There was also a movement among the Dacians. Never a trustworthy people, they had now nothing to fear as the Roman army had been withdrawn from Moesia. They studied the initial phases of the civil war but took no action for the moment. When, however, they heard that fighting had flared up in Italy and that the whole world was at loggerheads, they stormed the winter-quarters of the cohorts and cavalry, and proceeded to make themselves masters of both banks of the Danube. They were on the point of moving in upon the legionary bases when Mucianus barred their way with the Sixth Legion.[3] He had not yet heard of the victory at Cremona and was anxious to forestall the overwhelming and double threat which would have been presented by a Dacian and

1. Caratacus was captured in A.D. 51; but Claudius had already celebrated a triumph over Britain eight years earlier, shortly after the invasion began.
2. In Book Four.
3. On his journey from Byzantium to Italy: see p. 131.

German invasion at two different points. As so often, it was the luck of Rome that saved the day by bringing Mucianus and the forces of the East upon the scene, and because we meantime settled the issue at Cremona. Fonteius Agrippa, who had governed Asia as a proconsul for the normal period of one year, was appointed to administer Moesia, and was given additional forces from the army of Vitellius. To distribute this army among the provinces and to tie it down in a foreign war was an act at once of statesmanship and peace.

47. Nor did the other peoples of the Empire keep quiet. In Pontus there had been a sudden uprising led by a foreign slave and one-time commander of the royal fleet called Anicetus. He was a freedman of Polemo,[1] and having once wielded great influence could not stomach the changed circumstances caused by the conversion of the kingdom into a Roman province. So, in the name of Vitellius, he called to arms the tribes which border on the land of Pontus, luring on the destitute to hope for plunder. At the head of a considerable force, he swooped down on Trapezus, an ancient and famous city founded by the Greeks at the farthest point on the coast of Pontus. Here they cut to pieces a cohort which had once formed part of the royal army but had later been given Roman citizenship as well as Roman standards and equipment, while retaining the idle and licentious habits of the Greeks. Fresh fuel was added to the blaze by a rebel fleet, sailing where it pleased over a Black Sea which, thanks to Mucianus' action in withdrawing the best of the galleys and all the crews to Byzantium, had been left unpoliced. Even the uncivilized natives insolently roved the seas in hastily constructed boats. These they call 'arks': they are narrow above the waterline, but broad in the beam,[2] and neither bronze nor iron rivets are used in their construction. When the sea is choppy, they increase the freeboard by adding planks successively according to the height of the waves, until they are wholly enclosed by a sort of roof. In this fashion, they ride the waves. Identical in shape fore and aft the boats can be rowed in both directions since it does not matter whether they are beached stern or bow first: either way is equally safe.

48. This state of affairs alerted Vespasian. He put together a special force drawn from his legions and placed it under the command of an

1. Polemo II was the last king of independent Pontus (A.D. 38–63), and later ruler of parts of Cilicia: see p. 82, n. 1.
2. They had walls sloping inwards above water-level, but a broad beam at or beneath it.

experienced soldier called Virdius Geminus. As the undisciplined hordes were scouring the countryside in an eager search for loot, Virdius surprised them, and forced them to take to their ships. Then, hurriedly building galleys, he came up with Anicetus at the mouth of the River Chobus, where the fugitive was safe under the protection of the king of the Sedochezi, whom he had induced to become his ally by a money bribe and other gifts. It is true that at first the king employed threats and armed force to save his guest. But when the choice between the wages of a traitor and outright war was dangled before his eyes, loyalty melted away in typical native fashion. He struck a bargain for the death of Anicetus, and surrendered the refugees. That was the end of this police action.

Everywhere, the tide now seemed to be turning in Vespasian's favour beyond his wildest dreams. He was congratulating himself on the success of the Pontus expedition when the news of the Battle of Cremona reached him in Egypt.[1] He hurried all the faster to Alexandria, for, now that Vitellius' army was shattered, his intention was to follow this up by a blockade of the capital, which depended on its imports. To this end he was already making preparations for a naval and land invasion of the province of Africa that lies farther along the same coast. By withholding the grain supplies, he aimed at sowing famine and dissension among his enemies.[2]

1. In November 69.
2. The province of Africa supplied two-thirds of Italy's corn imports: cf. p. 149, n. 1.

# The March on Rome

49. The imperial power was thus passing into new hands amid world-wide convulsions. Meanwhile, the behaviour of Antonius Primus degenerated sharply after Cremona. He felt he had broken the back of the war and the rest would be easy – or perhaps, in a character like his, it needed success to reveal the greed, pride and other vices that lurked beneath the surface. He pranced through Italy as if it were a conquered country, ingratiated himself with the legions as if they were his own, and in everything he did and said tried to build up a position of strength and influence. To give the troops a taste for licence, he accorded the legions the right of appointing centurions to replace those who had been killed. The posts were filled by a show of hands, and the most unruly candidates elected. Thus, so far from the troops being at the disposal of their officers, the latter were hurried along by the violence of their men. These were the methods of an agitator who sought to ruin discipline. But it was not long before Antonius adapted them to the task of filling his own pockets. He had no fear of the approaching Mucianus, though this was a more dangerous mistake than it would have been to slight Vespasian.

50. However, as winter approached and the Po valley became water-logged, a light expeditionary force set off. At Verona were left the H.Q.s and main parties of the victorious legions, the wounded or those too old for action, and a number of fit soldiers as well. It was thought that the cohorts, cavalry and some picked legionaries would be enough to cope with the situation, as the war was by this time practically won. The Eleventh Legion[1] had now joined in. It had hesitated at first, and then, when things turned out well, became uneasy because of its failure to cooperate. It was accompanied by a recent levy of 6,000 Dalmatian recruits. This whole force was led by the

1. From Burnum (on River Krka) in Dalmatia.

governor, Pompeius Silvanus, though decisions were actually made by Annius Bassus, the legionary commander. Silvanus, too lazy to be a fighter, frittered away the time for action in talk, but Bassus knew how to manage him by a show of deference, and whenever there was work to be done, he was always on the spot and ready to act with quiet efficiency. These units were reinforced by the pick of the naval personnel at Ravenna, who were anxious to transfer to service in the legions.[1] Their places were taken by the Dalmatians.

The army and its leaders halted at Fanum Fortunae. They were hesitant about strategy, for they had heard that the pretorian cohorts had moved out from the capital, and imagined that the passes of the Apennines were by this time manned. What also alarmed the leaders was the lack of supplies in a region devastated by war, and the mutinous demand of the troops for a bounty called 'nail-money'.[2] The commanders had not made provision for pay or food, either. Haste and greed neutralized their efforts, for the men stole what they could have had as a gift.    51. I find that some widely-read historians vouch for the truth of the following story. The victors displayed such disregard for right and wrong that a trooper claimed that he had killed his brother in the recent battle, and demanded a reward from his leaders. Common morality deterred them from honouring the murder, and the very nature of civil war from punishing it. In the end, it seems, they decided to put the man off by saying that the reward he deserved was too great to be paid on the spot. And there the story ends. However, according to Sisenna, an equally ghastly act had occurred in a previous civil war, for in the battle against Cinna on the Janiculum,[3] a soldier of Pompeius Strabo killed his brother, and then, when he realized what he had done, committed suicide. Thus in earlier generations merit evoked keener appreciation, and wicked actions keener remorse. Anyhow, it will not be inappropriate for me to cite these and similar anecdotes from ancient history when the context calls for lessons in right conduct or consolation for evil.

1. Because legionary pay and terms of service were better than those enjoyed by the fleet.

2. Roman soldiers were made to pay for their kit by stoppages against pay, and excessive marching wore out their hob-nailed boots more quickly.

3. In 87 B.C., when the Marian army under Cinna captured Rome, which was defended by Pompeius Strabo in the city and by Octavius on the right bank (including the Janiculan Hill). The historian Cornelius Sisenna (d. 67 B.C.) dealt with the period 91–78 B.C., but survives only in fragments.

52. Antonius and the other Flavian leaders decided that the cavalry should be sent forward and a general reconnaissance of Umbria made in the hope of finding some way of access to the summit of the Apennines by a fairly gentle gradient. A summons was also to be sent to the H.Q.s and main parties of the legions and whatever other troops were at Verona, and the Po and the Adriatic were to be crowded with supply ships.

Certain senior officers tried to drag their feet, feeling that Antonius was now too powerful, and that it would be safer to pin their hopes on Mucianus. The latter was in fact worried at such a rapid advance, and was convinced that he would be debarred from the campaign and the distinctions it offered unless he were personally present at the entry into Rome. So the tone of his dispatches to Primus and Varus was non-committal, sometimes stressing the need for exploiting any opening, sometimes enumerating the advantages of delay. His language was carefully chosen so that in the light of events he could either disclaim responsibility for failure or take credit for success. A certain Plotius Grypus had recently been given senatorial status by Vespasian, and placed in command of a legion.[1] He, and other reliable adherents, were given clearer hints by Mucianus, and all of them sent back unfavourable reports on the excessive haste of Primus and Varus, which was just what their correspondent wanted. By forwarding these accounts to Vespasian, Mucianus soon made sure that Antonius' intentions and achievements were not valued as highly as he had hoped.

53. Antonius resented this, and in his turn blamed Mucianus, whose accusations, he said, had robbed his own desperate endeavours of their value. In general conversation, too, he expressed himself with the freedom of a man who was not disposed to mince his words or submit to control. The dispatches he sent to Vespasian had too arrogant a tone for an emperor's hearing and contained veiled attacks on Mucianus. He pointed out that it was he, Antonius, who had got the legions of Pannonia to fight, who had spurred the Moesian commanders to action, and by steady persistence forced the Alps, seized Italy, and headed off enemy reinforcements coming from Germany and Raetia. He had routed Vitellius' legions while they were disunited and separated, first by a whirlwind cavalry charge, and then by a day

1. Probably the Seventh (Claudian), in place of its temporary commander, Vipstanus Messalla.

and a night of hard infantry fighting. This was no mean achievement, and the credit belonged to him. The sack of Cremona must be regarded as a war liability, and civil dissensions in the past had involved the country in greater loss and in the destruction not of one city but of several. His method of serving his emperor was not to send messages and write despatches, but to act and fight. What he had done did not eclipse the fame of those who, in the meantime, had established order elsewhere. These officers had been concerned for the tranquillity of Moesia, he for the rescue and relief of Italy. It was thanks to his own promptings that the various provinces of Gaul and Spain, constituting one of the most powerful areas in the world, had gone over to Vespasian. But all these endeavours would have been reduced to a hollow mockery if the rewards for facing danger were to go only to those who had not faced it.

These complaints came to the ears of Mucianus, and they caused a serious rift between the two, in which Antonius showed what he felt with greater frankness, whereas Mucianus hugged his grievances with wily, and hence more implacable, cunning.

54. As for Vitellius, after the disaster to his cause at Cremona, he foolishly tried to hush up the news of defeat. In so doing, he was postponing the remedy for the disease rather than the disease itself. The fact is that he still had some prospects and resources if only he had confessed the truth and taken advice. But by pretending that all was well, which was the exact opposite of the facts, he merely aggravated his condition by falsehood. In the emperor's presence, there was an uncanny conspiracy of silence about the war, while throughout the country rumour was prohibited, and therefore multiplied. Men who would have told the truth, if this had been permitted, immediately set about circulating more sensational accounts to spite the censorship. The Flavian commanders, too, did their bit to increase gossip. Their method was to take captured Vitellian spies on conducted tours of the victorious army to give them an insight into its strength, and then send them back to Rome. Vitellius interrogated all these men in secret, and had them put to death. A remarkable example of inflexible courage is provided by the story of the centurion Julius Agrestis. Despite many conferences with Vitellius, he had failed to get him to act like a man. But at last the emperor was prevailed upon to allow Agrestis to be sent in person to reconnoitre the enemy strength and see what had happened at Cremona. The centurion made

no attempt to hide his commission from Antonius, but revealed the emperor's instructions and his own attitude, and asked permission to have a look at everything. Officers were detailed to show him the site of the battle, the ruins of Cremona, and the legions who had capitulated. Agrestis then made his way back to Vitellius. When the emperor refused to admit the truth of his story and actually alleged that he had been bribed, the centurion replied: 'Well, since you need overwhelming proof and have no further use for me whether alive or dead, I will supply you with evidence you must believe.' With these words, he left the emperor, and confirmed the truth of his report by committing suicide. Some authorities have stated that he was put to death on the orders of Vitellius, but all tell the same story of his fidelity and unwavering resolution.

55. Vitellius was like a sleeper awakened. He ordered Julius Priscus and Alfenus Varus to hold the Apennines with fourteen praetorian cohorts and all the available cavalry units. In their wake followed the legion[1] recruited from the sailors of the fleet. Under different leadership, a force of so many thousands – picked men and picked horses – was quite strong enough to launch an offensive, to say nothing of defending Rome. The remaining cohorts were allotted to the emperor's brother Lucius for the protection of the capital. Vitellius himself continued to lead his usual life of dissipation, and his very lack of confidence led to hasty decisions. He held hurried elections, appointing consuls in advance for a number of years. He lavished treaty status on the provincials, and Latin rights on foreigners.[2] Some were excused payment of tribute, others assisted by various exemptions. In short, with total unconcern for the future, he hacked the empire to pieces. But the lower classes gaped open-mouthed at such lavish bounty. Fools purchased his favours with money, but wise men regarded as null and void concessions which could neither be offered nor accepted without ruining the country. Finally, he yielded to the demand of the army, which had by now taken up its position at Mevania. Assembling a great retinue of senators, many of whom wanted to curry favour, while still more were induced by fear, he

1. Perhaps the Second (Support) Legion, which served in Britain, A.D. 71–86.
2. By 'provincials' Tacitus seems to mean provincial communities whose status was to be raised by the granting of a treaty defining their rights and obligations. In a community enjoying 'Latin rights' Roman citizenship could be gained by those elected to local office: they were then no longer 'foreigners'.

travelled with them to army headquarters, where his indecision put him at the mercy of unreliable advisers.

56. During a speech of his to the assembled troops, an incident occurred which was spoken of as a prodigy: a flock of birds of ill omen[1] flew overhead in such numbers that they seemed like a dark cloud blotting out the daylight. Then, too, there was the sinister escape from the altar of an ox that scattered the implements of sacrifice and was felled some distance away in a manner contrary to the ritual prescribed for the killing of victims. But the chief portent was Vitellius himself. He knew nothing about active service, and had formed no plans for the future. He was perpetually asking others about the proper march-order, the arrangement for reconnaissance, and the extent to which a military decision should be forced or postponed. Whenever a dispatch arrived, his very looks and movements betrayed panic; and, to crown all, he drank. Finally, bored with camp life, and learning of the defection of the fleet at Misenum, he returned to Rome, frightened by each new blow he suffered but blind to the supreme danger. It was perfectly open to him to cross the Apennines with his army intact and fall upon an enemy exhausted by wintry conditions and lack of supplies. But by dissipating his resources, he consigned to slaughter and captivity a devoted army that was ready to face any odds. His most experienced centurions disagreed with him, and would have told the truth if consulted. But they were refused access to the emperor by his courtiers, and his own character was such that he listened to sound advice with an ill humour and lent a ready ear only to what was agreeable – and fatal.

57. The influence which can be exerted in times of civil strife by a single, unscrupulous individual is illustrated by the story of the Misenum fleet. A centurion who had been cashiered by Galba, one Claudius Faventinus, induced the sailors to rebel. He did this by dangling before their eyes the offer of a reward for treachery contained in a forged letter purporting to come from Vespasian. The fleet was commanded by Claudius Apollinaris, an officer who was neither steadfast in loyalty nor enterprising as a rebel. An ex-praetor, too, Apinius Tiro, happened to be at Minturnae at the time, and put himself at the head of the renegades. Incited by these two, the Italian communities in the area contributed their local rivalries to the confusion of civil war. Of these, Puteoli was particularly attached to

1. Vultures (on this occasion).

Vespasian, while Capua remained faithful to Vitellius. The latter now chose Claudius Julianus, who had recently commanded the fleet at Misenum without much insistence on discipline, for the task of smoothing the sailors' ruffled feelings, and for this purpose gave him one urban cohort and some gladiators. When the two forces encamped within striking distance of each other, Julianus lost little time in going over to Vespasian. The rebels thereupon occupied Tarracina, a town whose walls and situation protected it more effectually than the temper of its garrison.

58. On hearing of this, Vitellius left part of his forces at Narnia with the pretorian prefects, and sent off his brother Lucius with six cohorts and 500 cavalry to deal with the offensive which was being mounted throughout Campania. The emperor himself was depressed, but found some encouragement in the enthusiasm of his troops and the clamour of the populace for arms, giving the specious name of 'army' and 'legions' to a cowardly mob unlikely to translate its boasts into action. At the instance of his freedmen – for at Vitellius' court loyalty stood in inverse proportion to rank – he caused the people to be mustered by wards, and had volunteers sworn in. The response was overwhelming, so he shared the responsibility for the levy between the two consuls. He imposed upon the senators specific contributions of slaves and money. The equestrian order offered its services and wealth, and freedmen too actually asked to shoulder the same burden. Thus a pretended devotion born of fear had turned into real attachment, and it was not so much the man Vitellius as the disastrous position of the emperor that aroused men's pity. Besides, Vitellius did his best to angle for sympathy by looks, words and tears, for he was lavish with his promises and displayed the emotional extravagances of panic. Indeed, he consented to be addressed as 'Caesar', a title which he had previously refused. Now the magic of the name appealed to his superstition, and in moments of fear the voice of wisdom and the gossip of the mob are listened to with equal alacrity. But mere emotional impulses, however strong originally, always grow weaker in the long run. So senators and knights gradually melted away, at first reluctantly and in his absence, later without respect or distinction. In the end, Vitellius grew ashamed of his fruitless endeavours and ceased to demand what no one offered.

59. Though Italy had been shocked by the occupation of Mevania and by the impression that fighting was starting all over again, yet the

panic-stricken departure of Vitellius caused a clear swing of public opinion in favour of the Flavian cause. The Samnites, Paeligni and Marsi, furious that Campania had stolen a march upon them, were naturally eager to emphasize their new-found loyalty by performing every kind of military service. But the severe winter gave the army a rough time throughout the passage of the Apennines, and the difficulty it experienced in forcing a way through the snow, even when unmolested, showed the extent of the danger which it would have had to face but for Vitellius' retreat. This was one more example of the good fortune that helped the Flavian leaders no less often than cool calculation. In the mountains they were met by Petilius Cerialis,[1] who had eluded the Vitellian guards by disguising himself as a peasant and making use of his personal knowledge of the area. Cerialis was closely related to Vespasian, and a distinguished soldier in his own right. For these reasons he was co-opted as one of the leaders. According to many accounts, Flavius Sabinus and Domitian had a chance to escape too, and by means of various subterfuges messengers from Antonius repeatedly found their way in with information of a rendezvous where an escort would be waiting. Sabinus pleaded that he was a sick man and not fit enough to undertake such an exhausting and desperate venture. Domitian had the will to act, but Vitellius had put him in custody and, though his gaolers promised to join him in the escape, it was feared that this was a trap. What is more, Vitellius himself avoided any ill-treatment of Domitian out of consideration for his own relatives.

60. On reaching Carsulae, the Flavian leaders took a few days' rest, and waited for the main parties of the legions to catch up. The site of the camp appealed to them, too, for it commanded a wide and distant prospect,[2] and the presence of some very prosperous towns in the rear assured a flow of supplies. Furthermore, there was a chance of conversations with the Vitellians ten miles away which might lead to their surrender. This was not much to the taste of the Flavian rank-and-file, who preferred to win a victory rather than negotiate a peace. They were not prepared to wait even for their own legions, feeling that these would share the prize rather than the peril. Antonius had his men paraded, and pointed out that Vitellius still disposed of

1. Commander of the Ninth Legion in Britain in A.D. 61, consul and commander in the Rhineland A.D. 70–1, governor of Britain A.D. 71–4.
2. To north, west and south. The Narnia gap is visible from Carsulae.

considerable forces, which might well prove to be of doubtful loyalty if
they were given time to think things over, but would offer desperate resistance if hope were denied them. The opening moves of a civil war, he
claimed, must be left to chance, but final victory came with planning
and calculation. The fleet at Misenum and the finest part of the coast of
Campania had already fallen away, and nothing was left to Vitellius of
a world-wide empire but the strip of territory between Tarracina and
Narnia. The glory gained by the battle of Cremona was enough, and
more than enough the dishonour earned by Cremona's ruin. Their
dearest wish should be to save Rome, not capture it. Greater rewards
and supreme glory would be theirs if they tried to secure the preservation of the senate and people of Rome without bloodshed.

These and similar arguments succeeded in mollifying their feelings.
61. Soon after, the legions arrived. Then, as the alarming news of
this increase in strength spread, the Vitellian cohorts began to waver.
No one encouraged them to fight, but many urged them to go over
to the Flavians. Their officers competed with one another in surrendering their companies and squadrons to the victor as a free gift that
would earn them his gratitude in the future. Thanks to them, it was
learnt that Interamna, in the flat country nearby, was garrisoned by
a force of 400 cavalry. Varus was instantly sent off with a battle
group. He killed the few who resisted, and the majority threw down
their arms and asked for quarter. A few found their way back to the
Vitellian camp, spreading demoralization everywhere and telling
exaggerated tales of the fighting spirit and numbers of the enemy in
order to excuse the scandal of losing the place they were supposed to
defend. In any case, on the Vitellian side unsoldierly conduct went
unpunished, and the rewards earned by defection killed loyalty. All
that remained was a competition in perfidy. There were constant
desertions, at any rate on the part of tribunes and centurions. The
rank-and-file, on the other hand, stubbornly adhered to Vitellius
until Priscus and Alfenus, by leaving the camp and going back to
him, freed everyone[1] from the need to be ashamed of giving up.
62. It was during this period[2] that Fabius Valens was put to death at
Urvinum, where he had been confined. His head was displayed to the
Vitellian cohorts to prevent their indulging any further hopes, for
they imagined that Valens had got through to the German provinces

1. i.e. every member of the Vitellian forces at Narnia.
2. About 10 December 69.

and was mobilizing existing and newly recruited armies there. The gory sight effectually disillusioned them. The Flavian army for its part triumphantly greeted the death of Valens as marking the end of the war.

Valens was born at Anagnia of an equestrian family. Undisciplined in character but not without talent, he had tried to pass himself off as a man of fashion by behaving extravagantly. During Nero's reign, he appeared on the music-hall stage at the emperor's coming-of-age party, ostensibly at the imperial command, then voluntarily. In this he displayed some skill, but little sense of decorum. As the commander of a legion,[1] he both supported Verginius and blackened his name. It was thanks to him that Fonteius Capito met his end, after Valens had lured his victim into treachery – or perhaps because his allurements had failed. False to Galba, he displayed towards Vitellius a loyalty which contrasted favourably with the perfidy of others.

63. The position was now hopeless everywhere, and the Vitellian troops decided to go over to the enemy. Even this act was not to be performed without a certain dignity. They marched down to the flat land beneath Narnia with banners flying and standards borne aloft. The Flavian army, ready and armed as if for battle, had formed up in closed ranks on either side of the main road. The Vitellians marched forward until they were enveloped by them, and were then addressed by Antonius in a conciliatory tone. Some were told to stand fast at Narnia, others at Interamna. One or two of the victorious legions were also left behind with them to provide a force which would be inoffensive if the ex-enemy troops behaved, yet strong enough to quell any insubordination.

During this period, Primus and Varus made a point of sending Vitellius a stream of messages offering him his life, a competence, and retirement in Campania, if he would lay down his arms and throw himself and his children on the mercy of Vespasian. This was also the general tenor of Mucianus' letters to him. On the whole, Vitellius took the offer seriously, and talked of the number of servants to be allotted him and the best seaside resort to choose. Indeed, his whole attitude was so spineless that, if his courtiers had not remembered that he was an emperor, he would have forgotten it himself.

64. The leading political figures however were engaged in secret conversations with the city prefect. Flavius Sabinus, urging him to

1. The First, at Bonn: see p. 56.                2. e.g. Caecina.

claim his share of victory and renown. They pointed out that he had his own military force in the urban cohorts, and could rely upon the cohorts of the city watch, their own slaves, the luck of the Flavians, and the fact that nothing succeeds like success. He should not allow himself to be elbowed out of the limelight by Antonius and Varus. Vitellius' cohorts were few in number[1] and upset by bad news from every quarter. The populace was easily swayed, and, given a lead, would be quick to transfer its flattery to Vespasian. As for Vitellius, he had been unable to cope with success, and was now inevitably prostrated by disaster. Credit for bringing the war to an end would go to the one who was the first to gain control of Rome. It was incumbent on Sabinus to stake a claim to the imperial power on behalf of his brother, and not less incumbent on Vespasian that others should take second place in his esteem to Sabinus.

65. His response to these remarks was luke-warm, for age had enfeebled him. But some critics made him the target for their secret suspicion that it was envy and jealousy that prompted him to stand in the way of his brother's rise. It is a fact that, when both were subjects, Flavius Sabinus had the greater standing and wealth of the two, as being the elder. There was also a story that he had once demanded a mortgage upon Vespasian's house and land as a condition of saving him from bankruptcy; hence, although they were outwardly friendly, it was feared that there was secret ill-feeling. A more charitable interpretation was that his gentle character made him hate bloodshed and killing, and that this was why he took part in repeated interviews with Vitellius to discuss peace and an armistice upon agreed terms. They often met in private, and finally made a solemn compact, it was said, in the Temple of Apollo. Only two men, Cluvius Rufus and Silius Italicus,[2] were technically witnesses and could vouch for the actual terms of the agreement and the words exchanged between them, but observers at a distance marked their looks – Vitellius hang-dog and degenerate, Sabinus with an expression suggesting sympathy rather than a desire to humiliate.

66. If Vitellius had found it as easy to convert his followers as to give way himself, the army of Vespasian would have entered the capital

1. There were only three pretorian cohorts in Rome at the moment.
2. See p. 25 and n. 3 for Cluvius. Silius Italicus (consul A.D. 68, later governor of Asia) was an orator and poet whose *Punica* is still extant. Both were dead by the time Tacitus was writing the *Histories*.

without bloodshed. As it was, the greater their fidelity to Vitellius, the more vigorously they opposed the notion of peace terms, pointing out the danger and discredit of a pact whose faithful observance depended on the whim of the conqueror. Vespasian, they said, was not so conceited as to tolerate Vitellius in the role of subject, and even the beaten side would not accept such a situation. So there was no safety in the mercy of the conqueror. No doubt Vitellius himself was no longer young,[1] and had had his fill of success and failure. But what name and status would his son Germanicus inherit? For the moment, there was an offer of money, servants and the delightful bays of Campania. But when Vespasian had consolidated his power, neither he nor his court, nor indeed his armies, would regain their peace of mind unless the rival emperor were destroyed. After being taken prisoner and kept for a few days, Fabius Valens had proved too great a burden for them. It was clear therefore that Primus, Varus, and that typical Flavian Mucianus would have no alternative but to kill Vitellius. Caesar had not spared the life of Pompey, nor Augustus that of Antony.[2] What hope was there then that Vespasian would be above such things when he had been the dependant of a Vitellius when that Vitellius was a colleague of Claudius?[3] Indeed, even if he had no thought for his father's position as censor and three times consul, or for the many other high offices filled by his distinguished family, despair at least should arm him for a desperate bid. The troops stood firm, and there was still support for him among the people. In any case, the upshot could be no more dreadful than the fate to which they were hurrying of their own accord. If they were beaten, they must die. If they surrendered, they must die. What alone mattered was whether they were to breathe their last amid mockery and insult, or on the field of honour.

67. But Vitellius had no ears for bold policies. He was overwhelmed by pity for his family and by concern lest, by fighting to the bitter end, he might leave his widow and children to face a victor less disposed to mercy. He also had an elderly mother in poor health, but happily she died a few days before the ruin of her family, having gained nothing by her son's reign but grief and men's esteem.

On 18 December, after learning of the defection of the legion and cohorts which had surrendered at Narnia, he walked down from the

1. See p. 199.        2. Neither of these assertions is strictly true.
3. See p. 54 and n. 1.

palace dressed in black and surrounded by his sorrowing servants. His little son was borne in a tiny litter, as if to his funeral. The greetings of the public were ingratiating and ill-timed. The troops maintained a sullen silence. 68. No one, however heartless and inhuman, could have failed to be deeply touched by the scene. An emperor of Rome, until recently the acknowledged master of the world, was leaving the imperial palace which had been his and passing through the people and city of Rome on the way to abdication. This was something they had never seen, never heard of. Julius Caesar had been the victim of sudden assassination, Gaius of a secret plot. Night and a solitary countryside had hidden the flight of Nero. Piso and Galba met their deaths in circumstances which recalled a field of battle. The abdication of Vitellius, however, took place at a public meeting summoned by himself, amid his own troops, before an audience which included women. He made a short speech suited to the melancholy occasion, saying that he was abdicating in the interests of peace and of his country. He merely urged them to remember him and deal mercifully with his brother, his wife and his innocent children. As he spoke, he held up his son and appealed to them, sometimes as individuals, sometimes collectively, to look after the child. In the end, his tears prevented further speech. Drawing from his belt the dagger which symbolized the power of life and death over his subjects, he offered it to the consul standing by him, Caecilius Simplex. The latter refused to take it, and the nearer members of the crowd protested indignantly. He then moved away with the intention of giving up the insignia of empire in the Temple of Concord and of making for his brother's house. At this, the cries increased. They barred his access to a mere private house, and called upon him to go back to the palace. Every other road was blocked except that which took him along the Sacred Way.[1] Thereupon, not knowing what to do, he returned to the palace.

69. A rumour of Vitellius' intended abdication had already leaked out, and Flavius Sabinus had issued written orders to the tribunes of the cohorts[2] to confine their men to barracks. Assuming, therefore,

1. The Sacred Way led through the Forum and past the Palatine with its palace.

2. Tacitus does not make it clear whether he is alluding only to the urban cohorts, which Sabinus commanded *ex officio*, or to the pretorian, urban and watch cohorts in general, as is historically more probable.

that there had been a complete transfer of sovereignty to Vespasian, the leading senators, a number of knights, and representatives of all the urban troops and of the watch crowded the house of Flavius Sabinus. While they were there, news came of the pro-Vitellian sympathies of the populace, and of the threatening attitude of the cohorts from Germany. But by this time Sabinus had gone too far to allow of retreat, and every one of his supporters was selfishly afraid that the Vitellians might hunt them down while they were separated and consequently weaker. So they urged the reluctant Sabinus to use force. It is typical of a situation of this sort that everybody offered advice, but only a few took the initiative and faced the danger.

Near the Basin of Fundanus, as the armed escort of Sabinus came down the hill, it was confronted by the most active of Vitellius' supporters. The fracas was unexpected, and there was not much fighting, though it told in favour of the Vitellians. Sabinus took the safest course open to him in the emergency: he occupied the Capitoline Hill with a mixed force and a number of senators and knights. (It is not easy to establish their identity without much research, because after Vespasian's victory many people pretended to have served his cause in this way.) There were even some women among the besieged, notably Verulana Gratilla, who followed the call to action and not the claims of her children and relatives.

The cordon which the Vitellian troops threw round the besieged was a loose one and that is why, late at night, Sabinus was able to get his children and his nephew Domitian to join him on the Capitol. He also managed to send a messenger through a carelessly guarded sector in the enemy lines to give the Flavian leaders news of the siege and say how desperate his plight would be unless help were forthcoming. The night was so quiet that Sabinus could have got away without loss, for Vitellius' men, though full of dash in a tight corner, were pretty slack when it came to fatigues and guard-duties, and a sudden wintry rainstorm made seeing and hearing difficult.

70. At first light, before either side could begin hostilities, Sabinus sent a senior centurion, one Cornelius Martialis, to protest to Vitellius against this breach of the agreement. The act of abdication, he complained, appeared to have been no more than a pretence, an empty show, designed to deceive many persons of quality. Why, otherwise, on leaving the rostra, had Vitellius made for his brother's house which stood in the public eye provocatively close to the Forum,

rather than the Aventine and his wife's home? The latter course of action would have been correct for one who was a subject trying to avoid any appearance of still being emperor. Far from doing this, Vitellius had returned to the very stronghold of empire, the palace. From this an armed column had been sent out, a crowded area of the city had been strewn with the bodies of innocent victims, and not even the Capitol was to be spared. After all, he, Sabinus, was merely a civilian, an ordinary senator. While the issue between Vespasian and Vitellius was being settled by the clash of legions, the capture of cities and the surrender of cohorts, and even when the Spanish and German provinces and Britain were already renouncing their allegiance, he, Vespasian's brother, had remained a loyal subject until Vitellius took the initiative and invited him to negotiate. Peace and agreement were essentials for the beaten. On the victors they merely reflected credit. If Vitellius regretted the pact, he had no business to launch an armed attack on Sabinus, whom he had perfidiously tricked, or on the son of Vespasian, who was little more than a child.[1] What was to be gained by murdering one old man and one youth? Vitellius should go and face the legions, and fight it out there. The result of such a battle would determine everything else.

Vitellius was upset by these reproaches and made a short speech of apology, throwing the blame on the troops, whose impetuosity had, he said, overborne his own restraint. He also warned Martialis to leave by a remote corner of the palace to avoid being murdered by the soldiers as the intermediary of a pact that they detested. Vitellius himself was in no position either to command or to prohibit. Emperor no longer, he was merely the cause of the fighting.

71. Martialis had scarcely regained the Capitol when the infuriated troops appeared. They had no leader, and each man followed his own devices. At a rapid pace, the column galloped past the forum and the temples abutting on it, and charged up the slope opposite as far as the outer gate of the Capitoline Hill.[2] At that time, there was a row of porticoes on the right-hand side of the Clivus Capitolinus as you go up. The defenders got on to the roof of the colonnade and assailed the Vitellians with stones and tiles. The enemy for their part were armed

---

1. He was now eighteen years old.
2. The troops came from the pretorian barracks and crossed the north-west end of the forum, passing the Temples of Concord and Saturn. The slope or ramp is the Clivus Capitolinus, some of which still remains.

only with swords, and thought it would take too long to bring up artillery or missiles. So they hurled firebrands at a projecting portico, followed the flames as they spread uphill, and would have forced the charred gates of the Capitol, had not Sabinus uprooted the statues with which past generations had adorned the whole area, and so formed an improvised barricade at the actual entrance. Then the Vitellians attacked at two opposite approaches to the Capitol, next to the Grove of Refuge and where access is gained to the Tarpeian Rock by the Hundred Steps. Both onslaughts were unforeseen, but that delivered by way of Refuge was closer and more violent. Nor could the enemy be prevented from climbing up through the adjoining buildings which, naturally enough in a time of profound peace, had been allowed to attain a considerable height, on a level with the surface of the Capitol. At this point it is a matter of controversy whether it was the attacking force that set fire to the houses or whether – and this is the more common version – it was the besieged who did so in an attempt to dislodge their enemies, who were forcing their way up and had made some progress. From the houses the fire spread to the porticoes adjoining the temple. Then the rafters made of well-seasoned timber caught alight and fed the flames. Thus the Capitoline temple, its doors locked, was burned to the ground undefended and unplundered.

72. This was the most lamentable and appalling disaster in the whole history of the Roman commonwealth. Though no foreign enemy threatened, though we enjoyed the favour of heaven as far as our failings permitted, the sanctuary of Jupiter Best and Greatest solemnly founded by our fathers as a symbol of our imperial destiny – a temple which neither Porsenna on the capitulation of the city nor the Gauls on its capture[1] had been able to desecrate – was now, thanks to the infatuation of our leaders, suffering utter destruction. It had already been burnt down in a previous civil war,[2] but by an individual and mysterious act of arson. But on this occasion it was besieged in the broad light of day, and in the broad light of day fired. One might well ask, for what military reasons? What advantage could compensate Rome for this heavy sacrifice? So long as we fought in the defence

1. Roman tradition did not always admit that Rome had capitulated to the Etruscan Porsenna (in the fifth century B.C.). In 390 or 387 B.C. the Gauls captured the city, but not the Capitol.
2. On 6 July 83 B.C.

of our country and not against it, the Capitoline temple stood four-square.

It owed its origin to a vow made by Tarquin the Elder in the Sabine War, and the scale upon which he had laid its foundations was prompted rather by a hope of coming greatness than by the then modest resources of Rome. The construction of the building was carried further by Servius Tullius, thanks to the support of our allies, and later by Tarquin the Proud with spoils taken from the enemy at the capture of Suessa Pometia. But the distinction of completing the structure was reserved for the free republic. On the expulsion of the kings, it was dedicated by Horatius Pulvillus in his second consulship.[1] Such was its magnificence that the enormous increase in Rome's wealth in later days served rather to adorn than to enlarge it. Four hundred and twenty-five years later, in the consulship of Lucius Scipio and Gaius Norbanus, it was burnt down, to be rebuilt on the same site. Sulla undertook this responsibility after his victory, but he did not live to perform the dedication. This was the only instance in which his proverbial good luck deserted him. The inscription recording the name of Lutatius Catulus[2] survived amid all the great works of the Caesars until the reign of Vitellius. Such, then, was the temple which was now being reduced to ashes.

73. But the fire caused more terror among the besieged than the besiegers. The fact was that in this crisis the Vitellian soldiers showed both cunning and determination, whereas on the opposing side were panicky troops and a leader who was slow to act and seemed mentally paralysed. Incapable of using either tongue or ears, he neither listened to the views of others nor made clear his own. Turning now this way, now that in answer to each enemy shout, he countermanded what he had ordered, and ordered what he had countermanded. Soon the typical signs of collapse appeared: everybody gave instructions and no one carried them out. Finally, throwing down their arms, they started looking around them for an escape route and methods of concealment. The Vitellians forced their way in, creating a confused turmoil of blood, iron and flames. A few of the professional soldiers – the most notable being Cornelius Martialis, Aemilius Pacensis, Casperius Niger and Didius Scaeva – ventured to resist, and were struck down.

1. 507 B.C. Other sources place the dedication two years earlier.
2. Lutatius Catulus (d. 61 or 60 B.C.) was consul in 78 B.C. Placed in charge of the rebuilding of the Capitoline temple, he dedicated this in 69 B.C.

Flavius Sabinus was unarmed and made no attempt to run. He was surrounded together with the consul Quintius Atticus, who had attracted notice by the pretentious way in which he had showered edicts upon the people, glorifying Vespasian and insulting Vitellius. The rest got away by various hazardous means, some dressed as slaves, others hidden by loyal dependants and secreted amid the lumber of their store-rooms. Some few, again, overheard the Vitellian watchword and by actually challenging the enemy or giving the correct answer found concealment in daring.

74. As soon as the defences were breached, Domitian had hidden himself in the house of the caretaker of the temple. Then, prompted by an ingenious freedman, he put on a linen mantle, eluded recognition by joining a throng of priests and lay low near the Velabrum at the home of one of his father's dependants, Cornelius Primus. This is why, during Vespasian's reign, he demolished the caretaker's lodge and put up a small chapel to Jupiter the Preserver and a marble altar carved with a representation of his own adventure. Later, on becoming emperor in his turn, he built a large temple dedicated to Jupiter the Guardian, with an effigy of himself under the protecting arm of the god.

Sabinus and Atticus were heavily chained and taken to Vitellius, who received them with words and looks that showed little hostility, though there was a noisy clamour from those who insisted upon the right to execute them, and demanded a reward for services rendered. The cries, which were first raised among the bystanders, were taken up by the dregs of the city mob, who howled for Sabinus' execution with a mixture of menace and flattery. Vitellius was standing at the top of the palace steps preparing to appeal to their better feelings, but they forced him to give up the attempt. Then Sabinus was stabbed and hacked to death, his head cut off and the decapitated body dragged to the Gemonian Steps.

75. Such was the end of a man of undeniable importance. He had served his country for five-and-thirty years, winning distinction in the civilian and military spheres. His honesty and fair-mindedness are beyond question. He talked too much: but this was the one and only charge levelled against him by gossip during the seven years in which he governed Moesia and his twelve-year tenure of the city prefecture.[1]

1. Sabinus was governor of Moesia A.D. 49–56 and city prefect A.D. 56–60, 62–8 and in 69.

At the end of his life, he seemed to some unenterprising, to many a man of moderation who sought to spare Roman lives. All observers agree that before Vespasian's accession Sabinus was the most distinguished representative of his house. We are told that his murder gave pleasure to Mucianus. A widely held theory was that peace actually gained from the cessation of rivalry between two men, of whom one might well have reflected that he was the emperor's brother, and the other that he was his colleague.

Vitellius resisted a popular demand for the execution of the consul, however. He was mollified by Atticus' attitude, and this seems to have been a way of showing his thanks. For when asked who had set fire to the Capitol, Atticus had accepted responsibility. By this admission (unless it was a lie devised to suit the occasion) he had, so it appeared, shouldered the odium and guilt himself, thus exonerating Vitellius and his followers.

76. By this time, Lucius Vitellius had encamped at Feronia[1] and was threatening Tarracina. The gladiators and seamen were confined to the town, and did not venture to expose themselves in the open outside the walls. As I have already mentioned, the gladiators were commanded by Julianus and the seamen by Apollinaris. These two were so dissolute and idle that they resembled brigands more than officers. There was no question of keeping watch or reinforcing weak points in the walls. Night and day, the pleasant beaches[2] rang with cries of revelry. The men were scattered everywhere on errands of pleasure, and fighting was merely a subject discussed at the banqueting-table. Apinius Tiro had gone off a few days earlier and by his merciless exaction of gifts and money throughout the towns of the area earned the cause more unpopularity than support.

77. Meanwhile, a slave belonging to Vergilius Capito[3] deserted to Lucius Vitellius. Promising to betray the undefended citadel[4] of Tarracina if given men, he took some cohorts in battle order along the top of the hills late at night and planted them on a height immediately overlooking the enemy. From this point, they rushed down to

1. A shrine of the harvest and water goddess Feronia, with a grove and a spring, some three miles from Tarracina in the direction of Rome.
2. But the beaches lay outside the walls.
3. Capito was governor of Egypt in A.D. 47–52. He came from Capua, but seems to have had property at Tarracina.
4. On Monte S. Angelo (225 m.) on the north-east side of the town. The attack took place at first light on 18 December 69.

inflict a massacre rather than fight a battle. The defenders were struck down while still unarmed or feeling for their weapons. Some indeed had only just been roused from sleep, and were dazed by the darkness, panic, trumpet-calls and enemy cries. A few of the gladiators offered resistance and inflicted some losses before they fell. But the rest of them made a rush for the ships. Here the scene was one of general panic and confusion, in which civilians were mixed up with troops and shared their fate at the hands of the Vitellians. Six galleys got away at the first alarm, with the admiral Apollinaris on board. The rest were captured on the beach, or were overloaded by the mad press of fugitives and went to the bottom. Julianus was taken before Lucius Vitellius, and suffered the indignity of flogging before being strangled under the victor's eyes. Some criticized Triaria, Lucius' wife, for wearing a soldier's sword and behaving with arrogance and cruelty amid the grief and suffering of captured Tarracina. Lucius himself sent a laurelled dispatch to his brother announcing his victory and asking whether he wanted him to return immediately or to complete the subjugation of Campania. The delay involved was providential for Vespasian's followers, and indeed for the whole state. For the Vitellian troops, naturally stubborn, were now flushed by success as well, and if they had made for Rome immediately after the battle, there would have been a desperate struggle entailing the destruction of the capital. For Lucius Vitellius, despite his shady reputation, did get things done, and as good men derive their effectiveness from their virtues, so he, like all who are really evil, derived his from his vices.

78. While these events were in progress on Vitellius' side, the army of Vespasian, which had left Narnia, was celebrating the festival of the Saturnalia in idleness at Ocriculum.[1] This fatal delay was caused by the desire to wait for Mucianus. There have been some who have suspected Antonius of wilfully and maliciously wasting time after the receipt of a secret communication from Vitellius. This did in fact offer to reward him with a consulship, the hand of Vitellius' daughter (now of marriageable age) and a rich dowry, provided he would change sides. Others have held that this account of the delay was a fiction invented to please Mucianus. In the view of certain writers, all the generals were agreed that, as the most powerful cohorts had

1. The Flavians left Narnia on 16 December. The festival of the Saturnalia (17 December and some days thereafter) normally meant a holiday for soldiers as well as civilians.

deserted from Vitellius, it was policy to confront Rome with the threat rather than the reality of armed occupation. Vitellius' abdication seemed imminent, now that he was deprived of all his defences. But, according to this view, everything was spoilt by the haste and subsequent weakness of Sabinus, who had rashly resorted to arms and then proved unable to defend the strongly-fortified Capitoline Hill, impregnable even to large armies, against no more than three cohorts. It is difficult to blame any one leader for what was the responsibility of them all. Mucianus persistently held up the victors by his ambiguously-phrased letters, while Antonius' misplaced deference earned him condemnation in the very act of forestalling criticism. As for the other leaders, their belief that the war was over served to mark its final stages with tragedy. Even Petilius Cerialis, who had been sent on with a force of 1,000 cavalry to cut across country through the land of the Sabini and enter the city by the Salarian Way, had failed to make sufficient haste. Finally, the news that the Capitol was beleaguered shocked all the Flavian commanders alike into action.

79. The night[1] was far advanced before Antonius, marching to the rescue down the Flaminian Way, reached Saxa Rubra. It was too late. There he heard the news of the execution of Sabinus, the burning of the Capitol, the panic in Rome – a story of unrelieved disaster. There were also tidings of the arming of the lower classes and slaves in defence of Vitellius. Furthermore, Petilius Cerialis' cavalry engagement had resulted in defeat.[2] Hurling himself recklessly on an enemy he believed beaten, he had run into a mixed Vitellian force of infantry and cavalry. The encounter took place in the suburbs, amid buildings, gardens and winding lanes familiar to the Vitellians but formidable to the enemy, who were strangers to the area. Nor did the Flavian cavalry cooperate well, owing to the presence among them of some who had just surrendered at Narnia and were watching to see which side was the lucky one. The commander of a cavalry regiment, Julius Flavianus, was captured. The rest suffered ignominious rout, though the victors did not keep up the pursuit beyond Fidenae.

80. This success made the people more enthusiastic than ever. The city mob armed. Only a few had proper shields; the majority caught up

1. The night of 19–20 December 69. The distance from Ocriculum to Saxa Rubra is about thirty-seven (Roman) miles; see p. 157 and n. 1.
2. Probably early on the morning of 19 December.

whatever weapons they could find and insisted upon the order to advance. Expressing his thanks, Vitellius told them to throw a screen out in front of the city. Then the senate was summoned and a delegation chosen to meet the Flavian armies and urge a peace settlement, ostensibly in the interests of the country.

The envoys had a mixed reception. Those who had approached Petilius Cerialis faced an extremely hazardous situation, for the troops flatly refused terms. The praetor Arulenus Rusticus was wounded. What made this particularly scandalous was his high personal reputation, quite apart from the violation of his status as an ambassador and praetor. His fellow negotiators were roughly handled, and his senior lictor was killed when he ventured to clear a way through the press. Indeed, if they had not been protected by an escort provided by the commander,[1] in the mad passion of civil strife the diplomatic immunity enjoyed by ambassadors even among foreign nations would have been infringed with fatal consequences outside the very walls of Rome. A calmer attitude marked the reception of the envoys to Antonius, not because the troops were more restrained but because their general had more hold over them.   81. Among these envoys was Musonius Rufus, a knight and a keen student of philosophy and Stoicism. Mixing with the troops in their companies, he now proceeded to lecture armed men on the blessings of peace and the dangers of war. Many of them laughed in his face, more still found him tedious, and a few were even ready to knock him down and stamp on him. But luckily the warnings of the best-behaved men and the threatening attitude of the rest induced him to abandon his untimely moralizing. The Flavians also received a deputation of Vestal Virgins carrying a letter from Vitellius addressed to Antonius. In this, he asked for one day's grace before the final conflict, suggesting that the hold-up would make it easier for them to negotiate a general settlement. The Vestals were sent away with due courtesy, and Vitellius was informed in the reply that with the murder of Sabinus and the firing of the Capitol all exchanges normal in war were at an end. 82. However, Antonius did assemble the legions and try to modify their resentment, urging them to camp for the night by the Milvian Bridge and enter Rome the next day.[2] His motive for waiting was the fear that, once exasperated by resistance, the troops would have no

1. The Flavian commander, Cerialis.
2. 21 December. Rome was captured on 20 December.

regard for the people and senators or even for the temples and shrines of the gods. But the men were suspicious of any postponement, thinking it would prejudice victory. Besides, the glint of banners displayed along the high ground,[1] though in fact only untrained civilians were massed behind them, gave the impression that the enemy had a sizeable army.

The Flavians advanced in three columns. One went down the Flaminian Way on which they had been marshalled, a second advanced along the bank of the Tiber, and a third approached the Colline Gate by the Salarian Way. The militiamen were routed by a cavalry charge, but the Vitellian regulars moved up to face the attack, also in three battle-groups. There was a good deal of fighting outside the city boundaries, the upshot being varied but mostly favourable to the Flavians, who were helped by better leadership, However stiff resistance was encountered by those who turned off towards the eastern areas of the city and the Sallustian Park, using narrow and slippery tracks. The Vitellians, standing on the park walls, hurled back the attackers below them with stones and javelins until the evening. Finally the cavalry forced the Colline Gate and enveloped the position. There was fierce fighting in the Campus Martius, too. Here their good luck and tradition of victory helped the Flavians, while it was despair alone that drove the Vitellians wildly forward, and, though routed, they reformed repeatedly inside the city.

83. Close by the fighting stood the people of Rome like the audience at a show, cheering and clapping this side or that in turns as if this were a mock battle in the arena. Whenever one side gave way, men would hide in shops or take refuge in some great house. They were then dragged out and killed at the instance of the mob, who gained most of the loot, for the soldiers were bent on bloodshed and massacre, and the booty fell to the crowd.

The whole city presented a frightful caricature of its normal self: fighting and casualties at one point, baths and restaurants at another, here the spilling of blood and the litter of dead bodies, close by prostitutes and their like – all the vice associated with a life of idleness and pleasure, all the dreadful deeds typical of a pitiless sack. These were so intimately linked that an observer would have thought Rome in the grip of a simultaneous orgy of violence and dissipation. There

1. Now called the Monti Parioli.

had indeed been times in the past when armies had fought inside the city, twice when Lucius Sulla gained control, and once under Cinna.[1] No less cruelty had been displayed then, but now there was a brutish indifference, and not even a momentary interruption in the pursuit of pleasure. As if this were one more entertainment in the festive season,[2] they gloated over horrors and profited by them, careless which side won and glorying in the calamities of the state.

84. The heaviest fighting took place in the attack on the pretorian barracks, which the most determined Vitellians still held as their last hope. This spurred the victors, and particularly the ex-pretorians, to redouble their efforts. They applied to the task every invention ever designed to storm the most powerful cities – the penthouse and artillery, the mound and firebrands – and repeatedly exclaimed that this operation was the climax of all the toil and danger they had endured in many a battle. Rome, they cried, had been handed back to senate and people, their temples to the gods. But the special glory of the soldier lay in his barracks, for this was his country and this his home. If they were not immediately recovered, the night would have to be spent under arms. On the opposing side, the Vitellians, outnumbered and doomed, set themselves to trouble victory, delay peace, and desecrate homes and altars with blood, grasping at the last consolation granted to the beaten. Many of them lost consciousness and breathed their last while hanging from the towers and crenellations, and when the gates were torn from their sockets, the survivors formed a compact body and charged the victors. They all fell with their wounds in front, facing the enemy – the measure of their anxiety, even at the moment of extinction, to die an honourable death.

As for Vitellius, on the capture of the city he was taken in a chair through the back of the palace to his wife's house.[3] His intention, provided he could lie low during the remaining hours of daylight, was to get away to his cohorts and his brother at Tarracina.[4] Then with characteristic fickleness of purpose, and – true to the psychology

---

1. Sulla: 88 and 82 B.C. (but on the latter occasion the fighting took place outside the city). Cinna: 87 B.C.: see p. 176 and n. 3.

2. See p. 194 and n. 1.

3. See p. 189.

4. The capture of Tarracina must have been known to Vitellius by the evening of 18 December.

of panic – amid all his fears least happy about what he was doing at
the moment, he returned to the palace. The building was forlorn and
deserted, for even the humblest of his menials had slipped away, or
avoided encountering him. The solitude and silence of the place were
frightening. He tried locked doors, and shuddered to find rooms
empty. Exhausted by miserable wanderings and hidden in an ignominious refuge,[1] he was hauled from his hiding-place by a cohort
tribune named Julius Placidus. His hands were tied behind his back.
Presenting a revolting spectacle with his clothes in ribbons, he was led
away amid curses from many and tears from none. The squalor of his
end had robbed it of pity. On the way, one of the men from the army
of Germany met him. It was not clear at the time whether he was
aiming a blow at Vitellius – either in fury or else in order to spare him
further humiliation – or attacking the tribune. In any event, he cut off
the tribune's ear, and was immediately run through.

85. At the point of the sword, Vitellius was at one moment forced to
look up and face the jeering, at the next to fix his eyes not only on
the statues of himself as they were pulled down but above all on the
rostra or the spot where Galba was murdered. Finally, they drove
him to the Gemonian Steps where the body of Flavius Sabinus had
lain. One remark of his, and one only, was overheard which showed
a not wholly degenerate spirit. When a tribune mocked him, he
retorted 'Whatever you may say, I was your emperor.' Thereupon
he fell lifeless beneath a rain of blows. And still the mob reviled him
in death as viciously as they had flattered him while he lived.

86. His father, as I have already recorded, was that Lucius Vitellius
who was censor and three times consul. His home town was Luceria.
At the time of his death, he was fifty-seven years old, having won the
consulship, various priesthoods and a name and place among the
leading figures of Rome, all thanks to his father's eminence and
without the slightest effort on his own part. The post of emperor was
offered to Vitellius by men who did not know him personally. Few
commanders have made themselves so popular with the army by
good actions as he did by doing nothing. However, he displayed
frankness and generosity, though these are qualities which can prove
disastrous if exaggerated. Imagining that friendship is secured not by
steadiness of character but by lavish presents, he deserved rather than
achieved it. There is no doubt that Rome gained by Vitellius' defeat,

1. A janitor's office or, according to another account, a kennel.

but credit for betraying him cannot be claimed by those who sacrificed Vitellius to Vespasian after proving false to Galba.[1]

It was now almost dusk, and owing to the panic of the magistrates and senators, who had slipped out of the city or were taking cover in the houses of their various dependants, it was impossible to call a meeting of the senate. As for Domitian, when there was nothing more to fear from the enemy, he presented himself to the Flavian leaders and was greeted with the title 'Caesar'. The troops crowded round and just as they were, still armed, escorted him to his father's home.

1. e.g. Caecina and Bassus.

*Book Four*

# A Divided Senate

1. The execution of Vitellius marked the end of hostilities rather than the beginning of peace. The victors roamed through the city sword in hand, hunting the vanquished down with relentless hate. The streets were choked with bodies, the squares and temples stained with blood. The Flavians slaughtered their victims wherever they happened to come across them. Soon discipline went to pieces, and they set to work to search for skulkers and drag them from their hiding places. Whenever a man of tall and military appearance came in sight, they cut him down regardless of whether he was a soldier or a civilian. While feeling still ran high, their brutality glutted itself with blood. Then it was transformed into an appetite for loot. They left no lurking-place untouched, no door unopened: the excuse was that supporters of Vitellius might be hidden there. This was a signal for breaking into private mansions or, if resistance was offered, an excuse for murder. There were plenty of destitute Romans or vicious slaves ready to betray rich masters. Others again were denounced by their friends. Rome was filled with wailing and lamentation, and suffered the plight of a captured city. Indeed the unruly behaviour of the Othonian and Vitellian troops, which had been resented at the time, now seemed tolerable in retrospect. The Flavian generals had been keen enough to start the civil war, but they were incapable of exercising control in the day of victory. The truth is that revolution and strife put tremendous power into the hands of evil men, whereas peace and quiet call for good lives.

2. The title of Caesar, and the imperial palace, had been taken over by Domitian. While not yet prepared to give his mind to his official responsibilities, he was already playing the part of an emperor's son so far as seducing girls and women went. The post of pretorian prefect was assigned to Arrius Varus, but supreme control rested with Antonius Primus. The latter helped himself to money and servants

from the emperor's palace as if they were the spoil of Cremona. As to the remaining commanders, their modest pretensions or humble birth had robbed them of the limelight in the fighting, and now deprived them of its profits.

The frightened and cringing populace of Rome urged that Lucius Vitellius should be intercepted on his way back from Tarracina with the cohorts, and the last remaining embers of war extinguished. The cavalry were sent on to Aricia, while the legions marched out and took up a position short of Bovillae. Vitellius, for his part, lost no time in surrendering himself and his cohorts to the victors at discretion, and his men threw down their luckless arms as much in disgust as fear. A long line of prisoners of war hedged in by armed guards marched through the city, none with looks of entreaty, but rancorous and resentful, facing unflinchingly the clapping and insults of the jeering mob. A few tried to break away but were dealt with by their escorts. The rest were put in a place of confinement. None of them said anything that could earn him discredit, and in the hour of calamity they kept their honour. Lucius Vitellius was then executed. As unprincipled as his brother, he showed the greater vigour during the latter's reign, and, while not closely associated with the emperor's success, he was swept irresistibly away by his fall.

3. In the course of these same days, Lucilius Bassus was sent off with a force of cavalry in battle order to restore peace in Campania. Here feeling ran high between the different communities, and this, rather than any act of insubordination against the new emperor, was the reason for the expedition. The sight of the troops had a calming effect, and the smaller towns were not penalized. But Capua had the Third Legion billeted upon it, and the leading families suffered severely. Tarracina, on the other hand, got no compensation, which shows that men are more inclined to repay injury than kindness: the truth is that gratitude is irksome, while vengeance is accounted gain. Some comfort was derived from the punishment meted out to Vergilius Capito's slave, who, as I have mentioned, had betrayed Tarracina to the enemy. He was nailed to the gallows, still retaining the very rings which Vitellius had given him to wear.[1]

At Rome, however, the senate awarded Vespasian all the usual imperial titles. It felt pleased and confident. The civil war, begun in

1. The slave must have reported to Vitellius after the capture of Tarracina: see p. 198. 'Gallows' is often merely a synonym for 'cross'.

the Gallic and Spanish provinces, spreading to Upper and Lower
Germany and then the Balkans, finally traversing Egypt, Judaea,
Syria and every province and garrison, now seemed to have purged
the whole world of evil and run its course. The senate was further
encouraged by a message from Vespasian written under the impression that the war was not ended. That at any rate was how it looked
at the first glance. But he spoke as if he were truly emperor, modestly
concerning himself, and on public issues like a statesman. The senate
in its turn showed a proper respect. By its decree Vespasian received
the consulship with his son Titus as colleague, and Domitian was
accorded the praetorship and the powers of a consul.

4. Mucianus, too, had sent the senate a dispatch. This gave rise to
comment. If he was not the emperor, why, it was asked, did he speak
with the voice of authority?[1] He could have given the same report
verbally in a few days' time when called upon to speak in the senate
in the usual order of precedence. Besides, even his criticism of
Vitellius came too late and was no proof of independence. But what
really showed an attitude of contempt for the state and insult towards
the emperor was his boast that the principate had been at his disposal,
and had been handed to Vespasian as a gift. However, hard feelings
were concealed, and flattery displayed. With many fine words, Mucianus was granted triumphal honours for a war waged against fellow-
Romans, though his campaign against the Sarmatians was made the
excuse.[2] Antonius Primus, too, received the insignia of consul, and
Cornelius Fuscus and Arrius Varus those of praetor.[3] After that, it
was heaven's turn: a motion for the restoration of the Capitol was
approved.[4]

All these proposals were made by the consul-designate, Valerius
Asiaticus, the rest of the senators signifying assent by a mere glance
and gesture. A few who were especially prominent or had talent for
flattery supported the resolutions with elaborate and hollow rhetoric.
When it was the turn of the praetor-designate Helvidius Priscus to
speak, he expressed himself in language which, while paying due
respect to the new emperor, was remarkable for its frankness. There

1. See p. 114 and n. 2.
2. A triumph could not be celebrated over one's fellow-Romans. Mucianus
in fact deserved his: see p. 172          3. See p. 69, n. 2.
4. Religious business usually took precedence over secular on the agenda of
the senate.

was no trace of insincerity, and the senate gave him a tremendous reception. For Helvidius this day above all others marked the beginning of great offence – and great glory.[1]

5. Since this is the second time that I have had occasion to refer to a man who must often recur in my narrative, it seems appropriate to provide a short review of his career and interests, and of how he fared in life. Helvidius Priscus came of an Italian family from the town of Cluviae, and his father had been the senior centurion of a legion. From early youth he devoted his brilliant gifts to academic studies. His aim was not – as so often happens – to disguise ease and idleness under a pretentious name, but to arm himself more stoutly against the unpredictable chances of a public career. He adhered to the school of philosophy[2] by which moral virtue is counted the only good and wickedness alone evil, while power, rank and other accidentals which do not lie within a man's will are reckoned neither good nor evil. When he had occupied no higher office than that of quaestor, he was chosen by Thrasea Paetus[3] for his daughter's hand. From his father-in-law's character he learnt, above all, the courage to be free. As citizen, senator, husband, son-in-law and friend, he met the varied obligations of life duly and consistently, contemptuous of wealth, unfaltering in his devotion to the right, and inflexible in the face of danger. 6. Some critics felt that he was too eager to make a name, for the last of all human infirmities to be shed, even by a philosopher, is a longing for glory. The fall of his father-in-law drove him into exile, but he returned on the accession of Galba and proceeded to impeach Thrasea's prosecutor, Eprius Marcellus.[4] This act of retaliation, perhaps excessive, perhaps justified, deeply divided the senate at the time. If Marcellus were convicted, it meant the downfall of a whole army of potential defendants. The case opened with a stormy encounter, as the brilliant speeches of the two opponents

1. Helvidius Priscus, son-in-law of Thrasea Paetus, was exiled with him in A.D. 66, recalled by Galba, occupied a praetorship in A.D. 70 and was again exiled in A.D. 74 or 75 and put to death as a determined opponent of the principate.

2. Stoicism.

3. Thrasea Paetus, consul, A.D. 56, leader of the Stoic opposition to Nero, by whom he was put to death in A.D. 66.

4. Eprius Marcellus, consul A.D. 60 or 61, and 74, governor of Asia A.D. 70-3, had accused Thrasea Paetus in A.D. 66. He finally conspired against Vespasian in A.D. 79 with Caecina, and committed suicide.

show. But as time went on, the ambiguous attitude of Galba and the protests of a number of senators caused Priscus to drop the charge. Reactions varied, like men's characters. Some praised his restraint, others found him lacking in determination.

However, at the meeting of the senate that recognized Vespasian as emperor, it had been decided that a deputation should wait upon him. This led to a bitter altercation between Helvidius and Eprius. Priscus demanded that the members of the deputation should be chosen individually by the magistrates under oath, while Marcellus called for the use of lot in accordance with the motion of the consul designate. 7. But Marcellus' eagerness was really prompted by a desire to spare his own blushes and the fear that, if others were chosen, this would be interpreted as a reflection upon himself.

From brief exchanges, they gradually passed on to prolonged and bitter speeches, Helvidius asking why Marcellus was so frightened of the verdict of the magistrates. After all, he had money and eloquence sufficient to give him a lead over many of his competitors but for the handicap that men remembered his crimes. If lots were drawn, no distinction was made between men's characters. A senatorial vote and expression of opinion, on the other hand, was designed to probe the life and reputation of each and every candidate. Consideration for Vespasian, as well as for the public interests, required that the deputation should consist of the most irreproachable members of the senate – men who could accustom the emperor's ear to the language of honour. Vespasian had been friendly with Thrasea, Soranus and Sentius. However inadvisable it might be that their prosecutors should be punished, they had no business to be paraded before him. A verdict of the senate in this matter would be a hint to the emperor as to whom he should favour, and whom fear. Good advisers were the most valuable instrument of good government. Marcellus should be satisfied with having driven Nero to execute so many innocent victims. Let him make the most of his ill-gotten gains and his immunity from punishment, and resign Vespasian to better men.

8. Marcellus retorted that the policy under attack did not originate with him. It was the consul-designate who had put forward the proposal, he said, in accordance with long-standing precedents which fixed lot as the method employed to choose deputations, in order to give no loophole for self-seeking or personal vendettas. Nothing had happened to render an established principle obsolete, or to transform

what was a tribute to the emperor into a reflection upon any particular person. They were all qualified to do homage. A more vital matter was to see that the stubbornness of certain individuals did not irritate susceptibilities which, in the early days of a reign, were inevitably on edge, anxiously eyeing everybody's remarks, and even glances. For his part, he added, he remembered the age in which he was born, and the constitution devised by their fathers and grandfathers. Earlier times earned his admiration, the present his allegiance. He prayed for good emperors, but took them as they came. The fall of Thrasea was attributable quite as much to a decision of the senate as to the speech he had himself made. This was the sort of fiction designed by the tyranny of Nero to mock them, and his friendship with such an emperor had been just as agonizing an experience for himself as exile had been for others. In short, Helvidius was welcome to boast of his resolution and intrepidity, and class himself with Cato, Brutus and their like. He, Marcellus, was merely a single member of a senate that had endured a common yoke. He had one further piece of advice for Priscus. Let him not seek to climb above his sovereign, or try to play the schoolmaster to a man like Vespasian who, no longer young, had held the honours of a triumph and was the father of grown-up sons. Evil emperors wanted unrestricted power, but even the best of them welcomed some limit to independence.

These conflicting views were debated with great vigour on both sides, and met with varying reactions. The voting went in favour of those who wanted the deputation elected by lot, even the moderates supporting tradition. The leading senators also came down on this side because they were afraid of their colleagues' jealousy if elected themselves.

9. This was followed by another dispute. The praetors of the treasury, who were at that time the officials responsible for its administration, had complained of the low state of the public finances, and asked for a limit on expenditure. The consul-designate suggested that the emperor should handle a situation where commitments were so heavy and the problem so intractable. Helvidius proposed senatorial action. When the consuls proceeded to invite other members to express their opinion in order of seniority, a tribune of the plebs called Vulcacius Tertullinus used his veto to prevent any decision being taken on this important issue in the absence of the emperor. Helvidius had already proposed that the restoration of the Capitol should be

shouldered by the state with the assistance of Vespasian. This proposal was passed over, and afterwards forgotten, by the moderates. In certain quarters, however, it was remembered all too well.

10. Then Musonius Rufus attacked Publius Celer,[1] alleging that he had secured the fall of Barea Soranus[2] by false testimony. It looked as if an inquiry into this would revive the bitterness aroused by the period of accusations. But in this case the defendant was despicable and guilty, and there was no question of shielding him. Soranus was remembered with reverence, while Celer, who claimed to be a philosopher, yet testified against Barea, had betrayed and dishonoured the ideal of friendship which he preached. The hearing was fixed for the next meeting of the senate. But now that there was a movement for settling old scores, it was not so much Musonius or Publius they were waiting for as Priscus, Marcellus and the rest of them.

11. Against this background – conflicts within the senate, a sense of grievance among the beaten, an inability on the part of the victors to command respect, Rome uncontrolled by either laws or emperor – Mucianus entered the capital and concentrated all power in his own hands. Antonius Primus and Arrius Varus now lost the control they had previously exercised. The resentment which Mucianus felt towards them was obvious, though his looks did not betray it. But Rome was shrewd enough to detect when a man had lost favour. Before long there was a swing of public opinion to the new master. Men courted and flattered Mucianus, and Mucianus alone. He in turn played up by constantly moving from one palace or park to another, closely surrounded by an armed escort. This taste for ostentation, processions and military guards shows how eagerly he assumed the reality of imperial power while waiving the title of emperor.

The greatest alarm was caused by the execution of Calpurnius Galerianus, the son of Gaius Piso.[3] He had kept out of political adventures, but his distinguished name and the good looks of youth made him the subject of popular gossip, and in a city which was still unsettled and always relished the latest rumours, idle tongues talked of him as a possible emperor. On the orders of Mucianus, he was put

1. Publius Egnatius Celer was a Stoic philosopher from Berytus.
2. Barea Soranus, consul A.D. 52 and later governor of Asia, was charged with sedition and condemned to death in A.D. 66: see Tacitus, *Annals* xvi, 32–3.
3. Gaius Calpurnius Piso Galerianus had been exiled by the emperor Gaius, but was restored and given the consulship by Claudius.

under military arrest. Within the walls of the city, his end would have attracted more notice, so that it was at a point forty miles from Rome along the Appian Way that his veins were opened and he bled to death. Julius Priscus, the prefect of the pretorian cohorts under Vitellius, committed suicide less from compulsion than a sense of shame, but Alfenus Varus managed to survive his cowardice and disgrace. Asiaticus, being a freedman, paid for his evil influence at court by suffering the execution appropriate to a slave.[1]

1. Crucifixion.

## Civilis Revolts

12. It was at this moment that rumours of disaster in Germany began to multiply. Rome received them with unconcern. The annihilation of armies, the capture of permanent legionary camps and the defection of the Gallic provinces were indeed discussed – but not as if they were calamities. In order to explain the reasons for this war and the widespread rebellion of foreign and allied peoples which marked the conflagration, I shall refer to its antecedents.

The Batavians,[1] so long as they lived beyond the Rhine, formed a branch of the Chatti. Driven out by domestic dissensions, they occupied the uninhabited riverine fringes of Gaul together with the 'Island' in the lower reaches, washed by the North Sea on the west, and on the other three sides by the Rhine. They were not exploited financially despite the Roman supremacy and their alliance with a stronger power, but contributed only men and arms to the empire. After a long and hard training in the German campaigns,[2] the Batavian cohorts were moved across the Channel to Britain[3] where they added to their laurels, still commanded according to long-standing practice by their own nobles. In the home country, they also had a picked cavalry force specially trained for amphibious operations. These men were capable of swimming the Rhine while keeping hold of their arms and mounts, and maintaining perfect formation. 13. By far the most prominent of the Batavians were Julius Civilis and Claudius Paulus, who were of royal descent. Fonteius Capito executed Paulus on a trumped-up charge of rebellion,[4] while Civilis was put in irons and sent to Nero. Although acquitted

1. See Key to Place-Names, under 'Batavians' and 'Chatti'.
2. The campaigns of Drusus, Tiberius and Germanicus between the Rivers Rhine and Elbe in 12 B.C.–A.D. 16.
3. In A.D. 43 when the invasion of Britain took place, or in A.D. 60–1 during the rebellion of Boudicca.
4. Paulus may have been suspected of complicity with Vindex.

by Galba, he found himself once more in danger under Vitellius, whose army clamoured for his head. This was why he hated Rome and hoped for great things from our difficulties. But Civilis was unusually intelligent for a native, and passed himself off as a second Sertorius or Hannibal, whose facial disfigurement he shared.[1] Open rebellion involved the risk of being attacked as an enemy of Rome, so he posed as a friend and supporter of Vespasian. It must be admitted that Antonius Primus sent him a letter with instructions to divert the reinforcements called up by Vitellius and to immobilize the legions by the fiction of a German revolt. He had received the same hint in a personal interview with Hordeonius Flaccus, who was sympathetic to Vespasian and seriously perturbed by a situation in which his country faced disaster if fighting were resumed and thousands of armed men invaded Italy.

14. So Civilis determined to rebel. But for the time being he concealed his ultimate purpose, intending to shape his future course in the light of events. The way in which he set about his revolutionary enterprise was the following. At the time, Batavians of military age were being conscripted on the instructions of Vitellius. The levy was by its nature a heavy burden, but it was rendered still more oppressive by the greed and profligacy of the recruiting sergeants, who called up the old and unfit in order to exact a bribe for their release, while young, good-looking lads – for children are normally quite tall among the Batavians – were dragged off to gratify their lust. This caused bitter resentment, and the ringleaders of revolt got together and succeeded in inducing their countrymen to refuse service. Civilis invited the nobles and the most enterprising commoners to a sacred grove, ostensibly for a banquet. When he saw that darkness and merriment had inflamed their hearts, he addressed them. Starting with a reference to the glory and renown of their nation, he went on to catalogue the wrongs, the depredations and all the other woes of slavery. The alliance, he said, was no longer observed on the old terms: they were treated as chattels. How long would they have to wait for the arrival of the governor, who, despite his burdensome and overbearing suite, did exercise real control? The Batavians were at the mercy of prefects and centurions who, when glutted with spoil

1. i.e. the loss of an eye. Sertorius was a distinguished adherent of Marius who as governor of Spain was in rebellion against the Sullan régime in Rome during the years 80–72 B.C. Hannibal lost an eye during the invasion of Italy.

and blood, were replaced by others looking for fresh pockets to pick and new labels for plunder. They were faced with a levy which parted children from parents and brothers from brothers, apparently for ever. The Roman state had never been in such low water. The permanent legionary camps contained nothing but loot and old men past service. They had only to lift up their eyes. They should have no fear of the legions: these were merely names without substance. The Batavians, on the other hand, could rely on a strong body of infantry and cavalry, kinship with the Germans and identity of purpose with the Gallic provinces. Even the Romans would welcome such a war, in which a doubtful issue would at any rate secure the rebels credit with Vespasian, and an outright victory call for no apology.

15. Civilis was listened to with whole-hearted approval. He exacted from all his hearers an oath of loyalty marked by barbarous ritual and traditional curses upon the perjuror. Negotiations for a joint plan of action were made with the Cannenefates. This is a tribe occupying part of the Island[1] and closely resembling the Batavians in origin, language and fighting spirit, though less numerous. Then he sent secret agents to win over the auxiliaries from Britain, that is, the Batavian cohorts, which, as I have already mentioned,[2] had been moved to Germany, and were now stationed at Mogontiacum.

Among the Cannenefates was a foolish desperado called Brinno. He came of a very distinguished family. His father had taken part in many marauding exploits, and had snapped his fingers at Gaius' bogus expeditions without being brought to book.[3] The mere fact that his son was the heir of a rebel family secured him votes. He was placed upon a shield in the tribal fashion and carried on the swaying shoulders of his bearers to symbolize his election as leader.[4] Immediately calling upon the Frisii, a tribe beyond the Rhine, he swooped down on two Roman cohorts in their nearby quarters[5] and simultaneously overran them from the North Sea. The garrison had not

1. See map 7.
2. See p. 121.
3. Brinno's father seems to have refused to contribute troops to Gaius' military build-up in Gaul in autumn A.D. 39–spring A.D. 40. The enterprise, whatever its nature, came to nothing.
4. The German tribes elected *ad hoc* military leaders as and when the need arose.
5. Probably the forts were those at Valkenburg and Katwijk or De Woerd near Leiden at the mouth of the (Old) Rhine.

expected the attack, nor indeed would it have been strong enough to hold out if it had, so the posts were captured and sacked. Then the enemy fell upon the Roman supply-contractors and merchants who were scattered over the countryside with no thought of war. The marauders were also on the point of destroying the frontier forts,[1] but these were set on fire by the cohort-prefects because they could not be defended. The headquarters of the various units and such troops as they could muster rallied to the upper[2] part of the Island under a senior centurion called Aquilius. But this was an army on paper only, lacking real strength. It could hardly be otherwise, for Vitellius had withdrawn the bulk of the cohorts' effectives and saddled with arms a bunch of loafers from the nearest Nervian and German districts.

16. Civilis decided on a ruse. He took it upon himself to criticize the prefects for abandoning their forts, and offered to deal with the outbreak of the Cannenefates in person with the help of the cohort under his command. As for the Roman commanders, they could get back to their respective stations. But the Germans are a nation that loves fighting, and they did not keep the secret for long. Hints of what was afoot gradually leaked out and the truth was revealed: Civilis' advice concealed a trick, scattered cohorts were more liable to be wiped out, and the ringleader was not Brinno, but Civilis. When the plot came to nothing, the latter resorted to force and enrolled the Cannenefates, Frisii and Batavians in separate striking forces. On the Roman side, a front was formed at no great distance from the Rhine,[3] and the naval vessels which had put in at this point after the burning of the forts were arrayed to face the enemy. Fighting had not lasted long before a Tungrian cohort went over to Civilis, and the Roman troops, disarrayed by this unforeseen treachery, went down before the combined onslaught of allies and foes. The naval force was equally disloyal. Some of the rowers were Batavians, and they feigned incompetence in order to hinder the sailors and marines in the performance of their duties. Then they began to resist, and tried to steer the ships towards the enemy-held bank, finally murdering the helmsmen and centurions who refused to throw in their lot with them. In the end the whole fleet of twenty-four ships either deserted or was captured.

1. Along the (Old) Rhine; a number of sites have been determined.
2. i.e. eastern.
3. Perhaps in north-east Betuwe, between Driel and Huissen.

17. This success earned the rebels immediate prestige, and provided a useful basis for future action. They had obtained the arms and ships they needed, and were acclaimed as liberators as the news spread like wild-fire throughout the German and Gallic provinces. The former[1] immediately sent an offer of help. As for an alliance with the provinces of Gaul, Civilis used cunning and bribery to achieve this, returning the captured cohort-prefects to their own communities and giving the men the choice between discharge and soldiering on. Those who stayed were offered service on honourable terms, those who went received spoil taken from the Romans. He also talked to them privately and reminded them of the ill-treatment they had endured for so many years in a condition of subjection which it was wrong for them to describe as 'peaceful development'. The Batavians, he said, despite exemption from tribute, had risen against the tyranny they all endured. The Romans had been routed and vanquished in the very first encounter. What if the Gallic provinces shook off the yoke? What reserves were left in Italy? It was at the cost of provincial blood that the provinces were crushed. They should not worry about the battle fought by Vindex.[2] In this, the Aedui and the Arverni had been trampled underfoot by Batavian cavalry. Among the auxiliaries of Verginius had figured Belgians, and sober reflection showed that Gaul had succumbed to Gallic forces. Now they were all on the same side, with the added advantage of such military discipline as had prevailed in the Roman army in the past. They were supported by veteran cohorts, fresh from the defeat of Otho's legions. Slavery was good enough for Syria and Asia and the Orient with its tradition of kingship, but in Gaul there were many men still living who had been born before the Roman tribute was imposed.[3] It was beyond question that the annihilation of Quintilius Varus[4] had saved Germany from enslavement, and this had been a challenge presented to an emperor who was not Vitellius, but Caesar Augustus. Nature had given even the dumb brutes freedom, and courage was the peculiar

1. Tacitus seems to allude to the Germans across the Rhine (cf. p. 218), who did not, however, except in theory, form part of the Roman province of Germany at this time.

2. The defeat of Vindex by Verginius Rufus at Vesontio (Besançon) in May 68.

3. Probably a reference to the imposition by Tiberius, in, or after, A.D. 14, of a tribute upon Gauls previously immune.

4. In Lippe (the 'Teutoburger Forest') in A.D. 9 at the hands of Arminius and the Germans.

excellence of man. Heaven helped the braver side. So, with vigour
untrammelled and unimpaired, let them fasten upon a distracted and
exhausted enemy. While rival groups supported Vespasian and
Vitellius, there was scope to attack both.

18. Civilis in this way kept an eye on Gaul and Germany. If his plan
worked, he hoped at any moment to become king of the strongest
and richest nations in the world. As for Hordeonius Flaccus, he
hushed up the initial moves of Civilis and in so doing gave them
sustenance. But when panic-stricken messengers arrived with news of
the storming of forts, the wiping-out of cohorts and the expulsion of
everything Roman from the Island of the Batavians, Flaccus instructed the legate Munius Lupercus to move out against the enemy.
Lupercus, who commanded a camp[1] containing two legions, assembled a force consisting of legionaries from the garrison, Ubii from
adjacent units, and Treviran horse stationed at no great distance.
These units he rapidly put across the river,[2] together with a Batavian
cavalry regiment which, though long disaffected, pretended to be
loyal in order to betray the Romans in the face of the enemy and
derive greater profit from its flight. Near Civilis were massed the
captured Roman standards: his men were to have their eyes fixed
upon the newly-won trophies while their enemies were demoralized
by the recollection of defeat. He also caused his mother and sisters,
accompanied by the wives and young children of all his men, to take
up their station in the rear as a spur to victory or a reproach to the
routed. Then the battle chant of the warriors and the shrill wailing
of the women rang out over the host, evoking in response only a
feeble cheer from the legions and cohorts. The Roman left front was
soon exposed by the defection of the Batavian cavalry regiment,
which immediately turned about to face us. But in this frightening
situation the legionaries kept their arms and ranks intact. The Ubian
and Treviran auxiliaries disgraced themselves by stampeding over the
countryside in wild flight. Against them the Germans directed the
brunt of their attack, which gave the legions a breathing-space in
which to get back to the camp called Vetera. The prefect of the Batavian cavalry regiment, Claudius Labeo, was involved in some petty
local rivalry with Civilis. As his murder might be unpopular with
the Batavians and his continued presence encourage dissension,

1. Vetera, the station of the Fifth and Fifteenth Legions.
2. The River Waal.

Civilis had him removed to a place of exile among the Frisii.
19. At about the same date, the cohorts of Batavians and Cannenefates
were overtaken by Civilis' messenger as they were starting off on the
way to Rome at the orders of Vitellius.[1] They promptly assumed an
intractable and high-handed attitude towards the Romans. As a bribe
for making the march, they proceeded to ask for a bounty, double
pay and an increase in the cavalry element of their units.[2] No doubt
these were privileges promised by Vitellius, but the men were less
concerned to obtain them than to secure an excuse for mutiny. Moreover, by his many concessions Flaccus had merely encouraged them
to clamour more noisily for what they knew he would refuse. Paying
no attention to him, they made for Lower Germany to join Civilis.
Hordeonius[3] called his tribunes and centurions together and consulted
them on the desirability of bringing the insubordinate troops to heel
by force. But he was not by nature a man of action, and his staff were
worried by the ambiguous attitude of the auxiliaries and the dilution
of the legions by hasty conscription. So he decided against risking his
troops outside the camp. Afterwards he changed his mind, and as his
advisers themselves went back on the views they had expressed, he
gave the impression that he intended pursuit, and wrote to Herennius
Gallus, stationed at Bonn in command of the First Legion, telling him
to bar the passage of the Batavians and promising to follow closely
on their heels with his army. The rebels could in fact have been
crushed if Hordeonius and Gallus had moved up from opposite
directions and caught them between two fires. But Flaccus abandoned
his plan, and in a fresh dispatch to Gallus warned him not to molest the
departing cohorts. This bred a suspicion that the command wanted an
extension of the fighting, and that everything that had already happened or was feared in the future sprang not from the slackness of
the army or the enemy's violence but from a conspiracy by
the generals.
20. On approaching the camp at Bonn, the Batavian cohorts sent a
representative ahead to lay their views before Herennius Gallus.
There was no question, they said, of their waging war against the

1. See p. 139.
2. The auxiliary cavalry enjoyed more pay and prestige than the auxiliary
infantry.
3. At Mogontiacum (Mainz), from which the Batavian cohorts had started out.

Romans, for whom they had fought many a time. They were wearied by long and fruitless service, and longed for their homeland and retirement. If no resistance were offered, they would march on without doing damage, but if faced with armed force, they intended to cut their way through. This attitude made the legate hesitate, but his troops induced him to risk a fight. He had 3,000 legionaries and some untrained Belgian cohorts, together with a number of civilians and camp-followers who had no fight in them, though they were boastful enough before the hour of danger. This force burst from all the various gates of the camp, with the intention of surrounding the numerically inferior Batavians. The latter were old hands at fighting. They formed up into squares, compact masses of men presenting an impregnable defence everywhere, front, rear and sides. In this formation they broke the thin Roman line. As the Belgians gave way, the legion was driven from the field and the fugitives made helter-skelter for the rampart and gates of the camp. This was where the heaviest losses occurred. The ditches were choked with bodies, and the Romans suffered death and wounds not only at the hands of the enemy but as a result of falling and, in many instances, by their own weapons. The victors gave Cologne a wide berth and ventured on no further hostile act during the rest of the march. Their excuse for the fight at Bonn was that they had asked for peace and the rejection of their request had forced them to act in self-defence.

21. The arrival of the veteran cohorts meant that Civilis now commanded a proper army. But he still hesitated on his course of action, and reflected that Rome was strong. So he made all the men he had swear allegiance to Vespasian, and sent an appeal to the two legions which had been beaten in the previous engagement and had retired to the camp at Vetera, asking them to accept the same oath. Back came the reply. They were not in the habit of taking advice from a traitor nor from the enemy. They already had an emperor, Vitellius, and in his defence they would maintain their loyalty and arms to their dying breath. So it was not for a Batavian turncoat to sit in judgement on matters Roman. He had only to await his deserts – the punishment of a felon. When this reply reached Civilis, he flew into a rage, and hurried the whole Batavian nation into arms. They were joined by the Bructeri and Tencteri, and as the tidings spread Germany awoke to the call of spoil and glory.

22. In the face of this threatening concentration, the legionary

legates Munius Lupercus and Numisius Rufus[1] proceeded to reinforce the rampart and stockades. A settlement just outside the camp had grown during the long peace to the size of a small town.[2] This was now demolished to deny its use to the enemy. But they had forgotten to arrange for the conveyance of the food-supplies into the camp, and allowed them to be looted. Thus stocks which would have covered their needs for a long time were used up in a few days of licence. Civilis, himself commanding the central expeditionary force with the pick of his troops, the Batavians, filled both banks of the Rhine with disorderly bands of Germans in order to create a more ferocious appearance, while the cavalry careered over the plains nearby. At the same time the ships were moving upstream. The besieged were dumbfounded at the sight. In one direction their eyes fell upon the standards of veteran cohorts, in another upon the various tribal emblems normally carried into battle – representations of wild beasts brought from forest and sacred grove. This illustrated the twofold aspect of the war, civil and foreign.

The attacking force was encouraged by the length of the rampart, which, though designed for two legions, was in fact defended by barely 5,000 armed men.[3] But there were large numbers of camp-followers who had flocked to Vetera owing to the troubles and were available to help the war effort. 23. One end of the camp occupied a gentle slope, while the other was approached on the level.[4] The fact was that Augustus had imagined that this fortress was adequate to keep the provinces of Germany under supervision and control. He had never envisaged a situation so desperate that they would actually dare to march on Vetera and attack our legions. Consequently neither the site nor its defences had had labour spent upon them.[5] A

1. If both commanders were at Vetera, and not merely Lupercus (see p. 216), Numisius must have been seconded from the legion, the Sixteenth, which lay at Novaesium (Neuss). But Tacitus may be confused.

2. Birten near Xanten. It is now a village.

3. The fort was exceptionally large: 902 m. × 621 m. The strength of two legions at full establishment would be about 10,000 men.

4. The slope is at the north end towards Xanten, the level ground at the south end towards Birten.

5. Untrue: archaeology shows that the defences were undergoing continual improvement during the first century, and now included a ditch, rampart, gates and towers, as is clear from Tacitus' own account. There was aslo a well-designed H.Q. building, as well as a military hospital and the usual barrack-blocks.

numerous garrison and a well-stored arsenal seemed to meet the case.

The Batavians and the Germans from across the Rhine formed up in separate national contingents to show what each could do on its own, and challenged us with long-distance volleys. But most of their missiles sank harmlessly into the towers and merlons of the wall, and the enemy for their part were the target of a plunging fire of stones which inflicted some wounds. So with a yell and a rush they then made for the rampart, most of them putting ladders against it, others clambering over a 'tortoise' formed by their comrades. A few had already climbed some way when, under a rain of blows from swords and other arms, they were sent hurtling down to be buried under stakes and javelins. Natives are always full of fight at the start, and if successful they get out of control. But in this case their greed for booty made them put up with reverses as well. They even risked employing engines-of-war, unfamiliar as they were with such things. Not that they had any technical knowledge themselves. Deserters and prisoners showed them how to build a long timber shed like the super-structure of a bridge, put it on wheels and then move it forward, in such a way that some of the assailants posted themselves on top of it and so did battle from a kind of mound, while others concealed inside set about undermining the walls. But an artillery bombardment of stones soon flattened this crazy contraption. As they were preparing hurdles and mantlets, the guns shot burning spears at them, and the besiegers were themselves assailed with flames. In the end, despairing of storming Vetera, they revised their tactics and played a waiting game, being perfectly aware that the camp held only a few days' provisions and a mass of non-combatants. With luck, too, famine might encourage treason, sap the loyalty of the slaves, and provoke the unpredictable accidents of war.

24. Flaccus, meanwhile, hearing that Vetera was beleaguered, had sent officers to scour the Gallic provinces for reinforcements. He then entrusted the commander of the Twenty-Second Legion, Dillius Vocula, with a selected body of legionaries. The plan was that Vocula should march along the bank of the Rhine at top speed, while the governor travelled on board a naval squadron, being unfit physically and unpopular with his men. Indeed, the latter did not mince matters. They claimed that the Batavian cohorts had been allowed to leave Mogontiacum, while Civilis' movements had been hushed up and an alliance was now being made with Germans. Not even Antonius

Primus or Mucianus had done more to encourage the rise of Vespasian. Undisguised hostility and armed attack could be repelled in the open, but treachery and deceit worked in darkness and were for that reason hard to parry. There, opposite them, stood Civilis, marshalling his men for the fray, while Hordeonius from the pillows of a sick-room issued orders perfectly calculated to play into the enemy's hands. Thousands of sturdy fighters, ready for action, were controlled by a single elderly invalid. They had better kill the traitor, and free their luck and valour from this incubus. By exchanging these remarks they fanned each other's indignation, and it found further fuel in a letter from Vespasian which Flaccus, because he could not hide it, read out to the assembled troops, and sent its bearers to Vitellius under guard.

25. This succeeded in quietening them for the march to Bonn, which was the headquarters of the First Legion. The men there were even more resentful, and blamed Hordeonius for their defeat. It was his orders, so they claimed, that had been responsible for their being deployed against the Batavians under the impression that the legions from Mogontiacum were in pursuit; and his, too, was the treachery that had caused their discomfiture when no units turned up to help them. This episode was not known to the other armies, nor was it being communicated to their emperor, though it would have been quite possible to nip the treason in the bud by rushing up reinforcements from the many provinces within reach.

Hordeonius read out to the army copies of all the letters he had sent asking Britain and the provinces of Gaul and Spain for help, and introduced the disastrous practice of handing dispatches over to the legionary standard-bearers, by whom they were read to the troops before they were to the officers. Then he had one of the mutineers arrested, less because the fault lay with a single man than in order to assert his rights. The army was now moved from Bonn to Cologne. Gallic recruits were by this time streaming in, for at first the Gauls assisted the Roman cause with vigour, though later, as German strength increased, a number of the states rebelled against us, nourishing hopes of liberty and the ambition to acquire an empire for themselves once they were free. Among the legions there was growing resentment, and they had not been intimidated by the confinement of one solitary soldier. Indeed, this fellow actually tried to incriminate the governor, alleging that he had himself carried

messages between Civilis and Flaccus, and was being got rid of on a
trumped-up charge because he knew too much. Vocula showed
remarkable firmness. He got up on a platform and ordered the man
to be seized and taken away, still yelling, to execution. This gave the
trouble-makers a shock, and the better sort obeyed orders. Then, as
they called unanimously for Vocula to lead them, Flaccus handed
over the command to him.

26. But unity was lacking, and there were many irritants. Pay and
rations were short. The Gallic provinces refused to provide either
men or tribute. Owing to a drought unusual in these latitudes, the
Rhine was scarcely navigable and this restricted the movement of
supplies. Moreover, pickets had been posted along the whole length
of the river to prevent the Germans from fording it, and thus one
and the same cause reduced the supply of food and increased the
number of consumers. Ignorant minds found something sinister in
the very shortage of water, feeling that even the rivers on which the
empire had so long relied for defence were now deserting us. In time
of peace, this might have been attributed to chance or natural causes.
Now it was called 'fate' and 'the anger of heaven'.

On entering Novaesium, they were joined by the Sixteenth Legion.
The commanding officer, Herennius Gallus,[1] was added to Vocula's
staff, and took some of the burden of responsibility from his shoulders.
Not venturing to continue their advance against the enemy, they
encamped at a place called Gelduba. Here a training programme which
included manoeuvres, fortification and the construction of a rampart
helped them to steady the troops. Wishing to raise morale by a
plundering foray, Vocula led the army against the lands of the
nearby Cugerni, who had accepted Civilis' offer of alliance.

27. Part of the force remained behind with Herennius Gallus. One
day, it happened that a heavily-laden corn-ship had run aground a
little way from the camp, and the Germans proceeded to tow it to
their side of the river. Gallus was not prepared to stand this, and sent
a cohort to the rescue. The Germans, too, brought up reserves, and as
more and more newcomers joined in on either side, a regular fight
developed. The Germans inflicted heavy losses on us, and got the ship
away. The beaten troops adopted the now fashionable expedient of
blaming their commander for treachery rather than themselves for
cowardice. They dragged him out of his tent, tore his uniform and

1. But Herennius was commander of the First Legion at Bonn: p. 217.

assaulted him violently, telling him to say what he had got for betraying the army, and who his accomplices were. They then rounded on Hordeonius, describing him as the arch-plotter and Gallus as his tool. In the end, repeated threats of murder frightened Gallus into echoing their accusations against Hordeonius. He was then put in irons, and only freed on the arrival of Vocula, who on the following day had the ringleaders of the mutiny executed – a striking proof of the extremes of insubordination and submissiveness in this particular army. It is clear that the rank-and-file were loyal to Vitellius, while the senior officers favoured Vespasian. This is why crime and punishment alternated, and outbreaks of violence consorted so strangely with willingness to obey that it was possible to punish the men but impossible to restrain them.

28. Civilis for his part was now finding his strength immeasurably increased by reinforcements from Germany at large. A firm alliance was sealed by an exchange of hostages of the highest rank. The Batavian leader ordered the Ubii and Treviri to be plundered by their respective neighbours, and another force was sent beyond the Maas to strike a blow at the Menapii and Morini in the north of Gaul. In both theatres booty was gathered, and they showed special vindictiveness in plundering the Ubii because this was a tribe of German origin which had renounced its nationality and preferred to be known by the Roman name of 'Agrippinenses'.[1] Some cohorts of theirs were cut to pieces in the village of Marcodurum, caught napping because they were so far from the Rhine. The Ubii themselves joined the fray. Their aim was to plunder Germany, and this they did scot-free at first. But they were later rounded up, and indeed throughout this war they were less lucky than loyal.

The crushing of the Ubii made Civilis a more dangerous enemy, whose ambitions soared with success. He now pressed the siege of the legionary camp, keeping tighter watch so that no messenger with news of the relieving army should slip through his lines unobserved. He allotted the artillery and heavy engineering duties to the Batavians. The Germans from across the Rhine were clamouring for action, and these he ordered to advance in an attempt to cut the rampart. When repulsed, they were sent forward again, manpower being abundant and casualties of little consequence. 29. Nor did their exertion end

1. The official name of Cologne was *Colonia Claudia Ara Agrippinensium*: cf. Tacitus, *Annals* xii, 27.

with dusk. They not only heaped up a pile of logs by their positions, but held a carousal in the light of the bonfire. As the wine went to their heads, they would surge forward into battle with a reckless folly which failed to achieve anything, for their own shots went astray in the darkness and the Romans had the native ranks in full view and aimed at anyone who was conspicuous by his enterprise or glittering decorations. Civilis, realizing what was happening, ordered the fire to be put out, and staged a confused scene of darkness and battle. This was the signal for a pandemonium of discordant howling and blind rushes, in which it was impossible to see far enough to strike blows properly or to parry them. Whenever there happened to be shouting, they wheeled clumsily round in its direction and laid about them. Courage was useless, chance ruled the general chaos, and often heroes fell by the hand of cowards. The actions of the Germans were marked by incoherent fury, but the Roman soldier, who well understood his perilous position, hurled his iron-shod stakes and heavy stones to good effect. When the sound of climbing or the placing of ladders against the wall delivered the enemy into his hand, he would strike them back with his shield-boss and follow this up with the javelin. Many attackers surmounted the wall, but were stabbed by the Roman dirks. Thus the long night was endured, and dawn disclosed a new form of assault.

30. The Batavians had built a high tower with two superimposed platforms. This they brought up to the main gate, where the ground was flattest.[1] But the defenders countered this with sturdy poles and rammed it with beams until it fell to pieces, causing heavy losses to the men standing on it. A sudden sortie against the disorganized enemy achieved results, and the legionaries also used their greater experience and technical skill to outbid the enemy in the construction of engines of war. The most frightening of these was a grab capable of being elevated and depressed. This would suddenly be let down, and one or more of the enemy soldiers whisked up into the air before the eyes of their fellows, to be unloaded inside the camp by the rotation of the counter-weight. Despairing of assault, Civilis resumed his steady investment, attempting in the meantime to undermine the loyalty of the legions by messages and promises.

31. Such were events in Germany up to the Battle of Cremona,[2] the

1. See p. 219, n. 4.          2. i.e. up to the time when news of the Battle of Cremona reached the Rhine land (about 7 November 69).

outcome of which was made known by a letter from Antonius Primus
enclosing a proclamation issued by Caecina. Indeed, one of the cohort
commanders on the beaten side, Alpinius Montanus, testified personally to the success of the Flavian cause. Reaction to this was
varied. The auxiliaries from Gaul, who neither liked nor disliked the
contending sides and whose service implied no personal attachment,
lost no time in renouncing Vitellius at the prompting of their commanders. The seasoned troops held back. But when Hordeonius
Flaccus administered the oath of allegiance, they too accepted it under
pressure from the tribunes, though with little conviction in their looks
or hearts, and while firmly reciting the other formulae of the solemn
declaration, hesitated at the name 'Vespasian' or mumbled it, and
indeed for the most part passed it over in silence.

32. A missive from Antonius to Civilis was then read to the assembled
troops. Its tone inflamed their suspicions because the recipient was
addressed as if he were an ally of the Flavians, while the army of
Germany was alluded to as an enemy. When the news in due course
reached the camp at Gelduba, there was the same reaction in word
and deed, and Montanus was sent on to Civilis with a request that he
should cease hostilities and not disguise a national war under false
colours. If he had set out to help Vespasian, he was told, his mission
had already been fulfilled. Civilis' reply was diplomatic at first, but
when he realized that Montanus was a man of violent passions who
was ready to stir up trouble, he made an appeal to him. He prefaced
this with complaints and a reference to the dangers he had endured
for five and twenty years in Roman camps. 'A fine reward I got for
my efforts,' said he, '– the murder of my brother, my own imprisonment, and the vicious clamour of this army for my execution. For
this I seek satisfaction according to the law of nations. As for you
Treviri and your fellow craven spirits, what recompense do you
expect for the blood you have shed so often, other than unrewarded
service, endless taxation, flogging, the block and the devilish ingenu-
ities of tyranny? Look at me. I am the commander of a single
cohort, and rely on the Cannenefates and Batavians, who form only
a tiny fragment of the Gallic provinces. Yet together we have utterly
destroyed those vast but useless bases or are now cracking them in
the grip of war and hunger. One final argument: we shall either
achieve freedom if we venture or lose nothing by defeat.' With these
inflammatory words, but with instructions to take back a milder

reply, he dismissed Montanus, who returned with the story that his mission had failed, though he concealed the rest. The explosion was not long in coming.

33. Civilis held back a part of his forces, and sent the veteran cohorts and the keenest of his German troops against Vocula and his army, under the command of Julius Maximus and Claudius Victor, his sister's son. They sacked the headquarters of a cavalry regiment at Asciburgium as they passed by, and swooped upon the legionary camp so unexpectedly that Vocula was unable to address his men or deploy them in line of battle. All he could do when the alarm sounded was to urge them to form a central core of legionaries, around which the auxiliaries clustered in a ragged array. The cavalry charged, but were brought up short by the disciplined ranks of the enemy and forced back upon their fellows. What followed was a massacre, not a battle. The Nervian cohorts, too, were induced by panic or treachery to expose the Roman flanks. Thus the attack penetrated to the legions. They lost their standards, retreated within the rampart, and were already suffering heavy losses there when fresh help suddenly altered the luck of battle. Some Basque cohorts recruited by Galba had been summoned to the Rhineland. As they neared the camp, they heard the shouts of men fighting. While the enemy's attention was elsewhere, they charged them from the rear and caused a widespread panic out of all proportion to their numbers. It was thought that the main army had arrived, either from Novaesium or from Mogontiacum. This misconception gave the Romans new heart: confident in the strength of others, they regained their own. The pick of the Batavian fighters – at least so far as the infantry were concerned – lay dead upon the field; the cavalry got away with the standards and prisoners taken in the first phase of the engagement. In this day's work casualties in slain were heavier on our side, but consisted of the poorer fighters, whereas the Germans lost their very best. 34. The rival commanders were equally to blame: both deserved their defeat, and both threw away victory. If Civilis had offered battle in greater strength, he could not possibly have been surrounded by this small number of cohorts, but would have forced his way into the camp and destroyed it. Vocula, on the other hand, failed to inform himself of the enemy approach and was therefore beaten as soon as he came out, and then, distrusting his success, wasted several days to no purpose before moving against the enemy. Had he kept them on the run from the start

and exploited the situation while it was fluid, he could have gained sufficient momentum to raise the siege.[1]

Meanwhile, Civilis had tried a psychological approach with the beleaguered garrison, seeking to create the impression that the Romans were finished and that his own force had won a victory. The captured standards and flags were paraded round the camp, and even the prisoners were put on show. One of these ventured on an act of great courage: he shouted out what had really happened, and was cut down on the spot by the Germans. But this merely served to confirm his story, and moreover the sack and smoke of burning farmhouses told them that the victorious army was coming. When Vocula was within sight of the camp, he ordered a halt, and had his position surrounded by ditch and rampart. The general's instructions were that the baggage and heavy kit were to be dumped, so that the army could fight unimpeded. This evoked a storm of criticism. The troops clamoured for immediate action, and threatening their officers had by now become a habit. Without even giving themselves time to form up properly, the disarrayed and exhausted troops went into battle. Indeed, Civilis was by this time close upon them, relying as much on the enemy's blunders as upon the courage of his own troops. The Romans fought with mixed success, and the trouble-makers turned out to be cowards. Some men, however, remembered their recent victory. Standing firm and striking hard, they heartened themselves and their neighbours, and when the line was restored signalled to the besieged to seize their chance. From the walls the garrison could see everything, and they dashed out by every gate of the camp. Moreover, it happened that Civilis' horse fell, and its rider was thrown. Both armies believed the rumour that he was injured or killed, and this had a tremendous effect in dismaying the rebels and encouraging their enemies. But Vocula let the retreating Germans go, and set about strengthening the rampart and towers of the camp, as if the siege were soon to be renewed. After so many failures to exploit victory, there were good grounds for the suspicion that he preferred fighting.[2]

35. The most exhausting feature of this campaign for our armies was

1. Of Vetera.
2. The failures are three: at Gelduba; the slow advance; and the omission to pursue Civilis at Vetera. The absurd deduction is encouraged by the desire for an antithesis between 'victory' and 'fighting'.

the lack of supplies. The legionary baggage was sent to Novaesium with the non-combatants so that they could bring up grain from there by road, the river being controlled by the enemy. The first convoy got through without worries, for Civilis was still licking his wounds. But then he got wind that the supply train had again been sent off to Novaesium with its guard of cohorts and was proceeding on its way as if all were peaceful. Only a few men remained at the command posts, their arms were stowed away in the wagons,[1] and everybody was straying about with a complete absence of discipline. Civilis attacked in good order after sending parties ahead to hold the bridges, where the roads narrowed.[2] Fighting developed along the extended column of march, but it was indecisive, and finally night made them break contact. The cohorts rushed on to Gelduba, which still as previously had its camp, guarded by the garrison left there. It was quite obvious that the return trip would involve serious risk for the heavily-laden and demoralized train. Vocula therefore reinforced his troops with 1,000 men taken from the Fifth and Fifteenth Legions besieged at Vetera.[3] These soldiers were insubordinate and hated their officers. More started off than had been detailed, and on the march declared roundly that they had no intention of putting up any longer with short rations and the trickery of their commanders. Those who had stayed behind, however, complained that they had been left in the lurch by the withdrawal of a portion of the legions. Hence there was trouble in both places – one part asked Vocula to return to the camp, the other refused to do so.

36. In the meantime Civilis invested Vetera, while Vocula retreated to Gelduba and from there to Novaesium. He then won a cavalry engagement near Novaesium. But success was no less effective than defeat in stimulating the troops to destroy their leaders. When the addition of the detachments from the Fifth and Fifteenth had swelled their numbers, the legions demanded a bounty, having discovered that Vitellius had sent the money for this. Hordeonius lost little time in handing it over in the name of Vespasian, and it was this step which

1. See p. 155 and n. 1.

2. Probably in the neighbourhood of Rheinberg, where the River Mörs had to be crossed.

3. The account is confusingly abbreviated. The train had returned to Vetera with renewed supplies, and the transports were now making the third run southwards to Novaesium.

did more than anything else to foster mutiny. In a wild riot of pleasure, feasting and seditious gatherings at night, their old enmity for Hordeonius revived, and as none of the officers dared to resist a movement which darkness had robbed of the last vestige of restraint, the troops dragged him out of bed and murdered him. The same fate was in store for Vocula, but he disguised himself in the darkness by dressing as a slave, and managed to get away. 37. As the frenzy subsided, fear returned. They sent some centurions to ask the Gallic communities for reinforcements and pay. For themselves, with the impetuosity, panic and slackness which characterize a leaderless mob, they hastily prepared to resist the approaching Civilis, then promptly dropped their arms and fled. Failure bred dissension, for the contingents from the upper army took an independent line. However, the portraits of Vitellius were replaced in the camps and throughout the nearest communities in Belgica, though Vitellius was already dead. Then the men of the First, Fourth and Twenty-Second repentantly followed Vocula and in his presence once more swore allegiance to Vespasian. They were led off to relieve Mogontiacum, but by this time the besiegers, a mixed force of Chatti, Usipi and Mattiaci, had left the scene with their fill of spoil. Yet they paid in blood for the victory: some troops of ours had fallen upon them on their march, while they were scattered and off their guard. In addition, the Treviri built a battlement and rampart across their own territory, and fought the Germans with heavy losses on both sides. Their subsequent defection tarnished a fine record of service to Rome.

# The New Year, A.D. 70

38. While this was happening, Vespasian and Titus entered office as consuls, the former for the second time. This was done *in absentia*. Rome was depressed and distraught by a variety of fears. Quite apart from the calamities which were in fact impending, it fell victim to an imaginary panic in thinking that the province of Africa had revolted at the instigation of its governor, Lucius Piso. He was the last man to make trouble. But shipping was held up by severe winter storms, and the city populace, who usually bought their foodstuffs from day to day and whose one and only concern for public welfare centred on the corn-supply, were afraid that the coast of Africa was closed and sailings held up. Fear bred conviction, while the story was repeated by the Vitellians, as strongly partisan as ever, and the winners themselves welcomed the rumour – even foreign campaigns could not satisfy their ambition, and no victory in civil war ever did so.

39. The meeting of the senate called by the city praetor, Julius Frontinus, for 1 January passed decrees praising and thanking commanding officers, armies and client-kings. Tettius Julianus was deprived of his praetorship, ostensibly for abandoning his legion when it rallied to Vespasian,[1] in reality so that the vacant post could be transferred to Plotius Grypus. Hormus received the rank of knight.

Before long, Frontinus resigned office, and Caesar Domitian assumed the praetorship. It was his name that stood at the head of official letters and edicts,[2] but real power rested with Mucianus, apart from a number of measures upon which Domitian ventured at his friends' instigation or his own whim. But the men from whom Mucianus had most to fear were Antonius Primus and Arrius Varus. With their laurels fresh upon them, and owing their distinction to the fame of their achievements and the enthusiastic support of the troops,

1. See p. 132.
2. The consuls (Vespasian and Titus) were absent.

they were also the darlings of the people. This was because, once the fighting was over, they had avoided any act of violence.¹ (There was also a story that Antonius had approached Scribonianus Crassus, who derived his prominence from distinguished forebears and his brother's memory,² urging him to assume control of the state. Scribonianus could have relied on the support of a number of men who were in the plot, but he refused. Not an easy man to tempt, even if everything had been cut and dried, he was correspondingly nervous of a mere gamble.) So Antonius could not be publicly humiliated. Mucianus therefore heaped lavish praise upon him in the senate, and loaded him with secret offers, pointing to Nearer Spain, then vacant owing to the departure of Cluvius Rufus. He also distributed the posts of tribune and prefect on a generous scale among Antonius' friends. Then, having filled his mind with empty hope and ambition, he crippled him by removing to its winter camp³ the formation most devoted to Antonius – the Seventh Legion. The Third, too, long associated with Arrius Varus, was returned to Syria. Part of the army was already on its way to the German provinces. All troublesome elements were thus removed, and Rome regained its normal aspect, the rule of law, and the operation of civil authority.

40. During the sitting at which he took his place in the senate, Domitian made a short and restrained speech about his father's and brother's absence and his own youthfulness. He was good-looking, and as his character was still unknown, repeated blushes were taken as proof of modesty. When the prince consulted the house on the restoration of recognition to Galba, Curtius Montanus moved that Piso's memory should be honoured as well. Both proposals were approved by the senate, but so far as Piso was concerned, the thing was never put into effect. A committee was then chosen by lot to supervise the restoration of property stolen during the fighting, and others to survey and re-affix the bronze tablets which contained the text of laws and had suffered decay with the passage of time,⁴ to

1. Compare this admission with the rhetoric of p. 203.
2. Licinius Crassus Scribonianus was an elder brother of Galba's heir Piso; cf. pp. 30ff.
3. Carnuntum in Pannonia (Petronell, east of Vienna).
4. Bronze does not decay with the passage of time. This is probably a diplomatic way of saying that the firing of the Capitol (as it seems, by the Flavians) had damaged many of the tablets. Some were illegible, and their text had to be restored from other sources.

remove from the official calendars the flattery with which the period had disfigured them, and to impose restrictions on state expenditure. Tettius Julianus had his praetorship restored to him when it was discovered that he had taken refuge with Vespasian,[1] while Grypus retained his office. It was then decided to resume the hearing of the case between Musonius Rufus and Publius Celer. Publius was convicted, and satisfaction done to the spirit of the dead Soranus. A sitting notable for strict decisions in public matters did not fail to reflect credit on private individuals also. By bringing the action it was felt that Musonius had done his proper duty. But opinions were divided about the Cynic philosopher Demetrius, because his defence of an obviously guilty man seemed to have been prompted more by reasons of self-advertisement than honour. As for Publius himself, his hour of danger found him inert and speechless.

This was the signal for a hue and cry against the prosecutors. Junius Mauricus asked Domitian to put the imperial diaries at the disposal of the senate so that it could discover from them the identity of the victims whom various individuals had claimed the privilege of impeaching. He replied that, in matters of this sort, the emperor must be consulted.   41. The whole senate, following the lead given by its foremost members, formulated a solemn oath which was taken by all the officials in office without exception and in competition with one another, and by the remaining senators in the order of their seniority. In this they called heaven to witness that they had committed no action tending to anyone's hurt and had got neither reward nor preferment from the downfall of fellow Romans. Senators with guilty consciences were panic-stricken, and adopted various expedients to alter the phrasing of the oath. The chamber showed its approval of those who swore honestly, and stigmatized perjurors. This species of public degradation fell with special severity upon Sariolenus Vocula, Nonius Attianus and Cestius Severus, men notorious for their frequent appearance as prosecutors under Nero. Sariolenus had in addition to face the charge that he had recently engaged in the same activity under Vitellius, and the senators continued to shake their fists at Vocula until he left the chamber. They then transferred their attention to Paccius Africanus, and proceeded to hound him out as well for prompting Nero to destroy the Scribonii, two brothers who had

1. See p. 132.

been famous for their wealth and their devotion to each other.[1] Africanus did not dare to confess his part in this, nor could he deny it. But he rounded on Vibius Crispus, who had been tormenting him with questions. Implicating him in charges to which he had no reply, he parried odium by producing an accomplice.

42. It was on this occasion that Vipstanus Messalla won a great name for loyalty and eloquence. Though under senatorial age,[2] he ventured to plead for his brother Aquilius Regulus. The latter had attained a detestable eminence by engineering the ruin of the house of the Crassi and that of Orfitus.[3] It seemed that as a very young man Regulus had volunteered to take upon himself their prosecution not in order to save his own skin but in the hope of gaining power. Crassus' wife Sulpicia Praetextata and their four children were poised for vengeance, longing for the senate to take up the matter. So Messalla had avoided answering the charge or defending the accused. But he had made an impression on some of his hearers by the self-sacrifice with which he had shielded his brother in an evil hour. He was confronted with a fighting speech from Curtius Montanus, who went so far as to allege that after Galba's assassination Regulus had rewarded Piso's murderer, and had taken a bite at the murdered man's head. 'That action, at least,' he said, 'was not forced on you by Nero, and no purchase of rank or safety called for such fiendish behaviour. No doubt we must put up with the excuses of those who preferred ruining others to imperilling themselves. But in your case, the exile of your father and the division of his fortune among his creditors left you nothing to worry about. You were not old enough to stand for office. You possessed nothing capable of stimulating Nero's greed or fear. When your intellectual powers were still unexplored, when they were never yet put to the proof in the defence of an accused, it was blood-lust and open-mouthed covetousness that made you dabble them in the carnage of noble men. From your country's corpse you stole the spoils of consuls. Sated with seven million sesterces and clad in the shining robes of a

1. In A.D. 67 Scribonius Rufus and Scribonius Proculus, who had governed the provinces of Germany, were compelled to commit suicide by Nero.

2. Twenty-five years. Regulus was Messalla's half-brother.

3. One of the Licinii Crassi was accused by Regulus towards the end of Nero's reign (cf. p. 123, n. 1), as was Cornelius Salvidienus Orfitus. Details are obscure owing to the loss of the end of the *Annals*.

priest, in a career of indiscriminate destruction you trampled on innocent children, men old and distinguished, and women of high rank, blaming Nero for lack of vigour because he wore out himself and his prosecutors by attacking one family at a time. The whole senate, you cried, could be rooted out by a single sentence. Gentlemen, you must protect and preserve such a quick-witted counsellor for the instruction of each future generation. Our seniors imitate Marcellus and Crispus, so let our young folk model themselves on Regulus. Even when it fails, wickedness finds followers. What if it should flourish and wax strong? If we dare not offend one who is still of quaestor's rank, are we to bear the sight of him after he has become praetor and consul? Do you imagine that Nero will be the last of the tyrants? Those who survived Tiberius and Gaius thought likewise in their day, though a more frightful and pitiless ruler was to follow. We have no fear of Vespasian. Our present emperor is a man of maturity and moderation. But examples abide: men pass. We have lost our old vigour, gentlemen. We are no longer the senate which on Nero's death called down on his prosecutors and satellites the traditional punishment of our fathers. After an evil reign, the fairest dawn is the first.'[1]

43. Montanus' speech was listened to with such agreement that Helvidius was encouraged to hope that even Marcellus might be brought low. So he began his speech by praising Cluvius Rufus, who, he said, though just as rich and just as fine an orator as Marcellus, had never impeached a single individual in Nero's time. Then he proceeded to tax Eprius both with his offences and with this example, amid the eager approbation of the senators. Marcellus sensed their reaction, and made as if to leave the chamber, saying 'We shall withdraw, Priscus, and hand over to you your obedient senate. You can play the king in the presence of an emperor's son.' Vibius Crispus began to follow him. Both of them were furious, though their expressions were quite different, Marcellus looking daggers, Crispus all smiles. But their friends ran forward and pulled them back. The conflict of opinion grew more and more pronounced, and as the opposing parties – honest majority and powerful minority – fought it out with bitter determination, the day's sitting ended without agreement.

44. At the next meeting of the senate, the debate was opened by

1. See p. 23.

Domitian. He stressed the need to let bygones be bygones and forget the measures forced upon men by the previous régime, while Mucianus defended the professional prosecutors at length and also gave a warning to those who revived legal processes which they had set in action and then dropped. His language was mild, and sounded like an appeal. As for the senate, it quickly surrendered its newly-won freedom of speech as soon as it was questioned. Mucianus wished to avoid the appearance of flouting the senate's views and condoning every crime committed under Nero. So he compelled Octavius Sagitta and Antistius Sosianus (previously of senatorial rank) to return to their original place of exile in the islands from which they had escaped. Octavius had seduced one Pontia Postuma, and when she refused to marry him, her passionate lover had murdered her. Sosianus was a wicked man who had ruined many victims. Both of these had been condemned to exile by a severely framed decree of the senate, and their sentences were now confirmed, though other offenders were allowed to return home. This however did little to modify the resentment inspired by Mucianus. After all, Sosianus and Sagitta counted for nothing, even supposing they were pardoned. The real threat lay in the cleverness of the prosecutors, their wealth, and the power which they had learned to wield with diabolical skill.

45. An investigation conducted on lines which recalled the old days restored to the senate a brief period of cohesion. A complaint had been made by Manlius Patruinus to the effect that he had been roughly handled in the town of Sena by a rowdy mob, and indeed at the bidding of the local officials. Nor, it seemed, had the outrage stopped there. He had been cornered by a throng of groaning and wailing townsfolk who celebrated a mock funeral under his nose and hurled insults and abuse at the senate as a whole. The accused were summoned to appear, and after a hearing, convicted and punished. In addition, a senatorial decree was passed warning the common people of Sena to behave. In the course of these sittings, Antonius Flamma, who had been indicted by the inhabitants of Cyrene, was condemned under the extortion law and exiled for cruelty.

46. Amid these events a mutiny nearly flared up among the troops. The pretorians who had rallied to Vespasian after being dismissed by Vitellius were asking to be enrolled in their old corps, and legionaries selected for the same promotion demanded the lucrative service which

they had been promised. Even the Vitellian guards could not be got rid of without serious bloodshed. But the cost of maintaining such large numbers of men was likely to be immense. Mucianus entered the pretorian camp to form a more correct estimate of each claimant's seniority, and made the victorious Flavians parade in open order bearing their proper decorations and arms. Then the Vitellians whose surrender at Bovillae I have mentioned and the others who had been rounded up throughout the capital and its suburbs were led on to the parade ground in rags. Mucianus ordered these men to be segregated and formed up in separate parties according as they came from Germany, Britain or any other garrisons. From the first they had been dazed by the sight that greeted them. Facing them they observed what looked like an enemy front-line with a formidable display of arms and equipment, while they saw themselves encircled, naked and bedraggled. But when the process of sorting out began, fear gripped all of them, and the troops from Germany were particularly terrified as they imagined that they were being picked out for execution. They clasped their comrades to their hearts, put their arms round their necks, and kissed them farewell for ever, protesting that they should not be singled out from the rest and left to their fate, nor in a common cause suffer a different destiny. They appealed in turn to Mucianus, to the absent emperor, and finally to heaven and the gods. In the end, Mucianus addressed them all as soldiers of the same allegiance and the same emperor, and thus met their mistaken fears. Indeed, the victorious army added its shouts to their tears. This concluded events on that day. When they heard a speech from Domitian a few days later, they had already recovered their nerve. They now refused the offer of land, and pleaded for continued service and pay. This was a request – but a request which could not be gainsaid. They were therefore taken on the strength of the pretorian guard. Later, those who had reached the age limit and served their time were honourably discharged, while others were got rid of for misconduct. But the men were demobilized selectively and as individuals – the safest method of rendering a mass movement relatively harmless.

47. However, whether because of real financial stringency or to give the appearance of such, the senate resolved that a state loan of sixty million sesterces should be floated for public subscription. Responsibility for this was entrusted to Pompeius Silvanus. It was not long before the need disappeared or the pretence was abandoned. Then, a

law was passed on the motion of Domitian rescinding the consulships granted by Vitellius, and Flavius Sabinus was given a state funeral – striking proofs of the nature of fortune, whose treacherous surface combines the peak and the abyss.

48. These events coincided approximately with the murder of the senatorial governor Lucius Piso. The best way in which I can do justice to this bloodthirsty story is to go back and recall briefly its antecedents. They may have some bearing upon the origin and causes of crimes such as this.

During the reigns of Augustus and Tiberius, the control of the legion stationed in the province of Africa and the auxiliary troops intended to defend the imperial frontiers lay with the senatorial governor. Then Gaius Caesar's restless character and his fear of the official then in control of Africa, Marcus Silanus, induced him to remove the legion from the governor's control and entrust it to a commander sent out for the purpose. Patronage was shared equally between the two. Disagreement had been intentionally invited by the system of interlocking responsibilities, and it was further encouraged by an ugly spirit of competition. The power of the military commanders grew apace owing to their long terms of office,[1] or else because the smaller man always feels the greater urge to keep up with his rival. The senatorial governors on the other hand, being men of eminence, were more concerned for a quiet life than intrigue.

49. However, at the time of which I speak, the legion in Africa was controlled by one Valerius Festus, a young spendthrift who had ambitions and was worried by the fact that he was related to Vitellius. He was frequently closeted with Piso, but whether in these interviews Festus tempted the governor to rebel or himself resisted the other's enticement, it is difficult to say. No third person was present at their secret negotiation, and after Piso's murder the majority of those concerned were only too anxious to curry favour with the murderer. What is beyond dispute is that the province and its garrison had no use for Vespasian, and there were also certain Vitellian refugees from the capital who dangled inducements before Piso's eyes – the wavering loyalty of the Gallic provinces, the readiness of Germany for a change, his own peril, and the greater security which a governor

1. The available statistics hardly bear out this explanation. But Munatius Gallus was legionary commander in Africa for three years (A.D. 100–3) at the time when Tacitus was planning the *Histories*.

suspect in peace could achieve by resorting to war. While all this was afoot, the commander of the Petrian cavalry regiment, Claudius Sagitta, made a quick passage across the Mediterranean, and got to Africa before Mucianus' envoy, the centurion Papirius. Sagitta asserted that the centurion had received instructions to murder Piso. The governor's cousin and son-in-law, Galerianus, had already paid the price. The only hope of survival, he suggested, lay in acting boldly. There were, however, two such courses open to him: he might prefer an immediate military revolt, or he could sail for Gaul and offer his services to the Vitellian armies as their leader. Piso did not react to this at all. As for the centurion sent by Mucianus, when he put in to the harbour at Carthage, he behaved as though Piso were emperor, and was loud in good wishes to him. People who met the centurion were amazed at this sudden and surprising development, but he called on them to echo his acclamations. The mob was gullible enough. They made a rush for the main square, and clamoured for Piso to appear. Their noisy and exultant demonstrations created pandemonium, for they cared nothing for finding out the truth and gloried in flattery. Thanks to Sagitta's information or his own natural reserve, Piso refused to appear in public or countenance the eager plaudits of the crowd. He interrogated the centurion, and finding that the man's business was to incriminate him and secure his death, he had him executed. In doing this he was actuated less by the hope of saving his own life than by the disgust he felt for a cut-throat who had also helped to assassinate Clodius Macer, and who now, while his hands still dripped with the blood of the legionary commander, had re-turned to the scene of his crimes to murder the governor. Then he issued an agitated edict reproving the people of Carthage, and avoided even routine engagements, locking himself in his palace so as to give no excuse, however involuntarily, for a fresh disturbance.

50. But when the rioting of the mob, the centurion's execution and all the exaggerated medley of truth and falsehood typical of rumour came to the ears of Festus, he sent horsemen to kill Piso. They rode at speed, and in the half-light of dawn were already breaking into the governor's palace with drawn swords. Many of them were per-sonally unacquainted with Piso, for Festus had selected Punic and Moorish auxiliaries for this deadly work. Near the governor's bed-room they happened to encounter one of his slaves. They asked him who he was and inquired the whereabouts of Piso. The man's answer

was a gallant lie: 'I am Piso,' said he, and was instantly struck down.
Before long the governor too met his end, for there was somebody
on the spot who knew him.' This was one of the imperial agents in
Africa, Baebius Massa, already the deadly enemy of good men, and a
character destined to figure more than once in our story among the
causes of the sufferings we were later to endure.[1] Festus left Hadrume-
tum, where he had halted to survey the situation, and hurriedly re-
joining the legion, ordered the camp-commandant Caetronius
Pisanus to be clapped in irons. The real reason for this was a personal
feud, but he described him as Piso's accomplice. He punished some of
the soldiers and centurions and rewarded others – neither according
to their deserts, but to make people believe he had crushed an armed
rebellion.

Later on Festus settled a dispute between Oea and Lepcis. Its origin
had been petty – the stealing of crops and herds by the peasants of the
two states. But by this time it involved full-scale hostilities and set
battles. The reason was that the men of Oea, being outnumbered,
had called out the Garamantes, a wild tribe much given to plundering its neighbours. Thus the people of Lepcis had been reduced to
sore straits. Their lands had been extensively ravaged, and they were
now cowering behind the walls of their capital. But the intervention
of the Roman auxiliary horse and foot resulted in the utter defeat of
the Garamantes and the recovery of all the loot, apart from that
which the nomads had sold to the people of the interior as they
wandered from one inaccessible encampment to another.

51. Vespasian had already heard about the battle of Cremona. The
news was good everywhere. Now came word of the death of Vitellius,
brought to him by the many members of the two orders[2] who had
gambled successfully on the risks of a winter passage across the Mediterranean. Vespasian was attended by representatives of King Vologaeses,[3]
who offered him 40,000 Parthian cavalry. It was a flattering symbol of
prestige and success to have such a considerable force of allies at one's
disposal and yet be able to do without them. Vologaeses was thanked,
and told to send envoys to the senate and conclude a formal peace-
treaty. Vespasian, whose mind was set on Italy and events in the capital,
now heard ugly stories about Domitian, who was said to be exceeding

1. Tacitus is thinking of the years A.D. 93–6, when the senate was terrorized
by Domitian: see *Agricola* 45.          2. Senators and knights.
3. Vologaeses I, King of Parthia A.D. 51–79.

both the limits appropriate to his years and the privileges of a son. For these reasons the emperor handed over the main portion of his army to Titus for the winding-up of the campaign in Judaea.

52. There is a story that, before leaving his father, Titus appealed to him at some length not to be incensed by a too ready acceptance of the allegations against Domitian, but to adopt an unprejudiced and conciliatory attitude towards his son. Neither legions not fleets, he said, were such a sure defence to a ruler as a numerous family. Friends were not the same thing: time, chance, sometimes ambition or error cooled their affection, transferred it to others, or caused it to evaporate. But a man's family was inseparable, and this was above all true of emperors, for while their successes profited a wider circle, their misfortunes affected above all those nearest and dearest to them. Even brothers were unlikely to see eye to eye for ever unless their father set them an example.

Though Vespasian was not entirely mollified in his attitude to Domitian, he was certainly delighted by Titus' loyalty. He told him to be of good heart, and exalt his country by war and arms: peace and domestic matters would be his own concern, Then he loaded his fastest ships with corn and consigned them to the still stormy seas.[1] The reason was that the capital was in such dire straits that not more than ten days' supply was left in the granaries when Vespasian's shipments came to the rescue.

53. Responsibility for the reconstruction of the Capitol was delegated by the emperor to Lucius Vestinus. Though he belonged to the equestrian order, Vestinus' prestige and reputation had secured him a place among the leading men of Rome.[2] He summoned the diviners, who advised that the rubble of the earlier shrine should be dumped in the marshes[3] and the temple rebuilt on the same foundations, so far as these remained: it was the will of the gods that the ancient plan should be preserved unaltered. The whole area which was to be dedicated as the site of the temple was marked off by a continuous line of

1. Vespasian must have sent the ships immediately he heard of Rome's predicament (see p. 230). This must have happened in February, and before the normal opening of the summer sailing season in March. Titus left Alexandria *c.* 1 April. Tacitus has postponed the mention of the corn ships in order to secure an easy transition to the events marrated in ch. 53, which were themselves a consequence of orders conveyed to Rome in February.

2. Lucius Vestinus, a knight from Vienne, was governor of Egypt A.D. 59–62.

3. Near Ostia. What was sacred must not be put to profane use.

fillets and garlands, and on 21 June, under a tranquil sky, it was
entered by a procession of soldiers with auspicious names,[1] bearing
boughs of olive and laurel and followed by the Vestal Virgins with
boy and girl attendants who had both parents alive. All these carefully
sprinkled the site with water drawn from springs and rivers. Then the
praetor Helvidius Priscus, guided in the ritual by the pontifex Plautius
Aelianus, purified the area by the sacrifice of pig, sheep and ox, and
offered up the entrails upon a turf altar, praying to Jupiter, Juno and
Minerva, as the deities that ruled the empire, that they would vouch-
safe to prosper the labours now begun, and forasmuch as the building
of their holy house had been undertaken by the devotion of men, to
exalt the same by their divine assistance. Then the praetor laid his hand
upon the fillets around the Stone, to which ropes were secured.[2] In
the same instant, the other officials, the priests, senate, knights and a
large proportion of the populace eagerly and gladly took the strain
and hauled the enormous block into place. Everywhere they cast
into the foundations offerings of gold and silver – nuggets of
unrefined metal in the natural state. The diviners' instructions were
that the building should not be desecrated by the use of stone or
gold intended for any other purpose. Some addition was made to its
height. This, it was felt, was the only change that religious feeling
permitted, and the only respect in which the earlier temple had
been wanting in splendour.

1. Such as 'Faustus', 'Felix' or 'Valens'.
2. Perhaps the Stone or 'Terminus' had been dislodged by damage to the
Temple which incorporated it, and was to be ceremonially replaced in its
original position, symbolizing the irremovability and eternity of the Roman
state.

# The Rhineland Recovered

54. News of the death of Vitellius had meanwhile spread throughout the Gallic and German provinces and doubled the scale of operations. Civilis dropped the mask and threw himself headlong at Rome, while the Vitellian legions actually chose to serve a foreign power in preference to acknowledging Vespasian as emperor. The Gauls had screwed up their courage, imagining that our armies were in the same predicament everywhere. For the word had gone round that the bases in Moesia and Pannonia were under siege by the Sarmatians and Dacians, and a similar story, though false, was told of Britain. But it was above all the burning of the Capitol that had driven men to the belief that the empire's days were numbered. They reflected that Rome had been captured by the Gauls in the past, but as the house of Jupiter remained inviolate, the empire had survived.[1] Now, however, fate had ordained this fire as a sign of the gods' anger and of the passing of world dominion to the nations north of the Alps. Such at any rate was the message proclaimed by the idle superstition of Druidism. There was also a rumour abroad about the Gallic leaders who had been sent by Otho to fight Vitellius. Before they separated, it was alleged, they had sworn an oath to play their part in achieving independence if Rome crumbled under the impact of continued civil wars and internal disasters.

55. Until Hordeonius Flaccus was murdered, there was no overt action to give a hint of the conspiracy. But after his death, messages were exchanged between Civilis and Classicus, the commander of the Treviran cavalry regiment. The latter's rank and wealth put him in a class above others. He was descended from a line of kings, and his forebears had been prominent in peace and war. Classicus himself was in the habit of boasting that he counted among his ancestors more enemies of Rome than allies. Also involved were

1. See p. 190.

Julius Tutor and Julius Sabinus, the former a Treviran, the latter a
Lingon. Tutor had been placed by Vitellius in command of the west
bank of the Rhine. Sabinus for his part, naturally a conceited man,
was further inflamed by bogus pretensions to high birth. He claimed
that the beauty of his great-grandmother had attracted Julius Caesar
during the Gallic War and she had become his mistress.

These men had private and individual talks with other potential
rebels in order to explore their attitude. Then, having revealed their
plans to those whom they thought suitable and thus implicated them,
they met in Cologne, at a private house. This was because officially
the city would have nothing to do with such moves, although a few
Ubii and Tungri were present at the conference. But the Treviri and
Lingones carried most weight and were intolerant of long negotiations. They competed with each other in boastfulness. The Roman
nation, they declared, was in a fever of disunity, the legions cut to
pieces, Italy ravaged. The city of Rome was on the verge of being
captured and in every province the garrison was preoccupied with
fighting on its own doorstep. If the Alps were strongly manned, the
movement for independence would gather way and the Gallic
provinces decide the limits of their dominion at will.  56. These
views had only to be expressed to win instant approval. Dealing with
the rump of the Vitellian garrison was a more difficult problem. A
number of the council thought that they should be put to death as
trouble-makers and turncoats stained with the blood of their leaders.
But a policy of mercy won the day, as it was calculated to obviate the
desperate resistance which the refusal of quarter would inspire. It was
better to entice them into an alliance. If the legionary commanders
alone were killed, the rank-and-file in general would easily be induced
by a guilty conscience and the hope of impunity to come over to the
rebels.

Such, in outline, was their initial plan. A call to arms was issued
throughout the Gallic provinces, though the conspirators themselves
feigned obedience in order to give Vocula less warning of his doom.
Vocula did indeed get wind of what was afoot through certain informants but with his legions under strength and disloyal, he was in no
position to discipline the rebels by force. Caught between an unreliable army and a secret foe, he felt that the best course open to him
was to pay back deception in its own coin, and wield the very weapon
that threatened him. So he moved downstream to Cologne. To this

same city Claudius Labeo (whose capture and removal to Frisian
territory I have described)[1] made his escape after bribing his gaolers.
This man undertook, if given a bodyguard, to go to the Batavians
and force the better part of the tribe to return to their alliance with
Rome. Receiving a small infantry and cavalry force, he made no
attempt to carry out his venture against the Batavians, but induced a
few Nervii and Baetasii to take up arms and conducted less a regular
campaign than a series of stealthy raids against the Cannenefates and
Marsaci.

57. Lured on by the treacherous Gauls, Vocula now marched against
the enemy. He was already nearing Vetera when Classicus and Tutor
went ahead, ostensibly to reconnoitre, and came to a firm understanding with the German leaders. Then, for the first time, they
broke away from the legions and built their own walled camp,
though Vocula protested that Rome was not so racked with civil
strife that even the Treviri and Lingones could afford to despise her.
She still had at her disposal loyal provinces, victorious armies, her
imperial destiny and the vengeance of the gods. That was why
Sacrovir and the Aedui long ago,[2] and in recent times Vindex with
the Gallic provinces, had both been beaten in a single battle. Treaty-
breakers could expect to face the same divine forces and the same fate.
Julius Caesar and Augustus had been better judges of the Gallic
temper, and it was thanks to Galba and his tax concessions that they
had adopted an insolent air of hostility. At the moment the Gauls
were enemies because the yoke bore lightly on their shoulders; when
they had been despoiled and stripped, they would be friends.

This was a spirited speech on Vocula's part. But when he saw that
Classicus and Tutor persisted in their treachery, he turned round and
retired to Novaesium. The Gauls encamped two miles away on the
flat ground. Centurions and soldiers passed to and fro between the
camps, selling their souls to the enemy. The upshot was a deed of
shame quite without parallel: a Roman army was to swear allegiance
to the foreigner, sealing the monstrous bargain with a pledge to
murder or imprison its commanders. Though many of his staff
advised flight, Vocula held that courage was called for. He paraded
the troops, and spoke to them somewhat as follows:

    1. See pp. 216ff.
    2. Sacrovir led an abortive Gallic rebellion in A.D. 21: see Tacitus, *Annals* iii,
40–6.

58. 'I have never addressed you with such anxiety on your behalf or such unconcern for myself. I am content to be told that there is a plan to kill me. I welcome death without dishonour as the end of all my afflictions. It is for you that I feel shame and pity, for you are facing no ordinary array of battle – that is the privilege of a soldier and what one expects of the enemy – but war with Rome. This is what Classicus hopes to wage by your agency when he dangles before you a Gallic empire and asks you to swear allegiance to it. Even if luck and courage have deserted us for the moment, have things reached such a pitch that we have forgotten the lessons of the past when Roman legions chose to perish rather than abandon their post? Our very allies have often endured the sack of their cities and allowed themselves to be burnt to death with wives and children, when their only recompense for doom was fidelity and fame. At this very moment the legions at Vetera are facing hunger and siege, and neither intimidation nor promises can shift them. Our own position is quite different. Apart from munitions, men and excellent defences, we have adequate corn and supplies, however long the campaign. Our financial resources have just permitted the payment of a bounty, and whether you choose to regard this as coming from Vespasian or from Vitellius, you have in any case received it from a Roman emperor. If, after all your victorious campaigns, all the defeats inflicted on the enemy at Gelduba and at Vetera, you are frightened to engage them, this is of course an attitude unworthy of you. But you have a rampart, walls and the skill to hang on until reinforcements and armies gather from neighbouring provinces. Even if I am unpopular myself, there are other commanders and tribunes or in the last resort a centurion or a private. Choose one of these and prevent the whole world learning the monstrous news that you are proposing to offer your obsequious services to Civilis and Classicus for an invasion of Italy. Tell me, if the Germans and Gauls lead you to the walls of Rome, will you attack the mother-city? The imagination shudders at such wickedness. Shall Tutor the Treviran make you mount guard for him? Shall a Batavian lead you into battle, and the German hordes draw upon you for replacements? What will be the final chapter in this career of infamy, when Roman legions deploy against you? Turncoats fleeing from an army of turncoats and traitors from an army of traitors, will you hover between your new and old allegiance as an abomination to the gods? I address this prayer and supplication to you,

Jupiter Best and Greatest, to whom for 820 years we have paid the tribute of triumphs without number, and to you, Quirinus,[1] father of the city of Rome: if it was not your will that this camp should be preserved whole and inviolate while I commanded it, I ask that you will not suffer it to see pollution and outrage at the hands of Tutor and Classicus. Grant to the soldiers of Rome either innocence or a speedy repentance before it is too late.'

59. The speech was heard with emotions which varied between hope, fear and shame. Vocula withdrew and thought of committing suicide, but his freedmen and slaves foiled his desire to anticipate a hideous end. What happened was that Classicus sent Aemilius Longinus, a deserter belonging to the First Legion, and quickly secured his death. As far as the legionary commanders Herennius and Numisius were concerned, confinement seemed sufficient. Then Classicus dressed himself up in the uniform of a Roman general and appeared at the camp. Yet, hardened scoundrel as he was, he found that words failed him. All he could do was to read out the terms of the oath. Those present swore to uphold the Gallic Empire. He promoted Vocula's assassin to a high position among the centurions, and rewarded the rest according to their villanies.

Thereafter, Tutor and Classicus assumed separate responsibilities. Tutor surrounded Cologne with a strong force and compelled its inhabitants and all the troops on the Rhine in Upper Germany to swear the same oath. At Mogontiacum he executed the tribunes and expelled the camp commandant for refusing to swear. Classicus for his part picked out the most vicious of the troops who had capitulated and told them to approach the beleaguered garrison[2] and offer quarter if they were prepared to accept the situation. Otherwise there was no hope for them, for they would have to suffer famine, sword and death. The messengers reinforced their argument by pointing out that they had set the example themselves.

60. The besieged were torn between heroism and degradation by the conflicting claims of loyalty and hunger. While they hesitated, all normal and emergency rations gave out. They had by now consumed the mules, horses and other animals which a desperate plight compels men to use as food, however unclean and revolting. Finally they were reduced to tearing up shrubs, roots and the blades of grass growing

1. The deified Romulus.
2. At Vetera.

between the stones – a striking lesson in the meaning of privation and endurance. But at long last they spoiled their splendid record by a dishonourable conclusion, sending envoys to Civilis to plead for life – not that the request was entertained until they had taken an oath of allegiance to the Gallic confederacy. Then Civilis, after stipulating that he should dispose of the camp as plunder, appointed overseers to see that the money, sutlers and baggage were left behind, and to marshal the departing garrison as it marched out, destitute. About five miles from Vetera, the Germans ambushed the unsuspecting column of men. The toughest fighters fell in their tracks, and many others in scattered flight, while the rest made good their retreat to the camp. It is true that Civilis protested, and loudly blamed the Germans for what he described as a criminal breach of faith. But our sources do not make it clear whether this was mere hypocrisy or whether Civilis was really incapable of restraining his ferocious allies. After plundering the camp, they tossed firebrands into it, and all those who had survived the battle perished in the flames.

61. After his first military action against the Romans, Civilis had sworn an oath, like the primitive savage he was, to dye his hair red and let it grow until such time as he had annihilated the legions. Now that the vow was fulfilled, he shaved off his long beard. He was also alleged to have handed some of the prisoners over to his small son to serve as targets for the child's arrows and spears. However, he did not swear allegiance to the Gallic confederacy or allow any other Batavian to do so, relying as he did upon the resources of the Germans and his conviction that, if it came to a struggle for supremacy with the Gauls, the reputation he had acquired would give him the lead. The legionary commander Munius Lupercus was sent along with other presents to Veleda, an unmarried woman who enjoyed wide influence over the tribe of the Bructeri. The Germans traditionally regard many of the female sex as prophetic, and indeed, by an excess of superstition, as divine. This was a case in point. Veleda's prestige stood high, for she had foretold the German successes and the extermination of the legions. But Lupercus was put to death before he reached her. Some few of the centurions and tribunes – those born in Gaul – were retained as hostages for the security of the alliance. The winter quarters of the cohorts, cavalry regiments and legions were dismantled and burnt, with the sole exception of those at Mogontiacum and Vindonissa.

62. The Sixteenth Legion, together with the auxiliary units which surrendered with it, received orders to move from Novaesium to Trier, a time-limit being fixed for their departure from the camp. Throughout this interval the men occupied themselves with what each thought important. The cowards spent the time in dread of a repetition of the massacre at Vetera, the better sort in fear of their conscience and the scandal. What sort of march was this to be, they asked, and who would lead the way? Besides, everything would be done at the pleasure of those to whom they had surrendered absolute power of life and death. Others again, quite unconcerned about the disgrace, were busy stowing about them their money or favourite possessions. Some few got their equipment ready, and armed themselves as if they were going into battle. Amid such thoughts and preparations, the hour of departure arrived. It was even grimmer than they had anticipated. Inside the rampart, their sorry state had been less obvious, and the full extent of their ignominy was revealed only by the open country and the broad light of day. The emperors' portraits[1] had been ripped off and the standards thus dishonoured, while on either side of them fluttered the gaudy flags of the Gauls. Between marched the men in silence, like a long funeral procession. Their leader was the one-eyed Claudius Sanctus, ill-favoured in looks, and still less blessed with intelligence. Infamy was made doubly infamous when the other legion[2] joined them from the now abandoned camp at Bonn. Besides, the word had gone round that the legions had capitulated.

In the still recent past the natives had shuddered at the mere name of Rome. Now they all rushed out from their farms and houses in one great mob gloating over the novel spectacle. The triumph of the insolent populace proved too much for the Picentian cavalry regiment. Deaf to the promises or threats of Sanctus, they made off to Mogontiacum. Happening to come across Vocula's murderer, Longinus, they made him the target for their weapons and thus took the first step upon the road to redemption. The legions, however, held on their way and in due course encamped before the walls of Trier.

63. Elated by success, Civilis and Classicus debated whether they should not give their armies licence to plunder Cologne. By incli-

1. The portraits are medallions fixed to the poles of the standards.
2. The First.

nation cruel and greedy for booty, they were strongly attracted to the idea of sacking the city. But this course was barred by strategic considerations and the desirability of acquiring a name for clemency in the early stages of establishing a new state. Civilis was further influenced by the recollection of services rendered. At the outbreak of hostilities his son had been arrested at Cologne, but the local authorities had kept him in honourable custody. The tribes east of the Rhine, however, hated the city for its opulence and rapid growth, and only contemplated making peace on one of two conditions: either the settlement was to be opened up to all Germans without discrimination or else it would have to be demolished and the Ubii scattered in the process.

64. So the Tencteri, a tribe separated from Cologne by the Rhine, sent a deputation to lay their demands before the assembled townsfolk. The most vigorous envoy acted as spokesman and expressed himself somewhat as follows: 'We thank the gods whom we all worship, and the greatest of them, Mars,[1] that you have returned to the fold and assumed once more the name of Germans. We congratulate you on the fact that you will at last be free in an association of free peoples. Until today, by barring the rivers, the earth and in a sense the very sky, the Romans prevented conversation and contact between us, or else – and this is a greater insult to born fighters – saw to it that we met disarmed and practically defenceless under the gaoler's eye and on payment of a price.[2] But in order to confirm our friendship and alliance for all time, we call upon you to dismantle the defences that marked your slavery – your city-walls. Even the creatures of the wild lose their spirit in confinement. We also require you to put to death all the Romans in your territory, for liberty is incompatible with the notion of a master race. When they are dead, let their property be shared among the community, so that no one is in a position to hide anything or remain uncommitted to our cause. We and you must have the right to settle on either bank of the Rhine, as our fathers did in the past. Nature has granted every man the privilege of light and day: not less has she given brave warriors access to every land. Go back to your fathers' practices and their way of life, and tear yourselves from those pleasures which the Romans find to be a more effective instrument of domination than arms. As a people

1. The war-god Ziu or Tiu (cf. Tuesday=Fr. mardi).
2. Octroi or customs duty.

sound and uncorrupted, forgetting your past enslavement, you will confront your fellows as their equals, or as their leaders.'

65. The citizens of Cologne took their time to think the matter over. Then, as submission to the terms was rendered impossible by fear of future consequences, and outright rejection no less so by their present plight, they replied to this effect: 'As soon as we had a chance of freedom, we seized it with greater eagerness than caution, for the sake of union with you and the rest of the Germans, who are our kinsfolk. As regards our city-walls, at a moment when the armies of Rome are concentrating, safety demands that we should strengthen rather than demolish them. All the aliens from Italy or the provinces who previously lived among us have become casualties of war, or have fled to their various countries. The original settlers intermarried with us and raised families: their home is here. We do not believe that you are so ungenerous as to want us to kill our parents, brothers and sisters and children. We are prepared to abolish customs-dues and charges upon trade, and to allow unsupervised crossing of the Rhine into Cologne, provided that this takes place by day and no arms are carried, at least until with the passage of time what is now a novel concession develops into a tradition. We shall submit our proposals to the arbitration of Civilis and Veleda, and they shall negotiate and witness the agreement.' This reply satisfied the Tencteri, and a deputation sent to Civilis and Veleda with gifts secured a decision fully satisfactory to Cologne. But any personal approach to Veleda or speech with her was forbidden. This refusal to permit the envoys to see her was intended to enhance the aura of veneration that surrounded the prophetess. She remained immured in a high tower, one of her relatives being deputed to transmit questions and answers as if he were mediating between a god and his worshippers.

66. The alliance with Cologne strengthened Civilis' hand, and he decided to invite the support of nearby communities or to attack them if they offered opposition. Having taken over the Sunuci and embodied their fighting men in cohorts, he found further advance blocked by the resistance of Claudius Labeo and his irregular body of Baetasii, Tungri and Nervii. Labeo relied on his position astride a bridge[1] over the River Maas which he had seized in the nick of time. The battle fought in this confined space gave neither side the advantage until the Germans swam the river and took Labeo in the rear. At

1. Perhaps near the mŏdern Maastricht.

the same moment, greatly daring or by prior arrangement, Civilis rode up to the Tungrian lines and exclaimed loudly: 'We have not declared war to allow the Batavians and Treviri to lord it over their fellow-tribes. We have no such pretensions. Let us be allies. I am coming over to your side, whether you want me as leader or follower.' This made a great impression on the ordinary soldiers and they were in the act of sheathing their swords when two of the Tungrian nobles, Campanus and Juvenalis, offered him the surrender of the tribe as a whole. Labeo got away before he could be rounded up. Civilis took the Baetasii and Nervii into his service too and added them to his own forces. He was now in a strong position, as the communities were demoralized, or else felt tempted to take his side of their own free will.

67. Meanwhile Julius Sabinus demolished any visible reminders of the alliance with Rome, and claimed the title 'Caesar'. He then hastily led a large and ill-disciplined mob of his countrymen against the Sequani, a neighbouring state faithful to us. Nor did the Sequani decline the challenge. Fortune favoured the better side and the Lingones were routed. Sabinus' rashness in forcing an encounter was equalled by the panic which made him abandon it. In order to spread a rumour that he was dead, he set fire to the farmhouse where he had taken refuge, and people thought that he had committed suicide there. However, the ingenious method of concealment by which he kept alive for another nine years, the unflagging fidelity of his friends, and the remarkable example set by his wife Epponina form a story which I shall relate in its proper context. With the Sequanian victory the war movement came to a halt. Gradually the communities began to recover their senses and honour their obligations and treaties. In this the Remi took the lead by issuing invitations to a conference which should decide whether they wanted independence or peace.

68. At Rome, however, pessimistic and exaggerated stories about all these events gave Mucianus much anxiety. He was afraid that, however eminent the commanders – and he had already selected Annius Gallus and Petilius Cerialis – they would be unequal to supreme command in the field. Nor could the capital be left without supervision. Lastly, he feared the ungovernable passions of Domitian, and, as I have said, he had his suspicions of Antonius Primus and Arrius Varus. The latter, as pretorian prefect, was still powerful, and still had a military force under his orders. So Mucianus removed him from

his post, and made him controller of the corn supply as a consolation-prize. To pacify Domitian, who was well disposed towards Varus, he appointed one Arrecinus Clemens, who was connected by marriage with Vespasian and stood high in favour with Domitian, to command the pretorians. The reasons Mucianus more than once gave for this appointment were that Clemens' father had held it with distinction in Gaius' reign, that a familiar name would be popular with the troops, and that, while belonging to the senatorial order, Clemens was quite competent to discharge both functions.[1]

The most distinguished men at Rome were selected to assist in the operations, and others not so distinguished used their influence. Domitian and Mucianus prepared themselves too, though their attitudes differed. Domitian had all the impatience of ambitious youth, while Mucianus kept putting the brake on the young prince's enthusiasm. His fear was that if Domitian once got among the troops the impetuosity natural to his years and the prompting of bad advisers would not help him to act in the best interests of peace or war. The expeditionary force consisted of the victorious Eighth, Eleventh and Thirteenth Legions, the Twenty-First (which had been one of those supporting Vitellius), and, of the recently recruited legions, the Second. These were led across the Alps by the Great St Bernard and Mont Genèvre passes, though part of the army took the Little St Bernard. The Fourteenth Legion was summoned from Britain, and the Sixth and First[2] from Spain.

Thus the news of the army's approach conspired with their own inclinations to induce a change of heart in the Gallic peoples as they assembled for the conference at Reims. Here they were greeted by the Treviran deputation led by the warmongering Julius Valentinus. In a carefully rehearsed speech, he gave vent to the usual criticisms of imperialism, and to his abuse and hatred of Rome, for he was a skilled agitator whose senseless rhetoric won him many admirers.  69. But one of the notables of the Remi, Julius Auspex, stressed Rome's power and the advantages of peace. Even men who were no fighters, he said, found it easy enough to declare war, but in its conduct it was the men of action who bore the brunt, and already the legions were poised to strike. Julius impressed the most sensible of his hearers by his considerate and loyal attitude, while he restrained the younger

1. The pretorian prefecture was normally held by a knight, not a senator.
2. The First (Naval Support) Legion: see pp. 24 and 120.

ones by the appeal to danger and their fears. So while applauding Valentinus' spirit, they followed the advice of Auspex. It is clear that the Treviri and Lingones were prejudiced in the eyes of the Gallic provinces by the circumstance that they had sided with Verginius during the revolt of Vindex. Many were disturbed by the mutual jealousy of the provinces. Where would headquarters be set up? What religious and moral sanctions could they appeal to? If all turned out as they wished, which city would be chosen as capital? While victory was still far away, dissension was already upon them. They squabbled among themselves, some boasting of their alliances, and others of their wealth and manpower or the antiquity of their origin. This tiresome future effectively reconciled them to the present. In a letter addressed to them in the name of the Gallic provinces, the Treviri were invited to refrain from arms, since there was still the possibility of pardon and others were ready to intercede for them if they regretted the past. But resistance came from the same Valentinus, who stopped the ears of his countrymen, though he devoted himself less to the war effort than to a campaign of public speeches.

70. Hence the Treviri, Lingones and other rebellious communities did not prove equal to the highly dangerous situation they had brought upon themselves. Even their leaders failed to make a common plan. Civilis was scouring remote parts of Belgica in an effort to capture Claudius Labeo or dislodge him. Classicus spent most of his time in idleness as if he had won his empire and were making the most of the winnings. Even Tutor did not bestir himself to man the Rhine in Upper Germany and close the Alpine passes. In the meantime, moreover, the Twenty-First Legion invaded the country from Vindonissa, and Sextilius Felix with some auxiliary cohorts effected an entry by way of Raetia, to say nothing of a composite cavalry regiment which had been mobilized by Vitellius and had then gone over to Vespasian's side. This latter unit was commanded by Julius Briganticus, the son of Civilis' sister, who with the bitter animosity often felt by near relatives cordially returned his uncle's dislike. Tutor's Treviran contingent had been reinforced by a recent levy of Vangiones, Caeracates and Triboci, and he now stiffened it with veteran infantry and cavalry, enticing or threatening some legionaries to join him. At first these troops were successful in annihilating a cohort sent on ahead by Sextilius Felix, but when in due course the

Roman army and its commanders approached, they returned to their
original allegiance by an act of honourable desertion, followed by the
Triboci, Vangiones and Caeracates. Tutor, accompanied by the
Treviri, avoided Mogontiacum and fell back on Bingium. Here he
thought he was in safety because he had cut the bridge over the River
Nahe. But some cohorts under Sextilius hurried forward, and finding
a ford, turned the position and put Tutor to flight. This defeat broke
the morale of the Treviri, and the great mass of them threw down
their arms and scattered over the countryside. Some of their chiefs,
to give the impression that they were the first to cease hostilities, fled
to those communities which had not renounced their alliance with
Rome. The legions which, as I have already mentioned, had been
transferred from Novaesium and Bonn to Trier took the oath to
Vespasian of their own volition. These events occurred in the absence
of Valentinus. When he was on the point of regaining Trier in a
frenzy, bent on reducing everything to ruin and confusion, the
legions retired to the friendly Mediomatrici. Valentinus and Tutor
hounded the Treviri back to arms, murdering the legionary commanders Herennius and Numisius to lessen the chances of pardon and
strengthen the bond of crime.

71. This was the war situation when Petilius Cerialis reached
Mogontiacum. On his arrival there was a resurgence of hope.
Petilius was spoiling for a fight, and his strength lay rather in his
contempt for the enemy than in any wariness he displayed in his
dealings with them. His impassioned language fired the troops' enthusiasm, and it was clear that he would engage the enemy as soon as
he could make contact. He sent back to their homes the levies raised
throughout Gaul, and told them to announce that the legions could
cope with the defence of the empire: the allies might return to their
peace-time tasks in the conviction that a war taken in hand by the
Romans was as good as over. This made the Gauls more obedient.
Now that they had their men back at home, they found that the
taxes weighed less heavily, the mere fact of being despised making
them more obsequious. Civilis and Classicus, on the other hand,
learning of Tutor's rout, the Treviran disaster and the generally
favourable prospects opening before the Romans, were thrown into
a fever of panic and haste. While concentrating their own scattered
forces  they sent a stream of messages to Valentinus urging him not
to risk a decisive engagement.

The same considerations induced Cerialis to act quickly. Sending
officers to the land of the Mediomatrici to lead the legions back
against the enemy by the direct route, which was shorter,[1] and
gathering such troops as were available at Mogontiacum and the
force he had brought with him over the Alps, he marched in three
days to Rigodulum.[2] This village had been occupied by Valentinus
with a large contingent of Treviri, since it was protected on one side
by hills and on another by the River Mosel. He had reinforced the
position with trenches and rock barricades. These defences could not
frighten a general of Rome. Petilius ordered his infantry to force a
passage, and sent his cavalry up the rising ground,[3] telling himself that
any advantage such a ramshackle bunch of enemies derived from its
position was more than outweighed by that which his own men could
expect from their gallantry. The climb held up things for a time, as
the cavalry rode past the opposing fire on the flank.[4] But when the
Romans got to grips with them, the enemy were dislodged from
their perch and sent tumbling down the hillside like an avalanche.
Moreover a detachment of the cavalry rode round along the lower
contours[5] and captured the leading Belgians, including their commander Valentinus.[6]

72. On the next day Cerialis entered Trier. His men were agog to
destroy the city, and it is not hard to guess their thoughts. This was
the home of Classicus and of Tutor, the criminals who had encircled
and slaughtered Roman legions. Cremona's fault had been nothing in
comparison, yet it had been torn from the bosom of Italy for delaying
the victors for a single night. Still standing intact upon the borders
of Germany was a place which gloated over armies despoiled and
murdered generals. By all means let the booty pass to the exchequer.
They, the troops, felt that the firing and destruction of a rebellious
town was compensation enough for the sack of all their camps. But
Cerialis was afraid he might become notorious if he gave the troops
a taste for licence and brutality, and so he restrained their bitterness.
What is more, they obeyed, for the ending of the civil war had
improved their discipline in the face of foreign enemies.

1. Than the distance that Cerialis had to cover: Metz–Trier = sixty miles;
Mainz–Trier = ninety miles.        2. See map 8 and Introduction, p. 14.
3. East of point 201, first phase.        4. Second phase.        5. Third phase.
6. The Roman cavalry could remain out of sight of Riol until they reached
point 230.

Their attention was then arrested by the pitiful appearance of the legions brought from the land of the Mediomatrici. The men stood about, miserably conscious of their offence, their eyes fixed on the ground. No words of greeting were exchanged between the armies as they met, nor would the newcomers respond to consolation or encouragement, but hid themselves in their tents and shunned the very daylight. What had petrified them was not so much their predicament or fear as the shame and scandal. Even the victors were nonplussed. Without venturing upon speech or entreaties, they pleaded for pardon with tears and in silence. In the end Cerialis reassured them by repeatedly blaming destiny for events actually caused by the feud between the troops and their leaders or the low cunning of the enemy. They should regard this day as a fresh start in their military service and sworn allegiance. Neither the emperor nor he, Cerialis, wanted to dwell upon the past. Then his hearers were admitted to the same camp, and orders were issued in company details that in the event of an argument or dispute no one should taunt a fellow soldier with sedition or defeat.

73. Then Cerialis assembled the Treviri and Lingones,[1] and thus addressed them: 'I am no orator, and have always supported Rome's reputation for bravery by force of arms. But as you attach great importance to mere words, and judge of good and evil according to the utterances of agitators rather than in the light of their real nature, I have made up my mind to point out a few things. Now that the fighting is over, you may get more help from hearing these facts than we shall from stating them.

'The occupation of your land and that of the other Gauls by Roman generals and emperors was not prompted by self-interest, but happened at the invitation of your forefathers, whose quarrels had exhausted them to the point of collapse, while the Germans summoned to the rescue had imposed their yoke on friend and foe alike. The nature of our German campaigns is not entirely unknown – the many battles against the Cimbri and Teutoni,[2] the strenuous exertions of our armies, and the final upshot. We planted ourselves on the Rhine not to protect Italy but to stop a second Ariovistus dominating

1. Despite the events narrated at p. 251, the Lingones had not yet surrendered, and some must have joined Valentinus, if our text is sound.

2. In the time of Marius the Teutoni invaded Narbonese Gaul and the Cimbri north Italy. But they were defeated respectively at Aquae Sextiae (Aix-en-Provence) in 102 B.C. and at Vercellae (Vercelli) in 101 B.C.

Gaul.[1] Do you imagine that Civilis, the Batavians and the tribes east of the Rhine care any more for you than their ancestors did for your fathers and grandfathers? It is always the same motive that impels the Germans to invade the Gallic provinces – their lust, greed and roving spirit. What they have really wanted is to abandon their marshes and deserts, and gain control of this rich soil and of yourselves. But "liberty" and other fine phrases serve as their pretexts. Indeed, no one has ever aimed at enslaving others and making himself their master without using this very same language.

74. 'Throughout the whole of Gaul there were always despots and wars until you passed under our control. We ourselves, despite many provocations, imposed upon you by right of conquest only such additional burdens as were necessary for preserving peace. Stability between nations cannot be maintained without armies, nor armies without pay, nor pay without taxation. Everything else is shared equally between us. You often command our legions in person, and in person govern these and other provinces. There is no question of segregation or exclusion. Again, those emperors who are well spoken of benefit you as much as they do us, though you live far away, whereas tyrants wreak their will upon such as are nearest to them. You adopt an attitude of resignation towards natural disasters like bad harvests or excessive rainfall: in the same way you must put up with spending and avarice on the part of your masters. There will be faults as long as there are men. But the picture is not one of uninterrupted gloom. From time to time there are intervals of relief by way of compensation.

'You are surely not going to tell me that you expect a milder régime when Tutor and Classicus are your rulers, or that less taxation than now will be required to provide the armies to defend you from the Germans and Britons? For if the Romans are expelled – which Heaven forbid! – what else will result but world-wide war in which each nation's hand will be turned against its neighbour? The good luck and good discipline of eight hundred years secured the erection of this imperial fabric, whose destruction must involve its destroyers in the same downfall. But yours will be the most dangerous situation, for you have the riches and resources which are the main causes of

1. The occupation of Gallic territory in Upper Alsace by the German king Ariovistus was one of the immediate causes for Julius Caesar's conquest of Gaul.

war. At present, victors and vanquished enjoy peace and imperial citizenship on an equal footing, and it is upon these blessings that you must lavish your affection and respect. Learn from your experience of the two alternatives not to choose insubordination and ruin in preference to obedience and security.'

75. Cerialis' hearers had been fearing harsher treatment, and a speech of this sort reassured and encouraged them. Trier was still being garrisoned by the victorious army when Civilis and Classicus sent Cerialis a missive whose substance was as follows: Vespasian, though the news was silent on the matter, was dead; the resistance of Rome and Italy had been sapped by civil conflict; and Mucianus and Domitian were merely helpless puppets. If Cerialis saw fit to take over control in the Gallic provinces, Civilis and Classicus would for their part be content with the present boundaries of their two states. If, however, he were to prefer a fight, then they were ready for that too. To this Cerialis gave Civilis and Classicus no answer. The bearer of the offer and the letter itself he sent on to Domitian.

The enemy now advanced on Trier in several bodies and from every direction. Many critics blamed Cerialis for allowing them to concentrate when he might have dealt with the separate contingents before they effected a junction. The Roman army dug a ditch and built a rampart round their camp,[1] which they had hitherto occupied without fortifying it as prudence required.

76. Among the Germans opinions were divided. Civilis suggested waiting for the tribes from across the Rhine, so that their formidable reputation could complete the annihilation of the shattered Roman forces. The Gauls were merely booty which fell into the lap of the victors. And in any case, the Belgians, who constituted the sole element of strength among them, sided with the confederates openly or at heart. Tutor, however, asserted that delay favoured Rome, since her armies were concentrating from all quarters. One legion[2] had been shipped across the Channel, others had been summoned from Spain or were arriving from Italy. Nor were these legions hastily raised troops, but veterans with experience of war. As for the Germans to whom his colleague looked, they did not know what orders or obedience meant, but invariably acted as the fancy took them. Money and gifts were the only means of bribing such people, and these were

1. On the left or west bank of the River Mosel opposite Trier: see map 9.
2. See p. 252.

available in greater quantity on the Roman side. No man was so
keen on fighting as not to prefer idleness to danger if the profit were
the same. If they closed with the enemy immediately, Cerialis had
nothing but the legions composed of left-overs from the army of
Germany, and these were in any case committed to the Gallic alliance.
Again, the very circumstance that the Romans, much to their amaze-
ment, had just routed Valentinus' scrappy force would serve to
accentuate their recklessness and that of their commander. They
would try another gamble, and this time fall into the hands, not of an
inexperienced youth more practised in words and speeches than in
fighting and the sword, but of Civilis and Classicus. Seeing them
would revive in their imaginations a picture of fear, flight and famine,
and the realization that men who had surrendered so often as they had
done only survived on sufferance. Nor were the Treviri or Lingones
restrained by real affection. They would rise once more when their
fear left them.

77. This conflict of opinion was settled by Classicus' support of
Tutor's view, and the plan was immediately put into effect. The centre
was assigned to the Ubii and Lingones. On the right front were the
Batavian cohorts, on the left the Bructeri and Tencteri.[1] One division
moved up over the hills, a second by the road, and a third along the
ground between the road and the River Mosel. They fell upon the
Romans so unexpectedly that Cerialis was still in his bedroom and in
bed (he had not spent the night in camp) when he got simultaneous
news that the battle had begun and that his men were being worsted.
At first he reprimanded the messengers for being panic-mongers. But
soon the whole extent of the catastrophe was revealed before his eyes.
The legionary camp had been penetrated, the cavalry had fled, and
the intervening bridge over the Mosel which links the further
suburbs with the city was in the hands of the enemy. Cerialis was not
the man to lose his wits in a tight corner. He caught hold of the
fugitives and forcibly drove them back towards the bridge, showing
great dash and exposing himself in the front line, although unprotected by body-armour. Thanks to this reckless but successful energy
and to the rapid concentration of his best fighters, he recovered the
bridge and made sure that it was strongly held by a picked force. Then,
returning to the camp, he found that the companies of the legions
captured at Novaesium and Bonn were wandering aimlessly about

1. See map 9.

while only a few soldiers were gathered around the standards and the eagles were practically cut off. Losing his temper, he exclaimed: 'This is no Flaccus or Vocula whom you are deserting. There is no question of treachery here. The only thing I have to apologize for is that I thought you had forgotten your alliance with Gaul but remembered your oath to Rome. I shall be another Numisius or Herennius, so that all your commanders will turn out to have died at the hands of their own troops or of the enemy. Off with you! Go and tell Vespasian – or Civilis and Classicus, they are nearer – that you have abandoned your commander on the field of battle. Other legions will come, and they will not leave me unavenged or you unpunished.'

78. This was the truth, and the same taunts were driven home by the tribunes and prefects. The men formed up in their cohorts and companies, there being no possibility of deploying in the normal line of battle as the enemy were everywhere and, since fighting was in progress inside the camp rampart, the tents and baggage got in the way. At their various command-posts, Tutor, Classicus and Civilis were spurring their men to battle, urging the Gauls to fight for liberty, the Batavians for glory and the Germans in the interest of plunder. Indeed, everything went in the enemy's favour until the Twenty-First Legion, having managed to mass in a more open space than was available to the other formations, first held the thrust and then threw their opponents back. The working of providence may be detected in the victors' sudden loss of nerve and in their retreat. Their own story was that they had been dismayed by the sight of the auxiliary cohorts which had been scattered at the opening of the attack; for these had now gathered once more on the top of the ridge,[1] giving the impression that they were a fresh reinforcing army. But the real obstacle to a rebel victory was the shocking way in which they scrambled among themselves for loot, for this diverted their attention from the Romans. Thus, though Cerialis had nearly ruined his chances by carelessness, he restored them by determination and exploited his success to the full, capturing the enemy camp on the same day and destroying it.

79. The troops were not allowed to rest for long. A call for help came from Cologne, whose inhabitants offered to hand over Civilis' wife and sister and Classicus' daughter, who had been left there as securities for the alliance. Moreover the townsfolk had in the mean-

1. The ridge between points 145 and 330 in map 9.

time put to death the Germans isolated from each other in their various billets. This step justified the anxiety and urgency with which they issued an appeal that help should reach them before the enemy could rally to achieve his ambition, or satisfy his vengeance. Civilis had moved in their direction too. He was not without striking power, for his crack cohort was intact. Comprising Chauci and Frisii, this unit was stationed at Tolbiacum in the territory of Cologne. But bad news deflected Civilis from his target. The cohort proved to have been destroyed by a cunning ruse. The men of Cologne had plied the Germans with lavish food and drink until they were stupefied, then shut the doors upon them, set fire to the building and burnt them to death. Moreover Cerialis came to the rescue at full speed. Yet a third threat confronted Civilis – the possibility that the Fourteenth Legion with the assistance of the British fleet might raid the Batavian homeland in so far as it was exposed to attack from the North Sea. But the legion's commander, Fabius Priscus, marched his men by land against the Nervii and Tungri, who capitulated to him. As for the fleet, the Cannenefates took the initiative and themselves launched an attack upon it which resulted in the sinking or capture of the majority of the ships. These same Cannenefates also routed a mob of Nervii who had volunteered to take the field in the Roman interest. Again, Classicus successfully engaged the cavalry sent ahead by Cerialis to Novaesium. These minor but repeated losses tended to spoil the glad news of the recent victory.

80. These events coincided with the execution of Vitellius' son at the command of Mucianus, whose excuse was that disunity would persist unless he stamped out the last embers of war.[1] Nor did he permit Antonius Primus to be given a staff appointment by Domitian, being worried by his popularity with the troops and by the conceit of a man who could not brook equals, let alone superiors. Antonius left to join Vespasian, and though his reception did not answer his expectations, the emperor did not rebuff him either. Vespasian was torn between two conflicting forces. On the one hand he appreciated Antonius' services, for there was no denying that it was his generalship that had won the war. On the other hand there were Mucianus' letters. Besides, the rest of them denounced Antonius for his spite and swollen-headedness, not forgetting the earlier scandals of his career. He made matters worse himself because he provoked ill-will by

1. Cf. p. 187.

arrogance and dwelt tediously upon his achievements. He abused Caecina as a prisoner who had capitulated unconditionally, and dismissed the others as men who had no fight in them. Thus little by little he lost ground at court, though outwardly the emperor remained friendly.

## Signs and Wonders

81. In the course of the months which Vespasian spent at Alexandria, waiting for the regular season of summer winds when the sea could be relied upon,[1] many miracles occurred. These seemed to be indications that Vespasian enjoyed heaven's blessing and that the gods showed a certain leaning towards him. Among the lower classes at Alexandria was a blind man whom everybody knew as such. One day this fellow threw himself at Vespasian's feet, imploring him with groans to heal his blindness. He had been told to make this request by Serapis, the favourite god of a nation much addicted to strange beliefs. He asked that it might please the emperor to anoint his cheeks and eyeballs with the water of his mouth. A second petitioner, who suffered from a withered hand, pleaded his case too, also on the advice of Serapis: would Caesar tread upon him with the imperial foot? At first Vespasian laughed at them and refused. When the two insisted, he hesitated. At one moment he was alarmed by the thought that he would be accused of vanity if he failed. At the next, the urgent appeals of the two victims and the flatteries of his entourage made him sanguine of success. Finally he asked the doctors for an opinion whether blindness and atrophy of this sort were curable by human means. The doctors were eloquent on the various possibilities. The blind man's vision was not completely destroyed, and if certain impediments were removed his sight would return. The other victim's limb had been dislocated, but could be put right by correct treatment. Perhaps this was the will of the gods, they added; perhaps the emperor had been chosen to perform a miracle. Anyhow, if a cure were effected, the credit would go to the ruler; if it failed, the poor wretches would have to bear the ridicule. So Vespasian felt that his destiny gave him the key to every door and that nothing now defied belief. With a smiling expression and surrounded by an

1. See p. 240, n. 1.

expectant crowd of bystanders, he did what was asked. Instantly the cripple recovered the use of his hand and the light of day dawned again upon his blind companion. Both these incidents are still vouched for by eye-witnesses, though there is now nothing to be gained by lying.[1]

82. This deepened Vespasian's desire to visit the holy house of Serapis, for he wished to consult the god on matters of state. He had everyone else excluded from the temple, and went in alone, fixing his mind on the deity. Happening to glance round, he caught sight of a leading Egyptian named Basilides standing behind him. Now he knew that this man was detained by illness far from Alexandria at a place several days' journey distant. He inquired of the priests whether Basilides had entered the temple that day. He also inquired of those he met whether he had been seen in the city. Finally he sent off a party on horse, and ascertained that at the relevant time he had been eighty miles away. Thereupon he guessed that the vision was a divine one and that the reply to his query lay in the meaning of the name Basilides.[2]

83. Where the god Serapis came from is a problem which has not yet been brought before the attention of the public by Roman writers. The Egyptian priests give the following account. It concerns Ptolemy, the first Macedonian king of Egypt, who did much to develop the country.[3] While he was engaged in providing the newly-founded city of Alexandria with walls, temples and religious cults, he dreamed that he met a young man of remarkable beauty and more than human stature, who instructed him to send his most trusty courtiers to Pontus to fetch a statue of himself. This, he said, would cause the kingdom to prosper, and whatever place gave the image shelter would become great and famous. Thereupon, continues the account, this same youth appeared to ascend into heaven in a blaze of fire.

These signs and wonders impelled Ptolemy to reveal the nocturnal vision to the Egyptian priests whose practice it is to interpret such things. As they knew little of Pontus and foreign parts, he consulted an Athenian of the clan of the Eumolpidae, one Timotheus, whom he had brought over to supervise ritual, and asked him about the nature of this worship and the identity of the god. Timotheus got into touch with regular travellers to Pontus and from them found out that the

1. See p. 27.                              2. Greek *Basilides* = 'King's son'.
3. Ptolemy I (?305–?282 B.C.), founder of the dynasty.

country contained a city called Sinope, near which was a temple long famous in the neighbourhood and dedicated to Jupiter Dis.[1] The identification was borne out, they added, by the presence nearby of the statue of a goddess commonly described as Proserpina. But Ptolemy was just like a king: though easily upset, on recovering his nerve he showed himself keener on pleasure than religion. Thus he gradually put the matter out of his mind and devoted himself to other business. But in the end the same vision appeared before him, now in a more terrifying and urgent aspect and threatening both king and kingdom with ruin unless its orders were obeyed. Then Ptolemy had ambassadors and gifts assembled for an approach to King Scydrothemis, the then ruler of Sinope, instructing his envoys as they embarked to visit the shrine of Pythian Apollo.[2] The travellers were granted a favourable passage and an unambiguous answer from the oracle. They were to go on their way and bring back the image of Apollo's uncle, leaving that of his sister where it was.

84. On reaching Sinope, they addressed the offerings, requests and instructions of their king to Scydrothemis. The latter found it hard to make up his mind. At one moment, he was frightened of the divine will, at another terrified by the threats of his people, who opposed the transaction; and often he found the gifts and promises of the deputation tempting. In this way three years passed by without any diminution in Ptolemy's enthusiasm and appeals. The status of his ambassadors, the size of his fleet and the weight of his gold were ceaselessly augmented. Then a dreadful apparition confronted Scydrothemis in a dream, forbidding him to delay further the purposes of the god. When he still hesitated, he was vexed by all manner of disasters, by plague and by the manifestation of a divine wrath which became daily more grievous. Then he called his people together and explained to them the orders of the deity, his own vision and that of Ptolemy, and their ever growing afflictions. The common folk, turning a deaf ear to their king and jealous of Egypt, staged a sit-down strike around the temple in self-defence. At this point, the story became even more impressive, telling how the god embarked of his own accord upon the fleet, which was moored by the coast. Then comes the remarkable account of their sailing into Alexandria after completing the long voyage in only three days. A temple

1. The god of the underworld, Pluto.
2. At Delphi.

worthy of a great metropolis was built in the quarter called Rhacotis, where there had long been a chapel dedicated to Serapis and Isis.

Such is the favourite version of where Serapis came from and how he reached Egypt. I am aware that some authorities hold that he was brought from the Syrian city of Seleucia during the reign of the third Ptolemy.[1] Yet another story speaks of the initiative as coming from the same Ptolemy, but makes the original home of the god Memphis, a city once famous as the capital of the Old Kingdom. As for the identity of the god, he is equated by many with Aesculapius because he heals the sick, by some with Osiris, who is the oldest deity known to the Near East, by not a few with Jupiter owing to his all-embracing powers. But the prevailing identification of Serapis as Prince Dis is based on the attributes clearly portrayed in his statues,[2] or on esoteric lore.

85. I return now to Domitian and Mucianus. Before their march brought them to the area of the Alps, they received the good news of the victory at Trier. This was strikingly confirmed by the presence of the enemy commander Valentinus. He was far from demoralized, and his looks were proof of the sort of spirit he had shown. His defence was heard – if only as a study in psychology – and he was condemned. At the moment of execution, someone taunted him with his country's defeat. Valentinus' reply was that he found comfort in death

Mucianus now broached a suggestion which he had long meditated in secret, pretending that it had just occurred to him. Since, by divine mercy, the main forces of the enemy had been crushed, he said it was unseemly for Domitian to come between other generals and their laurels now that the war was practically over. If the stability of the empire or the safety of the Gallic provinces were in jeopardy, Caesar's place would have been in the front line. The Cannenefates and Batavians should be consigned to minor commanders, while Domitian displayed the power and success of the dynasty from the proximity of Lyons, not involving himself in petty perils, though ready to face major ones.

86.   Domitian saw through this sophistry; but there was an element

---

1. Ptolemy III (246–221 B.C.)
2. The attributes are Cerberus and a snake, suggesting the underworld, together with a corn-measure which recalls Demeter, the earth goddess who was mother of Persephone, Pluto's bride.

of deference in Mucianus' careful choice of diplomatic language. In such an atmosphere they reached Lyons. From this town it is believed that Domitian sent secret messengers to seduce Cerialis from his allegiance and see if he would hand over the army and supreme command to himself when they met. He may have been toying with the idea of fighting his father, or it may have been a manoeuvre to gain support and vantage against his brother. No one could tell, for Cerialis steered a safe course and returned an evasive answer to what he took to be the idle fancy of a child. Domitian realized that his elders despised his youthfulness, and ceased to discharge even the slight official duties he had previously undertaken. Assuming an ingenuous air of abstraction and looking as if butter would not melt in his mouth, he posed as a connoisseur of literature and poetry. What he was after was to hide his real character and avoid competing with his brother, whose gentler nature, quite unlike his own, he totally misconstrued.

*Book Five*

# The Jews

1. At the beginning of the same year[1] Titus Caesar, who had been selected by his father to complete the conquest of Judaea and already enjoyed a reputation as a general when Vespasian and he began to be talked of, received added support and recognition, as provinces and armies vied in displaying their enthusiasm. He was anxious to live up to his new position by cutting a fine figure and showing enterprise in arms. His polite and affable manners gained him devoted followers. In military duties and on the march he often mixed with the ordinary soldiers without sacrificing the respect due to a commanding officer.

Awaiting him in Judaea were three legions that had long served under Vespasian – the Fifth, Tenth and Fifteenth. The emperor also allotted him the Twelfth from Syria and the drafts from the Twenty-Second and the Third brought up from Alexandria. He was attended by twenty cohorts of allied infantry and eight regiments of cavalry, as well as by the two kings Agrippa and Sohaemus and the supporting forces offered by King Antiochus.[2] Then there were strong levies of Arabs, who felt for the Jews the hatred common between neighbours, and many individual adventurers from Rome and Italy who for various reasons hoped to ingratiate themselves with an emperor whose ear might still be gained. This then was the army with which Titus entered enemy territory.[3] He advanced in an orderly fashion, maintaining good reconnaissance and a state of readiness for battle, and encamped at no great distance from Jerusalem.

2. As I am now to record the death-agony of a famous city, it seems appropriate to inform the reader of its origins. The Jews are said to have been refugees from the island of Crete who settled in the remotest corner of Libya in the days when, according to the story, Saturn was driven from his throne by the aggression of Jupiter. This

1. A.D. 70.          2. See pp. 129 ff.          3. In April.

is a deduction from the name 'Judaei' by which they became known: the word is to be regarded as a barbarous lengthening of 'Idaei', the name of the people dwelling around the famous Mount Ida in Crete. A few authorities hold that in the reign of Isis the surplus population of Egypt was evacuated to neighbouring lands under the leadership of Hierosolymus and Judas. Many assure us that the Jews are descended from those Ethiopians who were driven by fear and hatred to emigrate from their home country when Cepheus was king. There are some who say that a motley collection of landless Assyrians occupied a part of Egypt, and then built cities of their own, inhabiting the lands of the Hebrews and the nearer parts of Syria. Others again find a famous ancestry for the Jews in the Solymi who are mentioned with respect in the epics of Homer: this tribe is supposed to have founded Jerusalem[1] and named it after themselves.    3. Most authorities, however, agree on the following account. The whole of Egypt was once plagued by a wasting disease which caused bodily disfigurement. So Pharaoh Bocchoris[2] went to the oracle of Hammon to ask for a cure, and was told to purify his kingdom by expelling the victims to other lands, as they lay under a divine curse. Thus a multitude of sufferers was rounded up, herded together, and abandoned in the wilderness. Here the exiles tearfully resigned themselves to their fate. But one of them, who was called Moses, urged his companions not to wait passively for help from god or man, for both had deserted them: they should trust to their own initiative and to whatever guidance first helped them to extricate themselves from their present plight. They agreed, and started off at random into the unknown. But exhaustion set in, chiefly through lack of water, and the level plain was already strewn with the bodies of those who had collapsed and were at their last gasp when a herd of wild asses left their pasture and made for the shade of a wooded crag. Moses followed them and was able to bring to light a number of abundant channels of water whose presence he had deduced from a grassy patch of ground. This relieved their thirst. They travelled on for six days without a break, and on the seventh they expelled the previous inhabitants of Canaan, took over their lands and in them built a holy city and temple.

4. In order to secure the allegiance of his people in the future, Moses prescribed for them a novel religion quite different from those of the

1. In Latin, *Hierosolyma*.
2. C. 721–715 B.C. (24th Dynasty); the date is much too late.

rest of mankind. Among the Jews all things are profane that we hold sacred; on the other hand they regard as permissible what seems to us immoral. In the innermost part of the Temple, they consecrated an image of the animal which had delivered them from their wandering and thirst, choosing a ram as beast of sacrifice to demonstrate, so it seems, their contempt for Hammon.[1] The bull is also offered up, because the Egyptians worship it as Apis. They avoid eating pork in memory of their tribulations, as they themselves were once infected with the disease to which this creature is subject.[2] They still fast frequently as an admission of the hunger they once endured so long, and to symbolize their hurried meal the bread eaten by the Jews is unleavened. We are told that the seventh day was set aside for rest because this marked the end of their toils. In course of time the seductions of idleness made them devote every seventh year to indolence as well. Others say that this is a mark of respect to Saturn, either because they owe the basic principles of their religion to the Idaei, who, we are told, were expelled in the company of Saturn and became the founders of the Jewish race, or because, among the seven stars that rule mankind, the one that describes the highest orbit and exerts the greatest influence is Saturn. A further argument is that most of the heavenly bodies complete their path and revolutions in multiples of seven.

5. Whatever their origin, these observances are sanctioned by their antiquity. The other practices of the Jews are sinister and revolting, and have entrenched themselves by their very wickedness. Wretches of the most abandoned kind who had no use for the religion of their fathers took to contributing dues and free-will offerings to swell the Jewish exchequer; and other reasons for their increasing wealth may be found in their stubborn loyalty and ready benevolence towards brother Jews. But the rest of the world they confront with the hatred reserved for enemies. They will not feed or intermarry with gentiles. Though a most lascivious people, the Jews avoid sexual intercourse with women of alien race. Among themselves nothing is barred. They have introduced the practice of circumcision to show that they are different from others. Proselytes to Jewry adopt the same practices, and the very first lesson they learn is to despise the gods, shed

1. The Egyptian god Amon of Thebes is represented as horned, and the ram was only occasionally offered up to him.
2. Leprosy.

all feelings of patriotism, and consider parents, children and brothers as readily expendable. However, the Jews see to it that their numbers increase. It is a deadly sin to kill an unwanted child, and they think that eternal life is granted to those who die in battle or execution – hence their eagerness to have children, and their contempt for death. Rather than cremate their dead, they prefer to bury them in imitation of the Egyptian fashion, and they have the same concern and beliefs about the world below. But their conception of heavenly things is quite different. The Egyptians worship a variety of animals and half-human, half-bestial forms, whereas the Jewish religion is a purely spiritual monotheism. They hold it to be impious to make idols of perishable materials in the likeness of man: for them, the Most High and Eternal cannot be portrayed by human hands and will never pass away. For this reason they erect no images in their cities, still less in their temple. Their kings are not so flattered, the Roman emperors not so honoured. However, their priests used to perform their chants to the flute and drums, crowned with ivy, and a golden vine was discovered in the Temple; and this has led some to imagine that the god thus worshipped was Prince Liber,[1] the conqueror of the East. But the two cults are diametrically opposed. Liber founded a festive and happy cult: the Jewish belief is paradoxical and degraded.

6. Their country and its limits are bounded on the east by Arabia, on the south by Egypt, and on the west by Phoenicia and the sea; of the north they have a distant view on the side towards Syria. The health of the Jews is good, and their physique sturdy. A dry climate and a fertile soil enable them to grow all the crops familiar to us, and in addition, balsam and palm. While palm-groves are notable for height and beauty, the balsam is a small tree. From time to time its branches swell, and if a steel knife is applied to them, the tubes which convey the sap receive a shock; so an incision is made with a fragment of stone or a potsherd, the sap being put to medicinal uses. The highest mountain to which Palestine rises is Lebanon, which, surprisingly enough in this semi-tropical climate, is thickly wooded and keeps unfalteringly its covering of snow. Its slopes feed the tumbling waters of the Jordan. This river does not empty itself into the Mediterranean, but flows through two lakes without losing its identity until it is finally absorbed in a third. This third lake resembles a sea in the vast extent of its circumference, but its water is even nastier to the taste,

1. Bacchus, god of the vine.

and unhealthy exhalations cause disease among those who live on its banks. Never ruffled by the wind, it admits the presence of neither fish nor water-fowl. The water – if water it be – sustains objects thrown upon it as if it were solid, and swimmers and non-swimmers find it equally buoyant. At a fixed season of the year the lake discharges bitumen. Experience teaches every skill, and has shown men how to gather this substance too. In its natural state a black liquid, it solidifies when sprinkled with vinegar, and floats on the surface of the water. Those who have the job of gathering the bitumen take hold of it with their hands and haul it on deck. Thereupon it follows automatically in a continuous stream which fills the boat until it is severed. But to sever it is quite impossible with any tool of bronze or iron, though it shuns blood or a cloth contaminated with a woman's menses. This is the story told by ancient writers; but those who know the locality personally say that the floating masses of bitumen are propelled by hand over the water and dragged on land. Then, after it has dried out on the hot soil or in the blazing sun, it can be cut up with axes and wedges as if it were timber or stone.

7. Not far from the Dead Sea is a plain which tradition says was consumed by lightning, though it was once fruitful and supported great and populous cities.[1] It seems that the ruins of these cities can still be traced, and that the very earth looks scorched and has lost its fertility. All natural vegetation and all crops sown by the hand of man, no matter whether in the blade, in the flower, or apparently fully developed, are blackened and insubstantial growths that crumble into a species of powder. Personally I am quite prepared to grant that once-famous cities may have been burnt up by fire from heaven, but I also think that the exhalation from the lake infects the ground and poisons the atmosphere above it, and that this is the reason why the young corn and the harvests of autumn rot: both soil and air are unfavourable. I should add that one of the rivers flowing into the Jewish Sea is the Belius, at whose mouth are sands which are collected and fused with natron to form glass. The beach concerned is small and yet inexhaustible whatever the quantities removed.

8. Much of Judaea is thickly studded with villages, and the Jews have towns as well. Their capital is Jerusalem. Here stood their Temple with its boundless riches. Outer defences covered the city; then came the royal palace; and the Temple was enclosed by an inner bulwark.

1. See *Genesis* xix, 24.

The Jew, and the Jew alone, was allowed to approach the gate of the Temple, and all but priests were denied access within its threshold.

While the Assyrian, Median and Persian Empires dominated the East, the Jews were slaves regarded as the lowest of the low. In the Hellenistic period, King Antiochus[1] made an effort to get rid of their primitive cult and hellenize them, but his would-be reform of this degraded nation was foiled by the outbreak of war with Parthia, for this was the moment of Arsaces' insurrection.[2] Then, since the Hellenistic rulers were weak and the Parthians had not yet developed into a great power (Rome, too, was still far away), the Jews established a dynasty of their own. These kings were expelled by the fickle mob, but regained control by force, setting up a reign of terror which embraced, among other typical acts of despotism, the banishment of fellow-citizens, the destruction of cities, and the murder of brothers, wives and parents. The kings encouraged the superstitious Jewish religion, for they assumed the office of High Priest in order to buttress their régime.

9. Roman control of Judaea was first established by Gnaeus Pompey. As victor[3] he claimed the right to enter the Temple, and this incident gave rise to the common impression that it contained no representation of the deity – the sanctuary was empty and the Holy of Holies untenanted. Though the walls of Jerusalem were dismantled, the shrine remained intact. During the civil war which then afflicted the Roman world, the eastern provinces passed under the control of Mark Antony and Judaea was conquered by the Parthian king Pacorus. But the invader was killed by Publius Ventidius, and the Parthians driven back across the Euphrates, while Gaius Sosius brought the Jews to heel.[4] Antony gave the kingdom to Herod, and it was enlarged by the now victorious Augustus. At Herod's death, without waiting for the imperial decision, a certain Simon usurped the title of king. He was dealt with by the governor of Syria, Quintilius Varus,[5] while the Jews were disciplined and divided up into three kingdoms

---

1. Antiochus IV Epiphanes of Syria (176–164 B.C.)
2. False: the Arsacid dynasty of Parthia gained power about 250 B.C.
3. On constituting the province of Syria in 63 B.C. after defeating Mithridates of Pontus.
4. In 38 B.C. Ventidius and Sosius were lieutenants of Mark Antony.
5. Varus was governor of Syria, 6–4 B.C.

ruled by Herod's sons.[1] In Tiberius' reign all was quiet. Then, rather
than put up a statue of Gaius Caesar in the Temple as they had been
ordered, the Jews flew to arms, though the rebellion came to nothing
owing to the assassination of the emperor.[2] As for Claudius, he took
advantage of the death or declining fortunes of the Jewish kings to
commit the government of the province to Roman knights or
freedmen. One of these, Antonius Felix, played the tyrant with the
spirit of a slave, plunging into all manner of cruelty and lust, and
marrying Drusilla, granddaughter of Cleopatra and Antony. This
meant that while Claudius was Antony's grandson, Felix was his
grandson by marriage.   10. However, the Jews patiently endured
their fate until Gessius Florus became governor.[3] During his term of
office war broke out. An attempt by Cestius Gallus, governor of
Syria, to repress the movement led to indecisive battles and more
often to defeats. When Gallus died a natural death – or else committed
suicide in mortification – Nero sent out Vespasian. Good luck, a
distinguished record and excellent subordinates enabled him within
the space of two summers[4] to plant his victorious flag throughout the
whole of the flat country and in all the cities except Jerusalem. The
next year was preoccupied by the civil war and passed without activity so far as the Jews were concerned, but when peace reigned in
Italy foreign affairs once more claimed attention. Rising anger was
felt at the fact that by this time only the Jews had failed to submit. It
also seemed advisable that Titus should remain at the head of the
armies to cope with all the eventualities or mishaps which might
confront a new dynasty.

11. So after encamping, as I have said, before the walls of Jerusalem,
he paraded his legions in formation before the eyes of the enemy. The
Jews, marshalled close under their walls, were in a position to venture
further out if they were successful and had a place of refuge ready at
hand in case of defeat. Titus sent against them cavalry and some cohorts in battle order, but the encounter was indecisive. Then the
enemy gave ground, and for some days thereafter fought a succession
of engagements just in front of the gates. Finally, repeated losses drove
them behind the walls. The Romans then concentrated on an assault.
After all, it seemed beneath them to wait for hunger to do its work on

1. Archelaus, Herod Antipas and Philip.          2. 24 January A.D. 41.
3. Gessius Florus governed Roman Judaea in A.D. 65–6.
4. A.D. 67 and 68.

the enemy, and the troops actually asked to be allowed to risk their lives. Some did so because they had real courage, many from mere bravado and a desire for rewards. As for Titus, his imagination dwelt on Rome, wealth and pleasure: it would be long before these dreams were realized if Jerusalem were destined not to fall in the immediate future.

But the city occupied a commanding position, and it had been reinforced by engineering works so massive that they might have rendered even a flat site impregnable. Two lofty hills were enclosed by walls skilfully staggered and forming re-entrant angles designed to expose the flank of an attacker. At the edge of the crags was a sharp drop, and a series of towers dominated the scene, 105 feet high where the rising ground helped, and 135 or 120 feet high on the lower contours.[1] These presented an impressive appearance, and to the distant observer seemed to be on a level. There were further walls inside around the palace, and a conspicuous landmark was the lofty castle of Antonia, so named by Herod in honour of Mark Antony.

12. The Temple was like a citadel and had its own walls, which had been even more laboriously and skilfully constructed than the rest. The porticoes around it constituted in themselves an excellent defensive position. To these advantages must be added a spring of never-failing water, chambers cut in the living rock, and tanks and cisterns for the storage of rainwater. Its builders had foreseen only too well that the strange practices of the Jews would lead to continual fighting. Hence everything was available for a siege, however long. Moreover, after Pompey's capture of Jerusalem, fear and experience taught them many lessons. So taking advantage of the money-grubbing instincts of the Claudian period, they purchased permission to fortify the city, and in the days of peace built walls meant for war. Already the home of a motley concourse, its population had been swollen by the fall of the other Jewish cities, for the most determined partisan leaders escaped to the capital, and thereby added to the turmoil. There were three different leaders and three armies. The long outer perimeter of the walls was held by Simon, the central part of the city by John, and the Temple by Eleazar. John

---

1. The figures given here, in part conjectural, are based on Josephus' information. The first numeral reads in the manuscripts of Tacitus 'sixty', the symbol *cv* having perhaps been misinterpreted as *lx*.

and Simon could rely on numbers and equipment, Eleazar on his strategic position. But it was upon each other that they turned the weapons of battle, ambush and fire, and great stocks of corn went up in flames. Then John sent off a party of men, ostensibly to offer sacrifice but in reality to cut Eleazar and his followers to pieces, thus gaining possession of the Temple. Henceforward, therefore, Jerusalem was divided between two factions, until, on the approach of the Romans, fighting the foreigner healed the breach between them.

13. Prodigies had occurred, but their expiation by the offering of victims or solemn vows is held to be unlawful by a nation which is the slave of superstition and the enemy of true beliefs. In the sky appeared a vision of armies in conflict, of glittering armour. A sudden lightning flash from the clouds lit up the Temple. The doors of the holy place abruptly opened, a superhuman voice was heard to declare that the gods were leaving it, and in the same instant came the rushing tumult of their departure. Few people placed a sinister interpretation upon this. The majority were convinced that the ancient scriptures of their priests alluded to the present as the very time when the Orient would triumph and from Judaea would go forth men destined to rule the world. This mysterious prophecy really referred to Vespasian and Titus, but the common people, true to the selfish ambitions of mankind, thought that this mighty destiny was reserved for them, and not even their calamities opened their eyes to the truth.

We are told that the number of the besieged, old and young, men and women, amounted to 600,000. All who could bear arms did so, and more than their numbers warranted had the courage necessary. They displayed an inflexible determination, women no less than men, and the thought that they might be compelled to leave their homes made them more afraid of living than of dying.

This, then, was the city and nation which Titus faced. Since a headlong assault and the element of surprise were ruled out by the lie of the ground, he proposed to employ earthworks and mantlets. Each legion had its allotted task, and there was a lull in the fighting while they pushed on with the construction of every conceivable device for storming cities, whether invented long ago or due to the ingenuity of modern times.

# The Collapse of Civilis

14. After his ill-success at Trier, Civilis gathered reinforcements throughout Germany, and took up his position by the camp at Vetera. The site he had chosen was a safe one, and his idea was to hearten the barbarians with the memory of the successes they had won there. Cerialis followed him to the same spot, his forces doubled by the arrival of the Second, Sixth and Fourteenth Legions. Besides, the cohorts and cavalry regiments summoned long before had quickened their pace after the victory. Neither commander was a sluggard, but they were separated by a vast expanse of swampy ground. This was its natural state, and Civilis had also built a dam at an angle into the Rhine to hold up the river and cause it to flood the adjacent soil. Such, then, was the terrain: a slippery, treacherous waste of inundated land. It told against us, for while the Roman legionary was laden with arms and frightened of swimming, the Germans were familiar with rivers and could rely upon their height and the lightness of their loads to raise them above the level of the waters.

15. In answer to the Batavian challenge, therefore, those of our troops who were spoiling for battle threw themselves into the fight, but panicked when their arms and mounts sank into the dangerous depths of the morass. The Germans knew where the shallows were, and galloped through them, usually avoiding our front-line and surrounding the flanks and rear. There was no question of a normal infantry battle at close quarters. It resembled nothing so much as a naval engagement, as the men floundered about everywhere in the flood waters or grappled hand and foot on any patch of firm ground where they could stand. Wounded and unwounded, swimmers and non-swimmers, they were locked in mutual destruction. However, despite the wild confusion, losses were comparatively light, for the Germans did not venture beyond the flooded ground and returned to their camp. The result of this encounter prompted both comman-

ders, however different their moods, to force a final decision without delay. Civilis wanted to exploit success, and Cerialis to wipe out humiliation. While the Germans were elated by victory, a sense of outraged honour stimulated the Romans. The natives passed the night singing or shouting, our troops in sullenness and threats.

16. At dawn on the following day Cerialis formed his front of cavalry and auxiliary cohorts and posted the legions behind them, keeping a picked force under his personal command in case of emergencies. Civilis avoided extending his line and marshalled his force in compact battle-groups. The Batavians and Cugerni were on his right, while his left flank nearer the river was held by the Germans from across the Rhine. The two generals did not make the usual speech to their troops at large, but addressed each formation as they rode up to it. Cerialis dwelt on the ancient renown of Rome and alluded to past and present victories, calling for the total annihilation of a treacherous, cowardly and conquered enemy. What was wanted, he said, was vengeance, not battle. They had just fought an engagement in which they were themselves outnumbered; yet the pick of the Germans had been routed, and the survivors bore flight in their hearts and scars upon their backs. Then he found appropriate arguments to spur the courage of the various legions, calling the men of the Fourteenth the conquerors of Britain. Galba, he added, had owed his elevation to the lead given by the Sixth, and in the coming battle the men of the Second would handsel their new standards and new eagle. Riding further along the ranks towards the garrison of Germany, he stretched out his hands in an appeal to them to recover at the cost of the blood of the enemy a river-frontier and a camp rightfully theirs. There was a general shout of mounting enthusiasm. Some were impatient for battle after a long peace, others keen on peace from war-weariness, while for the future they looked forward to rewards and a quiet life.

17. Nor was it in silence that Civilis got his troops into position. He called upon the very site of the battle to bear witness to their courage, and told the Germans and Batavians that they stood upon the tokens of their triumph and trod the ashes and bones of legions. Wherever the Roman looked, he said, he was confronted by captivity, defeat and doom. They must not be dismayed by the fluctuating fortunes of the Battle of Trier when the Germans' own victory had stood in their way, making them drop their weapons and cumber their hands

with loot. But afterwards the story was one of unbroken success and enemy failure. Whatever advantages tactical skill could provide had been provided, including a sodden plain with which they were familiar and marshes which hampered the enemy. The Rhine and the gods of Germany were within sight. Under their divine protection they were to take the offensive, with thoughts of their wives, parents and country. This day would either win them a renown unparalleled in their past history, or humiliate them in the eyes of posterity.

When his words had been applauded with the usual war-dances and clashing of arms, a rain of stones, sling-shots and other missiles marked the beginning of the engagement. Our troops did not enter the marsh, and the Germans tried to taunt them into doing so. 18. When ammunition gave out and the fight grew hotter, the enemy charged forward with greater fury. Keeping out of reach themselves, they made use of their imposing stature and immense spears to stab the wavering and shaken Romans. Besides, a party of Bructeri managed to swim across the river from the mole which, as I have recorded, was built out into the Rhine. There was a confused scene here, and the front-line, consisting of allied cohorts, was on the point of being driven from the field when the legions took over and contained the enemy thrust, thus restoring the balance of advantage. While this was happening, a Batavian turncoat came up to Cerialis with an offer to take the enemy in the rear if some cavalry were sent round the far end of the marsh, where the ground was firm and the Cugerni assigned to its defence were off their guard. Two cavalry regiments were sent off with the man, and surrounded the unwary foe. When a burst of shouting told what had happened, the legions pressed forward on the main front, and the Germans turned and fled to the Rhine. This day's work would have marked the end of the war if the Roman fleet had been quick enough to follow it up. Nor did the cavalry press their advantage either, as rain suddenly poured down and dusk was at hand.

19. The next day the Fourteenth Legion was sent off to join Annius Gallus in the upper province, Cerialis' effectives being kept up to strength by the arrival of the Tenth Legion from Spain. As for Civilis, he received reinforcements from the Chauci, but not venturing to hold the Batavian capital, he hastily gathered up such property as was portable, set fire to the rest, and retreated to the Island. He was aware that the Romans had no ships for bridge-building, and that their army was not going to cross the river in any other way.

What is more, he dismantled the mole constructed by Drusus Germanicus, and thus the Rhine, which in any case tends to flow into the Gallic arm owing to the fall of the ground, poured down in spate when the barrier was removed. This was tantamount to diverting the course of the river, for a shallow bed was all that now separated the Island from Germany, presenting an apparently uninterrupted landscape. Others who crossed the Rhine were Tutor and Classicus and a hundred and thirteen Treviran senators, among them the Alpinius Montanus whom I have mentioned previously[1] as the officer sent by Antonius Primus to the Gallic provinces. He was accompanied by his brother Decimus Alpinius. The other leaders, too, by angling for sympathy and offering bribes, proceeded to gather recruits among tribes who thirsted for adventure.

20. In fact, the rebels had plenty of fight left in them, so much so that on one and the same day Civilis mounted a fourfold assault on the positions occupied by the cohorts, cavalry regiments and legions. His targets were the Tenth Legion at Arenacium and the Second at Batavodurum, together with Grinnes and Vada, where the cohorts and cavalry regiments were encamped. Civilis divided his troops into separate contingents under the command of himself, his sister's son Verax, Classicus, and Tutor. He was not so optimistic as to imagine that he would succeed everywhere. But the gamble might well come off at one of these several points. Besides, Cerialis was a reckless commander, and might be intercepted on the way as he rushed to and fro in response to the various alarms. The force detailed to deal with the camp of the Tenth thought that an outright assault would be too difficult. So when the Roman troops had gone out and were busy felling timber, they pounced upon them and threw them into disorder, killing the camp commandant, five senior centurions, and a few other ranks. The rest took refuge behind their defences. Meanwhile a German force tried to break down the bridge which was under construction at Batavodurum, but the action was indecisive and had to be broken off at dusk.

21. The situation was more dangerous at Grinnes and Vada. Vada was attacked by Civilis, and Grinnes by Classicus. The assailants could not be halted, and our best men were killed, including the cavalry commander Briganticus, who, as I have said,[2] was faithful to Rome and hated his uncle Civilis. But when Cerialis came to the rescue

1. See pp. 225 ff.        2. See p. 253.

with a picked body of horse, our luck changed, and the Germans were driven headlong into the river. Civilis attempted to halt the rout, but he was recognized, fired at, and compelled to abandon his mount and swim across the Rhine. Verax escaped in the same way, while Tutor and Classicus were taken off in some small boats which put in. The Roman fleet did not participate in this engagement either. Though ordered to intervene, it was hampered by fear and the dispersal of the crews on other military duties. Admittedly, Cerialis allowed insufficient time for the execution of his orders, being a man who improvised on the spur of the moment and yet in the upshot was brilliantly successful, luck supplying any deficiency of generalship. Hence neither he nor his army worried overmuch about discipline.

Indeed, a few days later an incident occurred which, though involving no risk of his capture, nevertheless earned him some discredit. 22. He had gone to Novaesium and Bonn to inspect the camps which were being put up to accommodate the legions for the winter,[1] and was returning with a naval flotilla. March discipline was poor, and his pickets careless. This was observed by the Germans, who made plans for a surprise attack. Choosing a dark and cloudy night, they swept downstream and penetrated the camp without interference. The massacre was initiated by an act of low cunning. They cut the guy-ropes and put the Romans to the sword while they were still fumbling about under their own tents.[2] Another party of assailants threw the naval force into disarray, and attached hawsers to the ships and towed them off by the sterns. The silence which had assisted surprise was succeeded, once the bloodshed began, by the wild clamour with which the enemy sought to spread dismay and confusion. The Romans were by this time roused by their wounds. They looked about for their weapons and scuttled down the lanes between the tents. Only a few had their proper equipment on. The majority rolled their clothing round their forearms and drew their swords. Their commander, half-asleep and practically defenceless, was saved by a mistake on the part of the enemy, who made haste to tow away the flagship, thinking that the commander was aboard. Cerialis had in fact spent the night elsewhere (according to general belief at the time, because of an intrigue with an Ubian woman called Claudia Sacrata). His guards tried to make excuses for their dereliction of duty by pointing to their commander's scandalous behaviour, alleging that it was because they

1. The previous camps had been destroyed: see p. 247.   2. Made of leather.

had been ordered not to make a noise which would disturb his rest that they had omitted to exchange their calls and had fallen asleep themselves. It was broad daylight by the time the enemy sailed away in the captured ships and proceeded to tow the Roman flagship up the River Lippe to present it to Veleda.

23. Civilis could not resist the urge to stage a naval demonstration. He manned all the biremes and single-banked vessels he had, and to these was added a large number of small craft carrying thirty to forty men apiece and fitted out like Liburnians.[1] Moreover, there were captured craft assisted by improvised sails made from coats of many colours. These presented a brave sight as they moved along their chosen course through a vast gulf, resembling the ocean, by which the mouth of the River Maas conveys the waters of the Rhine to the North Sea.[2] Quite apart from their native vanity, they had a motive for putting their fleet on a war footing: they hoped by this impressive array to intercept the convoys sailing from Gaul. Astonishment rather than fear was the emotion with which Cerialis mustered his fleet. Though inferior in numbers, it enjoyed the advantage of experienced rowers, skilled helmsmen, and ships of greater size. The Romans moved with the current, the enemy before the wind. Thus the two fleets sailed past each other in opposite directions and had only time for a tentative discharge of light weapons before they lost touch.

24. Civilis risked no further offensive, but retired across the Rhine. Cerialis ravaged the Island of the Batavians severely, employing the well-known stratagem of leaving Civilis' land and farms untouched. But by this time summer was turning to autumn, and repeated rain-storms at the equinox caused the river to inundate the marshy, low-lying island until it looked like a morass. Nor was there any sign of the Roman fleet or convoys in the offing, and the camps on the flat ground were being washed away by the violence of the river. It was claimed by Civilis that the legions could have been crushed at this moment, and he took credit for cunningly diverting the Germans from this aim when they were set upon it. This may be true, since a few days later he surrendered. The situation was that Cerialis, while sending secret messages offering the Batavians peace and Civilis a pardon, had been urging Veleda and her people to bring about a

1. Fast galleys.
2. The estuary of the Waal and Maas formed a large sheet of water called Helinium.

change in the fortunes of war, which had dealt them many heavy blows, by performing a timely service to Rome. The Treviri had been cut to pieces, the Ubii recovered, the Batavians robbed of their homeland. The friendship of Civilis had brought nothing but wounds, defeat and bereavement. As an exile and outlaw, he was a burden to those who harboured him, and the Germans had incriminated themselves quite enough by their many crossings of the Rhine. Any further plots would mean that wrongdoing and guilt on the one side would be confronted by vengeance and the gods on the other.

25. With threats went promises. The loyalty of the Germans across the Rhine was thus undermined, and there was murmuring among the Batavians too. It was no use putting off the evil day, they reflected. A single nation could not shake off a yoke common to the whole world. The fire and slaughter inflicted on Roman legions had merely resulted in bringing more and stronger ones upon the scene. If Vespasian was the man for whom they had fought, then Vespasian was now established as emperor. But if their warlike challenge were addressed to Rome, how small a fraction of the human race the Batavians represented! In contrast with Raetia, Noricum and the burdens borne by other provincials, they were assessed in terms not of taxes, but of courage and men. Such a status was the next best thing to independence, and if there were to be a choice of masters, it was more honourable to put up with Roman emperors than women of Germany.

This was how the ordinary people felt. Their leaders used more bitter language. It was Civilis' frenzy, they complained, that had plunged them into war. In order to ward off family troubles, he had destroyed his people. Heaven had turned against the Batavians in the hour in which they besieged the legions, killed their commanders and shouldered a war which, however necessary to a single individual, was fatal to themselves. Their situation was indeed desperate unless they came to their senses and demonstrated a change of heart by punishing the offender.

26. Civilis sensed the way public opinion was moving, and made up his mind to act first. He had had his fill of troubles, and moreover hoped to escape with his life – a prospect which often helps to sap great resolves. He asked for a conference. A bridge over the River Nabalia[1] was cut, the two commanders advanced to the edges of the

1. See Key to Place-Names.

gap, and Civilis began his speech in these terms: 'If I were pleading my defence before an officer of Vitellius, my actions would have deserved no pardon and my words no belief. The enmity between us was total. He began hostilities, and I extended them. But for Vespasian I have long felt respect, and while he was still a subject, we were called friends. This fact was known to Antonius Primus and it was his letters that drove me into a war designed to prevent the passage of the Alps by the legions of the German garrison and the warriors of Gaul. What Antonius said in his letters was re-echoed by Hordeonius Flaccus personally. The war I declared in Germany was the war fought by Mucianus in Syria, by Aponius in Moesia and by Flavianus in Pannonia. . . .'[1]

1 At this point, or earlier, our MSS break off. It is clear, however, that the Roman position in the Rhineland was fully restored in A.D. 70, and the frontier defencies reformed and reorganized. Tacitus' reference to the Batavians in the *Germania* (published in A.D. 98) suggests that they suffered no reprisals and retained their status as untaxed subjects of the empire supplying only military levies. The troubles of A.D. 69/70 were never repeated here, and this in itself is a vindication of Roman imperialism.

# BIBLIOGRAPHY

## ABBREVIATIONS

| | |
|---|---|
| AA | *Anzeiger für die Altertumswissenschaft* |
| AAntHung | *Acta Antiqua Academiae Scientiarum Hungarlcae* |
| AArchttung | *Acta Archaeologica Academiae Scientiarum Hungarlcae* |
| AC | *Antiquité Classique* |
| AE | *Année Épigraphique* |
| AJP | *American Journal of Philology* |
| ANRW | *Aufstieg und Niedergang der römischen Welt*, ed. H. Temporini (–W. Haase), Berlin & New York, 1972– |
| Ath | *Athenaeum* |
| BCAR | *Bullettino della Commissione Archeologica Comunale di Roma* |
| BJ | *Bonner Jahrbücher* |
| BphW | *(Berliner) Philologische Wochenschrift* |
| Burr | V. Burr, *Tiberius Julius Alexander*, Bonn, 1955 |
| CAH | *Cambridge Ancient History* |
| CIL | *Corpus Inscriptionum Latinarum* |
| CJ | *Classical Journal* |
| CP | *Classical Philology* |
| CQ | *Classical Quarterly* |
| CR | *Classical Review* |
| CRAI | *Comptes-rendus de l'Académie des Inscriptions* |
| CW | *Classical World (Classical Weekly)* |
| DLZ | *Deutsche Literatur-Zeitung* |
| EC | *Les Études Classiques* |
| EHR | *English Historical Review* |
| F96 | P. Fabia, 'L'adultère de Néron et de Poppée', *RPh* 20 (1896) 12–22 |
| F01 | id., 'La préface des Histoires', *REA* 3 (1901) 41–76 |
| F02 | id., 'La querelle des Lyonnais et des Viennois en 68–69 après J.-C.', *Revue d'histoire de Lyon*, 2 (1902) 106–18 |
| F03 | id., 'Vitellius à Lyon', ibid. 3 (1903) 89–105 |
| F04 | id., 'La lettre de Pompeius Propinquus à Galba et l'avènement de Vitellius en Germanie', *Klio* 4 (1904) 42–67 |
| F10 | id., 'Le premier consulat de Petilius Cerialis', *RPh* 34 (1910) 5–42 |

# Bibliography

F12      id., 'La journée du 15 janvier 69 à Rome', *RPh* 36 (1912) 78–129

F13      id., 'L'ambassade d'Othon à Vitellius', *RPh* 38 (1913) 53–8

F14      id., 'Les prétoriens de Vitellius', *RPh* 38 (1914) 32–75

F41      id., 'La concentration des Othoniens sur le Pô', *REA* 43 (1941) 192–215

*Gn*      *Gnomon*

*GR*      *Greece and Rome*

*GS*      (Mommsen's) *Gesammelte Schriften*

*Gym*      *Gymnasium*

*H*      *Hermes*

Helbig      W. Helbig (H. Speier), *Führer durch die öffentlichen Sammlungen klassicher Altertümer in Rom*[4], I (1963), II (1966), III (1969)

*HSCP*      *Harvard Studies in Classical Philology*

*HZ*      *Historische Zeitschrift*

*ILS*      *Inscriptiones Latinae Selectae*, ed. Dessau

*IRT*      *Inscriptions of Roman Tripolitania*, ed. J. M. Reynolds and J. B. Ward-Perkins

*JEA*      *Journal of Egyptian Archaeology*

*JP*      *Journal of Philology*

*JRS*      *Journal of Roman Studies*

KIPW      Der kleine Pauly-Wissowa

*Lat*      *Latomus*

*LCM*      *Liverpool Classical Monthly*

*MAAR*      *Memoirs of the American Academy in Rome*

*MEFR*      *Mémoires de l'École Française de Rome*

*MH*      *Museum Helveticum*

*Mn*      *Mnemosyne*

MW      M. McCrum and A. G. Woodhead, *Select Documents of the Principates of the Flavian Emperors including the Year of Revolution, A.D. 68–96*, 1961 (no. of item follows)

MZ      Mainzer Zeitschrift

N      H. C. Newton, 'The Epigraphical Evidence for the Reigns of Vespasian and Titus', *Cornell Studies in Classical Philology* 16, 1901

Nash      E. Nash, *Pictorial Dictionary of Ancient Rome*, Tübingen–London I (1961; [2]1968), II (1962; [2]1968)

*NS*      *Notizie degli Scavi*

P      *Peake's Commentary on the Bible*, ed. M. Black and H. H. Rowley, 1962

*PACA*      *Proceedings of the African Classical Associations*

*PBSR*      *Papers of the British School at Rome*

*Ph*      *Philologus*

*PIR*      *Prosopographia Imperii Romani*[1] [2]

*PP*      *Parola del Passato*

PW      Pauly-Wissowa, *Realencyclopädie*

*RA*      *Revue Archéologique*

*RCCM*      *Rivista di Cultura Classica e Medioevale*

*REA*      *Revue des Études Anciennes*

*REG*      *Revue des Études Grecques*

*REJ*      *Revue des Études Juives*

| REL | *Revue des Études Latines* |
| RFC | *Rivista di Filologia e d'Istruzione Classica* |
| RhM | *Rheinisches Museum* |
| ROB | *Berichte van het Rijksdienst voor het Oudheidkundige Bodemonderzoek* |
| RPAA | *Rendiconti della Pontificia Accademia Romana di Archeologia* |
| RPh | *Revue de Philologie* |
| S | K. Scott, *The Imperial Cult under the Flavians*, Stuttgart, 1936 |
| SIFC | *Studi Italiani di Filologia Classica* |
| SO | *Symbolae Osloenses* |
| Syme | R. Syme, 'Consulates in Absence', *JRS* 48 (1958) 1–9 |
| SZG | *Schweizerische Zeitschrift für Geschichte* |
| T | Tacitus (Tacite, Tacito) |
| TAPA | *Transactions of the American Philological Association* |
| Turner | E. G. Turner, 'Ti. Julius Alexander', *JRS* 44 (1954) 54–64 |
| TZ | *Trierer Zeitschrift* |
| W | G. R. Watson, *The Roman Soldier*, 1969 |
| W56 | K. Wellesley, 'Three Historical Puzzles in *Histories* 3', *CQ* NS 6 (1956) 207–14 |
| W57 | id., 'Moonshine in Tacitus', *RhM* 100 (1957) 244–52 |
| W60 | id., 'Suggestio Falsi in Tacitus', *RhM* 103 (1960) 272–88 |
| W81(84) | 'What happened on the Capitol in December, A.D. 69?', *American Journal of Ancient History* 6 (1981), (1984), 166–190 |
| WJA | *Würzburger Jahrbücher für die Altertumswissenschaft* |
| WklPh | *Wochenschrift für klassische Philologie* |
| WS | *Wiener Studien* |
| YCS | *Yale Classical Studies* |
| ZPE | *Zeitschrift für Papyrologie und Epigraphik* |

## BIBLIOGRAPHY

G. Andresen, 'T' in the *Jahresberichte des Philologischen Vereins zu Berlin*, 1875–1924

(C. Bursian), *Jahresberichte über die Fortschritte der classischen Altertumswissenschaft* 3, 18, 39, 55, 59, 72, 121, 167, 224, 247, 282

C. W. Mendell, 'T: Literature 1948–1954', *CW* 48 (1955) 121–5

A. Briessmann, 'Auswahlbericht, T'. *Gym* 68 (1961) 64–80

H. W. Benario, 'Recent Work on T', *CW* 58 (1964) 69–83; 63 (1970) 253–67; 71 (1977) 1–32

R. Hanslik, 'T: Forschungsbericht', *AA* 13 (1960) 65–102; 20 (1967) 1–32

id., 'T, 1939–1972', *Lustrum* 16 (1971–2) 143–304; 17 (1973–4) 71–216

# Bibliography

## GENERAL STUDIES OF TACITUS

G. Bossier, *T and Other Roman Studies*, London 1906

P. Wuilleumier (d'après les notes de P. Fabia), *T*, Paris, 1949

E. Paratore, *T*, ¹1951, ²1962: *Lat* 11 (1952) 249–51 (Favez); *REL* 30 (1953) 423–28 (Bardon); *JRS* 43 (1953) 145–8 (Brink); *AJP* 75 (1954) 74–8 (Oliver); *CR* 14 (1964) 53–5 (Townend); *Gn* 26 (1954) 85–9 and 37 (1965) 422–4 (Güngerich)

I. Borzsák, 'T', *Das Altertum* 4 (1958) 32–52

id., 'T', PW: *REL* 47 (1969) 619 (Laugier)

R. Syme, *T*, Oxford, 1958: *CR* 9 (1959) 258–61 (Balsdon); *Phoenix* 13 (1959) 39–41 (Crook); *RCCM* 1 (1959) 403–8 (Questa); *JRS* 49 (1959) 140–6 (Sherwin-White); *Mn* 12 (1959) 369–75 (Thiel); *Gn* 33 (1961) 55–8 (Momigliano)

R. Hanslik, 'Die Ämterlaufbahn des T im Lichte der Ämterlaufbahnen seiner Zeitgenossen', *Anz. ph.-hist Kl., Öst. Ak. Wissen.*, 1965, 47–60

E. Koestermann, 'T und die Transpadana', *Ath* 43 (1965) 167–208

V. Pöschl, ed., *T* (*Wege der Forschung* xcvii), Darmstadt, 1969

T. A. Dorey, ed., *T*, London, 1969

I. Kajanto, 'T' 'Attitude to War and the Soldier', *Lat* 29 (1970) 699–718

H. W. Benario, *An Introduction to T*, Athens, Georgia, 1975

R. Martin, *T*, London, 1981

## COMMENTARIES

G. E. F. Chilver, *A Historical Commentary on T' Histories I and II*, Oxford, 1979; *cf.* reviews in *CR, Gn, Lat, JRS* etc.

G. E. F. Chilver and G. B. Townend, *A Historical Commentary on T' Histories IV and V*, Oxford, 1985

C. and W. Heraeus, ⁶Leipzig and Berlin, 1929, repr. Amsterdam, 1966

H. Goelzer, Paris, 1920

H. Heubner, *Die Historien: Kommentar*, Heidelberg: *Erstes Buch*, 1963; *Zweites Buch*, 1968; *Drittes Buch*, 1972; *Viertes Buch* (with W. Fauth), 1976; *Fünftes Buch* (with W. Fauth), 1982; *cf.* reviews in *CJ, CR, CW, Gn, Gym, JRS, MH* etc.

K. Wellesley, *The Histories:* Book iii, Sydney, 1972

E. Wolff²-G. Andresen, 1926

## TACITUS' USE OF SOURCES AND HIS HISTORICAL ATTITUDE AND METHODS

A. Briessmann, *T und das flavische Geschichtsbild*, Wiesbaden, 1955: *REL* 33 (1955) 412–16 (Béranger); *JRS* 46 (1956) 203–6 (Chilver); *Gn* 28 (1956) 519–27 (Drexler); *Mn* 10 (1957) 83–5 (den Boer); *CP* 52 (1957) 216–18 (Rogers); *HZ* 184 (1957) 191 (Treu); *CR* 8 (1958) 53–4 (Syme); *AAntHung* 6 (1958) 241–4 (Borzsák)

M. R. Comber, 'Parenthesis in T', *RhM* 119 (1976) 181–4

P. Fabia, *Les sources de T dans les Histoires et les Annales*, Paris, 1893

D. Flach, *T in der Tradition der antiken Geschichtsschreibung*, Göttingen, 1973

E. Groag, 'Zur Kritik von T' Quellen in den Historien', *Jahrbücher für klassische Philologie und Pädagogik* Supp.-Band 23 (1897) 709–99

F. Hampl, 'Beiträge zur Beurteilung des Historikers T', *Natalicium Carolo Jax oblatum*, Innsbruck, 1955

W. Kierdorf, 'Die Proömien zu T' Hauptwerken', *Gym* 85 (1978) 20–36

F. Klingner, 'T und die Geschichtsschreiber des I. Jahrhunderts n. Chr.', *MH* 15 (1958) 194–206

J. Martin, 'Zur Quellenfrage in den Annalen und Historien des T', *Würzburger Studien zur Altertumswissenschaft* 9 (1936) 21–58

F. A. Marx, 'T und die Literatur der exitus illustrium virorum', *Ph* 92 (1937) 83–103

T. Mommsen, 'Cornelius T und Cluvius Rufus', *GS* vii 224–52

F. Münzer, 'Die Entstehung der Historien', *Klio* I (1902) 300–30

H. Nesselhauf, 'T und Domitian', *H* 80 (1952) 222–45

H. Nissen, 'Die Historien des Plinius', *RhM* 26 (1871) 497–548

ed., G. Radke, *Politik und Literarische Kunst im Werke des T*, Stuttgart, 1971

J. S. Reid, 'T as an Historian', *JRS* 11 (1921) 191–200

R. T. Scott, *Religion and Philosophy in the Histories of T*, Rome, 1968

O. Seeck, 'Zur Quellenbenutzung des T', *Festschrift Hirschfeld*, 1903, 45–9

A. Stein, 'T als Geschichtsquelle', *Neue Jahrbücher für das klassische Altertum* 18 (1915) 361–74

G. H. Stevenson, 'Ancient Historians and their Sources', *JP* 35 (1920) 204–24

R. Syme, 'How T came to History', *GR* 4 (1957) 160–7

G. B. Townend, 'Cluvius Rufus in the *Histories* of T', *AJP* 85 (1964) 337–77

J. Vogt, *T als Politiker*, Stuttgart, 1924

id., 'T und die Unparteilichkeit des Historikers', *WJA* 9 (1936) 1–20; repr. in *T* ed. Pöschl, Darmstadt, 1969

E. Woelfflin, 'Zur Composition der Historien des T', *Sitzungsberichte Ak. Wiss. München* 1901, 3–52

## •TACITUS AS A LITERARY ARTIST

H. Bardon, 'A propos des *Histoires:* T et la tentation de la rhétorique', *Hommages Herrmann*, 1960, 146–51

E. Courbaud, *Les procédés d'art de T dans les Histoires*, Paris, 1918

S. G. Daitz, 'T's Technique of Character Portrayal', *AJP* 81 (1960) 30–52

E. C. Evans, 'Roman Descriptions of Personal Appearance in History and Biography', *HSCP* 46 (1935) 43–84

N. P. Miller, 'Virgil and T', Virgil Society Lecture no. 56, London, 1962; ead., 'Dramatic Speech in T', *AJP* 85 (1964) 279–96

I. S. Ryberg, 'T's Art of Innuendo', *TAPA* 73 (1942) 383–404

R. Syme, 'Obituaries in T', *AJP* 79 (1958) 18–31

## THE TOPOGRAPHY OF ROME AND ITALY

G. Lugli, *Roma antica: il Centro monumentale*, Rome, 1946

id., *Fontes ad Topographiam veteris urbis Romae pertinentes*, Rome, 1952–

H. Jordan (–C. Hülsen), *Topographie der Stadt Rom im Alterthum* I3, Berlin, 1907

# Bibliography

E. Nash, *Pictorial Dictionary of Ancient Rome*, Tübingen-London, I (1961; ²1968), II (1962; ²1968)

H. Nissen, *Italische Landeskunde*, Berlin, I (1883), II (1902)

S. B. Platner and T. Ashby, *A Topographical Dictionary of Ancient Rome*, London, 1929

P. Tozzi, 'T e la geografia della valle del Po', *Ath* 48 (1970) 104–31

id. *Storia padana antica*, Milan, 1972


## THE ARMY AND NAVY


G. Alföldy, *Die Hilfstruppen der römischen Provinz Germania Inferior*, Düsseldorf, 1968

id., *Die Legionslegaten der römischen Rheinarmeen*, Köln/Graz, 1967

G. L. Cheesman, *The Auxilia of the Roman Imperial Army*, Oxford, 1914

M. Durry, *Les cohortes prétoriennes*, Paris, 1938

B. Filow, 'Die Legionen der Provinz Moesia', *Klio* Beiheft 6 (1906)

G. Forni, *Il reclutamento delle legioni da Augusto a Diocleziano*, 1953

H. Freis, *Die Cohortes Urbanae*, Köln/Graz, 1967

B. Hallermann, *Untersuchungen zu den Truppenbewegungen in den Jahren 68/69 n. Chr.*, Diss. Würzburg, 1963

D. Kienast, *Untersuchungen zu den Kriegsflotten der römischen Kaiserzeit*, Bonn, 1966

*Legio VII Gemina*, León (Diputación provincial), 1970: various authors

H.M.D. Parker, *The Roman Legions*, Oxford, 1928, repr. Cambridge, 1958

D. B. Saddington, 'The Roman *auxilia* in T, Josephus and other early imperial writers', *Acta Classica* 13 (1970) 89–124

id., 'The Development of the Roman Auxiliary Forces from Augustus to Trajan', *ANRW* II 3, 176–201

C. G. Starr, *The Roman Imperial Navy, 31 B.C. to A.D. 324*², Cambridge, 1960

W. Wagner, *Die Dislokation der römischen Auxiliarformationen in den Provinzen Noricum, Pannonien, Moesien und Dakien von Augustus bis Gallienus*, Berlin, 1938

G. R. Watson, *The Roman Soldier*, London, 1969

G. Webster, *The Roman Imperial Army*, London, 1969

H. van de Weerd, *Trois légions romaines du Bas-Danube*, Louvain, 1907


## THE HISTORY OF A.D. 69–70


H. W. Benario, '*Imperium* and *Capaces Imperii*', *AJP* 93 (1972) 14–26

A. W. Braithwaite, ed., Suetonius, *Vespasianus*, Oxford, 1927

G. E. F. Chilver, 'The Army in Politics, A.D. 68–70', *JRS* 47 (1957) 29–35

D. Flach, 'Die Überlieferungslage zur Geschichte des Vierkaiserjahres', *Ancient Society* 4 (1973) 157–76

H. Fuchs, *Der geistige Widerstand gegen Rom in der antiken Welt*, Berlin, ²1964

H. R. Graf, *Kaiser Vespasian*, Stuttgart, 1937

H. Grassl, *Untersuchungen zum Vierkaiserjahr 68/69 n. Chr.*, Diss. Graz, 1972, Wien, 1973

S. Gsell, *Essai sur . . . Domitien*, Paris, 1894

M. Hammond, 'The Transmission of the Powers of the Roman Emperor', *MAAR* 24 (1956) 63–133, esp. 67–78

R. Hanslik, 'Vitellius', PW

E. G. Hardy, ed., Plutarch, *Galba* and *Otho*, London, 1890 id., *Studies in Roman History, First Series* ²1910, 294–333, *Second Series* ¹1909, 130–268; 36–73

B. W. Henderson, *Civil War and Rebellion in the Roman Empire, A.D. 69–70*, London, 1908: *REA* 11 (1909) 97 (Glotz); *EHR* 24 (1909) 327–30 (Jones); *JP* 31 (1910) 123–52 (Hardy); *BphW* 30 (1910) 136–43 (Wolff)

L. Holzapfel, 'Römische Kaiserdaten', *Klio* 12 (1912) 483–93; 13 (1913) 289–304; 15 (1918) 99–121

L. Homo, *Vespasien, l'empereur du bon sens*, Paris, 1949

C. Jullian, *Histoire de la Gaule*, Paris, 1909–26

P. H. Martin, *Die anonymen Münzen des Jahres 68 n. Chr.*, Mainz, 1974

A. Momigliano, 'Vitellio', *SIFC* 9 (1931) 117–61

T. Mommsen, *The Provinces of the Roman Empire*, London, 1909

M. P. O. Morford, 'The Training of Three Roman Emperors', *Phoenix* 22 (1968) 57–72

C. R. Murison, *A Commentary on Suetonius' Lives of Galba, Otho and Vitellius*, Diss. Edinburgh, 1976

id., 'Some Vitellian Dates: an exercise in methodology', *TAPA* 109 (1979) 187–97

D. Timpe, *Untersuchungen zur Kontinuität des frühen Prinzipats*, Wiesbaden, 1962, esp. 106–21

M. Treu, 'Marcus Antonius Primus', *WJA* 3 (1948) 241–62

P. Venini, *C. Suetonio Tranquillo, Vite di Galba, Otone, Vitellio*, Turin, 1977

K. H. Waters, 'The Second Dynasty of Rome', *Phoenix* 17 (1963) 198–218

W. Weber, *Josephus und Vespasian*, Berlin-Stuttgart-Leipzig, 1921

K. Wellesley, *The Long Year: AD 69*, London, 1975

M. St A. Woodside, 'The Role of the Eight Batavian Cohorts in the Events of 68–69 A.D.', *TAPA* 68 (1937) 277–83

P. Zancan, *La crisi del Principato*, Padova, 1939

# BOOK I

## GENERAL

G. J. D. Aalders, 'Keizer Galba', *Tijdschrift voor Geschiedenis* 86 (1973) 507–18

B. Walker, 'A Study in Incoherence: the First Book of T' *Histories*', *CP* 71 (1976) 113–18

1 A. Dihle, 'Sine ira et studio', *RhM* 114 (1971) 27–43

H. Drexler, 'Die Praefatio der Historien des T', *Helikon* 5 (1965) 148–56 Fo1

J. B. Hainsworth, 'The Starting Point of T' *Historiae*', *GR* 11 (1964) 128–36

A. D. Leeman, 'Structure and Meaning in the Prologues of T', *YCS* 23 (1973) 169–208, esp. 173–86

T. B. Macaulay, *Life and Letters of*, London, 1911, 363 (Tuesday, 18 December 1838)

O. Seeck, 'Der Anfang von T' Historien', *RhM* 56 (1901) 227–32

D. C. A. Shotter, 'The Starting-Dates of T' Historical Works', *CQ* 17 (1967) 158–63

# Bibliography

P. Steinmetz, 'Die Gedankenführung des Prooemiums zu den Historien des T', *Gym* 75 (1968) 251–62

K. Wellesley, *Gn* 37 (1965) 704f.

2 G. Macdonald, 'Britannia Statim Omissa', *JRS* 27 (1937) 93–8
  id., 'Verbum non amplius addam', ibid. 29 (1939) 5–27
  H. G. Pflaum, 'La chronologie de la carrière de L. Caesennius Sospes', *Historia* 2 (1953/4) 431–50
  T. D. Pryce and E. Birley, 'The Fate of Agricola's Northern Conquests', *JRS* 28 (1938) 141–52
  I. A. Richmond and R. M. Ogilvie, eds., *T, Agricola*, Oxford, 1967, 75f.

4 Z. Yavetz, 'Plebs sordida', *Ath* 43 (1965) 295ff.
  P. A. Brunt, 'The Roman Mob', *Past and Present,* December 1966, 3–27

4 E. Koestermann, 'Der Rückblick, T' Historien I 4–11', *Historia* 5 (1956) 213–37

5 R. Syme, 'Partisans of Galba', *Historia* 31 (1982) 460–83

6 T. Mommsen, 'Der letzte Kampf der römischen Republik', *GS* iv 333–47
  R. Syme, 'Some Friends of the Caesars', *AJP* 77 (1956) 271

7 J. Burian, 'L. Clodius Macer', *Klio* 38 (1960) 167–73
  H. von Heintze, 'Galba', *Römische Mitteilungen* 75 (1968) 149–53 with Taf. 48–51

8 P. A. Brunt, 'The Revolt of Vindex and the Fall of Nero', *Lat* 18 (1959) 531–59
  J. C. Fant, 'Verginius Rufus', *Historia* 30 (1981) 240–43
  J. van Ooteghem, 'Verginius et Vindex', *EC* 36 (1968) 18–27
  J. B. Hainsworth, 'Verginius and Vindex', *Historia* 11 (1962) 86–96
  L. Paul, 'L. Verginius Rufus', *RhM* 54 (1899) 602–30
  D. C. A. Shotter, 'T and Verginius Rufus', *CQ* 17 (1967) 370–81
  G. B. Townend, 'The Reputation of Verginius Rufus', *Lat* 20 (1961) 337–41
  F. Hertlein, *Germania*, 9 (1925) 15–17

10 E. G. Hardy, *CR* 3 (1889) 77; N5; S
  *PIR²* s.v. 'C. Licinius Mucianus'

11 Burr; Turner

12 Fo4

13 F96
  O. Schönberger, 'Ein Quellenproblem bei T', *Historia* 12 (1963) 500–509
  G. B. Townend, 'Traces in Dio Cassius of Cluvius, Aufidius and Pliny', *H* 89 (1961) 242–7

14 N 1
  H. Nesselhauf, 'Die Adoption des römischen Kaisers', *H* 83 (1955) 477–95

15 C. D. Fisher, *CR* 23 (1909) 223

15–16 K. Büchner, 'T und Plinius über Adoption des römischen Kaisers', *RhM* 98 (1955) 289–312
  E. Hohl, 'T und der jüngere Plinius', *RhM* 68 (1913) 461–4
  D. Kienast, 'Nerva und das Kaisertum Traians', *Historia* 17 (1968) 51–71
  H. Nesselhauf (cf. 14)

16 H. Heubner, *Gym* 62 (1955) 101–5
  W. Jens, 'Libertas bei T', *H* 84 (1956) 331–52, esp. 341–6

20 MW 355

22 P. Grenade, 'Le mythe de Pompée et les pompéiens sous les Césars', *REA* 52 (1950) 28–63, esp. 31

27 F12
P. Noyen and G. Sanders, 'Innixus liberto', *AC* 28 (1959) 223–31
MW 211

29 M. H. Prévost, *Les adoptions politiques à Rome sous la République et l'Empire*, Paris, 1949

31 MW 337
J. C. Rolfe, 'Seasickness in Greek and Latin Writers', *AJP* 25 (1904) 192–200

36 P. Boyancé, 'La main de Fides', *Hommages . . . Bayet*, 1964, 101–13
M. Durry, *Les cohortes prétoriennes*, Paris, 1938

37 H. Grassl, 'War Obultronius Sabinus Proconsul der Baetica und L. Cornelius Marcellus sein Legat?', *Historia* 25 (1976) 496–8

40 R. W. Husband, 'Galba's Assassination and the Indifferent Citizen', *CP* 10 (1915) 321–5
R. Waltz, 'Examen d'une phrase de T', *Mélanges Ernout*, 377–82

42 I. Prammer, *Zeitschrift für die österreichischen Gymnasien* 34 (1883) 167–71

45 D. C. A. Shotter, 'T and Marius Celsus', *LCM* 3 (1978) 197–200

46 N 6 = MW 97
A. H. M. Jones, 'The Aerarium and the Fiscus', *JRS* 40 (1950) 22–9

47 N 1 = MW 76 = *ILS* 240 (cf. A. E. Gordon, *Album of Dated Latin Inscriptions* I and plates I, 126)
J. B. Hall, 'Varia Critica', *PACA* 13 (1975) 12–13

48 D. Kuijper, 'De T. Vinii aetatis spatio et crimine', *Archaeologie en Historie: opgedragen aan H. Brunsting*, Bussum, 1973, 145–51
G. V. Sumner, 'The Career of T. Vinius', *Ath* 54 (1976) 430–36
R. Syme, 'Missing Persons III', *Historia* 11 (1962) 153

49 H. Hill, 'Nobilitas in the Imperial Period', *Historia* 18 (1969) 230–50
E. Koestermann, 'Das Charakterbild Galbas bei T', *Naviula Chiloniensis* (Festschrift Jacoby) 1956, 191–206 = V. Pöschl, ed., *T* 413–31
G. Rickman, *Roman Granaries and Store Buildings*, Cambridge, 1971, 166ff.
id., *The Corn Supply of Ancient Rome*, Oxford, 1980
P. Schunck, 'Studien zur Darstellung des Endes von Galba, Otho und Vitellius in den Historien des T', *SO* 39 (1964) 38–82
W67

50 R. F. Newbold, 'Vitellius and the Roman Plebs', *Historia* 21 (1972) 308–19
F. Paschoud, 'T Histoires I 50: art de la composition et vérité historique', *Argos* 3 (1979) 7–19

51 P. Boyancé: cf. 36
H. Heubner *Gym*, 70 (1963) 226–30

54 A. Piganiol, 'Fides et mains de bronze', *Mélanges Lévy-Bruhl*, Paris, 1959, 471–3
V. v. Gonzenbach, 'Fides Exercituum: eine Hand aus Vindonissa', *Jahrb. der Gesellschaft Pro Vindonissa* 1951–2, 5ff.
K. Oehler, 'Der Consensus Omnium', *Antike und Abendland* 10 (1961) 103–29, esp. 115

59 G. Alföldy, *Hilfstruppen* 45ff. (cf. 'The Army and Navy')
M. W. C. Hassall, 'Batavians and the Roman Conquest of Britain', *Britannia* 1 (1970) 131–6

# Bibliography

61–66    F. Koester, *Der Marsch der Invasionsarmee des Fabius Valens*, Diss. Münster, 1927

62    H. Mattingly, *JRS* 10 (1920) 39

63    J. J. Hatt, 'Fouilles stratigraphiques à Metz', *CRAI* 1958 (1959) 98 and *Histoire de la Gaule romaine*, Paris, 1959, 143

65    F02

     M. Rambaud, 'L'origine militaire de la colonie de Lugdunum', *CRAI* 1964 (1965) 232–77

67–68    C. Dürr, 'Mons Vocetius', *Ort und Wort*, Okt. 1973, 1–27

     F. Stähelin, *Die Schweiz in römischer Zeit*,[3] Basel, 1948, 188ff.

     E. Täubler, 'Die letzte Erhebung der Helvetier', *Neue Schweizerische Rundschau* 1926, 789–97; id., *Tyche*, Leipzig, 1926, 167ff.

     H. Bögli, 'Aventicum', *BJ* 172 (1972) 175–84

70    G. Alföldy, *Noricum*, London, 1974, 242

     G. Walser, 'Das Strafgericht über die Helvetier im Jahre 69 n. Chr.', *SZG* 4 (1954) 260–70

     id., *Die römischen Strassen in der Schweiz*, I (1967)

     id., *Summus Poeninus*, Wiesbaden, 1984

73    K. R. Bradley, 'A *Publica Fames* in A.D. 68', *AJP* 93 (1972) 451–8

74    F13

77    *PIR*[2] s.v. 'T. Flavius Sabinus'

     G. B. Townend, 'Some Flavian Connections', *JRS* 51 (1961) 54

79    J. W. Eadie, 'The Development of Roman Mailed Cavalry', *JRS* 57 (1967) 161–73

     R. M. Rattenbury, 'An ancient armoured force', *CR* 56 (1942) 113–16; 57 (1943) 67–9; cf. 58 (1944) 43 (Brink)

     H. R. Robinson, *The Armour of Imperial Rome*, London, 1975

     R. Syme, *JRS* 43 (1953) 154

     R. D. Milns, 'The Career of M. Aponius Saturninus', *Historia* 22 (1973) 284–94

80    E. Hohl, 'Der Prätorianeraufstand unter Otho', *Klio* 32 (1939) 307–24

     H. Heubner, 'Der Prätorianertumult vom Jahre 69 n. Chr.', *RhM* 101 (1958) 339–53

87    N 76 = MW339; MW404

     J. F. Gilliam, 'Numeri', *Eos* 48 (1956) 207–16

     R. W. Davies, 'Joining the Roman Army', *BJ* 169 (1969) 208–32

     D. Gaspár, 'The Concept *in numeros referre* in the Roman Army', *Acta arch. ac sc. Hung.* 26 (1974) 113–16

89    J. P. V. D. Balsdon, 'The Salii and Campaigning in March and October', *CR* 16 (1966) 146–7

90    F. Millar, 'Emperors at Work', *JRS* 57 (1967) 9–19 esp. 19

## BOOK II

GENERAL

       *Archeologia e storia nella Lombardia Padana: Bedriacum nel xix centenario delle battaglie: Atti del convento . . . giugno 1969*, Como, 1972

H. Drexler, 'Zur Geschichte Kaiser Othos bei T und Plutarch', *Klio* 37 (1959) 153–78

J. Gerstenecker, *Der Krieg des Otho und Vitellius in Italien im Jahre 69*, Progr. München, 1882

R. Hanslik, 'Die Auseinandersetzung zwischen Otho und Vitellius bis zur Schlacht von Bedriacum nach T', *WS* 74 (1961) 113–25

F. Klingner, 'Die Geschichte Kaiser Othos bei T', *Ber. Verh. Sächsischen Ak. (phil.-hist. Kl.)* 92 (1940) 3–27 = *Studien zur griechischen und römischen Literatur,* 1964, 605–24 = V. Pöschl ed., *T,* 1969, 388–412

E. Koestermann, 'Die erste Schlacht bei Bedriacum, 69 n. Chr.', *RCCM* 3 (1961) 16–29

E. Kuntze, *Beiträge zur Geschichte des Otho-Vitellius Krieges,* Karlsruhe, 1885

A. Momigliano, 'Vitellio', *SIFC* 9 (1931) 117–61

T. Mommsen, 'Die zwei Schlachten von Bedriacum', *GS* iv 354–65

J. Nicols, *Vespasian and the Partes Flavianae,* Wiesbaden, 1978

A. Passerini, 'Le due battaglie presso Bedriacum', *Studi . . . offerti a E. Ciaceri,* Genova, etc., 1940

L. Paul, 'Kaiser Marcus Salvius Otho', *RhM* 57 (1902) 76–136

C. Préaux, 'Le règne de Vitellius en Egypte' in *Mélanges Georges Smets,* Brussels, 1952, 571–8

M. Puhl, *De Othone et Vitellio imperatoribus quaestiones,* Diss. Halle, 1883

E. R. Schwinge, 'Die Schlacht bei Bedriacum' in *Silvae, Festschrift f. Ernst Zinn,* Tübingen, 1970, 217–32

K. Wellesley, 'A Major Crux in T', *JRS* 61 (1971) 28–51

2  MW 177

J. A. Crook, 'Titus and Berenice', *AJP* 72 (1951) 162–75

J. F. Gilliam, 'Titus in Julian's "Caesares"', *AJP* 88 (1967) 203–8

3  E. Hartmann in Heubner's Commentary

8  L. Urlichs, *RhM* 11 (1857) 32

P. A. Gallivan, 'The False Neros: a Re-examination', *Historia* 22 (1973) 364f.

11  MW 355; W60, F41

H. R. Robinson (above, on I 79)

14  W 174–5

14–15  K (above, on I 61–66)

16  MW 455

18–19  W60

19  E. Wolff, *WklPh* 2 (1885) 1558

27–30  Koester (above on I 61–66)

35  H. Heubner, *Gym* 62 (1955) 105–8

38  C. A. Powell, 'Deum ira, hominum rabies', *Lat* 31 (1972) 833–48

40  K. Wellesley, *supra* and *The Long Year* 75

46  W60

46–  B. F. Harris, 'T on the Death of Otho', *CJ* 58 (1962) 73–7

P. Schunck (cf. i 49)

49  MW 34

J.-C. Richard, 'Les aspects militaires des funérailles impériales', *MEFR* 78 (1966) 313–25

# Bibliography

50    MW 78; A. Degrassi. 'Il Sepolcro dei Salvii a Ferento', *RPAA* 34 (1961–2) 59–77

54–5    W60; S. Mitchell, 'Requisitioned Transport . . .' *JRS* 66 (1976) 106–31

58    *PIR*² s.v. 'Lucceius Albinus'

59    MW 277; 372
     Fo3

62    MW 79ff.; W60

63    MW 89, 262; G. W. Houston, 'M. Plancius Varus and the Events of A.D. 69–70', *TAPA* 103 (1972) 167–80

64    T. Ashby and R. A. L. Fell, 'The Via Flaminia', *JRS* 11 (1921) 125–90 esp. 173ff.

66    F14

71    R. Syme, *JRS* 43 (1953) 161
     G. B. Townend, 'The Consuls of A.D. 69/70', *AJP* 83 (1962) 113–29

74    A. Schalit, 'Die Erhebung Vespasians nach Josephus, Talmud, Midrasch', *ANRW* II 2, 208–327

75    A. Degrassi, *Scritti Vari* II, 951ff.

78    W. Fauth in Heubner's Commentary
     H. Volkmann, 'Die Pilatusinschrift von Caesarea Maritima', *Gym* 75 (1968) 125

79    MW 41, 328–30
     Burr; Turner
     A. Stein, *Die Präfekten von Ägypten,* Bern, 1950, 37f.
     R. Syme, *AJP* 77 (1956) 269

81    A. A. Barrett, 'Sohaemus, King of Emesa and Sophene', *AJP* 98 (1977) 152–9
     P. M. Rogers, 'Titus, Berenice and Mucianus', *Historia* 29 (1980) 86–95: cf. J. A. Crook (above on II 2)

82    C. S. Walton, 'Oriental Senators', *JRS* 19 (1929) 38–66

85    P. Fabia, 'L'adhésion de l'Illyricum à la cause flavienne', *REA* 5 (1903) 329–82
     Syme

86    N 7 = MW 274; N 317 = MW 275; *AE* 1965, 39 *bis*
     J. Colin, 'Le préfet de prétoire Cornelius Fuscus', *Lat* 15 (1956) 56–82
     A. Ferrill, 'Otho, Vitellius and the Propaganda of Vespasian', *CJ* 60 (1965) 267–9
     D. C. A. Shotter, 'T and Antonius Primus', *LCM* 2 (1977) 23–7
     R. Syme, *Danubian Papers,* Bucharest, 1971, 82
     H. Hill, *CR* 41 (1927) 124

89    J. Curle, *A Roman Frontier Post,* Edinburgh, 1911, 299
     E. Sander, 'Die Kleidung des römischen Soldaten', *Historia* 12 (1963) 144–66, esp. 155

92    D. M. Jones, *CR* 59 (1945) 12

92–94    F14

100    C. Cichorius, 'Ein römisches Porträtbild' in *Römische Studien* (²1922, repr. 1961) 402–6
     R. H. Martin, 'Caecina's Meeting with Bassus', *Eranos* 49 (1951) 174–6
     *PIR*² s.v. 'Sex. Lucilius Bassus'

BOOK III

GENERAL See: Book II General; K. Wellesley, ed. 1972; and W81 (84)

1   J. Šašel etc., (eds.), *Claustra Alpium Iuliarum I: Fontes* (Catalogi . . . Musei
    . . . Labacensis), Ljubljana, 1971
5   *AE* 1966,68
6   G. Brusin, *Aquileia e Grado,*[5] Padova, 1964
7   J. Gagé, 'Vespasien et la mémoire de Galba', *REA* 54 (1952) 290–315
8   I. A. Richmond and W. G. Holford, 'Roman Verona', *PBSR* 13 (1935)
    69–76
    G. Radke, 'Verona', PW
    F. Sartori, *Verona Romana,* Verona, 1960; id., 'Colonia Augusta Verona
    Nova Gallienana', *Ath* 42 (1964) 361–72
9   R. Syme, 'Missing Persons III', *Historia* 11 (1962) 153f.
    W56
10  N 87; MW 269
12  C. G. Starr, *The Roman Imperial Navy* (cf. 'The Army and Navy')
13  G. B. Townend, 'Some Rhetorical Battle-pictures in Dio', *H* 92 (1964)
    467–81
    W67
14  N 8; W56, 57
21  L. Valmaggi, 'Sulla campagna flavio–vitelliana del 69', *Klio* 9 (1909) 252–3
23–25  W57
29  D. Baatz, 'Ein Katapult der Legio IV Macedonica aus Cremona', *Römische
    Mitteilungen* 87 (1980) 283–99
    id., 'Recent Finds of Ancient Artillery', *Britannia* 9 (1978) 1–17
36  W57
38  P. Grimal, *Les jardins romains,* Paris, 1942
41  F 14, W56
42  G. Radke, 'Volaterrae,' PW
43  R. Syme, *AJP* 77 (1956) 272
45  E. Harrison, 'A Passage in British History', *CQ* 1 (1907) 305–7
    I. A. Richmond, 'Queen Cartimandua', *JRS* 44 (1954) 43–52
    D. Braund, 'Observations on Cartimandua', *Britannia* 15 (1984) 1–6; cf.
    ibid. 9 (1975) 1ff.
    S. Mitchell, 'Venutius & Cartimandua', *LCM* 3 (1978) 215–19
47  R. and R. C. Anderson, *The Sailing Ship* (esp. ch. iv: 'The Double-Ended
    Ship'), London, 1926
    J. Hornell, *Water Transport,* Cambridge, 1946
48  P. Jouguet, 'Vespasien acclamé dans l'hippodrome d'Alexandrie', *Mélanges
    . . . Alfred Ernout,* Paris, 1940, 201–10; id., 'L'arrivée de Vespasien à
    Alexandrie', *Bulletin de l'Institut d'Egypte* 24 (1941–2) 21–32
    A. Henrichs, 'Vespasian's Visit to Alexandria', *ZPE* 3 (1968) 51–80
    O. Montevecchi, 'Vespasiano acclamato dagli Alessandrini', *Aegyptus* 61
    (1981) 155–70
50  N 83 = MW 451
    W. Eck, 'M. Pomponius Silvanus', *ZPE* 9 (1972) 259–76
56  S

# Bibliography

57 F 14; G. Lugli, *Forma Italiae, Regio* I, Vol. 1, *Pars* 1 (Anxur-Tarracina), 1926

58 F14

59–62 G. B. Townend, 'Some Flavian Connections', *JRS* 51 (1961) 54–61

61–3 F14

66 W67

67–73 F14

68 MW 323, 455

69 H. Jordan (–C. Hülsen), *Topographie der Stadt Rom im Alterthum* I3, Berlin, 1907, 402–25

71 W81 (84)
  G. Lugli, *JRS* 36 (1946) 3
  Nash I, 250, pls. 292–4; II pl. 1320

74 K. Christ, 'Zur Herrscherauffassung und Politik Domitians', *SZG* 12 (1962) 187–213
  J. C. Anderson Jnr., 'Domitian's Building Activity', *Historia* 32 (1982) 93–105, esp. 95
  W56

75 MW 97

76–7 F14

78–85 F14

81 C. E. Lutz, 'The Roman Socrates', *YCS* 10 (1947) 3–147

82 Ministero della Pubblica Istruzione, *Carta archeologica di Roma* II (1964)
  Nash I 491–9; pls. 605–15

84 Nash I 221; pls. 254–8
  I. A. Richmond, 'The Relation of the Praetorian Camp to Aurelian's Wall of Rome', *PBSR* 10 (1927) 12–22 with pls. vii and viii

86 Ministero, etc. (cf. 82)
  W56

## BOOK IV

### GENERAL

P. A. Brunt, 'T on the Batavian Revolt', *Lat* 19 (1960) 494–517

A. W. Byvanck, 'De Opstand der Bataven', *Antiquity and Survival* 3 (1960) 15–27

E. G. Hardy, *Studies in Roman History*, Second Series 1909, 36–73

H. Hettema, *De Nederlandse Wateren en Plaatsen in de Romeinse Tijd*, 's-Gravenhage, ²1951, 209–19

F. Münzer, 'Die Quelle des T für die Germanenkriege', *BJ* 104 (1899) 67–111

H. Nissen, 'Die Geschichte von Novaesium', *BJ* 111/12 (1904) 1–96, esp. 60–80

W. Sprey, *T over de Opstand der Bataven*, Groningen, 1953

1–2 F14

2 R. Urban, 'Historische Untersuchungen zum Domitiansbild des T', Diss. München, 1971

K. H. Waters, 'The Character of Domitian', *Phoenix* 18 (1964) 49–77

3   L. Lesuisse, 'T et la lex de imperio des premiers empereurs romains', *EC* 29 (1961) 157–65

MW 1 = *ILS* 244 (cf. Helbig [4]II 220; and A. E. Gordon, *GR* 20 (1951) 80–82 with pl. cvi)

A. Vassileiou, 'Deux remarques sur l'anneau d'or', *AC* 40 (1971) 649–57

4   MW 257

J. Malmoux, 'C. Helvidius Priscus', *PP* 30 (1975) 23–40

5   P. A. Brunt, 'Stoicism and the Principate', *PBSR* 43 (1975) 1–35

6   MW 271, 272

K. R. Bradley, 'The Career of Titus Clodius Eprius Marcellus, cos II A.D. 74', *SO* 53 (1978) 171–81

9   P. A. Brunt, 'The Fiscus and its Development', *JRS* 56 (1966) 75–91

D. E. Strong, 'The Administration of Public Buildings in Rome . . .', *Bull. Institute of Classical Studies, London* 15 (1968) esp. 104f.

12   J. E. Bogaers, 'Civitas en stad van de Bataven en Canninefaten', *ROB* 10–11 (1960–1) 263–317; id., 'Einige opmerkingen over het Nederlandse gedeelte van de limes van Germania Inferior (Germania Secunda)', *ROB* 17 (1967) 99–114

13   M. W. C. Hassall (cf. i, 59)

T. W. Africa, 'The One-Eyed Man against Rome', *Historia* 19 (1970) 528–38

W. O. Müller, 'Once More the One-Eyed Man against Rome', *Historia* 24 (1957) 402–10

J. H. D'Arms, 'Hordeonius Flaccus', *Historia* 23 (1974) 497–54

14   *Konsthistorisk Tidskrift* 25 (1956) 3–112 (various authors)

15   K. H. Esser, 'Mogontiacum', *BJ* 172 (1972) 217–27

J. E. Bogaers, 'Praetorium Agrippinae', *Bull. Kon. Ned. Oudheidk. Bond* 17 (1964) 210–39; id., 'Forum Hadriani', *BJ* 164 (1964) 45–52

L. A. W. C. Venmans, 'De incendio castrorum Romanorum quae fuerunt in media urbe Traiecto ad Rhenum', *Mn* 3 (1935–6) 83–7

K. Wellesley, *CR* 12 (1962) 119

17   A. J. Christopherson, 'The Provincial Assembly of the Three Gauls', *Historia* 17 (1968) 351–66, esp. 365

19   W 191

22   H. Beck, *Das Ebersignum im Germanischen,* Berlin, 1965

H. Nissen (cf. iv 'General') 68

23   H. von Petrikovits, *Das römische Rheinland* . . . Köln/Opladen, 1960, 38 and Tafel 1; id., 'Vetera', PW

F. K. Kiechle, 'Die Entwicklung der Brandwaffen im Altertum', *Historia* 26 (1977) 253–6

24   P. Fabia, 'Dillius Vocula', *Studi Romani* 2 (1914) 153–88

C. D. Fisher, *CR* 23 (1909) 223

N 23 = MW 40

26   M. E. Carbone, 'The First Relief of Castra Vetera', *Phoenix* 21 (1967) 296–8

30   H. Lehner, *Vetera,* Berlin, 1930, 34 and Abb. 23

33   T. Bechert, *Asciburgium* (Duisburger Forschungen 20) 1974, with *BJ* 179 (1979) 475–98

36   E. Fraenkel, 'Eine Form römischer Kriegsbulletin', *Eranos* 54 (1956) 189–94

# Bibliography

38  T. Mommsen, 'Das Verhältnis des T zu den Acten . . .', *GS* vii 253–63

39  Syme; *MW* 389

40  J. Gagé, 'Vespasien et la mémoire de Galba', *REA* 54 (1952) 290–315

41  *IRT* 342; *AE* 1949, 76

    H. W. Benario, 'C. Paccius Africanus', *Historia* 8 (1959) 496–8

    P. A. Gallivan, 'The Fasti for the Reign of Nero', *CQ* NS 24 (1974) 290–311, esp. 304

42  R. H. Martin, 'The Speech of Curtius Montanus', *JRS* 57 (1967) 109–14

    R. Syme, *JRS* 43 (1953) 161

44  R. S. Rogers, 'A Criminal Trial of A.D. 70', *TAPA* 80 (1949) 347–50

45  P. A. Brunt, 'Charges of Provincial Maladministration', *Historia* 10 (1961) 189–227

    N 166

47  *MW* 97 = *ILS* 984

48  M. Benabou, 'Proconsul et légat en Afrique: le témoignage de T', *Antiquités africaines* 6 (1972) 129–36

    M. P. Speidel, 'The Singulares of Africa', *Historia* 22 (1973) 125–7, esp. 126

49  N 27 = *MW* 266; N 28 = *MW* 84; N86 = *MW* 443

50  H. G. Pflaum, 'La nomenclature des villes africaines de Lepcis Magna et Lepti Minus', *Bull. Soc. Ant. France* 1959 (1961) 85–92

    M. F. Squarciapino, *Leptis Magna*, Basel, 1966

    C. Daniels, *The Garamantes of Southern Libya*, New York and North Harrow, 1970

    E. Müller-Graupa, 'Mera mapalia', *Ph* 85 (1930) 303–12

53  N 260 = *MW* 261; *AE* 1956, 208; D. M. Pippidi, *Studii . . . Istorie Veche* 6 (1955) 355–83

    H. Bardon, 'La naissance d'un temple', *REL* 33 (1955) 166–82

    S. Schlossmann, 'Stipulari, stips', *RhM* 59 (1904) 357f.

    A. Stein (cf. ii 79) 34f.

54  A. Mócsy, PW Supplement-Band ix 550

61  M. Guarducci, *RPAA* 21 (1945–6) 163–76; 25–6 (1949–51) 75–87 (cf. *AE* 1953, 25)

    P. Mingazzini, *BCAR* 74 (1951–2) 71–6

    E. des Places, 'Description grecque métrique concernant Veleda', *REG* 61 (1948) 381–90

62  *MW* 391 = *ILS* 2497

63  P. La Baume, 'Das römische Köln', *BJ* 172 (1972) 271–92

64  O. Brogan, 'Trade between the Roman Empire and the Free Germans', *JRS* 26 (1936) 195–222

    R. E. M. Wheeler, *Rome beyond the Imperial Frontiers,* London, 1954

67  F. Görres, 'Zur Kritik einiger Quellenschriftsteller der Römischen Kaiserzeit', *Ph* 39 (1880) 459–74

    J. Martin (cf. 'T's Use of Sources')

68  *MW* 302, 514, 519

    J. E. Bogaers, 'De Romeinse helm van Buggenum', *ROB* 9 (1959) 85–93

    F10 (cf. E. Wolff, *WklPh* 1911, 10–15; R. Syme, *JRS* 48 (1958) 6)

    P. Fabia in *Mélanges Boissier,* Paris, 1903, 191–6

    H. S. Jones, *EHR* 24 (1909) 329

# Bibliography

H. Heubner, 'Mucians Reisevorbereitungen' in *Latinität und Alte Kirche (Festschrift . . . Hanslik)*, Wien–Köln–Graz, 1977, 150–58

70    K. Schumacher, 'Beiträge zur Topographie und Geschichte der Rheinlande', *MZ* 6 (1911) 8–19

72    E. M. Wightman, *Roman Trier and the Treveri*, London, 1970

      R. Schindler, 'Augusta Trevirorum', *BJ* 172 (1972) 258–70

74    P. A. Brunt (cf. i 8)

      R. Syme, *The Roman Revolution*, Oxford, 1939 (repr. 1951, pb 1960–), 155

76    C. D. Gordon, 'Subsidies in Roman Imperial Defence', *Phoenix* 3 (1949) 60–69

77    E. Gose, 'Neue Beobachtungen an der Römerbrücke', *TZ* 27 (1964) 153–9

      E. Sadée, 'Die Örtlichkeit der Schlacht bei Trier im Bataverkriege, 70 n. Chr.', *BJ* 132 (1927) 165–84

      K. Schumacher (cf. iv 70)

81–82    H. I. Bell, *Cults and Creeds in Graeco-Roman Egypt*, Liverpool, 1953, repr. 1957

      P. Derchain and J. Hubaux, 'Vespasien au Sérapéum', *Lat* 12 (1953) 38–52

      H. Dieterich, *Archiv für Religionswissenschaft* 8 (1905) 500n1

      P. M. Fraser, 'Two Studies on the Cult of Serapis', *Opuscula Atheniensia* III = *Acta Instit. Ath. Regni Sueciae* 7 (1960) 1–54

      P. M. Fraser, *Ptolemaic Alexandria*, Oxford, 1970

      D. Hume, *An Enquiry concerning Human Understanding*, Section x, Part 11

      S. Morenz, 'Vespasian, Heiland der Kranken', *WJA* 4 (1950) 370–8

      P 807

      A. Rowe, 'Discovery of the Famous Temple and Enclosure of Serapis at Alexandria', *Supplément aux Annales du Service des Antiquités de l'Égypte*, 1946; id., 'A Visit to the Soma', *Bull. J. Rylands Library* 38 (1955) 139–155

      K. Scott, 'The Role of Basilides in the Events of A.D. 69', *JRS* 24 (1934) 138–40

      J. E. Stambaugh, *Sarapis under the Early Ptolemies*, Leiden, 1972

      D. Tarrant, 'The Touch of Socrates', *CQ* 8 (1958) 95–8

      O. Weinreich, *Antike Heilungswunder* (*Religionsgeschichtliche Versuche* VIII, I) Giessen, 1909, esp. 66, 68, 75

      C. B. Welles, 'The Discovery of the Serapeum and the Foundation of Alexandria', *Historia* 11 (1962) 271–98

83    J. Krall, *T und der Orient*, Wien, 1880

      P. Jouguet in *Hommages Bidez et Cumont*, Brussels, 1949, 159–66

      J. H. Oliver, *The Athenian Expounders of the Sacred and Ancestral Law*, Baltimore, 1950

86    K. H. Waters (cf. iv 2)

# Bibliography

1–13   *Only a very small selection of the enormous literature which in one way or another throws light upon the subject-matter of these chapters can be given here.*

## THE JEWS IN THE ROMAN WORLD

M. Friedländer, 'La propagande religieuse des Juifs grecs avant l'ère chrétienne', *REJ* 30 (1895) 161–81

M. Friedländer, 'Les prophéties sur la guerre judéo-romaine de l'an 70', *REJ* 30 (1895) 122–4

J. A. Hild, 'Les Juifs à Rome devant l'opinion et dans la littérature, III', *REJ* 11 (1885) 161–94

T. J. Hunt, 'T and the Jews', *Pegasus* 2 (1964) 17–19

J. Juster, *Les Juifs dans l'empire romain*, Paris, 1914

A. Momigliano, *Ricerche sull' organizzazione della Giudea sotto il dominio romano, 63 a.C.–70 d.C.*, Bologna, 1934, repr. Amsterdam, 1967

M. Radin, *The Jews among the Greeks and Romans*, Philadelphia, 1915

T. Rajak, *Josephus*, London, 1983

T. Reinach, *Textes d'auteurs grecs et romains relatifs au Judaisme*, Paris, 1895

A. Schalit (cf. ii 74)

E. M. Smallwood, ed. Philo, *Legatio ad Gaium*, Leiden, ¹1961, ²1970

ead., *The Jews under Roman Rule*, Leiden, 1976

## JUDAEA: HISTORY, CUSTOMS, TOPOGRAPHY

G. Dalman, *Arbeit und Sitte in Palästina*, Gütersloh, 1928–37

id., *Jerusalem und sein Gelände*, Gütersloh, 1930, repr. Hildesheim, 1966

K. M. Kenyon, *Jerusalem*, London, 1967

E. Schürer, *A History of the Jewish People in the Age of Jesus Christ*, rev. edition (– G. and P. Vermes, F. Millar, M. Black), Edinburgh, 1973–9

H. Graetz, *The History of the Jews*, tr. B. Löwy, etc., London, 1891–2

W. Weber, *Josephus und Vespasian*, Berlin, 1921

## TACITUS AND JUDAEA

G. Boissier, 'Le jugement de T sur les Juifs', *Mélanges Cabrière* I, 81–96

W. Fauth in Heubner's Commentary V

A. M. A. Hospers-Jansen, *T over de Joden* (with extensive summary in English), Groningen, 1949

I. Lévy, 'Tacite et l'origine du peuple juif', *Lat* 5 (1946) 331–40

J. Morr, 'Die Landeskunde von Palästina bei . . . T .ʾ. .', *Ph* 81 (1926) 265–71

M. Stern, *Greek and Latin Authors on the Jews II*, Jerusalem, 1980

C. Thiaucourt, 'Ce que T dit des Juifs au commencement du livre V des Histoires', *REJ* 19 (1889) 57–64 and 20 (1890) 312–14

THE SIEGE OF JERUSALEM

F. M. Abel, 'La topographie du siège de Jérusalem en 70', *Revue Biblique* 56 (1949) 238–58

R. Cagnat, 'L'armée romaine au siège de Jérusalem', *REJ* 22 (1891) xxviii–lviii

P. Fabia, 'Pline l'ancien a-t-il assisté au siège de Jérusalem par Titus?', *RPh* N.S. 16 (1892) 149–55

3– J. G. Gager, *Moses in Greco-Roman Paganism,* Nashville and New York, 1972, esp. 127f.

4   P 252

5   E. M. Smallwood, 'The Legislation of Hadrian and Antoninus Pius against circumcision', *Lat* 18 (1959) 334–47

A. Büchler, 'La fête des cabanes chez Plutarche et T', *REJ* 37 (1898) 181–202

6   R. Macmullen, *CQ* N.S. 12 (1962) 279

T. Klauser, *Reallexikon,* s.v. 'Asphalt'

9   E. M. Smallwood, 'Some Notes on the Jews under Tiberius', *Lat* 15 (1956) 314–29; id., 'The Chronology of Gaius' Attempt to Desecrate the Temple', *Lat* 16 (1957) 3–17

P 731; 922

11   Sœur Marie-Aline de Sion, *La forteresse Antonia à Jérusalem et la question du Prétoire,* Diss. Paris, 1956

13   D. S. Barrett, 'T *H V* 13, 2 and the Dead Sea Scrolls Again', *RhM* 119 (1976) 366

J. G. Griffiths, 'T and the Hodayot in the Dead Sea Scrolls', *RhM* 122 (1979) 99–100

A. Schalit, above

14–15   T. Woodman, 'Self-Imitation and the Substance of History' in *Creative Imitation and Latin Literature* (ed. D. West and T. Woodman), Cambridge, 1979, 143–55; 231–5

16   J. S. Rainbird, 'Tactics at Mons Graupius', *CR* N.S. 19 (1969) 11f.

17   E. A. Thompson, *The Early Germans,* Oxford, 1965, 115

19   W. Vollgraff, 'Les travaux de Drusus dans la Germanie Inférieure', *REA* 42 (1940) 686–98

20–21   J. E. Bogaers, 'Twee Romeinse wijmonumenten uit Alem, Noord-Brabant', *ROB* 12–13 (1962–3) 39–56

26   A. Dederich, 'Über die Nabalia von T', *Monatsschrift für die Geschichte Westdeutschlands* 4 (1878) 213–19

# KEY TO TECHNICAL TERMS

AUXILIARIES: cavalry regiments and infantry cohorts (battalions), each about 500 or 1,000 men strong, raised from non-Roman provincials and commanded by 'prefects', Roman officers who had served in the legions. These units were more mobile than the legions, to which they gave support on the flanks, front and rear. Their total strength throughout the territory of the empire was some 180,000 men.

CAPITOL: *either* the Capitoline Hill, with or without the adjacent Arx (see map 10).
*or* the principal building on it, the Temple of Jupiter Best and Greatest.

CENTURION: commander of a legionary half-company ('century') of some eighty men. The centuries were paired to form a full company ('maniple'), one centurion being senior to the other.

CLIENT: a dependant such as a freedman (or his descendant), who remained after emancipation under a legal and moral obligation to render services to his ex-master ('patron') in return for favours and protection. Rulers of small kingdoms on the fringe of the empire, 'client-kings', stood in a similar relationship to the emperor, and could rely on Roman support so long as they retained the confidence of the suzerain.

CONSUL: the highest executive official or 'magistrate' of the Roman People, and president of the senate. At any one time, there were two consuls acting as colleagues. Elected by the senate and with the emperor's approval for terms of two, four or six months, they were called 'suffect' if entering office after the initial pair of each year, after whom it was named. After election and before the assumption of the consulship, a consul-elect was called 'designate'. A repeated, and particularly a third, tenure was a proof of high status and imperial favour. An ex-consul ('consular') was competent to hold the most senior commands abroad.

FREEDMAN: an ex-slave who had bought or been given his emancipation or 'manumission'; see client. The 'freedmen of Caesar' formed a class of senior civil servants wielding considerable power as members of the emperor's secretariat.

## Key to Technical Terms

IMPERIAL AGENT: a financial officer (knight or freedman) administering the imperial domain in a province, subordinate in rank and status to the governor but responsible directly to the emperor.

KNIGHT: a member of the 'equestrian order', a class of Romans determined by birth and financial position, and inferior to the 'senatorial order'. No obligation lay upon knights to serve the state, but if they chose an official career, a wide range of the less important executive and military positions lay open to them.

LEGION: a heavy infantry formation numbering some 5,000 men who were Roman citizens recruited from Italy and the more-highly Romanized provinces. It was officered by a commander ('legate'), normally of the rank of praetor, by six staff-officers ('tribunes'), and by sixty company commanders ('centurions'). The men were equipped with spear, sword, dagger, helmet, body-armour and semi-cylindrical shield, and were used as a heavy thrusting force designed to cut a way through any opposition. When not actively campaigning, the legion was regularly employed on fortification, road-building and other ancillary tasks. It possessed a cavalry and artillery element. At the time with which the *Histories* are concerned there were some thirty legions with a total strength of about 150,000 men.

MAGISTRATE: an official elected by the senate for a yearly term (in the case of consuls, for less than a yearly term) to conduct the deliberative, judicial and executive functions of the Roman People. The main grades, in ascending order of seniority, are: Quaestor, Praetor, Consul. After serving in Rome, they could expect promotion to posts of appropriate seniority abroad.

PALACE: a complex of buildings of many kinds occupying most of the Palatine Hill south west of the forum, and including the residence of the emperor.

PRAETOR: one of *c.* eighteen annual 'magistrates' with judicial functions. The minimum age of tenure was normally thirty years.

PRETORIAN GUARD: a *corps d'élite*, mostly serving in a ceremonial capacity in Rome and in immediate attendance on the emperor. There were nine (under Vitellius sixteen) cohorts of 1,000 men each, whose barracks lay outside the walls of Rome on the north east (see map 11). Each cohort was commanded by a 'tribune', and the whole body by one or more 'prefects', usually of equestrian rank.

QUAESTOR: one of *c.* twenty annual 'magistrates' with minor executive and financial functions. The minimum age of tenure was normally twenty-five years, and election to the quaestorship conveyed membership of the senate.

ROSTRA: a high platform or tribunal in the forum from which magistrates addressed the assembled Roman People.

TRIBUNE: *either* a legionary staff-officer

or a commander of a pretorian, urban or watch cohort

or (as tribune of the plebs) an annually elected official who under the republic exercised a check upon the administrative powers of magistrates by virtue of his veto and legal inviolability; under the principate the office was overshadowed by the 'tribunician power' enjoyed by the emperor.

TRIUMPH: a ceremonial procession of troops, commander, prisoners and booty through Rome to the Temple of Jupiter Best and Greatest at the conclusion of a successful campaign. Under the emperors, who were themselves the supreme commanders, only the 'ornaments' were awarded to the field commander (see p. 69, n. 1).

URBAN COHORTS: gendarmerie units (four in number and with a strength of 1,000 men each under Vitellius) serving mostly in Rome. Each of these was commanded by a tribune, and the whole force by the chief-of-police ('city prefect').

WATCH: seven cohorts of police and firemen, each 1,000 men strong and commanded by a tribune, responsible for the fourteen 'regions' into which the city of Rome was divided. The whole force was headed by an equestrian 'prefect of the watch'.

# KEY TO PLACE-NAMES

| Ancient Name | Modern Name (or Description of District) | Map No. |
|---|---|---|
| Achaia | Central and Southern Greece | – |
| Actium | At mouth of Gulf of Amvrakia, Greece | – |
| Aedui | Round Autun | 6 |
| Africa | Tunisia and Tripolitania | – |
| Alani | Don–Volga Steppes | – |
| Albani | Azerbaijan | – |
| Albingaunum | Albenga | 1 |
| Albintimilium | Ventimiglia | 1 |
| Allia, River | Fosso della Bettina, c. 11 miles north of Rome | – |
| Allobroges | Rhône–Lake of Geneva | 6 |
| Altinum | Altino | 1 |
| Anagnia | Anagni | 5 |
| Antioch | Antakya | – |
| Antipolis | Antibes | 6 |
| Appian Way | Rome–Benevento–Brindisi | 5, 11 |
| Aquinum | Aquino | 5 |
| Aquitania | France south-west of River Loire | 6 |
| Arenacium | Probably Rindern near Kleve | 7 |
| Aricia | Ariccia | 5 |
| Ariminum | Rimini | 1, 5 |
| Arverni | Auvergne | 6 |
| Asciburgium | Asberg, near Mörs | 7 |
| Asia | West Anatolia | – |
| Ateste | Este | 1 |
| Atria | Adria | 1 |
| Aventicum | Avenches | 1 |
| Baetasii | Between Louvain, Diest, Hasselt and St Truiden | 6 |

| Ancient Name | Modern Name (or Description of District) | Map No |
|---|---|---|
| *Baetica* | Andalucía | – |
| *Batavians* | Old Rhine-Waal, with Land van Maas en Waal, Bommelerwaard and some land south of River Maas | 7 |
| *Batavodurum* | North-east suburbs of Nijmegen | 7 |
| *Bedriacum* | Probably Tornata, west of Bozzolo | 1, 2 |
| *Belgica* | North and east France, with west Switzerland | 6 |
| *Belius, River* | Nahr Na'aman, near Acre | – |
| *Berytus* | Beyrout | – |
| *Bingium* | Bingen | 6 |
| *Boii* | Between Adda and Po | 1 |
| *Bononia* | Bologna | 1 |
| *Bovillae* | Near Frattocchie | 5 |
| *Brigantes* | Between Hadrian's Wall and River Trent | – |
| *Brixellum* | Brescello | 1 |
| *Brixia* | Brescia | 1 |
| *Bructeri* | Between Lippe and Ems | 7 |
| *Brundisium* | Brindisi | – |
| *Byzantium* | Istanbul | – |
| *Caeracates* | Upper Germany | – |
| *Caesarea* | Between Tel Aviv and Haifa | – |
| *Calabria* | Province of Lecce | – |
| *Campania* | Lazio and Campania | 5 |
| *Campus Martius* | Corso area of Rome | 11 |
| *Cannenefates* | Inland from The Hague | 7 |
| *Capitolium* | Campidoglio | 10, 11 |
| *Cappadocia* | East Anatolia | – |
| *Capua* | Santa Maria di Capua Vetere | 5 |
| *Carsulae* | 3 km. north of Sangémini | 5 |
| *Castores* | Near Ronca de' Golférami | 2 |
| *Chatti* | Upper Weser | – |
| *Chobus, River* | River Khobi or Inguri, Caucasus | – |
| *Cilicia* | South-east Anatolia | – |
| *Cimbri* | North Jutland | – |
| *Cottiae Alpes* | Round Susa | 6 |
| *Cremera, River* | Fosso Valchetta or Fosso d'Aquatra-versa | 11 |

| *Ancient Name* | *Modern Name (or Description of District)* | *Map No.* |
|---|---|---|
| Cremona | Cremona | 1, 2, 3 |
| Cugerni | Near Krefeld | 7 |
| Curtius, Basin of | In the Foro Romano | 10 |
| Cyrene | Shahhat, Libya | – |
| Cythnus | Kythnos (Thermia) | – |
| Dacia | Romania | – |
| Dalmatia | Yugoslavia | – |
| Divodurum | Metz | 6 |
| Dyrrachium | Durrës (Durazzo) | – |
| Emerita | Merida | – |
| Eporedia | Ivrea | 1 |
| Etruria | Tuscany | 1, 5 |
| Fanum Fortunae | Fano | 1, 5 |
| Ferentis | Ferento | 5 |
| Fidenae | Castel Giubileo | 11 |
| Flaminian Way | Rome–Narni–Bevagna–Rimini | 5, 11 |
| Forum Alieni | Perhaps Legnago | 1 |
| Forum Iulii | Fréjus | 6 |
| Frisii | North Holland and Friesland | 7 |
| Fundanus, Basin of | A little to south of Quirinal Palace | 11 |
| Galatia | Central Anatolia | – |
| Garamantes | Fezzan | – |
| Gelduba | Gellep, near Krefeld | 7 |
| Gemonian Steps | Via dell'Arco di Settimio Severo | 10 |
| Germany, Lower | The Rhineland north of Vinxtbach near Niederbreisig | 6, 7 |
| Germany, Upper | The Rhineland south of Vinxtbach, to Vosges | 6 |
| Graian Alps | Round Little St Bernard Pass | 6 |
| Grinnes | Perhaps Rossum | 7 |
| Haemus, Mt | Stara Planina and Rodopi Planina | – |
| Hadrumetum | Sousse | – |
| Helvetii | West Switzerland | 1, 6 |
| Hispalis | Seville | – |
| Histria | Istria | 1 |
| Hostilia | Ostiglia | 1 |
| Ianiculum | Ianicolo | 11 |
| Iazyges | Between Danube and Theiss Rivers | – |
| Ida, Mt | Psiloriti Range, Crete | – |
| Interamna | Terni | 5 |

| Ancient Name | Modern Name (or Description of District) | Map No. |
|---|---|---|
| Lepcis | Near Homs, Libya | – |
| Leuci | Round Toul | 6 |
| Liguria | Liguria with parts of Piedmont | 1, 6 |
| Lingones | Round Langres | 6 |
| Lucania | Lucania and south Campania | 5 |
| Luceria | Lucera | 5 |
| Lucus | Luc-en-Diois | 6 |
| Lusitania | Portugal and west Spain | – |
| Marcodurum | Perhaps Merken near Düren | 7 |
| Marsaci | Perhaps Zeeland | 7 |
| Marsi | South of Upper Lippe | – |
| Mattiaci | Round Wiesbaden | – |
| Mauretania Caesariensis | East Morocco and west Algeria | – |
| Mauretania Tingitana | Morocco west of River Moulouya | – |
| Medi | North Iran | – |
| Mediomatrici | Round Metz | 6 |
| Memphis | Near Bedrashen, south of Cairo | – |
| Menapii | West Flanders | 7 |
| Mevania | Bevagna | 5 |
| Minturnae | Near mouth of River Garigliano | 5 |
| Misenum | Miseno | 5 |
| Moesia | South bank of River Danube in Bulgaria and Yugoslavia | – |
| Mogontiacum | Mainz | 6 |
| Mons Vocetius | Bözberg (or Ütliberg?) | 1 |
| Morini | West Pas-de-Calais | 6 |
| Mutina | Modena | 1 |
| Nabalia, River | River Ijssel or Vecht | 7 |
| Narbonese Gaul | Provence and Languedoc | 6 |
| Narnia | Narni | 5 |
| Nervii | Between Scheldt and Meuse, round Bavai | 6 |
| Noricum | East Austria | 1 |
| Novaesium | Neuss | 7 |
| Novaria | Novara | 1 |
| Numidia | East Algeria and west Tunisia | – |
| Ocriculum | Otricoli | 5 |
| Oea | Tripoli | – |
| Opitergium | Oderzo | 1 |
| Ostia | Ostia-Scavi | 5 |

| Ancient Name | Modern Name (or Description of District) | Map No. |
|---|---|---|
| Paeligni | Abruzzi | 5 |
| Pamphylia | South Anatolia | – |
| Pannonia | West Hungary and North Yugoslavia | – |
| Paphos | Paphos | – |
| Parthi | Iraq and Iran | – |
| Patavium | Padua | 1 |
| Perusia | Perugia | 5 |
| Pharsalia | In Thessaly | – |
| Philippi | Near Kavalla | – |
| Picenum | Marche and Abruzzi | 5 |
| Placentia | Piacenza | 1 |
| Poetovio | Ptuj | – |
| Pontus | North Anatolia | – |
| Portus Herculis Monoeci | Monaco | 1, 6 |
| Portus Pisanus | S. Stefano near Livorno | 1 |
| Postumian Way | Genoa–Piacenza–Verona–Aquileia | 1 |
| Puteoli | Pozzuoli | 5 |
| Raetia | East Switzerland, west Tirol, and Germany within the Danube and Inn Rivers | 1 |
| Ravenna | 5 km. south-east of Ravenna | 1 |
| Regium Lepidum | Reggio Emilia | 1 |
| Remi | Round Reims | 6 |
| Rhacotis | South-west quarter of Alexandria | – |
| Rigodulum | Riol | 6, 8 |
| Sabini | North-east of Rome | 5 |
| Salarian Way | Rome–Rieti–Ascoli Piceno–Porto d'Ascoli | 5 |
| Samnites | South Apennines | 5 |
| Sarmatians | North of Lower Danube | – |
| Saxa Rubra | Probably Grottarossa | – |
| Scythians | South Russia | – |
| Sedochezi | Caucasus | – |
| Seleucia | Samandag | – |
| Sena | Siena | 5 |
| Sequani | Between Saône, Jura, Vosges and Rhine | 6 |
| Sinope | Sinop | – |
| Sinuessa Spa | I Bagni near Mondragone | 5 |
| Stoechades Islands | Îles d'Hyères | 6 |

## Key to Place-Names

| Ancient Name | Modern Name (or Description of District) | Map No. |
|---|---|---|
| Suebians | Elbe Valley, Brandenburg, Bohemia and Moravia | – |
| Suessa Pometia | In area of Latina | – |
| Sunuci | Dutch Limburg | 7 |
| Tarentum | Taranto | – |
| Tarracina | Terracina | 5 |
| Tencteri | South of River Lippe | 7 |
| Teutoni | Perhaps Jutland | – |
| Thrace | Bulgaria | – |
| Ticinum | Pavia | 1 |
| Tingitana v. 'Mauretania' | | – |
| Tolbiacum | Zülpich | 7 |
| Transpadane Region | North Piedmont and west Lombardy | 1 |
| Trapezus | Trabzon | – |
| Treviri | Round Trier | 6, 9 |
| Triboci | Alsace | – |
| Tungri | Round Tongres | 6 |
| Ubii | Round Cologne | 7 |
| Umbria | Umbria | 5 |
| Urvinum | Collemancio, 14 km. north-west of Bevagna | 5 |
| Usipi | South-east of Bonn, between Sieg and Lahn Rivers | 7 |
| Vada | Perhaps Heerewaarden, east of Rossum | 7 |
| Vangiones | Round Worms, on both sides of Rhine | – |
| Vascones | Navarre and Guipuzcoa | – |
| Vercellae | Vercelli | 1 |
| Verona | Verona | 1 |
| Vetera | Birten near Xanten | 7 |
| Vicetia | Vicenza | 1 |
| Vindonissa | Windisch | 1, 6 |
| Vocontii v. 'Lucus' | | 6 |

# INDEX OF PERSONAL
# NAMES

Aegialus, 44

Aemilius Longinus, 246, 248

Aemilius Pacensis, 35, 75, 89, 191

Aerias, King, 82

Agrestis, see Julius Agrestis

Agricola, see Julius Agricola.

Agrippa (son-in-law of Augustus), 31

Agrippa II, King, 130, 271

Albinus, see Lucceius Albinus

Alfenus Varus, 98, 167, 179, 183, 210

Alienus Caecina, see Caecina Alienus

Alpinius, Decimus, 283

Alpinius Montanus, 166, 225–6, 283

Amullius Serenus, 40

Anicetus, 173–4

Annius Bassus, 176

Annius Faustus, 86–7

Annius Gallus, 75, 88, 95, 101, 107, 251, 282

Antiochus, King of Commagene and Cilicia, 129, 271

Antiochus (IV), King of Syria, 276

Antistius Sosianus, 235

Antonius Felix, 277

Antonius Flamma, 235

Antonius Naso, 35

Antonius Novellus, 75, 89

Antonius Primus
  Career and character, 132–3
  Italian campaign, 145–66 and 175–205 passim; 225, 283
  Relations with Mucianus and Vespasian, 13, 149, 175, 177–8, 194–5, 209, 220, 230–1, 251, 261–2
  Relations with Civilis, 212, 225, 287

Antonius Taurus, 35

Antony, Mark, 84, 160, 186, 276–8

Apinius Tiro, 180, 193

Apollinaris, see Claudius Apollinaris

Aponianus, see Dillius Aponianus

Aponius Saturninus, Marcus, 69, 132, 139, 147, 150, 152, 287

Aquilius (centurion), 214

Aquilius Regulus, 233–4

Argius, 50

Ariovistus, 256

Arrecinus Clemens, 252

Arrius Antoninus, 68

Arrius Varus, 148, 154–5, 177, 183–6, 203, 205, 209, 230–1, 251–2

Arruntius, Lucius, 119

Arsaces, 276

Arsacids, 45

Arulenus Rusticus, 196

Asiaticus (Gallic leader), 138

Asiaticus (Vitellius' freedman), 115, 139, 210

Asinius Pollio, 116

Asprenas, see Calpurnius Asprenas

Atilius Varus, 158

Atilius Vergilio, 46

Augustus (emperor 31 B.C.–A.D. 14), 10, 11, 27, 31, 33, 51, 77, 126, 186, 215, 219, 237, 244, 276

Aurelius Fulvus, 69

Auspex, see Julius Auspex


Baebius Massa, 239

Barbius Proculus, 37

Barea Soranus, 207, 209, 232

Basilides (Egyptian), 264

# Index of Personal Names

Basilides (priest of Mt Carmel), 128

Bassus, see Lucilius Bassus

Berenice, Queen, 82, 130

Betuus, Cilo, 44

Blaesus, see Junius Blaesus

Bocchoris, Pharaoh, 272

Briganticus, see Julius Briganticus

Brinno, 213–14

Brutus, 51, 84

Cadius Rufus, 68

Caecilius Simplex, 117, 187

Caecina Alienus
  Career and character, 53–4, 141–2
  Gallic and Italian campaigns, 58–64 and 77–169 passim; 225, 262

Caecina Tuscus, 168

Caelius Sabinus, 68

Caetronius Pisanus, 239

Calpurnius Asprenas, 86

Calpurnius Galerianus, 209, 238

Calpurnius Repentinus, 56, 58

Calvia Crispinilla, 66

Calvisius Sabinus, 49

Campanus, 251

Camurius, 46

Caninius Rebilus, 168

Capito, see Fonteius Capito

Caratacus, King, 172

Cartimandua, Queen, 172

Casperius Niger, 191

Cassius Longus, 154

Cato, 208

Celer, Publius, 14, 209, 232

Celsus, see Marius Celsus

Cepheus, 272

Cerialis, see Petilius Cerialis

Cestius Gallus, 277

Cestius Severus, 232

Cetrius Severus, 40

Cingonius Varro, 24, 44

Cinna, 176, 198

Cinyras, 82

Civilis, see Julius Civilis

Classicus, see Julius Classicus

Claudia Sacrata, 284

Claudius (emperor A.D. 41–54), 11, 27, 32, 49, 50, 54, 68, 126, 171, 186, 277

Claudius Apollinaris, 180, 193–4

Claudius Cossus, 63

Claudius Faventinus, 180

Claudius Julianus, 181, 193–4

Claudius Labeo, 216, 244, 250–1, 253

Claudius Paulus, 211

Claudius Pyrrhicus, 91

Claudius Sagitta, 238

Claudius Sanctus, 248

Claudius Severus, 62

Claudius Victor, 226

Clemens, see Arrecinus Clemens

Cleopatra, 277

Clodius Macer, 25, 27, 44, 66, 140, 238

Cluvius Rufus, 25, 67, 115, 119, 185, 231, 234

Cocceius Proculus, 37

Coelius, see Roscius Coelius

Coenus, 113

Corbulo, 11, 126, 148, 160

Cornelius Aquinus, 25

Cornelius Dolabella, 75, 118

Cornelius Fuscus, 133, 147, 152, 170, 205

Cornelius Laco, 24, 29, 30, 34, 38, 42, 45, 49

Cornelius Marcellus, 44

Cornelius Martialis, 188–9, 191

Cornelius Primus, 192

(Cornelius) Scipio, Lucius, 191

Cornelius (Scipio), Publius, 165

Crassus (brother of Piso Licinianus), 49

Crassus (father of Piso Licinianus), 30

Crassus, Marcus (triumvir), 31, 84

Crescens, 67

Crispina, 49

Crispinus, 57

Crispus, see Vibius Crispus

Curtius Montanus, 231, 233–4

Decimus Alpinius, see Alpinius Decimus

Demetrius, 232

Didius Scaeva, 191

Dillius Aponianus, 150, 152
Dillius Vocula, 220, 223-3, 226-9, 243-4, 246, 260
Dolabella, *see* Cornelius Dolabella
Domitian (emperor A.D. 81-96), 9, 21, 182, 188, 192, 200, 203, 205, 230, 235-7, 239, 240, 251-2, 258, 261, 266-7
Domitius Sabinus, 40
Donatius Valens, 56, 58
Drusilla, 277
Drusus Germanicus, 283
Ducenius Geminus, 30

Eleazar, 278-9
Epiphanes, Prince, 97
Epponina, 251
Eprius Marcellus, 112, 139, 206-8, 234

Fabius Fabullus, 154
Fabius Priscus, 261
Fabius Valens
   Career and character, 25, 53-4, 184
   Gallic and Italian campaigns, 56-66 *and* 89-186 *passim*
Felix, *see* Antonius Felix
Festus (cohort commander), 116
Festus, *see* Valerius Festus
Flaccus, *see* Hordeonius Flaccus
Flavianus, *see* Tampius Flavianus
Flavius Sabinus (city prefect), 48, 114, 118, 141, 182, 184-5, 187-9, 190, 192-3, 195-6, 199, 237
Flavius Sabinus (consul A.D. 69), 68, 102, 112
Flavus, 138
Fonteius Agrippa, 173
Fonteius Capito, 25-6, 44, 53, 57, 184, 211
Frontinus, *see* Julius Frontinus
Fuscus, *see* Cornelius Fuscus

Gaius (emperor A.D. 37-41), 32, 50, 76, 126, 187, 213, 234, 237, 277
Gaius Marius, *see* Marius, Gaius
Gaius Norbanus, *see* Norbanus, Gaius
Gaius Piso, *see* Piso, Gaius

Gaius Plinius, *see* Pliny the Elder
Gaius Sosius, *see* Sosius, Gaius
Gaius Volusius, *see* Volusius, Gaius
Galba (emperor A.D. 68-9)
   Career and character, 9-11, 21, 27-8, 36, 50-1, 81, 126
   Reign before arrival in Rome, 23-6, 48, 50-4, 61, 65, 68, 84, 86, 88, 115, 123, 140, 158, 206-7, 212, 226, 244, 281
   Reign after arrival in Rome, 29-35, 44, 55-6, 65-6, 75, 133, 142, 184
   Fall and death, 16, 38-46, 51, 60, 100, 187, 199, 233
   Reputation after death, 47, 114, 135, 148-9, 231
Galeria, 119, 186, 189, 198
Galerianus, *see* Calpurnius Galerianus
Galerius Trachalus, 77, 117
Gallus, *see* Annius, Herennius Gallus
Germanicus (son of the emperor Vitellius), 116, 168, 186-7, 261
Gessius Florus, 277
Geta, 123
Gnaeus Pompey, *see* Pompey
Grypus, *see* Plotius Grypus

Hannibal, 165, 212
Helvidius Priscus, 14, 136, 205-8, 234, 241
Herennius Gallus, 217-18, 222-3, 246, 254, 260
Herod, 276, 278
Hilarus, 119
Horatius Pulvillus, 191
Hordeonius Flaccus, 26, 53, 55-6, 114, 140, 212, 216-17, 220-3, 225, 228-9, 242, 287
Hormus, 153, 162, 230, 260

Icelus (Marcianus), 29, 44, 49, 139
Italicus, 147, 158

John, 278
Julianus, *see* Claudius Julianus
Julius Agrestis, 178-9
Julius Alpinus, 63

# Index of Personal Names

Julius Atticus, 42

Julius Auspex, 252–3

Julius Briganticus, 95, 253, 283

Julius Burdo, 57

Julius Caesar, 46, 51, 77, 168, 186–7, 243–4

Julius Calenus, 166

Julius Carus, 46

Julius Civilis, 57, 211–29, 242, 245, 247–51, 253–4, 257–61, 280–6

Julius Classicus, 90, 242, 244–6, 248, 253–5, 257–61, 283–4

Julius Cordus, 67

Julius Flavianus, 195

Julius Frontinus, 230

Julius Fronto, 35, 97

Julius Gratus, 97

Julius Mansuetus, 160

Julius Martialis, 38, 71

Julius Maximus, 226

Julius Placidus, 199

Julius Priscus, 137, 179, 183, 210

Julius Sabinus, 243, 251

Julius Tutor, 243–6, 254–5, 257–8, 260, 283–4

Julius Valentinus, 252–5, 259, 266

Julius Vindex, 11, 24–5, 32, 52, 54, 61, 64, 76, 138, 215, 244, 253

Junius Blaesus, 58, 116, 168–9

Junius Mauricus, 232

Juvenalis, 251

Labeo, see Claudius Labeo

Laco, see Cornelius Laco

Laecanius, 46

Licinianus, see Piso Licinianus

Licinius Caecina, 112–13

Licinius Mucianus
  Career and character, 67, 83–4, 139, 186, 193
  As Flavian supporter, 85, 125–32, 221, 287
  March to Rome, 145, 149, 160, 172–3, 175, 177–8, 184, 193–5, 205, 209
  As master of Rome, 209, 230–1, 235–6, 238, 252
  March to north, 266–7

Licinius Proculus, 48, 71, 75, 101, 104–5, 107, 116

Longinus, see Aemilius Longinus

Lucceius Albinus, 115–16

Lucilius Bassus, 141–2, 152–3, 167, 169, 204

Lucius Arruntius, see Arruntius, Lucius

Lucius Piso, see Piso, Lucius

Lucius Scipio, see (Cornelius) Scipio, Lucius

Lucius Sulla, see Sulla, Lucius

Lucius Vestinus, see Vestinus, Lucius

Lucius Vitellius, see Vitellius, Lucius

Lupercus, see Munius Lupercus

Lutatius Catulus, 191

Macer, see Clodius, Martius Macer

Magnus, 49

Manlius Patruinus, 235

Manlius Valens, 60

Marcellus (nephew of Augustus), 31

Marcellus, see Cornelius, Eprius, Romilius Marcellus

Marcianus Icelus, see Icelus (Marcianus)

Marcus Aponius, see Aponius Saturninus, Marcus

Marcus Crassus, see Crassus (father of Piso Licinianus) and Crassus, Marcus (triumvir)

Marcus Silanus see Silanus, Marcus

Mariccus, 117

Marius, Gaius, 103

Marius Celsus, 30, 40–1, 45, 48, 64, 68, 75, 77, 95–6, 101, 104–5, 107, 117

Marius Maturus, 89, 170–1

Mark Antony, see Antony, Mark

Martialis, see Cornelius Martialis

Martius Macer, 95, 102, 123

Massa, see Baebius Massa

Maturus, see Marius Maturus

Memmius Rufinus, 153

Messalla, see Vipstanus Messalla

Mevius Pudens, 36

Minicius Justus, 148

Montanus, see Alpinius, Curtius Montanus

Moschus, 75
Moses, 272
Mucianus, *see* Licinius Mucianus
Munius Lupercus, 216, 219, 247
Musonius Rufus, 14, 196, 209, 232

Nero (emperor A.D. 54–68)
  Appearance, 25, 86
  Reign, 9–11, 27, 34–5, 49, 68, 126, 133, 232, 235, 277
  Military measures, 24, 41, 64, 88
  Fall and death, 23, 40, 61, 76–7, 84, 97, 187
  Following and courtiers, 30, 32, 36–7, 44, 48, 50, 65–7, 86, 113, 115, 123, 139, 148, 207–8, 232–4
Nero (false), 22, 85–6
Nerva (emperor A.D. 96–8), 21
Nonius Attianus, 232
Nonius Receptus, 56, 58
Norbanus, Gaius, 191
Numisius Lupus, 69, 150
Numisius Rufus, 219, 246, 254, 260
Nymphidius Sabinus, 24, 37, 44

Obultronius Sabinus, 43
Octavia, 30
Octavius Sagitta, 235
Ofonius Tigellinus, 36, 65
Onomastus, 37–8
Orfidius Benignus, 106, 108
Orfitus, 233
Otho (emperor A.D. 69)
  Career and character, 9, 10, 21, 30, 35, 39, 51, 81, 85, 94, 100, 111, 117, 139, 171
  Conspires against Galba, 29, 30, 35–8, 41–5
  Reign, 47–9, 60, 64–77, 84, 88–9, 91–2, 119, 123
  Campaign in N. Italy and death, 95, 97–100, 113, 115, 118, 126, 132–3, 151, 153, 161, 164, 215, 242

Paccius Africanus, 232–3
Pacorus, King, 45, 276
Papirius, 238
Patrobius, 50, 139

Paulinus, *see* Suetonius Paulinus
Paulus, *see* Claudius Paulus
Pedanius Costa, 123
Pedius Blaesus, 68
Petilius Cerialis, 182, 195–6, 251, 254–6, 258–62, 267, 280–5
Petronia, 118
Petronius Turpilianus, 24, 44
Petronius Urbicus, 64
Picarius Decumus, 91
Piso, Gaius, 209
Piso Licinianus, 30, 33–5, 39, 40, 42, 44–7, 49, 50, 187, 231, 233
Piso, Lucius, 230, 237–9
Plancius Varus, 118
Plautius Aelianus, 241
Pliny the Elder, 12, 14, 162
Pliny the Younger, 12, 13
Plotius Firmus, 48, 71, 109, 111
Plotius Grypus, 177, 230, 232
Polemo, King, 173
Polyclitus, 44, 139
Pompeius Propinquus, 29, 57
Pompeius Silvanus, 133, 176, 236
Pompeius Strabo, 176
Pompeius Vopiscus, 68
Pompey, 31, 51, 84, 104, 186, 276, 278
Pomponius Longinus, 40
Pontia Postuma, 235
Poppaea Sabina, 30, 36, 38
Porcius Septiminus, 147
Porsenna, 190
Primus, *see* Antonius Primus
Priscus, *see* Fabius, Helvidius, Julius Priscus
Proculus, *see* Licinius Proculus
Ptolemaeus, 36
Ptolemy I, Pharaoh, 264–5
Ptolemy III, Pharaoh, 266
Publilius Sabinus, 137, 167
Publius Celer, *see* Celer, Publius
Publius Cornelius, *see* Cornelius (Scipio), Publius
Publius Ventidius, *see* Ventidius, Publius

Quintilius Varus, 215, 276

# Index of Personal Names

Quintius Atticus, 192–3
Quintius Certus, 91

Regulus, see Aquilius Regulus
Romilius Marcellus, 56, 58
Romulus, 139, 246
Roscius Coelius, 58
Rosius Regulus, 168
Rubellius Plautus, 30
Rubrius Gallus, 112, 141
Rufinus, 138

Sabinus, see Julius, Flavius, Sabinus
Sacrovir, 244
Sagitta, see Claudius Sagitta
Salonina, 93
Salvius Cocceianus, 110
Salvius Titianus, 67–8, 77, 95, 101,
    104–5, 107, 117
Sanctus, see Claudius Sanctus
Sariolenus Vocula, 232
Saturninus, see Aponius Saturninus,
    Marcus
Scaevinus Paquius (?), 68
Scipio (cohort commander), 116
Scribonia, 30
Scribonianus (Furius Camillus), 70,
    126
Scribonianus Camerinus, 123
Scribonianus (brother of Piso Lici-
    nianus), 31, 49, 231
Scribonii, 232
Scydrothemis, King, 265
Seleucus, 128
Sempronius Densus, 46
Sempronius (Gracchus), Tiberius, 165
Sentius, 207
Sertorius, 212
Servius Tullius, King, 191
Sextilia, 119, 135, 186
Sextilius Felix, 147, 253–4
Sido, 147, 158
Silanus, Marcus, 237
Silius Italicus, 185
Simon, 278
Sisenna (centurion), 85
Sisenna (historian), 176
Sohaemus, King, 129, 271

Soranus, see Barea Soranus
Sosianus, see Antistius Sosianus
Sosius, Gaius, 276
Sostratus, 83
Spurinna, see Vestricius Spurinna
Statius Murcus, 47
Subrius Dexter, 40
Suedius Clemens, 75, 89
Suetonius Paulinus, 75, 77, 95–7,
    100–1, 103–5, 107, 116
Sulla, Lucius, 103, 198
Sulpicia Praetextata, 233
Sulpicii, 31
Sulpicius Florus, 47

Tamiras, 82
Tampius Flavianus, 133, 147, 150,
    287
Tarquin the Elder, King, 191
Tarquin the Younger, King, 191
Tatius, King, 139
Terentius, 46
Tettius Julianus, 69, 132, 230, 232
Thrasea Paetus, 137. 206–8
Tiberius (emperor A.D. 14–37), 9, 11,
    31–2, 76, 119, 126, 139, 234, 237,
    277
Tiberius Alexander, 27, 125, 128
Tiberius Sempronius, see Sempronius
    (Gracchus), Tiberius
Tigellinus, see Ofonius Tigellinus
Timotheus, 264
Titianus, see Salvius Titianus
Titus (emperor A.D. 79–81), 9, 16, 21,
    27, 81–4, 125, 128, 131, 205, 230,
    240, 271, 277–9
Titus Vinius, see Vinius, Titus
Trachalus, see Galerius Trachalus
Trajan (emperor A.D. 98–117), 21
Trebellius Maximus, 58, 119
Trebonius Garutianus, 25
Triaria, 118–19, 194
Turpilianus, see Petronius Turpilianus
Turullius Cerialis, 94
Tutor, see Julius Tutor

Umbricius, 38

Valens, *see* Fabius Valens

Valentinus, *see* Julius Valentinus

Valerius Asiaticus, 58, 205

Valerius Festus, 140, 237–9

Valerius Marinus, 123

Valerius Paulinus, 171

Varius Crispinus, 70

Varus, *see* Quintilius Varus

Vatinius, 44

Vedius Aquila, 107, 148

Veleda, 17, 247, 250, 285

Vellocatus, 172

Ventidius, Publius, 276

Venutius, 172

Verania, 49

Verax, 283–4

Vergilius Capito, 193, 204

Verginius Rufus, 11, 26, 53, 55, 68, 111–12, 121, 123, 184, 215, 253

Verulana Gratilla, 88

Vespasian (emperor A.D. 69–79)
Career and character, 9, 10, 13, 21, 83, 131, 140, 166, 182, 185–6, 192–3, 207–8, 212, 234, 237, 252, 279, 287
As governor of Judaea, 27, 48, 51, 67, 81, 83, 124, 271, 277
Elevation to principate, 15–17, 82, 84–5, 120, 124–9, 132–3, 139, 150, 152–3, 171, 188–9, 194, 200, 204–5, 209, 213, 216, 218, 223, 225, 228–30, 232, 235, 239, 242, 245, 253, 258, 260, 286–7
Strategy, 130–1, 134, 140–1, 145–6, 148–9, 151, 153, 168, 173–4, 177, 180, 221, 239–40, 261, 263–4, 271

Vestinus, Lucius, 240

Vestricius Spurinna, 12, 88, 92–3, 95, 102

Vettius Bolanus, 119, 140

Veturius, 37

Vibius Crispus, 86–7, 223–4

Vindex, *see* Julius Vindex

Vinius, Titus, 21, 24, 28–9, 30, 41–2, 44–7, 49, 50, 65, 139

Vipstanus Apronianus, 67

Vipstanus Messalla, 12, 150, 152, 156, 160, 162, 233

Virdius Geminus, 174

Vitellius (emperor A.D. 69)
Career and character, 9, 10, 15–16, 21, 26, 72, 85, 94, 99, 100, 110, 126–7, 136, 147, 151, 186, 193, 199, 204–5, 215, 237, 287
Elevation to principate, 30, 51–4, 56–7
Reign before arrival in Rome, 57–64, 66–8, 73–5, 77, 81, 84, 91, 94, 98, 104, 113–24, 129, 134–5, 145–6, 171, 212, 214, 216–17, 235, 253
Reign after arrival in Rome, 47, 130–3, 135–42, 149–50, 152–4, 163, 167, 169, 171, 173, 178–84, 203, 218, 223, 225, 228–9, 232, 245
Attempted abdication and death, 184–5, 187–9, 192–6, 198–200, 239, 242

Vitellius, Lucius (brother of the emperor), 76, 113, 167–8, 179, 181, 187–8, 193–4, 198, 204

Vitellius, Lucius (father of the emperor), 26, 54, 186, 199

Vitellius Saturninus, 71

Vocula, *see* Dillius Vocula

Volaginius, 126

Vologaeses, King, 45, 239

Volusius, Gaius, 163

Vulcacius Tertullinus, 208

**MAP I**

BOII = *Peoples*
—·—· = *Frontiers*

R. Inn

NORICUM

VENETIA

Alpes
Iuliae

Opitergium
Aquileia
POSTUMIAN WAY
Vicetia
Altinum
Verona
Patavium
Histria
Forum
Alieni
Ateste
Mantua
Bedriacum
Hostilia
R. Tartaro
Atria
Brixellum
R. Po
Regium Lepidum
Mutina
AEMILIAN WAY
Bononia
Ravenna
AEMILIA
Ariminum
ETRURIA
Fanum
Fortunae
FLAMINIAN WAY
UMBRIA

MAP I

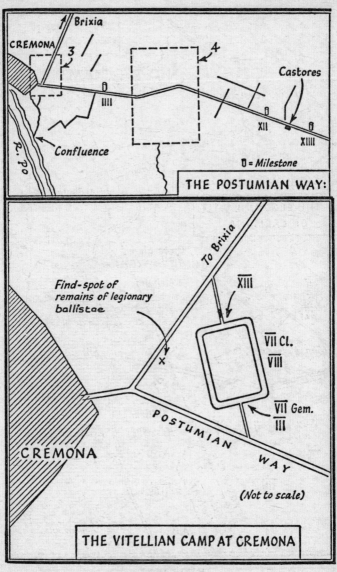

THE POSTUMIAN WAY:

THE VITELLIAN CAMP AT CREMONA

**MAPS 2 AND 3**

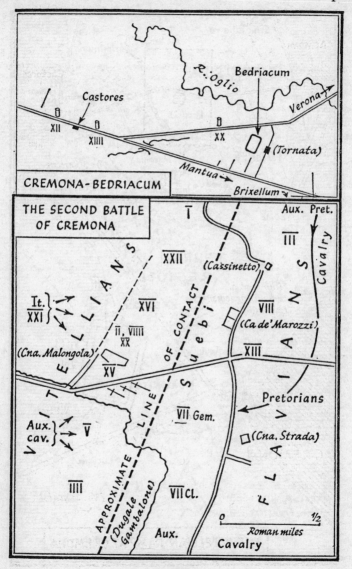

CREMONA-BEDRIACUM

THE SECOND BATTLE
OF CREMONA

MAPS 2 AND 4

MAP 5

MAP 6

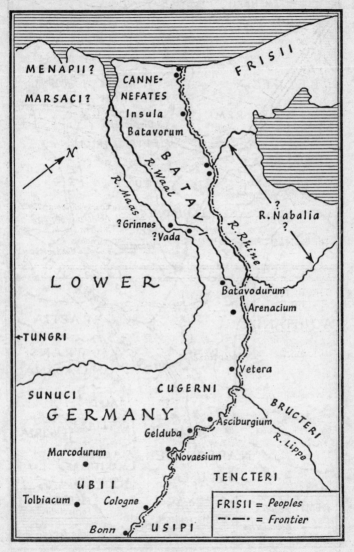

MAP 7

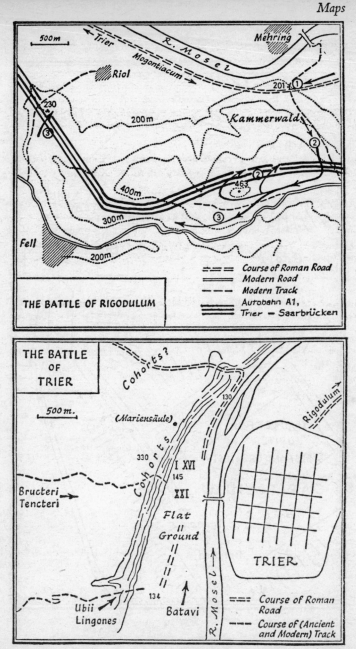

THE BATTLE OF RIGODULUM

500 m

R. Mosel
Trier
Mogontiacum →
Mehring

Riol
201
Kammerwald
230
200 m
463
400 m
300 m
Fell
200 m

=== Course of Roman Road
— Modern Road
--- Modern Track
Autobahn A1,
Trier – Saarbrücken

THE BATTLE
OF
TRIER

500 m.

Cohorts?

Cohorts
130
(Mariensäule)
330
I XVI
145
Rigodulum →
XXI
Flat
Ground

Bructeri
Tencteri →

Cohorts

134
Ubii
Lingones →
Batavi ↑

R. Mosel

TRIER

=== Course of Roman Road
--- Course of (Ancient and Modern) Track

MAPS 8 AND 9

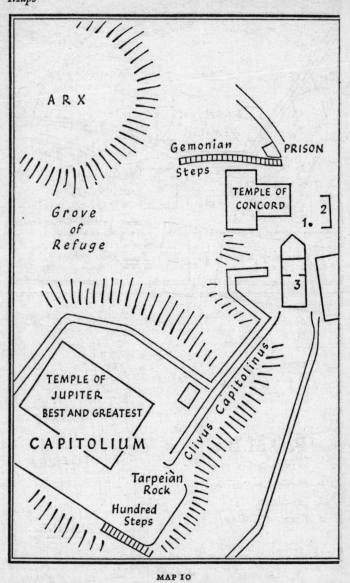

ARX

Gemonian
Steps

PRISON

TEMPLE OF
CONCORD

2

1.

Grove
of
Refuge

3

TEMPLE OF
JUPITER
BEST AND GREATEST

CAPITOLIUM

*Clivus Capitolinus*

Tarpeian
Rock

Hundred
Steps

MAP 10

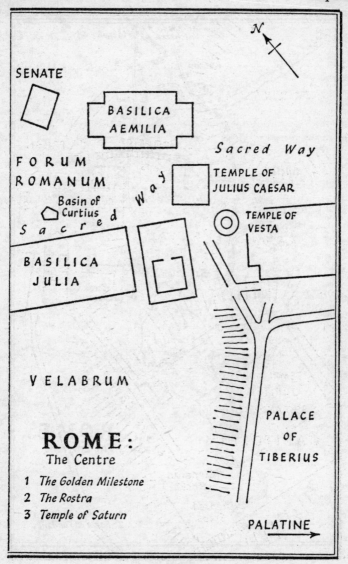

N

SENATE

BASILICA
AEMILIA

*Sacred Way*

FORUM
ROMANUM

Way

TEMPLE OF
JULIUS CAESAR

Basin of
Curtius

Sacred

TEMPLE OF
VESTA

BASILICA
JULIA

VELABRUM

PALACE

OF

TIBERIUS

# ROME:
The Centre

1 *The Golden Milestone*
2 *The Rostra*
3 *Temple of Saturn*

PALATINE →

MAP 10

ROME:
The Environs

1. *Flavian mansion*
2. *Basin of Fundanus*

1 km

MAP II